Empirical Bayes

Empirical Bayes methods as envisioned by Herbert Robbins are becoming an essential element of the statistical toolkit. In *Empirical Bayes: Some Tools, Rules, and Duals*, Roger Koenker and Jiaying Gu offer a unified view of these methods. They stress recent computational developments for nonparametric estimation of mixture models, not only for the traditional Gaussian and Poisson settings but for a wide range of other applications. Providing numerous illustrations where empirical Bayes methods are attractive, the authors give a detailed discussion of computational methods, enabling readers to apply the methods in new settings.

Roger Koenker is an honorary professor of economics at University College London. He was a member of the technical staff of Bell Labs and Professor of Economics and Statistics at the University of Illinois. He is a fellow of the Econometric Society, the British Academy, the ASA and the IMS.

Jiaying Gu is an Associate Professor of Economics at the University of Toronto.

Econometric Society Monograph Series

The Econometric Society is an international society for the advancement of economic theory in relation to statistics and mathematics. The Econometric Society Monograph series is designed to promote the publication of original research contributions of high quality in mathematical economics and theoretical and applied econometrics.

Books in the Series

R. Koenker & J. Gu, *Empirical Bayes: Some Tools, Rules and Duals, 2026*
M. Voorneveld (ed.), *One Hundred Years of Game Theory: A Nobel Symposium, 2026*
V. Chernozhukov (ed.), *Advances in Economics and Econometrics: Twelfth World Congress, Vols. I & II,* 2025
T. Strzalecki, *Stochastic Choice Theory*, 2025
C. Hsiao, *Analysis of Panel Data: 4th edn,* 2022
D. M. Kreps, *The Black–Scholes–Merton Model as an Idealization of Discrete-Time Economies*, 2019
W. Thomson, *How to Divide When There Isn't Enough: From Aristotle, the Talmud, and Maimonides to the Axiomatics of Resource Allocation*, 2019
O. Compte & A. Postlewaite, *Ignorance and Uncertainty*, 2018
I. Molchanov & F. Molinari, *Random Sets in Econometrics,* 2018
B. Honoré, A. Pakes, M. Piazzesi, & L. Samuelson (eds.), *Advances in Economics and Econometrics: Eleventh World Congress, Vols. I & II,* 2017
S. Maurer, *On the Shoulders of Giants: Colleagues Remember Suzanne Scotchmer's Contributions to Economics,* 2017
C. P. Chambers & F. Echenique, *Revealed Preference Theory,* 2016
J.-F. Mertens, S. Sorins, & S. Samir, *Repeated Games,* 2015
C. Hsiao, *Analysis of Panel Data: 3rd edn,* 2014
C. Cameron & P. Trivedi, *Regression Analysis of Count Data, 2nd edn,* 2013
A. Harvey, *Dynamic Models for Volatility and Heavy Tails, with Applications to Financial and Economic Time Series*, 2013
D. Acemoglu, M. Areilano, & E. Dekel (eds.), *Advances in Economics and Econometrics: Theory and Applications, Tenth World Congress, Vols. I, II, & III,* 2013
M. Fleurbaey & F. Maniquet, *A Theory of Fairness and Social Justice,* 2011
R. Vohra, *Mechanism Design: A Linear Programming Approach,* 2011
K. Samphantharak & R. Townsend, *Households as Corporate Firms: An Analysis of Household Finance Using Integrated Household Surveys and Corporate Financial Accounting,* 2009
I. Gilboa, *Theory of Decision under Uncertainty,* 2009
F. Vega-Redondo, *Complex Networks,* 2007
R. Blundell, W. Newey, & T. Persson, (eds.), *Advances in Economics and Econometrics: Theory and Applications, Ninth World Congress, Vols. I, II, & III,* 2006
J. Roemer, *Democracy, Education, and Equality,* 2006
C. Blackorby, W. Bossert, & D. Donaldson, *Population Issues in Social Choice Theory, Welfare Economics and Ethics,* 2005
R. Koenker, *Quantile Regression,* 2005
C. Hsiao, *Analysis of Panel Data, 2nd ed.,* 2003

Continued on page following the index

Empirical Bayes

Some Tools, Rules and Duals

Roger Koenker
University College London

Jiaying Gu
University of Toronto

CAMBRIDGE
UNIVERSITY PRESS

CAMBRIDGE
UNIVERSITY PRESS

Shaftesbury Road, Cambridge CB2 8EA, United Kingdom

One Liberty Plaza, 20th Floor, New York, NY 10006, USA

477 Williamstown Road, Port Melbourne, VIC 3207, Australia

314–321, 3rd Floor, Plot 3, Splendor Forum, Jasola District Centre, New Delhi – 110025, India

103 Penang Road, #05–06/07, Visioncrest Commercial, Singapore 238467

Cambridge University Press is part of Cambridge University Press & Assessment, a department of the University of Cambridge.

We share the University's mission to contribute to society through the pursuit of education, learning and research at the highest international levels of excellence.

www.cambridge.org
Information on this title: www.cambridge.org/9781009275330

DOI: 10.1017/9781009275354

When citing this work, please include a reference to the DOI 10.1017/9781009275354

First published 2026
First paperback edition 2026

A catalogue record for this publication is available from the British Library

ISBN 978-1-009-27536-1 Hardback
ISBN 978-1-009-27533-0 Paperback

To Hannah and Vera

Contents

Preface

Bayesians come in many varieties – 46,656, by the accounting of Good (1971). Among these, according to the infamous diktat of Dennis Lindley, in his discussion of Copas (1969) "there is no one less Bayesian than an empirical Bayesian." And yet the pragmatic origins of Bayesianism as developed in Ramsey (1931) would seem to encourage a less doctrinaire view. Our interest in empirical Bayes methods was sparked by a question that Larry Brown posed to one of us about shape-constrained density estimation and the monotonicity of Bayes rules in 2011. It has dominated our research agenda ever since. We cannot hope to do justice to the vast fabric of the empirical Bayes literature, so we will restrict our attention to a few threads that we feel are most relevant to econometric inquiry and may be underappreciated by the research community. Central to these, the golden thread, if you will, is the idea of nonparametric maximum likelihood estimation of mixture models, first announced in Robbins (1950) and greatly elaborated in Kiefer and Wolfowitz (1956). A pioneering application of this approach in econometrics was the work of Heckman and Singer (1984) on heterogeneity in duration modeling.

A crucial motivation for the empirical Bayes approach as conceived by Robbins (1956) is a desire to produce better methods for solving compound decision problems. We will emphasize this objective throughout since it provides a coherent way to address the inevitable question, "so what?" Decision problems often arise as a group of related problems, and while we might, at first, consider dealing with each of them in isolation, it is often better to recognize their similarity and try to exploit it. The typical formalism posits exchangeable random variables, $Y_i \sim \varphi(y|\theta_i)$ with θ_i drawn from some unknown distribution G and φ a known probability density. How related need the Y_i be? Robbins (1951) himself provocatively wrote,

> No relation whatever is assumed to hold among the unknown parameters θ. To emphasize this point, X_1 could be an observation on a butterfly in Ecuador, X_2 on an oyster in Maryland, X_3 the temperature of a star, and so on, all observations being taken at different times.

Efron (2010) refers to this as the paradox of "relevance" and notes that it features prominently in many early discussions of Stein shrinkage. Robbins takes a firm stand asserting the irrelevance of relevance. We will illustrate our own more prudential perspective on empirical Bayes methods with empirical examples drawn from our own research and that of others where relevance is always open to question.

The central focus of our monograph is a detailed treatment of empirical Bayes methods for nonparametric mixture models. This approach is broadly applicable to a wide variety of hierarchical models and leads to effective decision rules for solving compound decision problems that arise naturally in these models. In so doing the methods complement earlier parametric Bayesian methods for such models, methods that presume finite parameter prior structure. Like others, we focus primarily on quadratic loss and posterior mean decision rules, but we find considerable utility in other loss functions, and the Bayesian paradigm offers efficient mechanisms for solving these new problems as well.

Fortunately, there is a rich, related literature within which our own modest contributions can comfortably rest, untroubled by any guilt about errors of omission. What we lack in originality we have tried to make up for in the diligence with which we have pursued related literature. Of course, this is a Sisyphean task, and we apologize profusely to those we have overlooked.

Brad Efron's contributions constitute a rich vein of wisdom and technical innovation, from his *Scientific American* article with Carl Morris on Stein's paradox (Efron and Morris, 1977) to his influential monograph on "Large Scale Inference" (Efron, 2010) and the steady stream of articles since then; he has been an inspiration for us and many others.

Parametric empirical Bayes methods as ably surveyed in the texts of Maritz and Lwin (1989) and Carlin and Louis (2000) have been swallowed up under the rubric of hierarchical modeling and have undergone several generations of software development, bringing them into the mainstream of statistical practice: BUGS (Lunn et al., 2012), JAGS (Plummer, 2017) and culminating in the emergence of Stan (Carpenter et al., 2017). A fair question would be: How do these developments relate to our notion of empirical Bayes? Andrew Gelman, a leading proponent of the hierarchical approach, has written,

> Bayesian inference is already empirical. It is conditional on data. Using an approximation that involves point estimation does not add any "empirical" content. Historically the term "empirical Bayes" was used in contrast to a simpler Bayes in which the hyperparameters were chosen purely from prior information without reference to the data. But for several decades now we've had hierarchical Bayes, which can use as much or as little prior information as you'd like. (Gelman, 2021)

From this perspective "full Bayes," typically now relying on Markov chain Monte Carlo, produces joint posterior distributions for all lower level parameters as well as "prior" hyperparameters, while thereby avoiding the cardinal Bayesian sin: the plug-in estimator. Often in practice, however, priors are "calibrated" and their functional forms restricted in ways that are highly reminiscent of the ancien régime of Bayesian methods with conjugate priors. We have no quarrel with such methods, indeed they can be very effective when prior hierarchies are well adapted to empirical circumstances, but we will argue that more flexible priors can sometimes reveal features and improve decisions that more restrictive parametric modeling may miss. Likewise, parametric shrinkage and smoothing methods have spawned a vast literature and have elegant implementations in software. Again, we will argue that nonparametric empirical Bayes methods can provide a valuable complement to these parametric methods.

Some essential features of parametric empirical Bayes methods offer some familiar context: Gaussian panel data models, hierarchical models for discrete data, classical smoothing spline methods and some more recent developments with total variation penalized smoothing. In econometrics empirical Bayes has found increasing application in a wide variety of applications. Valuable recent surveys of related work in education and labor are available in Angrist et al. (2023) and Walters (2024), respectively. Nonparametric Bayesian methods for density estimation and regression problems involving Dirichlet process priors introduce a new element of flexibility along with new challenges for Markov chain Monte Carlo.

The discreet charm of the nonparametric maximum likelihood estimator for mixture models upon which we will focus much of our attention is that it is free of any tuning parameters, thus precluding embarrassing questions about how to choose them. Admittedly, tuning parameters creep back into the narrative when we address certain inferential problems. The infinite-dimensional problem of estimating mixing distributions in many empirical Bayes settings can be reduced to finding an atomic measure in a low-dimensional Euclidean space, typically approximated on a grid or lattice. The convexity of such problems ensures unique solutions that are supported on a small number of atoms. In some applications these discrete solutions may appear entirely natural, in others they may strain credulity, but in either case we believe that they offer valuable building blocks for subsequent inference and effective compound decision making.

More flexible models of response heterogeneity are a natural concomitant of expanding data availability throughout modern science: Richer data enables richer classes of models, but richer models typically require some form of regularization. We have become accustomed to shrinkage and model selection methods that rely on norm constraints on parameters interpretable as Bayesian (log) prior densities, but how to assess the strength of one's belief in such priors remains controversial. Typically, one resorts to some sort of data-driven selection mechanism, an empirical Bayes procedure like cross validation or Stein unbiased risk estimation. In contrast some shape-constrained maximum likelihood methods are self-regularizing in the sense that the constraints themselves are sufficient to produce a well-posed optimization problem, a feature shared by the nonparametric maximum likelihood estimator for mixture models.

Nonnegativity constraints on parameters act as a powerful regularization device and produce parsimonious estimates of mixing distributions that can be used as a foundation for solving a wide variety of compound decision problems. Robbins's vision of empirical Bayes methods and compound decision theory offers promising opportunities to deal with these challenges in econometrics and many other disciplines.

We have no philosophical aspirations, except perhaps to advocate for a more pragmatic form of data analysis attuned to the desire expressed by Cox (1962) "to formulate more realistic models that will enable scientifically more searching questions to be asked of data." We are content to revel in the illicit forms of prior elicitation that empirical Bayes has long been chastised for, while cheerfully admitting that more formal Bayesian methods can also contribute valuable prior information when it is available. Nor do we have any firm convictions when it comes to evaluating the performance of competing statistical procedures: Frequentist simulation evidence and asymptotics will commingle with Bayesian forms of inference and risk analysis.

Many diverse forms of data will be encountered in the course of our development of empirical Bayes methods. From the outset the classical Gaussian sequence model will play a prominent role, but models for count data also appear with some regularity. Modeling duration data has traditionally concerned itself with parametric heterogeneity, or frailty, but nonparametric empirical Bayes methods expand the flexibility of survival analysis. Longitudinal data offers a host of new challenges. Throughout we will meet opportunities to introduce new parametric effects that can be estimated by some form of profile likelihood method and raise intriguing questions about asymptotic efficiency. Finally, discrete data in its many forms has led us into some exotic new territories that deserve further exploration. We hope that this account of our foray into Robbins's domain of empirical Bayes will encourage others to pursue related paths.

Our exposition of empirical Bayes methods is strongly influenced by the practicalities of computational techniques and relies heavily on our parallel development of software in our R package **REBayes**. This package relies on the exceptional work of many contributors to the R language, R Core Team (2021), and the convex optimization language MOSEK (ApS, 2022a). In accord with recent initiatives to facilitate reproducibility, we have prepared a publicly available repository of files that will enable interested readers to reproduce all of the figures and tables that appear in the book.

Inevitably, there is inadequate space to thank all those who have contributed to our exploration of empirical Bayes methods. Our original impetus was the question posed by Larry Brown about shape-constrained density estimation and monotone Bayes rules. Herbert Robbins's influence permeates all of the subsequent work on empirical Bayes as does the work of Charles Stein, Brad Efron, Carl Morris, Bruce Lindsay, Cun-Hui Zhang and many others who have helped to lay the foundations of the subject. Ed Leamer's lively monograph *Specification Searches* Leamer (1978) and Bruce Hill's graduate decision theory course created a latent susceptibility to Bayesian ideas for one of us. Discussions with Steve Portnoy, Ivan Mizera, Stanislav Volgushev, Patrick Kline, Chris Walters, Joel Horowitz, Xiaohong Chen, Bodhi Sen, Asaf Weinstein, Dave Zhao, Aditya Guntuboyina, Nikos Ignatiadis and Yihong Wu have enriched our understanding of the empirical Bayes landscape. We were fortunate to receive reports from three extremely conscientious and constructive reviewers who saved us from many embarrassments and helped us to clarify the exposition in many places. Finally, we would like to thank Stéphane Bonhomme and Serena Ng who initially encouraged us to think that we might be capable of writing something worthwhile about empirical Bayes methods for an econometric audience. It remains to be seen whether they were right.

CHAPTER 1

Introduction

This chapter constitutes an overview of our subject and an attempt to motivate our enthusiasm for it. The research program laid out by Robbins (1951, 1956) has captured our imagination over the last decade, and we have come to believe that it will continue to have profound and far reaching positive influence in our present era of data prosperity.

1.1 INCIDENTAL PARAMETERS

Maximum likelihood is a central precept of modern statistics, and yet in large parameter spaces it may behave badly, yielding unreliable inferences and even inconsistent estimators. Incidental parameters, in the terminology of Neyman and Scott (1948), whose dimension grows proportionally to sample size, can seriously disrupt the elegant optimality theory of the classical Fisherian paradigm. Many examples of the ill effects of incidental parameters are familiar in econometrics. Some are relatively benign, and some have proven to be more intransigent. Some may be simply swept away by some form of differencing, and others cannot. We will encounter many forms of the incidental parameter problem in what follows. The empirical Bayes approach of Robbins (1956) advocates that rather than treating incidental parameters as fixed constants to be estimated one by one, it is often preferable to estimate their *distribution*.

Motivated by the findings of Neyman and Scott (1948), Kiefer and Wolfowitz (1956) demonstrated that joint maximum likelihood estimation of structural – or what might be called coincidental – parameters and the distribution of the incidental parameters can succeed in delivering consistent estimates of both, thereby resolving the paradoxes posed by Neyman and Scott. Treating the incidental parameters as random variables rather than fixed constants leads naturally into Bayesian territory. We will argue that the traditional view of incidental parameters as "fixed effects" can benefit from this distributional perspective. Econometrics has been traditionally suspicious about such "random effects" methods, as exemplified by the influential work of Mundlak (1961, 1978), so skeptical readers should be on their guard for points at which our enthusiasm for empirical Bayes methods impinges upon prior dogma. No paradigm is a panacea, and empirical Bayes is certainly no exception. Nonetheless, empirical Bayes methods offer new insights and approaches to a wide variety of econometric problems and is therefore worthy of renewed consideration. Lancaster (2000) has ably charted the ebb and flow of econometric interest in incidental parameters over the 50 years following Neyman and Scott (1948), but it is an unfinished story.

1.2 THE UR COMPOUND DECISION PROBLEM

The origins of empirical Bayes methods may be traced to a 1951 Berkeley Symposium paper (Robbins, 1951), "Asymptotically subminimax solutions of compound statistical decision problems." In this paper Robbins mounts a direct challenge to the formulation of statistical decision theory advanced by Wald (1950) a few years earlier. We begin with a simple estimation problem, where we observe a realization, y, of a Gaussian random variable with mean $\theta \in \Theta = \{1, -1\}$, and our goal is to estimate the parameter θ. A frequentist would naturally use the maximum likelihood estimator, which is simply

$$\hat{\theta} = \underset{\theta \in \{1,-1\}}{\operatorname{argmax}} \log \phi(y - \theta) = \operatorname{sgn}(y).$$

A Bayesian, assuming a prior distribution for θ, $\mathbb{P}(\theta = 1) = p$, would update their belief about θ through the posterior and obtain

$$\mathbb{P}(\theta = 1 | Y = y) = \frac{p\phi(y-1)}{p\phi(y-1) + (1-p)\phi(y+1)}.$$

The Bayesian would then estimate θ to be 1 if $\mathbb{P}(\theta = 1|Y = y) \geq 1/2$, which results in the estimator

$$\check{\theta} = \operatorname{sgn}(y + 0.5 \log(p/(1-p))).$$

Unless $p = 1/2$, the two estimators are clearly different. For the Bayesian, if there is strong belief that $\mathbb{P}(\theta = 1) = p \neq 1/2$, rather than focusing on the sign of y, they will shift y by a log-odds term and then evaluate the sign. For example, when told that $p = 3/4$, their estimator is $\operatorname{sgn}(y + 0.549)$, making it more likely that they would estimate θ to be 1 than the frequentist. For the frequentist, however, the reliability of the imagined prior is always questionable, so the debate continues.

In Robbins (1951), Robbins made a truly remarkable suggestion. His argument is based on a twist of the original setup: Suppose that instead of having only one observation and one parameter to estimate, we observe n independent realizations, $y_1, \ldots, y_n$, of Gaussian random variables whose respective means, θ_i, are either $+1$ or -1, each with variance one. Our objective is to choose $\hat{\theta} = (\hat{\theta}_1, \ldots, \hat{\theta}_n)$ to minimize the ℓ_1 loss,

$$L(\hat{\theta}, \theta) = (2n)^{-1} \sum_{i=1}^{n} |\hat{\theta}_i - \theta_i|.$$

We could, of course, ignore the fact that we now have n estimation problems and still use the maximum likelihood estimator by deciding $\hat{\theta}_i = \mathrm{sgn}(y_i)$, which would result in an expected loss of $\Phi(-1) \approx 0.15866$. The maximum likelihood estimator is, in fact, the unique minimax decision rule for any $n \geq 1$. It corresponds to the least favorable setting of the problem, in which the probability of ± 1 is $1/2$.

We are entitled to ask, however, "is the minimax rule reasonable?" Suppose we observe that three quarters of our sample observations are positive. Should we really stick with our pessimistic premise that ± 1 are equally likely? The reliability of a prior is always questionable, so maybe it would be preferable or rely on evidence provided by the observations at hand. Robbins suggests a method of moments approach to estimate p by $\hat{p} = (\bar{y} + 1)/2$, and simply plugging it into the Bayesian estimator:

$$\hat{\theta}_i = \mathrm{sgn}(y + 0.5 \log(\hat{p}/(1 - \hat{p}))).$$

This is the essential insight of Robbins's compound decision method: Given many similar decision problems, one can "borrow strength" from all of them to improve decision making for each.

Alternatively, one might adopt a more conventional Bayesian approach to obtain a $\hat{p}$. The log likelihood for p given the entire sample, y, is given by

$$\ell_n(p|y) = \sum_{i=1}^{n} \log(p\phi(y_i - 1) + (1 - p)\phi(y_i + 1)).$$

It is convenient to adopt a symmetric beta prior, $B(a, a)$, that becomes more concentrated around $1/2$ as the parameter a grows. The posterior mean for p can then be easily computed and used as an alternative plug-in estimator. This is similar to the idea behind hierarchical Bayes.

Figure 1.1 illustrates the advantages of such methods over the minimax rule for two sample sizes and several values of a. Of course, there is still a small risk penalty to be paid near $p = 1/2$, but this vanishes as the sample size grows, vindicating the phrase "asymptotically subminimax" in Robbins's title.

This compound statistical decision problem vividly illustrates the potential advantages of "borrowing strength" from the full sample to improve performance across multiple decision problems. Minimax procedures – and as we shall see, many likelihood based procedures – fail to exploit such opportunities. Robbins's crucial message is: When losses are aggregated over many seemingly related, or even seemingly unrelated, problems, we should be wary of decision rules that treat the problems in isolation and look for ways to treat them as an ensemble.

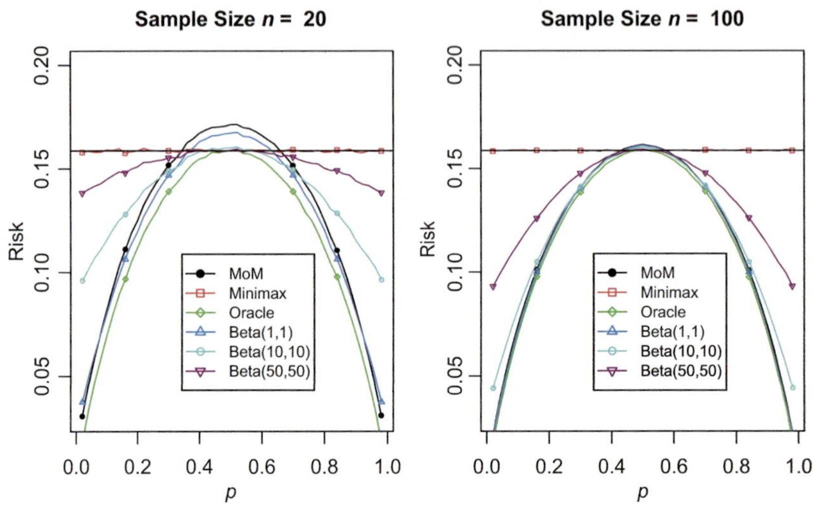

Figure 1.1. Empirical risk of several plug-in decision rules for the Ur Robbins problem. Mean loss is computed over 20,000 replications.

1.3 COMPOUND DECISIONS AND CLASSICAL DECISION THEORY

The final section of Robbins's seminal 1951 paper is devoted to embedding compound decision theory into the existing framework of Wald's decision theory. Formally, this seems straightforward; however its practical implications are quite revolutionary.

As in Wald (1950) we have a canonical problem with observations, y, on random variables, Y, from a sample space $\mathcal{Y}$, with probability distribution, P_θ, indexed by $\theta \in \Theta$. There are decision functions, $d \in \mathcal{D}$ that map actions, $a = d(y)$ from $\mathcal{Y} \to \mathcal{A}$ with loss function $L(d(y),\theta)$ and the expected loss denoted as

$$R(d,\theta) = \mathbb{E}_\theta L(d(Y),\theta) = \int L(d(y),\theta) dP_\theta(y).$$

Our objective is to choose d to minimize risk, either viewed from a Bayesian perspective as Bayes risk,

$$B(d) = \int R(d,\theta) dG(\theta),$$

where $G(\theta)$ is viewed as our prior distribution for θ, or from a minimax perspective simply as

$$\max_{\theta \in \Theta} R(d,\theta).$$

Compound decision problems expand upon this framework by considering ensembles of such problems with losses evaluated by aggregating in some fashion over the entire ensemble. The informal discussion here will be elaborated in the following chapter. For concreteness, we will consider independent instances of our canonical problem. They need not be closely related, but they should share the same problem structure, so each y_i is a realization of a Y_i that has a probability distribution P_{θ_i}. Loss is evaluated as

$$L(d,\theta) = n^{-1}\sum_{i=1}^{n} L(d_i,\theta_i).$$

If we consider decision rules of the general form $d_i(y_1,\ldots,y_n)$ and write the compound risk as

$$R_n(d,\theta) = n^{-1}\sum_{i=1}^{n}\int\cdots\int L(d_i(y_1,\ldots,y_n),\theta_i)dP_{\theta_1}(y_1)\ldots dP_{\theta_n}(y_n),$$

we can again try to minimize risk over this bigger class of decision rules. As a starting point, it is natural to assume that there is nothing special about the ordering of the problems so we can restrict attention to permutation-invariant rules. Following Robbins (1951), we will further restrict attention to what Robbins calls simple symmetric rules of the form $d_i(y_1,\ldots,y_n) = d(y_i)$. Subsequent authors, for example, Jiang and Zhang (2009), Weinstein et al. (2018) and Greenshtein and Ritov (2019), use the term "separable rules" for this class, and we will adopt this terminology.

When we restrict our decision rules d_i to depend only on their own y_i, risk is additively separable so it looks like we are led back to treating the compound problem as if it were just n independent problems. One's initial reaction to this observation is probably, "sure, why not?" The observations are assumed to be independent, so what could be gained by trying to use the y_i to inform our decision about θ_j? But we have seen that such borrowing of information across problem instances can be beneficial in the compound decision framework of the previous section. Is there a more general principle at work?

Assuming that the distributions P_θ have densities $\varphi(y|\theta)$, we can further write

$$\begin{aligned} R_n(d,\theta) &= n^{-1}\int\sum_{i=1}^{n} L(d(y),\theta_i)\varphi(y|\theta_i)dy \\ &= \int\left(\int L(d(y),\theta)\varphi(y|\theta)dG_n(\theta)\right)dy, \end{aligned}$$

where G_n denotes the empirical distribution of the θ_i's. Of course this G_n is unknown, so we would need to find a way to estimate it. Viewing the n problems as an ensemble allows us to improve upon the decision rules that would emerge from Wald's minimax approach that viewed each problem in isolation. In Robbins's Ur problem there were only two known support points for G_n, so estimation required only the relative probabilities of the two values ± 1, and this could be easily accomplished with Robbins's proposed method of moments estimator. What about the more general case?

At this point, Robbins makes a truly brilliant, yet remarkably simple, suggestion. Our sample consists of independent realizations of n random variables, each with a common density function,

$$f_G(y) = \int \varphi(y|\theta)dG(\theta),$$

and therefore the likelihood of the observed sample is

$$\ell(G) = \prod_{i=1}^{n} f_G(y_i),$$

which can then be maximized with respect to G. Solutions to problems of this type, albeit infinite-dimensional, can be efficiently computed by modern convex optimization methods that we will describe in detail in Chapter 12. We will refer to these solutions as nonparametric maximum likelihood estimators (NPMLE). We will encounter many varieties of these estimators for various mixing distributions in the remainder of the book.

Whether we choose to interpret G at this stage as the empirical distribution of "fixed" θ_i's or as a subjective prior distribution on them is entirely irrelevant. To support this proposal Robbins published an abstract, Robbins (1950), claiming the consistency of such a procedure. Unfortunately, no further details seem to have been provided. It would be another five years before Kiefer and Wolfowitz (1956) established firmer foundations for this claim. A practical implementation of this method of nonparametric maximum likelihood for mixture models required an even longer wait until Laird (1978) revealed how this could be done with the nascent EM (expectation maximization) algorithm. Modern computational tools relying on advances in convex optimization have made Robbins's suggestion much more practical, and this will prove to be an essential tool in our exposition of empirical Bayes methods.

1.4 EMPIRICAL BAYESBALL: SPRING TRAINING

As a preview of this approach we may consider the problem of evaluating the batting performance of US Major League baseball players, a mainstay of the empirical Bayes literature from its earliest days of Efron and Morris (1977).[1] Following Gu and Koenker (2017a), suppose we have data on the batting performance of 898 players, excluding pitchers, from 2002 to 2011. A complicating factor with this unbalanced panel is that players have different numbers of "at bats," so measures of past performance have differing precision. Let H_{it} be the number of hits of player i in period t, and N_{it} be the number of their "at bats." Rather than relying on binomial response directly, we

[1] It is a truth universally acknowledged that a statistician in possession of a good shrinkage estimator must be desirous of predicting baseball batting averages.

will consider, as in Brown (2008), the approximately Gaussian transformed response,

$$y_{it} = \arcsin\left(\sqrt{\frac{H_{it}+0.25}{N_{it}+0.5}}\right),$$

with means $\mu_i = \arcsin(\sqrt{p_i})$, where p_i is the individual specific (latent) batting success probability, and variances $\theta_i v_{it}^2 = \theta_i/(4N_{it})$. The additional individual specific scale parameter θ_i allows us to consider deviations, over or under dispersion, from the variances dictated by the binomial transformation. Following standard practice, we divide each season into two half-seasons, and for each player compute

$$\hat{\mu}_i = \left(\sum_{t=1}^{m_i} v_{it}^{-2}\right)^{-1} \sum_{t=1}^{m_i} y_{it}/v_{it}^2$$

and

$$S_i = \frac{1}{m_i - 1}\sum_{t=1}^{m_i}(y_{it} - \hat{\mu}_i)^2/v_{it}^2.$$

These sufficient statistics have Gaussian and Gamma distributions, respectively, $\hat{\mu}_i|\mu_i,\theta_i \sim \mathcal{N}(\mu_i,\theta_i v_i^2)$ and $S_i|\theta_i \sim \gamma(r_i,\theta_i/r_i)$, where we set $v_i^2 = \left(4\sum_{t=1}^{m_i} N_{it}\right)^{-1}$ and $r_i = (m_i - 1)/2$.

The likelihood of the joint density, g, of the latent parameters (μ,θ) can be written as

$$\ell(g) = K\prod_{i=1}^{n}\int\int \phi((\hat{\mu}_i-\mu)/\sqrt{\theta}v_i)/(\sqrt{\theta}v_i)\frac{e^{-R_i}R_i^{r_i}}{S_i\Gamma(r_i)}g(\mu,\theta)d\mu d\theta,$$

where $R_i = r_i S_i/\theta_i$. It is convenient at this point to make the further assumption that the mixing density $g(\mu,\theta)$ factors into $g = h_\mu h_\theta$. In this case, since the likelihood contribution of the S_i is independent of the μ_i's, we can solve the resulting (Kiefer–Wolfowitz) nonparametric maximum likelihood problem by first estimating the mixing density, h_θ, and then solving for h_μ. For the independent prior case this is especially convenient since the likelihood can be decomposed into Gamma and Student components. This independent prior case can be estimated with the function `WTLVmix` from the R package **REBayes** (Koenker and Gu, 2015–2024). Chapter 12 describes this computational strategy along with several other methods for computing the NPMLE. The independence assumption can also be alleviated, as we will discuss in Chapter 6.

In Figure 1.2 we show the resulting maximum likelihood estimates of h_μ and h_θ. Both are discrete distributions with only a few atoms. The h_θ is particularly simple with one large mass point somewhat above one indicating over-dispersion for most players, and a smaller mass point below one

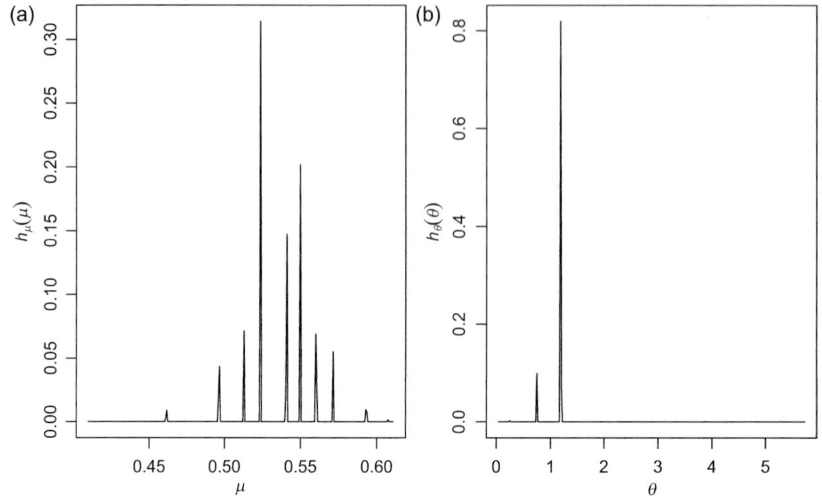

Figure 1.2. Nonparametric maximum likelihood estimates of the latent parameter distribution of a longitudinal model of baseball batting performance. Panel (a) depicts the estimated distribution of the mean of the transformed response, μ. Panel (b) shows the estimated distribution of the dispersion parameter of the transformed response, θ. The two components of the prior distribution, h_μ and h_θ, are assumed to be independent, so the likelihood can be factored into a Student component and a Gamma component, which can be estimated sequentially.

indicating under-dispersion for a smaller group of players. Under-dispersion in this setting reflects relatively stable performance over the sample period, while over-dispersion reflects more erratic batting. From these estimates it is easy to compute posterior mean estimates for μ, and after their transformation back to the original batting average scale for the parameters p_i. See Exercise 1.

It is plausible that better batting induces managers to give players more "at bats," casting doubt on the independent prior assumption. In Chapter 6 we will describe a model for longitudinal income dynamics that incorporates joint estimation of a bivariate prior for latent location and scale parameters. It is also possible to incorporate covariate effects employing profile likelihood methods: Gu and Koenker (2017a) introduce player's age as a quadratic effect; we find that batting performance is maximized at age 27.

Muting the dispersion factor θ_i and taking the model that $\hat{\mu}_i|\mu_i \sim \mathcal{N}(\mu_i, v_i^2)$, if we further assume that the latent μ_i follows a Gaussian distribution with mean μ_0 and variance σ_0^2, then we have

$$\hat{\mu}_i \sim \mathcal{N}(\mu_0, v_i^2 + \sigma_0^2).$$

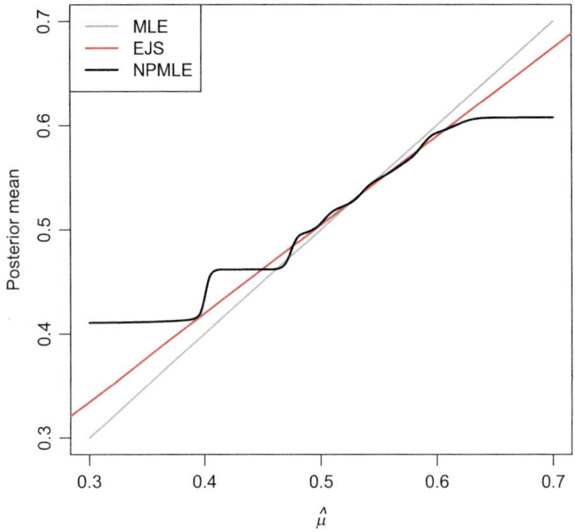

Figure 1.3. Comparison of posterior mean shrinkage rules for the Bayesball data. The linear Stein-type shrinkage rule (labeled EJS) is contrasted with the posterior mean rule derived from the NPMLE estimate shown in Figure 1.2. The gray 45° line (labeled MLE) represents the unshrunken maximum likelihood estimates.

We can estimate the unknown parameters (μ_0, σ_0^2) from the two equations

$$\bar{\mu} = n^{-1} \sum_i \hat{\mu}_i,$$

$$\bar{\sigma}^2 = n^{-1} S - n^{-1} \sum_i v_i^2,$$

with $S = \sum_i (\hat{\mu}_i - \bar{\mu})^2$. The empirical Bayes rule for estimating the latent μ_i's given the $\hat{\mu}_i$ and v_i^2 can be expressed as

$$\tilde{\mu}_i = \bar{\mu} + \left(\frac{\bar{\sigma}^2}{\bar{\sigma}^2 + v_i^2}\right)(\hat{\mu}_i - \bar{\mu}).$$

In Figure 1.3 we compare the shrinkage effects of this linear rule with the nonlinear shrinkage rule derived from the nonparametric maximum likelihood estimator, $\hat{h}_\mu$, both fixing $v_i = 0.01$. The two shrinkage procedures agree quite well for players in the middle of the distribution. Note that in the original "batting average" scale, players with $\hat{\mu} \in [0.5, 0.6]$ are those with hitting success rate between 0.23 and 0.319. The NPMLE posterior mean rule shrinks very aggressively in both tails, while in the shoulders of the distribution it is somewhat less aggressive than the linear rule. Efron (2010, p 9) refers to the tendency of linear Stein rules to over-shrink observations in the tails as the "tyranny of the majority." NPMLE rules, although more flexible, are obviously not fully exempt from this criticism.

1.5 FROM MOMENTS TO EXCHANGEABILITY TO MIXTURES

Moments play an important role in our subsequent developments, especially in the context of discrete response models. Method of moments estimators like Robbins's $\hat{p}$ for his 1951 problem will also appear with some regularity. A deeper connection between moment problems and the empirical Bayes paradigm is developed by Diaconis (1987) linking the Hausdorff moment problem to de Finetti's theorem.

Hausdorff (1921) considered moment sequences,

$$m_k = \int_0^1 x^k d\mu(x), \quad k = 0, 1, \ldots,$$

for probability measures, μ, on [0,1] and showed that such sequences must satisfy a strong monotonicity property. In particular, $\Delta m_k = m_{k+1} - m_k \leq 0$ and $\Delta^2 m_k = m_{k+2} - 2m_{k+1} + m_k \geq 0$. More generally, it follows that

$$(-1)^r \Delta^r m_k = \int_0^1 x^k (1-x)^r d\mu(x) \geq 0.$$

Hausdorff proved that such completely monotone sequences were the only ones that could be valid moment sequences.

Theorem 1.1 (Hausdorff). *A sequence, $\{1, m_1, m_2, \ldots\}$ can be a valid moment sequence for a probability measure μ on $[0,1]$ if and only if $(-1)^r \Delta^r m_k \geq 0$ for all k and r.*

De Finetti considered probability measures for infinite sequences of Bernoulli random variables and showed that such measures, P, were exchangeable, that is, were invariant to permutations,

$$P(e_1, \ldots, e_k) = P(e_{\pi(1)}, \ldots, e_{\pi(k)}),$$

for every sequence $e_1, \ldots, e_k$, all permutations, π and all k under strikingly similar conditions.

Theorem 1.2 (de Finetti). *P is exchangeable if and only if for all n,*

$$P(e_1, \ldots, e_n) = \int_0^1 x^r (1-x)^{n-r} d\mu(x),$$

where $r = e_1 + \cdots + e_n$, and μ is a unique probability measure on $[0,1]$ not depending on n or the e_i's.

Thus, P is exchangeable if and only if it can be expressed as a mixture of Bernoulli random variables with differing success probabilities. This brings us to a fundamental Bayesian decomposition that expresses the probability of elementary exchangeable events in terms of a likelihood, $x^r(1-x)^{n-r}$, and a prior μ over the parameter x. We have already seen that this is a canonical empirical Bayes setting in which likelihood is expressed in terms of some given parametric likelihood with mixing distribution represented by the prior.

Diaconis notes that Hausdorff's and de Finetti's theorems are equivalent. To show this, he defines, $m_k = P(1,\ldots,1)$, the probability of a sequence of k ones, and using $P(1) = P(1,0) + P(1,1)$, notes that

$$P(1,0) = P(1) - P(1,1) = m_1 - m_2 \geq 0,$$

and likewise,

$$\begin{aligned} P(1,0,0) &= P(1,0) - P(1,0,1) \\ &= P(1) - P(1,1) - P(1,1) + P(1,1,1) = \Delta^2 m_1 \geq 0. \end{aligned}$$

Continuing by induction, Diaconis shows that if the m_k have all such differences positive, they satisfy consistency requirements to be a valid probability, and from Hausdorff's theorem we obtain de Finetti's; conversely, if Hausdorff's condition is satisfied then de Finetti's theorem implies that $m_k = \int x^k d\mu(x)$. This is all very classical, appearing in Feller (1971), but has been greatly expanded to much larger classes of exchangeable processes that exhibit similar mixture structure. It will suffice for our purpose to note that infinite exchangeable sequences, $Y_1, Y_2, \ldots$, that is, those with joint distributions invariant to permutations, may be viewed as mixtures of conditionally iid[2] random variables. In our context this will generally be expressed by elements of the sequence, Y having common density,

$$f_G(y) = \int \varphi(y|\theta) dG(\theta)$$

with respect to some prior measure, G, on the parameter θ of some base density φ. This formalism is adequate for our present needs, but we should stress that the modern theory of exchangeable sequences and partitions thereof extends far beyond this domain. Interested readers are encouraged to consult Zabell (1992) for a more comprehensive view. A very readable introduction to modern developments is available in Diaconis and Skyrms (2018). Exchangeability and its consequential mixture representations serve as a foundation for all of Bayesian statistics, no less so than for empirical Bayes methods.

For multivariate arrays exchangeability generalizes nicely, but there are some unexpected subtleties when permutation invariance is restricted to marginal distributions. Consider P being a measure on matrices with 0–1 entries, Y_{ij}, such that

$$P(Y_{ij} \colon 1 \leq i,j \leq n) = P(Y_{\sigma(i)\tau(j)} \colon 1 \leq i,j \leq n)$$

[2] Independent and identically distributed.

for all permutations, σ and τ, and all n. In the univariate setting we can imagine constructing exchangeable Bernoulli sequences in the following way: First, a θ is drawn from the distribution μ on $[0, 1]$, then a coin is flipped which lands heads with probability θ; if heads is observed our entry is 1, otherwise 0. In the bivariate setting we consider an arbitrary Borel function $\psi : [0, 1]^2 \to [0, 1]$. We generate a pair of independent uniforms (U_i, V_j) on $[0, 1]$, and now flip a $\psi(U_i, V_j)$ coin, entering a 1 if it lands heads, 0 if tails. It transpires that any row/column-exchangeable Y is a mixture of such ψ-processes. See Diaconis (2009).

1.6 COMPOUND DECISIONS AND MULTIPLE TESTING

Another theme of our exposition will be the close connection between compound decision theory and multiple testing. Robbins's Ur problem for $\theta_1, \ldots, \theta_n \in \{-1, 1\}^n$ is essentially a multiple testing problem in which we weight Type I and Type II errors equally. Treating $\theta = -1$ as the null hypothesis and $\theta = 1$ as the alternative, we can construct a p-value procedure with individual p-value, $T_i = 1 - \Phi(Y_i + 1)$, cutoff $\Phi(-1)$, and decision rule,

$$\delta(T_i) = \text{sgn}(\Phi(-1) - T_i),$$

that is equivalent to our earlier minimax rule, $\delta(y) = \text{sgn}(y)$.

A p-value testing procedure that is equivalent to the empirical Bayes compound decision procedure described earlier can also be constructed. Under the null hypothesis, $Y_i \sim \mathcal{N}(-1, 1)$, we know that $T_i = 1 - \Phi(Y_i + 1)$ is uniformly distributed, $U[0, 1]$, while if $Y_i \sim \mathcal{N}(1, 1)$,

$$\mathbb{P}(T_i < u) = \mathbb{P}(Y_i + 1 > \Phi^{-1}(1 - u)) = 1 - \Phi(\Phi^{-1}(1 - u) - 2).$$

Thus, under the null, the density of T is $f_0(t) = 1$ for $t \in [0, 1]$, and under the alternative,

$$f_1(t) = \phi(\Phi^{-1}(1 - t) - 2)/\phi(\Phi^{-1}(1 - t)),$$

and the posterior probability of $\theta_i = 1$ given t_i and assuming for the moment that the unconditional probability, $p = \mathbb{P}(\theta_i = 1)$ is known, is given by

$$\mathbb{P}(\theta = 1 | t, p) = \frac{p f_1(t)}{p f_1(t) + (1 - p) f_0(t)}.$$

Under symmetric loss we were led to the decision $\hat{\theta}_i = 1$ if $\mathbb{P}(\theta_i = 1 | T_i, p) > 1/2$, which is equivalent to the p-value testing rule,

$$\delta(T_i) = \text{sgn}(\Phi(-1 + 0.5 \log(p/(1 - p))) - T_i).$$

Again, we are led back to the problem of estimating p. In these two-point mixture problems, ℓ_1 loss is equivalent to $0 - 1$ loss since the median and the mode are identical. We will see in Chapter 7 that when we consider more general settings beyond the point null and point alternative then we will need to depart from the realm of p-value multiple testing. Nevertheless, the link between estimation and multiple testing will provide a fruitful perspective throughout our exposition.

1.7 PARAMETRIC VS. NONPARAMETRIC EMPIRICAL BAYES

There is an extensive literature on hierarchical Bayes modeling with influential contributions by Lindley and Smith (1972) and Chamberlain and Leamer (1976) among many others. Early on such efforts were constrained to conjugate priors for latent effects, but the rapid development of Markov chain Monte Carlo methods have opened the way toward much more flexible formulations. Still, the modeling language available in Stan (Carpenter et al., 2017) and its predecessors is predominantly parametric in form. Because these methods have authoritative expositions elsewhere, we can afford to be quite brief in our treatment of them here. Any attempt to distinguish empirical from principled Bayes methods of this sort is fraught with pointless controversy. Indeed the distinction between likelihood and prior has become somewhat blurred as models become more complex and what might have been viewed as prior parameters are now routinely estimated and even, heaven forfend, plugged in. We make some comparisons with parametric hierarchical models in later chapters, especially with Dirichlet prior methods, which are more closely related to the mixture models that predominate our exposition.

We will focus much of our attention on nonparametric empirical Bayes methods that rely on the nonparametric maximum likelihood methods illustrated in the preceding baseball application. Efron (2014) has identified two basic modeling strategies for nonparametric empirical Bayes methods. The first he calls g-modeling. It proceeds by formulating a mixture model for some latent parameters like players' batting ability, and then derives decision rules that follow from estimating the mixing distribution, G, or its density, g, by some suitable method, typically maximum likelihood. The second approach, called f-modeling, exploits the fact that in many circumstances optimal Bayes decision rules can be formulated purely in terms of the marginal density of the observed response variable. In these cases, estimation of the mixing distribution, G, can be circumvented, and decision rules can be formulated entirely in terms of an estimated marginal density, f.

A leading example of this dichotomy is the classical Gaussian mixture model. We observe

$$Y_i = \theta_i + u_i, \quad i = 1, \ldots, n,$$

with independent $u_i \sim \mathcal{N}(0, 1)$ and $\theta_i \sim G$, so the Y_i's have marginal (mixture) density,

$$f_G(y) = \int \phi(y - \theta) dG(\theta).$$

The posterior mean of θ given $Y = y$, which is the optimal Bayes rule under squared error loss, is given by the Tweedie formula,

$$\mathbb{E}[\theta|Y = y] = y + f_G'(y)/f_G(y),$$

see Theorem 4.1. Thus, the analyst wanting to predict next season's batting average, y_{T+1}, from the average in the past season, y_T, might be inclined to estimate the marginal density, f_G, and to use it to predict

$$\hat{y}_{T+1} = y_T + \hat{f}_G'(y_T)/\hat{f}_G(y_T).$$

This would be an f-modeling strategy. Alternatively, we might instead favor estimating G with the NPMLE, constructing $f_{\hat{G}}$ and predicting with

$$\hat{y}_{T+1} = y_T + f_{\hat{G}}'(y_T)/f_{\hat{G}}(y_T).$$

This would be a g-modeling strategy. Both approaches have advantages and disadvantages that are application dependent. Like Efron, we will generally favor the g-modeling approach when it is feasible, but there will be several places where f-modeling makes an appealing appearance.

1.8 REGULARIZATION AND ITS TUNING

Modern statistical practice is replete with various forms of regularization intended to control smoothness, model selection and other irregularities. All such activity requires the choice of tuning parameters. From a Bayesian perspective this corresponds to a decision about how much you want to believe in your prior: How smooth should an estimated density be, or how sparse is sparse enough for an estimated regression model. Tuning parameter selection has spawned a small industry, perhaps not as scientific as piano tuning but probably employing more people. Since most of these choices are eventually resolved by some form of cross-validation or information criterion optimization, they naturally fall under the empirical Bayes rubric. And yet, we don't have anything original to add to the extensive existing literature that deals with these choices. Thus, while we will encounter various forms of tuning parameter selection in what follows, readers should not expect to encounter any magic elixirs.

Indeed, the whole idea of committing to a parametric prior up to but not including a scalar tuning parameter may seem a bit odd when it is first encountered. Why, we might ask, should we consider a prior, like that of Silverman (1982) for a univariate density, g, to look like

$$\left(\lambda \int ((\log g(x))''')^2 dx\right),$$

except that when one adjusts the λ knob one gets a nice transition from very wiggly $\hat{g}$ to very smooth, with a Gaussian limit estimate as $\lambda \to \infty$. Targeting a particular shape constraint like this is an appealing way to incorporate undogmatic forms of prior information. Parametric priors with estimated tuning parameters fall naturally into the empirical Bayes framework and will be discussed in Chapter 3.

1.9 ILLICIT PRIOR ELICITATION

In the mythical world of Savage (1954), subjective priors appear fully formed as from the head of Zeus, but as anyone who has tried to elicit prior distributions even in dimension one can attest, it's not easy, as acknowledged by no less than Lindley et al. (1979):

> ... the measurement of subjective probability is considerably more problematic and less satisfactory than the measurement of physical attributes such as length or mass and psychological attributes such as loudness or brightness. Indeed, the assessment of subjective probability is beset with severe problems of both theoretical and practical nature.

The review by Kadane and Wolfson (1998) provides a bracing description of various approaches, notably the earlier work by Kadane (1980) and Kadane et al. (1980) to extract Gaussian priors for regression settings. Thus, there has been a recent resurgence of interest in meta-analysis as a source for prior distributions. This is clearly in the spirit of Bayesian updating, and in settings with many similar problems it shares features with the mixture models we will consider. In general there seems to be a growing willingness to explore a variety of approaches to sensitivity of estimation and inference procedures to prior specifications. This may involve diagnostics, simulations or some form of external data validation.

The rigid prohibitions that one once saw regarding potential sources of prior beliefs have faded somewhat and left the field more open to empirical Bayes methods that quite explicitly confess to illicit elicitation of prior beliefs. In view of these developments, "objective Bayes" seems increasingly difficult to defend in the algorithmic climate of modern applied statistics. Empirical Bayes encompasses a wide variety of schemes to extract and use prior information from the data.

1.10 CONNECTIONS TO EMPIRICAL LIKELIHOOD

Empirical likelihood (Owen, 1990, 2001) especially in its Bayesian attire, Lazar (2003), shares many similarities with nonparametric empirical Bayes methods. However, rather than starting from a simple, scientifically plausible parametric mixture model and trying to construct a data-driven prior for the mixing distribution, empirical likelihood reverses this process and begins with a scientifically plausible prior in the form of moment conditions and seeks to estimate a data-driven likelihood. In this respect, empirical likelihood shares some features with approximate Bayesian computation, see for example, Marin et al. (2012). In both cases one arrives at nonparametric maximum likelihood procedures that promise a more flexible representation of the data than those offered by conventional parametric models. In both cases there are challenging profile likelihood problems and intriguing inferential questions. From a modeling perspective in which prior and likelihood are increasingly difficult to distinguish in many applications, it would be profitable to explore the interconnections of empirical Bayes and empirical likelihood more thoroughly. Unfortunately, we don't have anything novel to contribute to this intriguing topic.

1.11 THE WAY FORWARD

This brief introductory chapter is followed by a more detailed description in Chapter 2 of the Robbins compound decision paradigm and how it expands upon the classical framework of Wald. Parametric empirical Bayes methods exemplified by Stein estimators and hierarchical modeling are considered in Chapter 3 as a prelude to an extensive discussion of nonparametric empirical Bayes methods in Chapter 4, which constitutes the central focus of our exposition. Identification in nonparametric mixture models and profile likelihood methods are considered in Chapter 5. Heteroscedastic Gaussian mixture models are treated in Chapter 6. We return to compound decision making in Chapter 7 to consider a variety of ranking and selection applications. Empirical Bayes methods for survival and duration data are discussed in Chapter 8. Mixture models for categorical data are considered in Chapter 9. Random coefficient models for binary response and ecological inference are discussed in Chapter 10. Empirical Bayes methods have traditionally focused on prediction and point estimation, so the inference and confidence regions discussed in Chapter 11 are ripe topics for future research. Computational methods are discussed in the penultimate chapter including software implementations available in our R package **REBayes**.

Exercises

(1) Given the estimates in Figure 1.2, which can be reproduced in R with the commands: `library(REBayes); demo(Bayesball)`, transform the estimated distribution h_μ back to the original scale of p_i, the conventional batting average.

(2) Compute posterior mean estimates of μ_i as a function of $\hat{\mu}$ based on the Bayesball NPMLE using the `predict.GLmix` function of **REBayes**, and interpret the resulting "shrinkage" effects. Hint: This requires a somewhat arbitrary choice of the `newsigma` argument of the `predict` function. Try `newsigma = 0.01`, initially, and then suggest a more principled choice.

(3) Compare the posterior mean function of the previous problem with a version of the James-Stein estimator of the posterior mean.

(4) In early work on computer vision it was conjectured that 0-1 arrays generated so that (i) the chance of a one, appearing as a black pixel, in any given position was 1/2 and (ii) the chance that two ones appearing in any given pair of positions was 1/4 would be sufficient to ensure an appearance of randomness. Suggest a counterexample.

CHAPTER 2

The Empirical Bayes Paradigm

The foundations of modern decision theory were laid in a 1926 talk by Frank Ramsey called "Truth and Probability," eventually published as Ramsey (1931). Ramsey intended the talk as a critique of Keynes (1921); although highly original it was strongly influenced by prior work of the American polymath CS Peirce. A fascinating account of these early developments is provided by the recent biography of Ramsey by Misak (2020). Subsequent contributions by Wald (1950), Robbins (1951) and Savage (1954) have left us with a handful of conflicting principles for statistical decision making, each compelling on its own terms. We certainly do not aspire to reconcile these conflicting principles. The only safe general principle we would put forward is Le Cam's Basic Principle 0: "Do not trust any principle" (Le Cam, 1990). Instead, we will try to describe some special circumstances in which elements of the subjective Bayesian paradigm can be merged with conventional frequentist ideas to produce improved decision rules for ensembles of related problems.

This chapter will sketch a brief overview of the basic Wald framework of statistical decision theory and then contrast it with Robbins's compound decision paradigm. For more comprehensive exposition and critique of the Wald framework, the reader may consult Ferguson (1967) and Berger (1985). Manski (2004, 2007) has championed the use of minimax regret in econometrics. Hirano and Porter (2020) offer an elegant introduction intended for an econometric audience.

2.1 CLASSICAL STATISTICAL DECISION THEORY

In the beginning, before the chaos, there was the probability space, $(\mathcal{Y}, \mathcal{F}, \mathbb{P})$, with sample space $\mathcal{Y}$, σ-field of events $\mathcal{F}$, and probability measure $\mathbb{P}$. Only later was it recognized that there might be a multiplicity of probability models that could be used to describe a particular happenstance.

A statistical model is a collection, $\mathcal{M}$, of probability measures, $\{P_\theta : \theta \in \Theta\}$, indexed by a parameter θ that may be infinite-dimensional. A decision rule

$\delta(Y)$ is a mapping from the sample space $\mathcal{Y}$ to actions $a \in \mathcal{A}$. The consequence of taking action $a = \delta(y)$ in regime θ is that the decision maker incurs loss $L(a,\theta)$. The risk of using decision rule $\delta(y)$ is the expected loss

$$R(\delta,\theta) = \int L(\delta(y),\theta) dP_\theta(y).$$

We would like to choose δ to minimize this risk. This is inhibited, however, by the fact that it still depends upon the unknown, θ. Several options present themselves; see Milnor (1954) for a thorough comparison.

2.1.1 The Subjective Bayesian Option

Suppose we have an a priori assessment of the probability distribution of θ, say $G(\theta)$, with density $g(\theta)$, and for convenience let $dP_\theta(y) = \varphi(y|\theta)$; then we can average the risk over the parameter space, Θ, to obtain the Bayes risk,

$$\begin{aligned} B(\delta,G) &= \int_\Theta R(\delta,\theta) dG(\theta) \\ &= \int_\Theta \int L(\delta(y),\theta)\varphi(y|\theta) dy dG(\theta) \\ &= \int \left\{ \int_\Theta L(\delta(y),\theta) h(\theta|y) d\theta \right\} f_G(y) dy, \end{aligned}$$

where $h(\theta|y)$ denotes the posterior density of θ given $Y = y$, and $f_G(y)$ denotes the marginal density of Y. In effect we have updated our beliefs about θ, now reflected in the posterior density, $h(\theta|y)$, and we can now choose δ to minimize the inner expression in brackets. In the simplest cases when the decision is to choose a point estimator for θ and the loss function takes the form $L(\hat{\theta},\theta) = |\theta - \hat{\theta}|^p$, we obtain the following familiar solutions for $p \in \{1,2,\infty\}$:

$$\begin{array}{lll} p = 2 & \Rightarrow \quad \hat{\theta} = \int \theta h(\theta|y) d\theta & \text{mean,} \\ p = 1 & \Rightarrow \quad \hat{\theta} = \inf\{t | \int_{-\infty}^t h(\theta|y) d\theta \geq 1/2\} & \text{median,} \\ p = \infty & \Rightarrow \quad \hat{\theta} = \operatorname{argmax}\{h(\theta|y)\} & \text{mode.} \end{array}$$

The $p = 2$ case is easily seen by a familiar argument. Let Z be a random variable with density h and mean ζ; then minimizing $B(\delta, G)$ is equivalent to seeking $\hat{\theta}$ that minimizes

$$E(Z - \hat{\theta})^2 = E(Z - \zeta)^2 + (\zeta - \hat{\theta})^2,$$

which is obviously minimal when $\hat{\theta} = \zeta$, the mean of the posterior distribution.

The median example is a special case of the following more general asymmetric linear loss function: $L(\theta,\hat{\theta}) = \tau(\theta - \hat{\theta})^+ + (1 - \tau)(\theta - \hat{\theta})^-$. Minimizing the Bayes risk $B(\delta, G)$ is equivalent to finding $\hat{\theta}$ that minimizes $\int L(\theta,\hat{\theta}) h(\theta|y) d\theta$. This entails

$$-\tau \int_{\hat{\theta}}^{\infty} h(\theta|y)d\theta + (1-\tau)\int_{-\infty}^{\hat{\theta}} h(\theta|y)d\theta = 0$$

or

$$-\tau(1 - H(\hat{\theta}|y)) + (1-\tau)H(\hat{\theta}|y) = 0,$$

so $\tau = H(\hat{\theta}|y)$, or $\hat{\theta} = H^{-1}(\tau|y)$, the posterior τth quantile.

The $p = \infty$ loss function corresponds to $0 - 1$ loss. For a continuous parameter we can approximate this form of loss by

$$L(\theta, \hat{\theta}) = \mathbb{1}(|\theta - \hat{\theta}| > \varepsilon),$$

which for sufficiently small ϵ leads to choosing the mode of the posterior. In discrete parameter settings like Robbins's Ur problem, it leads to choosing the maximal a posteriori value of the parameter.

2.1.2 The Minimax Option

In the absence of a firmly held conviction about how to distribute probability mass over Θ prior to the revelation of Y, one is naturally led to a more paranoid, worst-case scenario mindset. How bad can things be if I adopt a given decision rule δ? This is one of the central ideas in Wald's decision theory. The minimax decision rule seeks to minimize over δ the maximal risk that occurs when using δ. This is often framed as a game in which the decision maker is paired with malevolent nature. For any decision rule, δ, that might be chosen, nature with malice aforethought is assumed to choose θ to make the decision maker's loss as large as possible. In such circumstances what other options could there be than to optimize against this "least favorable" θ? Obviously, this can be very pessimistic.

We have illustrated some pros and cons of the minimax approach in Section 1.2 with Robbins's binary compound decision problem. It is interesting to contrast this with a Gaussian model that is closer to a more conventional econometric setting. Suppose that we observe a sample, $Y_1, \ldots, Y_n$ from the model,

$$Y_i = \theta_i + \epsilon_n u_i,$$

with u_i drawn iidly[1] from $\mathcal{N}(0,1)$. Johnstone (2017, section 1.3) derives an approximately least favorable distribution (prior) for the θ_i's as the two-point distribution

$$\theta_i = \begin{cases} \epsilon_n \sqrt{\log n} & \text{with probability } \pi_n = 1/\sqrt{n \log n}, \\ 0 & \text{otherwise.} \end{cases}$$

[1] Drawn as independent and identically distributed, i.e., somewhere between idly and idyllically, although we shouldn't discount the Freudian connotation "drawn by the Id."

Thus, we would expect to face approximately $n\pi_n = \sqrt{n/\log n}$ nonzero θ_i's, while the remaining $n - \sqrt{n/\log n}$ bulk of the observations are pure noise. Nature is making it difficult to distinguish such a weak signal from all this noise. The minimax strategy that minimizes risk in such circumstances is a "hard thresholding" rule that sets

$$\hat{\theta}_{\lambda_n}(y_i) = \begin{cases} y_i & \text{if } |y_i| \geq \lambda_n \epsilon_n, \\ 0 & \text{otherwise,} \end{cases}$$

where $\lambda_n = \sqrt{\log(n \log n)}$. Taking $\epsilon_n = n^{-1/2}$, this decision rule achieves the asymptotically minimax risk

$$R_n \approx \sqrt{\log n/n},$$

but one is entitled to ask, isn't this too pessimistic? Some skepticism seems justifiable since it hasn't fully exploited the common structure of the problem. This minimax rule is still treating each coordinate of the problem in isolation.

A variant of the minimax formulation is minimax regret. Rather than evaluating loss at each θ with the original loss function, $L(\delta, \theta)$, we might instead ask how much worse off would we be than if we had used the best decision rule for that particular θ. Modifying the loss in this way and then recomputing the minimax procedure is called minimax regret. It has an attractive psychological interpretation, since after the fact (of experiencing the loss), we might be comforted by the thought that we couldn't have done much worse. However, in many statistical problems the original loss function specifies that the best we can do at any θ is to achieve zero loss, so in such cases minimax rules and minimax regret rules obviously coincide.

Another variant, Γ-minimax, restricts the class of competing decision rules and seeks a least favorable setting within this restricted class for which a minimax procedure is chosen. Such Γ-minimax procedures will be illustrated in Chapters 3 and 11.

2.1.3 The Plug and Play Option

Although lacking the illustrious axiomatic credentials of the preceding options, a more expedient mechanism for choosing a decision rule is the well-known "plug-in principle." A model is selected, an estimate, $\hat{\theta}$, of θ is produced, and thereafter we behave as if $\hat{\theta}$ *is* θ. However easily disparaged, plug-in rules are honored by their ubiquity in practice. Empirical Bayes procedures are often guilty of this sort of malfeasance, but we have tried to justify the practice where possible with asymptotic arguments.

2.2 ADMISSIBILITY, INVARIANCE AND ROBUSTNESS

Other considerations can be brought to bear to rule out certain decision rules. Each has an extensive literature, so we will keep our remarks very brief.

2.2.1 Admissibility

A decision rule δ is admissible if there is no other better rule δ' in the sense that $R(\delta,\theta) \leq R(\delta',\theta)$ for all $\theta \in \Theta$ with strict equality at least one θ. While it may seem obvious that we should discard inadmissible procedures, there are often trade-offs – ease of computation, for example – that may argue for their retention. There clearly have been some spectacular successes in identifying inadmissible decision rules, notably Stein's discovery that the sample mean of a multivariate Gaussian vector is inadmissible in dimensions larger than two as illustrated in Chapter 3. And yet the sample mean and its many progeny are alive and well in statistical practice. It seems fair to say that the initial enthusiasm for admissibility as a way forward in separating the wheat from the chaff of statistical decision rules has been dampened by the difficulty of its analysis in many settings. We will argue that the empirical Bayes approach to many of these problems offers an alternative lens through which they may be viewed more constructively.

2.2.2 Invariance

Invariance offers another compelling way to reduce the candidate decision rules. It has played a major role in the extensive literature on objective Bayesian methods and imposes plausible constraints on the choice of minimax rules. The monograph of Wijsman (1990) provides a comprehensive view of this subject, while Berger (1985) offers some cautionary qualifications. We will see that these arguments are especially compelling in the canonical dynamic panel setting in work by Lancaster (2000) and Moreira (2009). The permutation invariance of procedures we will consider follows naturally from exchangeability conditions and will play an important role in what follows.

2.2.3 Robustness

Having chosen a model and perhaps a prior for that model, there is always a residual concern that decisions based on strict adherence to one of the optimality principles described above may be overly sensitive to minor perturbations of the observed data. This concern was vividly raised in the early work of Tukey (1960) and advanced by Huber (1964) and the subsequent work of many others. As with admissibility, the finding that maximum likelihood estimation of Gaussian models was highly sensitive to small amounts of non-Gaussian contamination did little to quell the enthusiasm for least-squares methods in econometrics and applied statistics more generally. It should not be forgotten that the whole arsenal of robust methods is always available to the empirical Bayes practitioner concerned about the consequences of Gaussian hegemony. An interesting line of inquiry, which we will not fully pursue here, would be to consider the robustness of empirical Bayes procedures with respect to the specification of the conditional distribution of the response, $Y|\theta$. An initial exploration of this topic can be found in Koenker (2024).

Concern over the sensitivity of decision making to prior beliefs might be considered an infringement on personal belief and autonomy, but there is a growing recognition that the Gaussian tail behavior of commonly used priors can produce quite dogmatic posteriors. Following Jeffreys (1961) there has been interest in heavier-tailed priors like the Cauchy as a way to ameliorate this difficulty, and these suggestions have been elaborated in recent work on high-dimensional parametric models. We will return to this topic in Section 3.6.

2.3 COMPOUND DECISIONS

In the compound decision formalism of Robbins (1951), we face an ensemble of Wald decision problems. We observe exchangeable, that is permutation invariant, random variables $Y_1, \ldots, Y_n$. They are related to one another in that they are assumed to be generated by a common parametric density, $Y_i \sim \varphi(y|\theta_i)$, $i = 1, \ldots, n$, and each coordinate is entitled to its own parameter. In principle we could consider n distinct decision rules $d_i(y_1, \ldots, y_n)$ depending on the entire vector of observed Y_i's. Instead, we restrict attention to separable rules, $\delta_i(y_1, \ldots, y_n) = \delta(y_i)$ for some function $\delta\colon \mathbb{R} \to \mathbb{R}$. Crucially, the form of this function, δ, may depend upon the entire vector of observations. Compound risk is defined as expected loss over the ensemble:

$$
\begin{aligned}
R_n(\theta, \delta) &= n^{-1}\mathbb{E}\sum_{i=1}^{n} L(\delta(Y_i), \theta_i) \\
&= n^{-1}\sum_{i=1}^{n}\int L(\delta(y), \theta_i)\varphi(y|\theta_i)dy \\
&= \int\int L(\delta(y), \theta)\varphi(y|\theta)dG_n(\theta)dy,
\end{aligned}
$$

where $G_n(\theta) = n^{-1}\sum_{i=1}^{n} \mathbb{1}\{\theta_i \leq \theta\}$, the empirical distribution function of the latent, θ_i's. Thus, we can regard compound risk as a form of Bayes risk in which the prior, G, is replaced by the empirical distribution of the latent θ_i's:

$$
\begin{aligned}
B_n(\delta, G_n) &= \int\left\{\int_\Theta L(\delta(y), \theta)\varphi(y|\theta)dG_n(\theta)\right\}dy \\
&= \int\left\{\int_\Theta L(\delta(y), \theta)h(\theta|y)d\theta\right\} f_{G_n}(y)dy,
\end{aligned}
$$

where $h(\theta|y) = \varphi(y|\theta)dG_n(\theta)/f_{G_n}(y)$, is the posterior distribution of θ given y, and $f_{G_n}(y) = \int \varphi(y|\theta)dG_n(\theta)$ is the marginal density of the observed Y_i. From a frequentist viewpoint identifying the Bayesian prior, G, with the empirical distribution of the latent θ_i's may appear rather impractical. But we will see that salient features of G_n can often be effectively estimated and used to construct decision rules that improve upon naive decision rules that view each of the compound decision problems in isolation. This is the unique opportunity offered by the ensemble.

Theorem 2.1 (Fundamental Theorem of Compound Decisions). *For separable decision rules, compound risk is equal to the Bayes risk of a single copy of the compound decision problem with respect to the same prior.*

Separability is closely tied to the exchangeability of the underlying probability model. In Gaussian models with heterogeneous variances, for example, separability needs careful consideration. Independence of latent means and variances may appear convenient for exchangeability but implausible from a modeling perspective. This will be discussed in more detail in Chapter 6.

A potentially controversial aspect of the compound decision paradigm is the way losses are aggregated. The decision maker is entitled to make a few egregious errors as long as the *average* loss is small. This is fine as long as we are essentially indifferent about where the errors occur, but if there are one or two θ_i's that we especially care about then it will be little consolation that the remaining units achieve small losses, if large losses are incurred by our favorites. As in many corners of statistics, a fervent desire for uniformity can be very costly and push us toward decision making like the coordinate-wise MLE.

This crucial result in Theorem 2.1 leaves open the question: Is there a feasible version of the prior G_n? We will consider both parametric and nonparametric methods to estimate, G_n, and describe how to use such estimates to construct decision rules to minimize the compound risk.

When the θ_i's take only two values, as in Robbins's Ur problem, G_n reduces to a scalar parameter, and risk becomes

$$R_n(\theta,\delta) = p_n(\theta)\int L(\delta(y),1)\phi(y-1)dy + q_n(\theta)$$
$$\times \int L(\delta(y),-1)\phi(y+1)dy,$$

where $p_n(\theta) = n^{-1}\sum \mathbb{1}\{\theta_i = 1\}$ and $q_n(\theta) = 1 - p_n(\theta)$. Replacing p_n by the method of moments estimate, $\hat{p}_n = (\bar{y}+1)/2$, yields Robbins's rule,

$$\delta^*_{\hat{p}_n}(y) = \text{sgn}\left(y + \tfrac{1}{2}\log(\hat{p}_n/(1-\hat{p}_n))\right),$$

a decision rule that is asymptotically equivalent to the optimal Bayes rule obtained under the prior $\mathbb{P}(\theta_i = 1) = p_n(\theta)$. Granted $\delta^*_{\hat{p}_n}(y)$ is still slightly inferior to the minimax rule $\delta_{1/2}(y) = \text{sgn}(y)$ when $p_n = 1/2$ for any finite sample, but as we have seen in Figure 1.1, the magnitude of this disadvantage vanishes quickly as n grows, and its benefits can be substantial when $p_n \neq 1/2$.

Thus the firmly frequentist notion of the empirical distribution function is transformed in the context of compound decision making into that most Bayesian of constructs, a prior that underpins a Bayes decision rule. This "oracle Bayes rule" will serve as a benchmark for our subsequent evaluation of the performance of more pragmatic, empirical Bayes rules. It is as good as it gets. When there are only two known points of support for the parameter, θ, G_n only requires estimation of a scalar, p_n. Estimating p_n by the method of moments requires peeking at all the Y_i realizations before constructing Robbins's rule. This can be made to look more formally Bayesian by positing a beta prior for p_n and proceeding as in Chapter 1. In either case we can achieve a dramatic improvement by borrowing strength from the entire sample to inform each component decision. Priors can often be formulated as finite-dimensional parametric models as we will consider in the next chapter.

2.4 EMPIRICAL BAYES METHODS FOR A SCALAR PARAMETER

Although empirical Bayes methods are generally associated with compound decision problems involving simultaneous estimation of many parameters, this need not be considered their exclusive domain. In Anscombe et al. (1990), prompted by a question by Carl Morris, Robbins asserts,

> The usual interpretation of empirical Bayes involves the estimation of a lot of different parameters simultaneously. I use empirical Bayes methods to estimate just one parameter; let me tell you what the problem is. Suppose you have a lot of people who you are screening for high blood pressure and you decide that anyone whose blood pressure is above a certain level is at some risk. You have a new drug, and you want to study how effective it is to reduce blood pressure. . . . So everyone whose blood pressure is below the cutoff you give a placebo, and everyone above the cutoff you give the new drug. After a while you remeasure everyone's blood pressure. From the before and after data, we are to estimate the effect of the new drug for people who had high blood pressure. This violates the idea of controlled clinical trial . . . and yet I claim, if you will swallow my assumption, accept my model so to speak, I can estimate this parameter. . . . So in my opinion, it is a big mistake to limit empirical Bayes to estimation of parameters simultaneously.

We will see in Chapter 4 this line of inquiry that Robbins calls "biased allocation" is intimately connected to recent developments in both difference-in-differences and regression discontinuity methodology.

CHAPTER 3

Parametric Empirical Bayes Methods

In econometrics interest in parametric empirical Bayes methods begins with the work of Balestra and Nerlove (1966) on estimation of models for the demand for natural gas. They considered panel data models of the form

$$y_{it} = x_{it}^\top \beta + \alpha_i + u_{it},$$

which we can write in matrix form as

$$y = X\beta + Z\alpha + u,$$

where the matrix Z denotes an incidence matrix that identifies the n distinct cross-sectional units in the sample. Motivated by earlier, unpublished work of Hildreth, see Nerlove (2002), the α parameters are treated as random, independent of u and jointly normal. It should be noted that Goldberger (1962) had already considered closely related settings and coined the phrase "best linear unbiased predictor," later abbreviated BLUP by Robinson (1991), that incorporated prediction of random effects in regression.

Suppose that $u \sim \mathcal{N}(0, R)$ and $\alpha \sim \mathcal{N}(0, Q)$, and independent of u, so the covariance matrix Ω of $v = Z\alpha + u$ is $\mathbb{E}vv^\top = R + ZQZ^\top$, and we can immediately recognize the maximum likelihood estimator of β as

$$\hat{\beta} = (X^\top (R + ZQZ^\top)^{-1} X)^{-1} X^\top (R + ZQZ^\top)^{-1} y.$$

This is not a particularly friendly looking computational expression, but for spherical R and Q Nerlove (1971) derives a nice spectral decomposition of the covariance matrix whose Cholesky factorization leads to very efficient computations. An alternative computational perspective is provided by the following proposition.

Proposition 3.1 $\hat{\beta}$ solves $\min_{(\alpha,\beta)} \|y - X\beta - Z\alpha\|^2_{R^{-1}} + \|\alpha\|^2_{Q^{-1}}$, where $\|x\|^2_A = x^\top A x$.

Proof: Differentiating, we obtain the pair of normal equations,

$$X^\top R^{-1} X\hat{\beta} + X^\top R^{-1} Z\hat{\alpha} = X^\top R^{-1} y,$$

$$Z^\top R^{-1} X\hat{\beta} + (Z^\top R^{-1} Z + Q^{-1})\hat{\alpha} = Z^\top R^{-1} y.$$

Solving, we have $\hat{\beta} = (X^\top \Omega^{-1} X)^{-1} X^\top \Omega^{-1} y$, where

$$\Omega^{-1} = R^{-1} - R^{-1} Z (Z^\top R^{-1} Z + Q^{-1})^{-1} Z^\top R^{-1}.$$

Using the identity in Rao (1973, p. 33), we conclude $\Omega^{-1} = (R + ZQZ^\top)^{-1}$. ■

In the spherical case with $R = \sigma_u^2 I$ and $Q = \sigma_\alpha^2 I$, our optimization problem becomes

$$\min_{(\alpha,\beta)} \|y - X\beta - Z\alpha\|^2 + \lambda \|\alpha\|^2,$$

where $\lambda = \sigma_u^2/\sigma_\alpha^2$. Thus, the Nerlove procedure can be seen as a special form of Tikhonov regularization or ridge regression. Components of the vector, α, are shrunk toward zero by an amount controlled by the relative magnitudes of the two variance components. When the α_i's are very dispersed, so σ_α is large, relative to σ_u, then not much shrinkage occurs, but when the α dispersion is small, shrinkage is stronger, drawing the coordinates of α closer together. Note that this interpretation presumes that there is an intercept term in the X portion of the design matrix.

A longstanding controversy in econometrics surrounds the desirability of *any* shrinkage of this type. Mundlak (1978) famously argued that potential correlation of the α's with the remaining covariates of the model induces bias in $\hat{\beta}$ due to such shrinkage, and thus it is preferable to treat the α_i's as fixed effects, thereby transforming the original model into deviations from unit means.

Nerlove (2002) argues that this "fixed effects" fetish discards valuable information in the unit means. This controversy can be elaborated to consider more complex design assumptions, dynamic specifications and other features, but we will resist the temptation to do so since this is extensively litigated in the recent literature. Instead, we return to more fundamental issues involving the desirability of shrinkage.

3.1 STEIN SHRINKAGE AND ITS LEGACY

Charles Stein's revelation that the maximum likelihood estimator of the mean of a multivariate normal vector of dimension $n \geq 3$ was inadmissible under quadratic loss (Stein, 1956) came as a rude shock to most of the statistical profession. Perhaps not, however, to Herbert Robbins, who must have at least suspected this by the time of the 3rd Berkeley Symposium. Stein's result gave great impetus to the development of hierarchical models and thus to parametric empirical Bayes methods. We will briefly sketch the argument underlying the Stein result and some variations that flowed from it. In doing so we will follow closely the exposition of Stein (1986), for which we require the following lemma also attributed to Stein.

Lemma 3.2. *If $Y \sim \mathcal{N}(\mu, \sigma^2)$ and $g(\cdot)$ is a continuously differentiable function, then $Cov(g(Y), Y) = \sigma^2 \mathbb{E} g'(Y)$, provided both sides of this expression exist.*

Proof: Taking $\sigma^2 = 1$ and integrating by parts:

$$\begin{aligned}\mathrm{Cov}(g(Y),Y) &= \mathbb{E}[(Y-\mu)g(Y)]\\ &= \int (y-\mu)g(y)\phi(y-\mu)dy\\ &= -\int g(y)\phi'(y-\mu)dy\\ &= \int g'(y)\phi(y-\mu)dy\\ &= \mathbb{E}[g'(Y)].\end{aligned}$$

The result for general σ^2 then follows by substitution. ■

Let Y denote an n-dimensional multivariate normal vector with mean θ and unit covariance matrix I_n. Our objective is to estimate the vector θ subject to quadratic loss, $L(\hat{\theta},\theta) = \|\hat{\theta} - \theta\|^2$. Stein confines his attention to estimators that perturb each coordinate by functions $g = (g_1, \ldots, g_n)$, with each g_i a mapping $\mathbb{R}^n \to \mathbb{R}$, so

$$\hat{\theta}_i = Y_i + g_i(Y).$$

He proves the following result.

Theorem 3.3. *If $n \geq 3$ and g satisfies:*

(1) $\mathbb{E}g_i^2(Y) < \infty$,
(2) $\mathbb{E}|g_{ii}(Y)| \equiv \mathbb{E}|g_i'(Y)| < \infty$, *and*
(3) $\sum g_i^2(y) + 2g_{ii}(y) < 0$, *for almost all* $y \in \mathbb{R}^n$,

then $\hat{\theta}$ is everywhere better than the maximum likelihood estimator, that is

$$\mathbb{E}\sum(Y_i + g_i(Y) - \theta_i)^2 < \mathbb{E}\sum(Y_i - \theta_i)^2 = n.$$

Proof: By Stein's lemma we have the identity

$$\begin{aligned}\mathbb{E}\sum(Y_i + g_i(Y) - \theta_i)^2 &= n + \mathbb{E}\sum(g_i^2(Y) + 2(Y_i - \theta_i)g_i(Y))\\ &= n + \mathbb{E}\sum(g_i^2(Y) + 2g_{ii}(Y)).\end{aligned}$$

■

This may still look rather mysterious. What sort of g's actually satisfy these conditions, if any? Stein constrains g further to consider orthogonally equivariant estimators of the form

$$g(y) = h(\|y\|^2)y,$$

so risk becomes

$$\mathbb{E}\|Y + g(Y) - \theta\|^2 = n + \mathbb{E}\left[\|g(Y)\|^2 + 2\nabla g(Y)\right]$$
$$= n + \mathbb{E}\left[h^2(\|Y\|^2)\|Y\|^2 + 2nh(\|Y\|^2) + 4\|Y\|^2 h'(\|Y\|^2)\right].$$

Now if we choose, $h(t) = -c/t$, with $c > 0$, then for $n \geq 3$, we have

$$\mathbb{E}\left\|\left(1 - \frac{c}{\|Y\|^2}\right)Y - \theta\right\|^2 = n + \mathbb{E}\left(\frac{c^2 - 2(n-2)c}{\|Y\|^2}\right).$$

Minimizing with respect to c gives $c = n - 2$ and

$$\mathbb{E}\left\|\left(1 - \frac{n-2}{\|Y\|^2}\right)Y - \theta\right\|^2 = n - (n-2)^2\mathbb{E}\left(\frac{1}{\|Y\|^2}\right),$$

thereby establishing that the proposed estimator has strictly lower risk than the MLE, which is simply $\hat{\theta} = Y$ and has risk n. Stein (1986) describes an unbiased estimator of the risk of this estimator.

There are many variations on the form of this James and Stein (1961) estimator. For example, it may happen that $\|Y\|^2 < n - 2$, in which case coordinates of Y would alter in sign, so the "positive part" James–Stein estimator,

$$\hat{\theta}(Y) = \left(1 - \frac{n-2}{\|Y\|^2}\right)_+ Y,$$

might be preferred. When there is some a priori rationale for grouping coordinates of Y, one might consider grouped versions of the James–Stein estimator. If coordinates are thought to be similar to one another, but not necessarily close to zero, one can consider shrinking toward an estimate of their common value, as in Efron and Morris (1973b),

$$\hat{\theta}_i = \bar{Y} + \left(1 - \frac{n-3}{S}\right)(Y_i - \bar{Y}),$$

where $\bar{Y} = n^{-1}\sum Y_i$ and $S = \sum(Y_i - \bar{Y})^2$. When $Y_i \sim \mathcal{N}(\theta_i, \sigma^2)$, for $i = 1, \ldots, n$ with known σ^2, we have

$$\hat{\theta}_i = \bar{Y} + \left(1 - \frac{(n-3)\sigma^2}{S}\right)(Y_i - \bar{Y}).$$

Combinations of these variants and their progeny occupy a large swathe of the early literature on high-dimensional models in statistics. As we will see in Chapter 4, the Stein shrinkage estimators share a common feature: They are ideally suited to settings in which the parameter vector θ to be estimated exhibits some form of Gaussian structure. More general forms of shrinkage considered by Robbins (1956) and Brown (1971) depart from this Gaussian presumption.

3.1.1 Compound Decisions with Gaussian Sequence Model

Stein's problem can be viewed as a compound decision problem with $Y_i \sim N(\theta_i, 1)$ under squared error loss. This is often referred to as the Gaussian sequence problem and serves as a linchpin for much of the discussion that follows. Recalling the connection between compound risk and Bayes risk in Theorem 2.1: The compound risk, $R_n(\theta, \delta)$ is also the Bayes risk $B(\theta, G_n)$ for an estimator $\delta(Y)$ that uses the empirical distribution of $\theta_1, \ldots, \theta_n$ as the prior distribution G_n. If we restrict the class $\mathcal{D}$ to be linear shrinkage estimators, then we can view the James–Stein estimator as the optimizer of $\inf_{\delta \in \mathcal{D}} R(\delta, G_n)$ without any restriction on G_n. The Efron and Morris estimator in Efron and Morris (1973b), with their empirical Bayes interpretation of the James–Stein estimator, may be viewed as an optimizer of the same problem but restricting G_n to be Gaussian without any restriction on $\mathcal{D}$. Robbins's original empirical Bayes proposal in Robbins (1956), however, aims at putting no restriction on either $\mathcal{D}$ or G_n.

3.1.2 Stigler's Galtonian Perspective on Stein Shrinkage

Stephen Stigler's 1988 Neyman lecture, Stigler (1990), sought to demystify the Stein results by offering a new perspective based on Galton's early work on least squares regression. In Figure 3.1 we plot an imaginary sample of θ_i's and

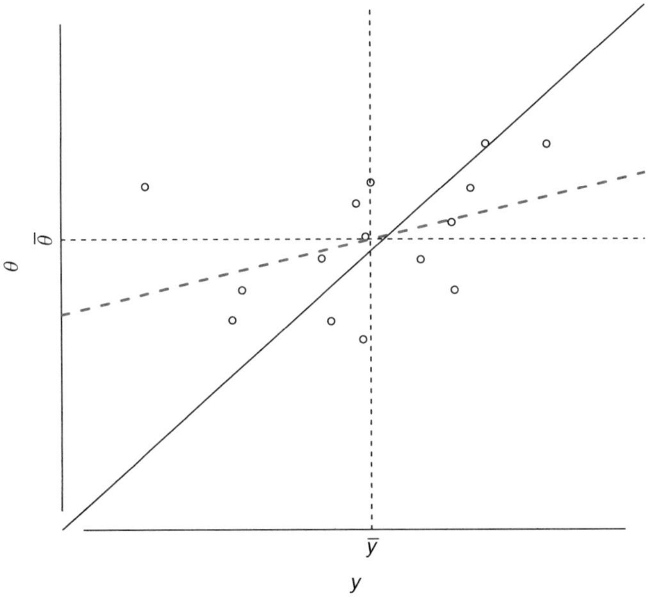

Figure 3.1. Stigler's Galtonian perspective on Stein shrinkage: The black solid line represents the $\hat{\theta} = y$ of the naive MLE; the red, dashed line is the best linear predictor of $\mathbb{E}(\theta | Y = y)$.

their corresponding y_i's. Admittedly we are not usually privy to seeing the θ_i's, but Stigler requests our forbearance about this. The black solid 45-degree line represents the naive maximum likelihood estimator. Projecting each of the y_i's vertically onto this line yields this estimator. In contrast, Galton would have us find the red, dashed regression line that passes through the point of sample means, $(\bar{y}, \bar{\theta})$. This line represents the best linear predictor of θ given $Y = y$, and it is indeed optimal if θ and Y happened to be jointly Gaussian. Of course, we need to keep reminding ourselves that we don't actually see the θ_i's, so this regression line is also a figment of our imagination.

What would we need to reconstruct an approximation of this regression line? It takes the form

$$\hat{\theta}_i = \bar{\theta} + \hat{\beta}(Y_i - \bar{Y}),$$

where $\hat{\beta} = \sum(Y_i - \bar{Y})(\theta_i - \bar{\theta})/\sum(Y_i - \bar{Y})^2$. We have assumed from the beginning that

$$Y_i = \theta_i + U_i,$$

with $U_i \sim \mathcal{N}(0,1), \quad i = 1,\ldots,n$, and independent of the θ_i's so we can estimate $\bar{\theta}$ by $\bar{Y}$, and

$$\mathrm{Cov}(Y,\theta) = \mathbb{V}(\theta) = \mathbb{V}(Y) - \mathbb{V}(U) = \mathbb{V}(Y) - 1.$$

An unbiased estimate of $\mathbb{V}(Y)$ is $(n-1)^{-1}\sum(Y_i - \bar{Y})^2$, so a natural estimate of our $\hat{\beta}$ becomes

$$\tilde{\beta} = \frac{\sum(Y_i - \bar{Y})^2 - (n-1)}{\sum(Y_i - \bar{Y})^2} = 1 - \frac{n-1}{\sum(Y_i - \bar{Y})^2} = 1 - \frac{n-1}{S},$$

and thus, we have a new estimator of the θ_i's, given by

$$\tilde{\theta}_i = \bar{Y} + \left(1 - \frac{n-1}{S}\right)(Y_i - \bar{Y}).$$

This is almost the Efron–Morris estimator, albeit with $c = (n-3)$ replaced by $n-1$. Nevertheless, it can be shown that it still dominates the MLE, provided that $n \geq 5$.

3.1.3 Reception of Stein Shrinkage

To gauge the prevailing attitudes about shrinkage of the type Stein proposed, it is sufficient to quote from the first paragraph of Dennis Lindley's discussion of Stein (1962), at a Royal Statistical Society meeting:

> When I first heard of this suggestion several years ago I must admit that I dismissed it as the work of one of these mathematical statisticians who are so entranced by the symbols that they lose touch with reality. It must, I argued, be due to the unbounded loss function, or it could be an ϵ-improvement, or the sample size was small. But it is none of these things. The estimate proposed by the author is realistic, a great improvement on the sample mean, and makes good practical sense. And I would

> urge those of you who may be put off by the author's rather severe mathematical style to persevere. We have here one of the most important original statistical ideas of the decade, destined, I feel sure, to influence our thinking and our practice.

Persevere they did, although there were always lingering doubts about the decision to combine problems in the way that Robbins and Stein proposed to do. As expressed by the English statistician George Barnard in the same JRSS discussion:

> I cannot resist the temptation to comment on the Bayesian attitude. Briefly, the difficulty here is to know what problems are to be combined together – why should not all our estimation problems be lumped together into one grand melee?

Efron's notion of relevance continues to be relevant despite Robbins's injunction that butterflies, oysters and stars may all be happily lumped together. For linear shrinkage rules of the Stein type, relevance isn't so much a matter of the similarity of the effects, θ_i, but rather how well as an ensemble they conform to a Gaussian sample, as we will see in Chapter 4.

Many refinements of the Stein admissibility results were developed in the subsequent literature ably surveyed from an econometric perspective by Judge and Bock (1978). The contributions of Brown (1966, 1968, 1971) have proven to be especially influential for the development of the theory. But we will resist the temptation to delve into these refinements. Instead, we will turn our attention to parametric hierarchical models, which have emerged as a highly successful mutation of the Stein shrinkage concept.

3.2 Γ-MINIMAX PARAMETRIC PRIORS

Another way to justify parametric priors is to adopt some form of restriction on the class of feasible decision rules and then try to identify an optimal rule for a least favorable element within this class. To illustrate this approach, suppose that $Y \sim \mathcal{N}(\theta, 1)$ and that we restrict attention to priors with known mean, μ, and variance, τ^2. Let

$$\Gamma = \left\{ G \colon \mu = \int \theta dG(\theta), \text{ and } \tau^2 = \int (\theta - \mu)^2 dG(\theta) \right\}.$$

An obvious candidate, $G \in \Gamma$, is $G^* = \mathcal{N}(\mu, \tau^2)$, with associated decision rule under quadratic loss,

$$\delta^*(y) = \frac{\tau^2}{1 + \tau^2} y + \frac{1}{1 + \tau^2} \mu,$$

and risk,

$$R(\theta, \delta^*) = \frac{\tau^4}{(1 + \tau^2)^2} + \frac{(\mu - \theta)^2}{(1 + \tau^2)^2}.$$

Thus, for any $G \in \Gamma$,

$$B(\delta^*, G) \equiv \int R(\theta, \delta^*) dG(\theta) = \frac{\tau^2}{1+\tau^2}.$$

Since δ^* is the Bayes rule for the prior, G^*, for any δ,

$$B(\delta, G^*) \geq B(\delta^*, G^*) = \frac{\tau^2}{1+\tau^2},$$

and

$$\sup_{G \in \Gamma} B(\delta, G) \geq B(\delta, G^*) \geq \frac{\tau^2}{1+\tau^2}.$$

It follows that

$$\sup_{G \in \Gamma} B(\delta, G) \geq \frac{\tau^2}{1+\tau^2} = \sup_{G \in \Gamma} B(\delta^*, G),$$

so δ^* is Γ-minimax, and the Gaussian prior, G^*, is least favorable in this moment based class, Γ. In the compound decision setting this leads us back to Stein rules. This example, adapted from Berger (1985), is generalized in Jackson et al. (1970) to exponential family models where Pearson family priors are conjugate and least favorable.

3.3 EFRON'S EXPONENTIAL FAMILY PRIOR

A much more flexible form of parametric prior introduced by Efron (2016) expresses the logarithm of the density of G, in the linear exponential family form,

$$\log g_\alpha(\theta) = \sum_{k=1}^{p} z_k(\theta)\alpha_k - \gamma(\alpha),$$

where $z_k(\theta)$ are elements of a basis expansion, and γ denotes the usual constant of integration of the exponential family. Letting $(t_1 < \cdots < t_m)$ be some relatively fine grid of $t_i \in \Theta$ and A an n by m matrix with typical element $\varphi(y_i - t_j)$, Efron proposes estimating the parameter vector $\alpha \in \mathbb{R}^p$ by maximizing the penalized log-likelihood,

$$\ell(\alpha) = \sum_{i=1}^{n} \log f_\alpha(y_i) + c_0 \|\alpha\|,$$

where the n vector $f_\alpha = (f_\alpha(y_1), \ldots, f_\alpha(y_n))$ can be written as, $f_\alpha = AZ\alpha$ with Z the m by p matrix with typical element $Z_{jk} = z_k(t_j)$. He refers to this procedure as "Bayesian deconvolution" although arguably one could also call it "Fisherian deconvolution." For relatively low-dimensional p this is a well-behaved optimization problem with a unique solution for fixed p and penalty parameter, c_0, on the Euclidian penalty $\|\alpha\|$. In contrast to the Kiefer–Wolfowitz NPMLE, the Efron $\hat{g}$ is smooth for typical basis expansions like the natural splines suggested by Efron. We will see in Chapter 12 that allowing the dimension of the expansion, p, to grow and the penalty parameter c_0 to tend to zero produces estimates increasingly similar to the NPMLE. This comes with the added advantage that the degree of smoothness is explicitly controlled by tuning parameters, in contrast to the early stopping EM computation of the NPMLE suggested by Laird (1978).

Another crucial advantage of the Efron $\hat{g}$ is that if one is willing to condition on the choice of tuning parameters, the elegant theory of inference for parametric maximum likelihood is available as developed in Efron (2016). Implementations of the Efron procedure are available in R from the package **deconvolveR**, Narasimhan and Efron (2018–2024) and from the function `BDGLmix` in the **REBayes** package of Koenker and Gu (2015–2024).

3.4 PARAMETRIC HIERARCHICAL MODELS

A Bayesian interpretation of Stein shrinkage arose quickly in the wake of the foregoing results and has continued to thrive since then. To see the connection in its simplest form, consider the canonical Stein problem: We observe $Y_i \sim \mathcal{N}(\theta_i, 1)$ with $i = 1, \ldots, n$. If we adopt the prior $\theta_i \sim \mathcal{N}(0, \tau^2)$ then the Y_i's are marginally $\mathcal{N}(0, 1 + \tau^2)$, and the Bayes rule for θ_i is

$$\hat{\theta}_i = \delta(y_i) = \mathbb{E}(\theta_i | y_i) = \left(1 - \frac{1}{1 + \tau^2}\right) y_i.$$

The prior variance, τ^2, controls the amount of shrinkage: When τ^2 is small the investigator is quite confident that all the θ_i's are clustered near zero and considerable shrinkage is justified; when τ^2 is large they are less confident, and less shrinkage is justifiable. What if we don't know τ^2? Lacking the courage of our own convictions, maybe we can cheat a bit. We may recall that $S = \sum Y_i^2 \sim (1 + \tau^2)\chi_n^2$, and perhaps with the aid of Wikipedia that the inverse χ_n^2 has expectation $(n - 2)^{-1}$, suggesting the already familiar

$$\hat{\delta}(y_i) = \left(1 - \frac{n - 2}{S}\right) y_i.$$

Thus, the James–Stein estimator is seen to be a method-of-moments empirical Bayes procedure. If we remove the zero mean restriction on the prior, so $\theta \sim \mathcal{N}(\theta_0, \tau^2)$, the Bayes rule becomes

$$\hat{\theta}_i = \delta(y_i) = \mathbb{E}(\theta_i | y_i) = \theta_0 + \left(1 - \frac{1}{1 + \tau^2}\right)(y_i - \theta_0),$$

and the empirical Bayes rule substituting $\bar{y}$ for θ_0 gives the Efron–Morris estimator,

$$\hat{\delta}(y_i) = \bar{y} + \left(1 - \frac{n - 3}{S}\right)(y_i - \bar{y}),$$

with one degree of freedom lost to estimation of θ_0.

Lindley and Smith (1972), appealing to results of de Finetti (1964) and Hewitt and Savage (1955), greatly elaborated this paradigm for Gaussian linear models and thus initiated the modern development of hierarchical models. They start from the compound decision premise that observations arise in an exchangeable fashion, so the Y_i's come from the mixture density, $\int \varphi(y \mid \theta) dG(\theta)$. When both conditional density $\varphi(y \mid \theta)$ and the mixing distribution G are Gaussian, this leads to some very elegant, tractable linear algebra.

Lemma 3.4 (Lindley and Smith). *Suppose, for $\theta_1 \in \mathbb{R}^{p_1}$, our observed response $y \in \mathbb{R}^n$ is multivariate Gaussian with mean vector $A_1\theta_1$ and covariance matrix C_1, that is, $y \sim \mathcal{N}(A_1\theta_1, C_1)$. Then, if θ_1 is also Gaussian, $\theta_1 \sim \mathcal{N}(A_2\theta_2, C_2)$, the marginal distribution of y is $\mathcal{N}(A_1A_2\theta_2, C_1 + A_1C_2A_1^\top)$ and $\theta_1|Y \sim \mathcal{N}(Bb, B)$, where $B^{-1} = A_1^\top C_1^{-1} A_1 + C_2^{-1}$, and $b = A_1^\top C_1^{-1} y + C_2^{-1} A_2\theta_2$.*

Their proof of this lemma yields a version of the Rao identity used in the proof of Proposition 3.1. The linear model structure makes these shrinkage formulae more complicated, but it is still possible to recognize that the posterior mean of θ_i is a matrix weighted average of the response vector, y, and the prior mean θ_2. The closely related papers of Chamberlain and Leamer (1976) and Leamer and Chamberlain (1976) offer further insight into this phenomenon.

Evidently, one can build hierarchies like these as deeply as one wishes. The only impediment is willingness to specify distributions for parameters at the next level. This is especially problematic for the covariance matrices that play a critical role in determining the relative weights of the matrix weighted averages. Lindley and Smith (1972) illustrate this with a two-way analysis of variance example:

$$y_{ij} = \mu + \alpha_i + \beta_j + u_{ij},\ 1 \le i \le n,\ 1 \le j \le J,$$

with only one observation per cell. Stephen Fienberg in his discussion of this paper extends this example to models with replication in the cells and suggests a method-of-moments estimator for the variance parameters. Like Lindley and Smith he assumes that C_1 the covariance matrix of the u_{ij} is $\sigma_0^2 I_{nJ}$ and that the α_i and β_j are iid $\mathcal{N}(0, \sigma_\alpha^2)$ and $\mathcal{N}(0, \sigma_\beta^2)$, respectively. When the design is balanced this leads to simple expressions for shrinkage estimators for the vectors α and β. The resulting point estimates can be considered maximum a posteriori, or MAP, estimates, and can be augmented to produce a full posterior distribution. A less dogmatic treatment of the variance parameters is proposed by expanding the hierarchical model to impose conjugate, inverse χ^2 distribution for the variances. MAP estimators are again proposed by iterating back and forth between location and scale parameters.

The rapid development of MCMC methods over the last 50 years has greatly expanded the flexibility of parametric hierarchical models and facilitated their efficient computation. Such methods underlie several generations of software development: BUGS, Lunn et al. (2012); jags, Plummer (2017); and most recently Stan, Carpenter et al. (2017). Careful language design, sophisticated Hamiltonian Monte Carlo algorithms, comprehensive documentation and copious illustrative applications have made Stan the default software for hierarchical Bayes modeling and estimation. Especially admirable is the attention paid to diagnostics designed to identify problematic performance of MCMC. Although Stan has been enthusiastically adopted in many other disciplines, it has been less warmly embraced in econometrics. Since regularization in other guises like machine learning has been welcomed in econometrics, this is puzzling. Perhaps the choice of parametric prior distributions is too traumatic. If so, nonparametric empirical Bayes might make a contribution toward relaxing the rather rigid structure of some more traditional forms of hierarchical Bayes modeling.

A prominent early exception to the econometric aversion to Stein shrinkage is the paper of Doan et al. (1984). As the use of structural macroeconomic models with their peremptory zero restrictions on coefficients receded, it became clear that the unrestricted vector autoregression models that replaced them needed some further discipline to control their profusion of parameters. Starting from the vector autoregression

$$y_t = A_t(L)y_{t-1} + c_t + u_t$$

for an m-dimensional response vector, the authors formulated a prior for $A_t(L)$ that effectively shrank these parameters toward a reference random walk with drift

$$y_t = y_{t-1} + c_t + u_t.$$

The Gaussian formulation of the prior facilitated a Kalman filtering approach to both estimation and prediction. While not delving into the details of the fitting procedures employed in this work, it can be viewed as a sophisticated form of penalized maximum likelihood. Penalty parameters were selected by exploring their impact on forecasting performance, and posterior inference about model parameters relied upon curvature of the posterior around the mode. This formulation of the prior, incorporating as it did constraints on the variability of time-varying coefficients, smoothness of distributed lag distributions and other features of macroeconomic conventional wisdom, became known as the "Minnesota prior" and continues to have resonance up to the present day. At the time it was written there was some debate about whether the approach was fully Bayesian or merely Stein-like. Since then, the idea of penalized Gaussian likelihood has become so ubiquitous that such distinctions seem pointless. More recently Bayesian methods in macroeconometrics have flourished, see for example, Del Negro and Schorfheide (2011).

3.4.1 Hierarchical Bayes versus Empirical Bayes

The hierarchical Bayes method does not always align with the empirical Bayes method, except in special circumstances. Consider the model with $Y_i \sim \mathcal{N}(\theta_i, 1)$ and $\theta_i \sim \mathcal{N}(\mu, 1)$. If μ were known, then under quadratic loss, the Bayesian estimator of θ_i is $\mathbb{E}(\theta_i | y_i) = \frac{1}{2}(y_i + \mu)$. When μ is unknown, the empirical Bayes method estimates μ by the sample mean $\bar{y}$, and thus the empirical Bayes estimator for θ_i becomes

$$\hat{\delta}(y_i) = \frac{1}{2}(y_i + \bar{y}).$$

Lindley and Smith (1972) shows that a hierarchical Bayesian approach, where μ is assumed to follow an improper uniform distribution over $\mathbb{R}$, leads to a hierarchical Bayesian estimator that coincides with the empirical Bayes estimator. However, this perfect agreement is an exception rather than the rule.

The uneasy coexistence of empirical Bayes and hierarchical Bayes methods is further highlighted in two papers by Petrone et al. (2014b,a) that ask the question: When do the two approaches merge? Unfortunately, the answer appears to be – only when their respective posteriors converge to degenerate distributions at the "true" parameter values. However, in the incidental parameter, compound decision framework this only happens when prior information is dominated by the information provided by the data thereby rendering any notion of the "borrowing of strength" from the ensemble of problems irrelevant. Before we reach this benign state of asymptopia, priors matter and posteriors will necessarily reflect their differences.

3.5 PARAMETRIC EMPIRICAL BAYES FOR HETEROSCEDASTIC GAUSSIAN MODELS

There are many variants of heteroscedastic Gaussian sequence models of the form

$$y_{ij} \sim \mathcal{N}(\mu_i, \sigma_i^2), \quad i = 1, \ldots, n, \; j = 1, \ldots, J.$$

The investigator observes pairs, $(\hat{\mu}_i, \hat{\sigma}_i^2)$ with $\hat{\mu}_i = J^{-1} \sum_j y_{ij}$ and $\hat{\sigma}_i^2 = (J - 1)^{-1} \sum_j (y_{ij} - \hat{\mu}_i)^2$; the objective is often to test the hypotheses: $H_0: \mu_i = 0$, or to select a subset that violate these hypotheses. In genomics this is often accomplished with a parametric empirical Bayes procedure implemented in the R package **limma** (Lönnstedt and Speed, 2002; Smyth, 2004). Rather than positing a prior on the full parameter space, **limma** assumes that the σ_i^2 are independent of the μ_i and drawn iidly from the inverse chi-squared distribution,

$$\sigma_i^{-2} \sim (\upsilon_0 s_0^2)^{-1} \chi^2_{\upsilon_0} \quad i = 1, \ldots, n.$$

The hyperparameters v_0 and s_0 can be estimated by the method of moments or maximum likelihood. The null hypotheses $H_0\colon \mu_i = 0$ have p-values

$$p_i = 2(1 - F_{t, v_0+v}(|\tilde{t}_i|)),$$

where $\tilde{t}_i = \hat{\mu}_i/\tilde{s}_i$, $\tilde{s}_i^2 = (v_0 s_0^2 + v\hat{\sigma}_i^2)/(v_0 + v)$, $v = J - 1$ and $F_{t,v}$ is the distribution function of a Student t random variable with v degrees of freedom. The parametric prior for the σ_i^2 shrinks the $\hat{\sigma}_i^2$ toward a common value and is intended to improve precision. The imposition of prior information on nuisance parameters while leaving the parameters of primary interest, in this case the μ_i, alone is referred to as "partially Bayes" by Cox (1975). See Ignatiadis and Sen (2025a) for a thorough investigation of this approach and extensions to nonparametric estimations of the prior. We will consider several other extensions including nonparametric estimation of a joint prior for the pairs, (μ_i, σ_i^2), in Chapter 4.

3.6 RIDGES, LASSOS, HORSESHOES AND OTHER COWBOY DIVERSIONS

Penalized maximum likelihood methods have expanded rapidly in response to growing demands for regularization of high-dimensional models. The influential work of Grace Wahba emphasized the Bayesian interpretation of these methods. In Kimeldorf and Wahba (1970) it was shown that in both interpolation and smoothing problems, shrinking solutions toward the null space of linear differential operators yielded tractable numerical solutions with an elegant general theory based on reproducing kernel Hilbert spaces. Given an mth order linear differential operator,

$$L = \sum_{j=0}^{m} a_j D^j,$$

and observations $\{(x_i, y_i)\colon \; i = 1, \cdots, n\}$, we can define an interpolating function μ as the solution of

$$\min_{\mu \in \mathcal{F}} \int (L\mu)^2 dx \quad \text{such that} \quad \mu(x_i) = y_i,\ i = 1, \ldots, n.$$

Similarly in the smoothing problem we have solutions to

$$\min_{\mu \in \mathcal{F}} \sum_{i=1}^{n} (y_i - \mu(x_i))^2 + \lambda \int (L\mu)^2 dx,$$

which shrink the estimated functions $\hat{\mu}$ toward the null space of L. Solutions take the form of L-splines, see for example, Ramsay et al. (1996), with absolutely continuous $(m-1)$ derivative and $L\mu \in \mathcal{L}_2$. The Bayesian interpretation of these solutions regards the integral contribution to the objective as a prior over the (Sobelev) space $\mathcal{F}$ of candidate functions. In the conventional case, $L = D^2$, solutions are cubic splines, piecewise cubic functions with a square integrable second derivative. Such priors are inherently improper since they impose no restriction on linear functions. This means that in the smoothing problem by letting $\lambda \to \infty$ we obtain the ordinary least squares solution of the bivariate regression of y on x. Smaller λ produce more flexible solutions, with $\lambda \to 0$ forcing solutions to interpolate the observed points. In conformity with other hierarchical Bayes estimators, we obtain a linear estimator. Denoting the function values at the observed x_i's as $\hat{\mu}_i = \hat{\mu}(x_i)$, we can write $\hat{\mu} = A(\lambda)y$, where $A(\lambda)$ is a known matrix depending only on λ and the spacings between adjacent x_i's. In the simplest case with equally spaced time series data, the matrix $A(\lambda)$ is just the second differencing operator, see Exercise 2.

This leaves the question: How should we select λ? To consider this, suppose we have the simple homoscedastic model,

$$y_i = \mu(x_i) + \sigma u_i,$$

with iid standard Gaussian u_i. We would like to minimize

$$\begin{aligned} R(\lambda) &= n^{-1}\mathbb{E}\|\mu - A(\lambda)y\|^2 \\ &= n^{-1}\mathbb{E}\|(I - A(\lambda))\mu\|^2 + n^{-1}\sigma^2\text{Trace}(A(\lambda))^2, \end{aligned}$$

but this isn't practical since we don't know μ. A possible approach if σ^2 is known would be to minimize

$$\begin{aligned} \hat{R}(\lambda) &= n^{-1}\|(I - A(\lambda))y\|^2 - n^{-1}\sigma^2[\text{Trace}(I - A(\lambda))^2 - \text{Trace}(A(\lambda))^2] \\ &= n^{-1}\|(I - A(\lambda))y\|^2 + n^{-1}\sigma^2\text{Trace}(A(\lambda))^2 - \sigma^2. \end{aligned}$$

This is a version of Mallows's C_p criterion (Mallows, 1973). It is obviously heroic to assume you know σ^2, except perhaps in some engineering applications, so a natural alternative is to minimize the leave-one-out cross-validation criterion,

$$V(\lambda) = n^{-1}\sum_{i=1}^{n}(y_i - \hat{\mu}^{(i)}(x_i))^2,$$

where $\hat{\mu}^{(i)}$, which depends upon λ, is the estimate of μ obtained by omitting the ith observation. It is known by the Sherman–Morrison–Woodbury formula that

$$V(\lambda) = n^{-1}\sum_{i=1}^{n}(y_i - \hat{\mu}(x_i))^2/(1 - A_{ii}(\lambda))^2.$$

$$V(\lambda) = \frac{n^{-1}\|(I - A(\lambda))y\|^2}{(n^{-1}\text{Trace}(I - A(\lambda)))^2}.$$

This is a variant of the cross-validation approach in which the quantities in the denominator are replaced by their sample average. Kimeldorf and Wahba called it generalized cross-validation, or GCV.

There are many variants of this approach. Connections to information criteria like AIC and SIC can be seen by considering

$$\nu(\lambda) \equiv 0.5 \log V(\lambda) = \log(\hat{\sigma}(\lambda)) - \log(1 - n^{-1}\text{Trace}A(\lambda)),$$

where $\hat{\sigma}^2 = n^{-1}\|(I - A(\lambda))y\|^2$. Now $A(\lambda)$ plays the role of the "hat" (projection) matrix in the theory of least squares regression. In the present case $\text{Trace}A(\lambda)$ varies from 2, when $\lambda \to \infty$, so $\hat{\mu}(x)$ is forced to be linear, to n, when $\hat{\mu}(x)$ interpolates the observed y_i's as $\lambda \to 0$. Thus $p(\lambda) = \text{Trace}A(\lambda)$ may be interpreted, loosely, as the "effective dimensionality" of the estimate $\hat{\mu}$. As long as $p(\lambda)$ is small relative to the sample size, n, we have the approximate criterion

$$\hat{\nu}(\lambda) = \log(\hat{\sigma}(\lambda)) + n^{-1}p(\lambda),$$

which is simply an "interpretation" of Akaike's AIC criterion for the present context. This observation was first made by Stone (1977) and immediately suggests a modification of the dimensionality penalty in accordance with the SIC criterion of Schwarz (1978):

$$\tilde{\nu}(\lambda) = \log(\hat{\sigma}(\lambda)) + \frac{1}{2}n^{-1}p(\lambda)\log n.$$

It should be admitted that trying to minimize any of these criteria to find a suitable λ can be a frustrating experience, but this is the price paid for asking the data to tell you how much you should believe in your (Gaussian) prior.

There is also a close connection of GCV to Stein unbiased risk estimation, or SURE, as shown in Li (1985). Stein (1981) showed that for Gaussian noise and squared error loss on μ, the estimator

$$\tilde{\mu}(\lambda) = y - \left[\frac{\sigma^2}{y^\top B(\lambda)y}\right] M(\lambda)y$$

dominates y and $\hat{\mu}$. Here $M(\lambda) = I - A(\lambda)$, and

$$B(\lambda) = (\text{Trace}(M(\lambda)I - 2M(\lambda)))^{-1}M(\lambda)^2.$$

The factor in square brackets is a "shrinkage factor," since if it were 1, $\tilde{\mu}$ would reduce to $\hat{\mu}$, whereas when it is less than 1 we can interpret $\tilde{\mu}$ as a compromise between $\hat{\mu} = A(\lambda)y$ and y,

$$\tilde{\mu} = (1 - v)y + v\hat{\mu},$$

where v denotes the scalar shrinkage factor. Further, Stein showed that

$$\text{SURE}(\lambda) = \sigma^2 - \frac{\sigma^4\|M(\lambda)y\|^2}{n(y^\top B(\lambda)y)^2}$$

is an unbiased estimator for the risk of $\tilde{\mu}(\lambda)$, that is, $\mathbb{E}n^{-1}\|\mu - \tilde{\mu}(\lambda)\|^2$, for any $\mu \in \mathcal{R}^n$, so to select a good λ it is natural to minimize SURE. This is obviously equivalent to minimizing

$$S(\lambda) = \frac{n(y^\top B(\lambda)y)^2}{\|M(\lambda)y\|^2}.$$

Now, in the same spirit as the AIC approximation, for n sufficiently large and $M(\lambda)$ balanced so its largest eigenvalue is small compared to its trace, we can approximate $B(\lambda)$ by $(\text{Trace}M(\lambda))^{-1}M^2(\lambda)$, and then

$$S(\lambda) \approx \frac{n(\text{Trace}M(\lambda))^{-2}\|M(\lambda)y\|^4}{\|M(\lambda)y\|^2} = \frac{\|M(\lambda)y\|^2}{n^{-1}(\text{Trace}M(\lambda))^2} = V(\lambda).$$

While we have presented these approaches to λ selection in the context of spline smoothing, it is evident that they apply more generally to the entire class of Gaussian hierarchical models in which Gaussian likelihoods are penalized by Gaussian priors. It is sometimes difficult to discern where the likelihood stops and the prior begins in such hierarchical models, which makes it difficult to distinguish Bayes from empirical Bayes procedures. Fortunately, this only matters in the higher echelons of statistical theology.

3.6.1 Total Variation Smoothing and the Lasso

Replacing squared L_2 norm (prior) penalties by L_1 norm penalties, for example trading

$$\min \sum (y_i - \mu(x_i))^2 + \lambda \int (\mu''(x))^2 dx$$

for

$$\min \sum (y_i - \mu(x_i))^2 + \lambda \int |\mu''(x)| dx,$$

produces another form of smoothing spline. It is piecewise linear, not piecewise cubic, and is better adapted to applications in which the target mean function exhibits sharp changes in derivative. The L_1 penalty can be interpreted as constraining the total variation of μ' to some fixed value controlled by the Lagrange multiplier λ. Like the Gaussian L_2 penalties, L_1 penalties are convex, facilitating efficient optimization. One can also replace the Gaussian log likelihood in such smoothing problems to produce estimates of conditional quantile functions. See Koenker et al. (1994) for further details.

L_1 penalization has become a standard tool for model selection following the influential work of Tibshirani (1996) and Donoho et al. (1998). One can interpret it as an independent (double exponential) Laplacian prior in the same way that the ridge penalties discussed earlier are seen as Gaussian priors. The heavier tails of the double exponential are more tolerant of large observations, while smaller observations are more aggressively shrunk toward zero. This is desirable from a selection point of view since researchers are often hoping that a small number of "interesting" effects can be identified among a large ex

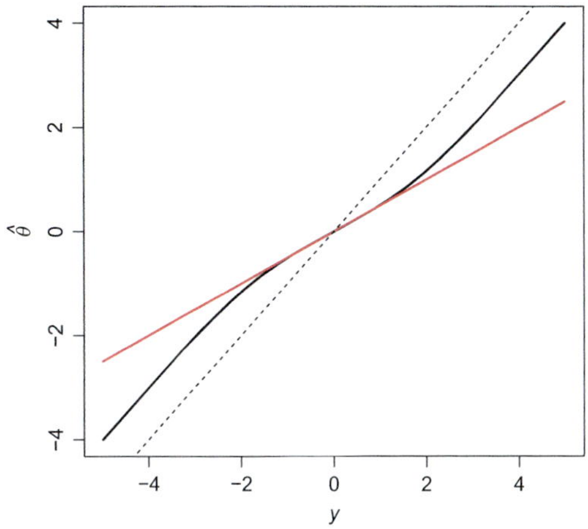

Figure 3.2. Comparison of Gaussian and Laplacian prior shrinkage: Posterior mean estimators for θ in the Gaussian sequence model; the red line represents shrinkage for the Gaussian prior, while the black curved line represents shrinkage for the Laplace prior.

ante set of possibilities. This is fancifully referred to as hunting for needles in a haystack and has been thoroughly explored in the influential paper of Johnstone and Silverman (2004).

Although the lasso is generally employed as a model selection device for high-dimensional regression settings, it is helpful to consider how it works in the simpler context of the Gaussian sequence model. In Figure 3.2 we contrast lasso shrinkage with ridge shrinkage in the simple model

$$Y_i = \theta_i + u_i,$$

with u_i iid $\mathcal{N}(0, 1)$. The red solid line represents linear shrinkage imposed by the prior $\theta_i \sim \mathcal{N}(0, 1)$, while the black curved line illustrates shrinkage with the prior when the prior is (standard) Laplace. The dashed line represents the naive MLE $\hat{\theta}_i = y_i$ 45-degree line. When the observed y is in $[-1, 1]$, the shrinkage is quite similar for the two priors, but when y is larger in absolute value, the linear shrinkage of the Gaussian prior is much more aggressive, while the Laplace prior exhibits bounded shrinkage. Old school robustniks will recognize this as a natural consequence of the form of the shrinkage component of the Tweedie formula, which coincides with the influence function of the respective influence functions of the Gaussian and Laplacian likelihoods.

Johnstone and Silverman (2004) consider an expanded class of priors that permit a positive mass, $1 - w$, at $\theta = 0$, often referred to as a spike and slab prior. This is natural in many needle and haystack settings. Denoting the Laplace density with median μ and scale a by $\gamma_{\mu,a}(y) = \frac{1}{2}a \exp(-a|y - \mu|)$, we have a two-parameter family of priors with density

$$g_a(\theta) = (1 - w)\delta_0(\theta) + w\gamma_{0,a}(\theta).$$

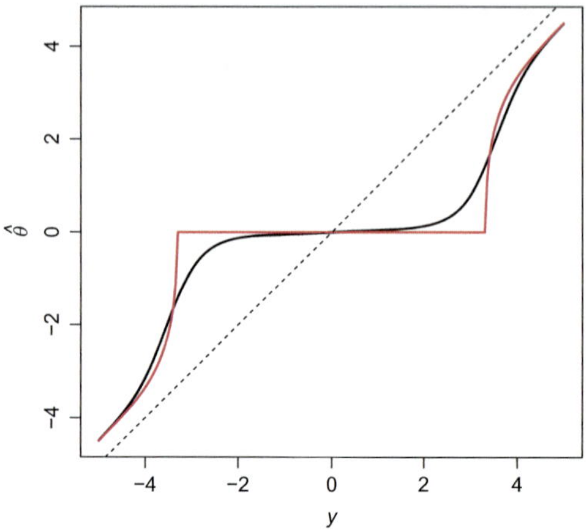

Figure 3.3. Comparison of posterior mean and median shrinkage for the Johnstone and Silverman Laplace prior with prior mass at zero. The black curve represents the posterior mean, while the red curve represents shrinkage with the posterior median.

The marginal density of Y given this prior is

$$f(y) = (1 - w)\phi(y) + wf_a(y),$$

where f_a denotes the convolution density,

$$f_a(y) = \int \phi(y - \theta)\gamma_{0,a}(\theta)d\theta = 0.5a\phi(y)[R(a - y) + R(a + y)],$$

and $R(y) = (1 - \Phi(y))/\phi(y)$.

Figure 3.3 illustrates posterior mean and posterior median shrinkage with this prior having set $w = 0.03$ and $a = 0.5$. Near zero, posterior median shrinkage forces $\hat{\theta}$ to zero, while for large absolute values of y the shrinkage of the two loss functions is indistinguishable. Despite the mass at zero the posterior mean with the Laplace prior doesn't manage to shrink observed y's all the way to zero, and for that reason its performance is slightly worse than the posterior median estimator in Johnstone and Silverman's simulations. The posterior median acts more like a hard thresholding estimator.

The obvious question at this point is: How should we go about choosing the tuning parameters w and a? In Johnstone and Silverman (2005) and the R package EBayesThresh that accompanies the paper, this is accomplished by maximizing the marginal log likelihood,

$$\ell(w,a) = \sum_{i=1}^{n} \log((1 - w)\phi(y_i) + wf_a(y_i)).$$

Thus, in the terminology of Efron, we can interpret these estimators as parametric empirical Bayes G-modeling methods. Prior parameters are simply estimated from the data by maximum likelihood.

3.6.2 Cauchy Priors and the Horseshoe Estimator

Johnstone and Silverman (2004) also consider a heavier-tailed "quasi-Cauchy" prior, for which they estimate the proportion of nonzeros but conclude that it is "always nearly, but not quite, as good as the [double] exponential method." Other heavy-tailed priors have also been considered in the literature. Carvalho et al. (2009) proposed a scale mixture of Gaussian priors for the θ_i's with hyperparameters drawn from half-Cauchy priors:

$$\theta_i|\lambda_i \sim \mathcal{N}(0, \lambda_i^2), \quad \lambda_i|\tau \sim C^+(0, \tau), \quad \tau \sim C^+(0, 1),$$

where $C^+(0, \tau)$ denotes the half-Cauchy distribution with scale τ. They suggest setting $\tau = 1$, but more recent literature and the R package **horseshoe** offer alternative MCMC proposals.

A more flexible variant of the Cauchy prior idea allows G to be a scale mixture of Gaussians or uniforms. Such methods have been proposed in Stephens (2017) and implemented in the R package **ashr**. This approach restricts $\hat{G}$ to be symmetric and unimodal, but it is more agnostic about the tail behavior of G than the Gaussian, Laplace or Cauchy choices would be.

A novel parametric empirical Bayes application is the Azevedo et al. (2020) study of large-scale A/B testing at Microsoft. To model the treatment effect of new "ideas" under test, the authors adopt a parametric prior for G as Student with unknown mean, scale and degrees of freedom parameter all estimated by maximum likelihood. Selection of implemented "ideas" is then determined by a positive posterior mean criterion. Some further discussion of this procedure can be found in Section 7.4.

It is instructive to reconsider the Johnstone and Silverman simulation experiment as a way to evaluate the efficacy of these priors compared to earlier thresholding methods and more recent nonparametric G-modeling methods. The main experiment fixed the sample size for each replication at $n = 1{,}000$; of these $k \in \{5, 50, 500\}$ are nonzero, and all the nonzero values take the same value, either 3, 4, 5 or 7. This design may seem unduly simple but perhaps can be motivated by the form of the minimax rule of Johnstone discussed in Section 2.1.2. In Table 3.1 we report average sums of squared errors for these experiments for 13 procedures: The horseshoe with hyperparameter τ fixed at one, several versions of the posterior mean and median with the Laplace prior of Johnstone and Silverman, the posterior mean based on the nonparametric maximum likelihood estimator of G, and finally the oracle Bayes rule posterior mean based on knowledge of the empirical distribution function of the true θ_i's for each sample.

One benchmark for these experiments might be considered to be that of the naive maximum likelihood decision rule. It has an expected loss of

Table 3.1. *Comparative performance of several estimators in standard Gaussian sequence model. Each entry in the table is a mean based on 1,000 replications. Each replication evaluates a sum of squared errors for* $n = 1{,}000$ *observations. The Horseshoe estimator of sets* $\tau = 1$. *Posterior means and medians using the Laplace prior of Johnstone and Silverman when the scale parameter, a, is estimated are denoted Lpmean(a) and Lpmed(a) respectively, and explicit values are given when a is fixed a priori. The posterior mean based on the Kiefer–Wolfowitz NPMLE is denoted KWpmean. And the oracle Bayes estimator, Oracle, is the posterior mean based on* $G = \hat{G}_n$, *the empirical distribution function of the true* θ_i*'s.*

	k = 5				**k = 50**				**k = 500**			
	3	4	5	7	3	4	5	7	3	4	5	7
Horseshoe	247	245	244	243	316	310	299	285	1,012	965	841	713
Lpmed(1.0)	35	30	20	15	214	164	140	133	993	1,101	1,125	1,130
Lpmed(0.5)	37	32	18	11	243	156	105	92	845	880	885	886
Lpmed(0.2)	38	35	19	8	298	189	96	70	1,065	731	666	658
Lpmed(0.1)	38	36	19	7	340	232	105	61	1,498	802	609	580
Lpmed(a)	36	31	18	9	215	155	101	73	857	876	785	660
Lpmean(1.0)	32	30	25	21	201	195	182	175	977	1,108	1,145	1,153
Lpmean(0.5)	32	29	19	14	203	162	129	115	853	896	904	905
Lpmean(0.2)	33	30	18	9	238	167	104	79	954	784	722	707
Lpmean(0.1)	33	30	18	8	275	192	104	66	1,190	809	651	613
Lpmean(a)	34	30	20	11	202	168	121	85	860	891	828	710
KWpmean	34	28	17	7	156	107	53	11	453	282	127	17
Oracle	27	21	11	1	149	100	45	3	445	274	119	9

1,000 in each setting. Alternatively, we have seen that the oracle rule based on the true prior is optimal among permutation-invariant procedures. The nonparametric empirical Bayes rule, KWpmean, has consistently superior performance relative to the other feasible procedures when k is 50 or 500. When $k = 5$, so there are very few needles, its performance is comparable to the Laplace procedures. The oracle of course is the best performer, but the KWpmean is always a close competitor.

It must be noted at this juncture that the Johnstone–Silverman simulation design is quite favorable to NPMLE. Because there are only two mass points for the true distribution, G, it is relatively easy for the NPMLE to produce a good estimate, $\hat{G}$. Often, especially when the non-null θ_0 is well separated from 0, $\hat{G}$ will itself have only two mass points, and in such cases the shrinkage effect of the posterior mean tends to attract observations to one or the other of these mass points as illustrated in Figure 4.2. In contrast, all of the other procedures involve priors that are symmetric about zero and therefore are only capable of shrinkage toward zero. Similar comments apply to the other estimators included in the simulations reported by Johnstone and Silverman, including the hard-thresholding procedures considered there. Although the NPMLE sacrifices a small advantage in not recognizing that the null value of zero is special, the location equivariance of the method also offers substantial advantages.

3.7 COMBINING "POSSIBLY RELATED" ESTIMATORS

Concern over the validity of combining disparate estimation problems as advocated by Robbins and Stein prompted a variety of new shrinkage proposals. Notable among these is the "relevance function" approach of Efron and Morris (1973a). They begin by considering the problem of estimating two vector-valued parameters, $\theta_1 \in \mathbb{R}^{n_1}$ and $\theta_2 \in \mathbb{R}^{n_2}$, in the model

$$Y_{ij}|\theta_{ij} \sim \mathcal{N}(\theta_{ij}, \sigma^2), \quad j = 1, \ldots, n_i, \; i = 1, 2,$$

for known σ^2, and suggest the rule

$$\delta_{ij} = \left[1 - \frac{(n-2)\sigma^2}{S}\rho_i(V_i)\right] y_{ij},$$

where $S_i = \sum_{j=1}^{n_i} Y_{ij}^2$, $S = S_1 + S_2$, $V_i = S_i/S$, and $n = n_1 + n_2$. When $\rho_i(V_i) = 1$ this reduces to James–Stein for the combined sample, while the choice of the "relevance function,"

$$\rho_i(V_i) = \frac{n_i - 2}{n - 2}\frac{1}{V_i},$$

yields separate James–Stein rules for each of the two groups. Intermediate choices are suggested that improve upon both estimators provided the ratios of prior variances are not too different in the two groups.

Combining estimators when one is biased is also of considerable practical importance. Green and Strawderman (1991) consider the case that X and Y are independent n-variate Gaussian random vectors, with covariance matrices $\sigma^2 I_n$ and $\tau^2 I_n$ respectively, and $\mathbb{E}X = \theta$ and $\mathbb{E}Y = \theta + \xi$. The mean squared error of linear estimators of the form

$$\delta_\alpha(X, Y) = \alpha X + (1 - \alpha)Y$$

is $\alpha^2 n\sigma^2 + (1-\alpha)^2(n\tau^2 + \xi^\top \xi)$, and choosing $\alpha^* = (n\tau^2 + \xi^\top\xi)/(n\sigma^2 + n\tau^2 + \xi^\top\xi)$ to minimize this expression, they consider estimators of the form

$$\delta_{\alpha^*}(X, Y) = \frac{(n\tau^2 + \xi^\top\xi)X}{n\sigma^2 + n\tau^2 + \xi^\top\xi} + \frac{n\sigma^2 Y}{n\sigma^2 + n\tau^2 + \xi^\top\xi}.$$

Noting that $\mathbb{E}\|X - Y\|^2 = n\sigma^2 + n\tau^2 + \xi^\top\xi$, they then write

$$\begin{aligned}\delta_{\hat{\alpha}}(X, Y) &= \frac{(\|X - Y\|^2 - n\sigma^2)X + n\sigma^2 Y}{\|X - Y\|^2} \\ &= X - \frac{n\sigma^2(X - Y)}{\|X - Y\|^2}.\end{aligned}$$

Thus, $\delta_{\hat{\alpha}}(X, Y)$ is interpretable as a linear shrinkage estimator that shrinks X toward Y. When the bias contribution, ξ, is small this reduces to the familiar variance-weighted average of the two estimators, while more substantial bias tends to reduce the influence of Y.

In the influential literature on educational value added, where empirical Bayes methods have been extensively employed, combinations of least squares estimators and instrumental variables estimators based on school lottery assignment have been recently used to mitigate the influence of selection bias, for example, Angrist et al. (2023).

3.8 EMPIRICAL BAYES DENSITY ESTIMATION

Penalized maximum likelihood is also a highly effective method for density estimation. Unlike more popular kernel methods it offers considerable flexibility to impose qualitative features on the target density. An early example is Good (1971) who proposed maximizing the penalized log likelihood,

$$\sum_{i=1}^{n} \log f(y_i) + \lambda \int \left(\left(\sqrt{f(y)}\right)'\right)^2 dy,$$

which shrinks the estimated density toward densities with small Fisher information for location. It is not entirely clear why this particular penalty might be desirable, but a variety of similar proposals emerged later. Interest naturally focused on the cubic smoothing spline alternative,

$$\sum_{i=1}^{n} \log f(y_i) + \lambda \int (f(y)'')^2 dy,$$

which shrinks toward exponential densities, that is, those with linear log density. The motivation for this too may seem obscure, so the proposal of Silverman (1982),

$$\sum_{i=1}^{n} \log f(y_i) + \lambda \int (f(y)''')^2 dy,$$

to shrink toward a Gaussian density, that is, those whose logarithm is quadratic, seems more appealing. Note that the Silverman penalty imposes no constraint on the mean or variance of the Gaussian limit as $\lambda \to \infty$. Consequently, in that limit we obtain the usual parametric Gaussian estimate.

As in the regression smoothing setting, the form of the L_2 penalty does enforce smoothness of derivatives, so kinks in $\log \hat{f}$ are prohibited. For kinky densities, L_1, or total variation, penalties on derivatives of $\log f$ are more appropriate. Penalizing total variation of $\log f$ itself has been considered by Davies and Kovac (2004), who provide a valuable geometric interpretation. Given iid observations, $Y_1, \ldots, Y_n$, imagine plotting its empirical distribution function and an associated Kolmogorov confidence band around it. Now attach a slack string to the left-most abscissa of the plot and pull the string taut so that it stays within the Kolmogorov band. This is illustrated in Figure 3.4. In panel (a) the empirical distribution function appears as the black step function with its red, dashed confidence band, and the taut string estimate is shown in blue as a piecewise linear curve that touches the confidence band at only a few distinct points. Panel (b) shows the taut string density estimate corresponding to the piecewise linear distribution in panel (a). Although the procedure produces a histogram-type density estimate, it should be emphasized that the choice of bin widths is automatic and controlled only by the parameter λ of the penalty, which in turn may be linked to the confidence level of the Kolmogorov band. It is a remarkably successful method for estimating the number of modes in a univariate density. These procedures have important antecedents in the celebrated Grenander (1956) estimator of monotone densities that also has a taut string interpretation as a least concave majorant of the observed empirical distribution function.

Smoother estimators can be achieved by penalizing the total variation of the first or second derivatives of the log density rather than log density itself. Total variation of the second derivative of log density gives a variant of the original Silverman proposal but permits more abrupt changes in the shape of the estimated density. Figure 3.5 illustrates two estimates of a univariate Gaussian density both based on total variation penalization of the second derivative of log density, one using $\lambda = 0.05$ and the other $\lambda = 1$. Not only is the former estimate under-smoothed, it exhibits an embarrassing upward tendency in both tails. More control over the tail behavior of such density estimators can be achieved by imposing stronger shape constraints.

The leading example of a shape-constrained density estimator is the Grenander (1956) estimator, which is extensively studied in Groeneboom and Jongbloed (2014). It too has a simple taut string interpretation since the least

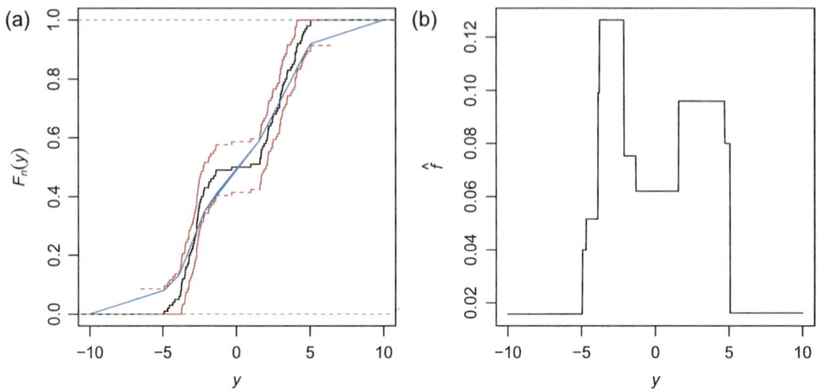

Figure 3.4. Taut string density estimator: Panel (a) illustrates the taut string interpretation of the estimator resulting in a piecewise linear estimate of the distribution function appearing in blue. Panel (b) shows the corresponding piecewise constant density estimate.

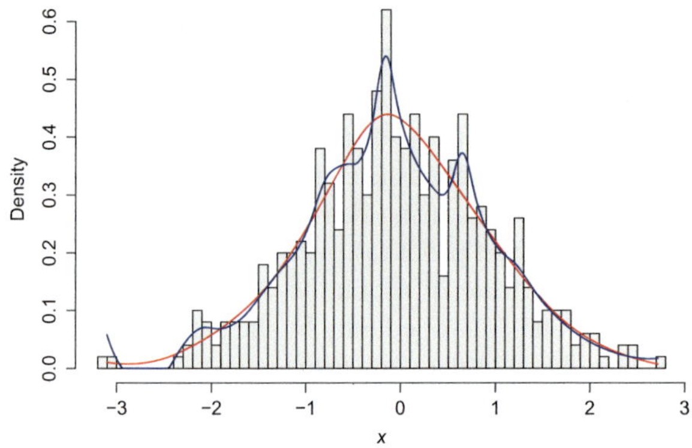

Figure 3.5. Two total variation estimates: The figure depicts a histogram of 500 iid Gaussian observations and two estimates of the density based on penalized maximum likelihood. Total variation of the second derivative of the log density is penalized in both cases, but the more wiggly estimate employs $\lambda = 0.05$, while the smoother one uses $\lambda = 1$.

concave minorant can be implemented by stretching a taut string over the top of the empirical distribution function to produce a piecewise linear distribution function estimate, and thus a piecewise constant and decreasing density estimate. To obtain unimodal density estimates one can try to estimate the mode and use this procedure twice, but it is probably simpler and more effective to consider strongly unimodal, that is, log concave, density estimation. In contrast to the other penalized maximum likelihood methods we have described for regression smoothing and density estimation, these shape-constrained methods are self-regularizing. They have no tuning parameters to select; they automatically produce sparse solutions with only a small number of distinct pieces. In this sense they are similar to the Kiefer–Wolfowitz NPMLE for estimating mixing densities described in earlier chapters and described in more detail in Chapter 12.

Log-concave densities must have lighter tail behavior than the exponential, and in some applications it is of interest to consider heavier-tailed unimodal densities. One way to do this is to consider ρ-concave densities as introduced by Avriel (1972). This is explored in detail in Koenker and Mizera (2010) and implemented in the R package **REBayes** by the function `medde`. This entails a slight departure from the strict maximum likelihood protocol and introduces a new tuning parameter that describes the desired tail exponent of the target density. Again, this brings us back to the empirical Bayes paradigm.

3.9 FINITE MIXTURE MODELS AND THEIR ESTIMATION

Mixture models occupy a prominent place in the empirical Bayes toolbox as we have already seen. Finite mixture models are often used to identify salient groupings of observations that have common structure and can be exploited to achieve improved precision for both estimation and inference. Finite mixture models are notoriously challenging computationally since their likelihood formulation is nonconvex and typically multimodal. The advent of the EM algorithm (Dempster et al., 1977) offered some relief from these difficulties, but serious reservations remain as reflected in the comments of Wasserman (2012). For a large class of infinite mixture models, convexity of the likelihood formulation is restored leading to efficient implementations of nonparametric empirical Bayes methods as we argue in subsequent chapters.

There is nothing sacred of course about the use of maximum likelihood estimation. Other criteria naturally suggest themselves in various applications. For finite mixture models the method of moments was employed by Karl Pearson for estimating a model for Weldon's crab data, as described in further detail in Chapter 12. Indeed, the James–Stein estimator may be viewed as a parametric method-of-moments empirical Bayes procedure. In Section 9.2 we contrast maximum likelihood and method-of-moments estimators for the Diaconis tack-flicking data.

Method of moments seems particularly well suited to finite mixture applications. Consider again the Gaussian sequence model

$$Y_i = \theta_i + U_i,$$

where U_i is standard Gaussian and θ_i is independent of U_i and follows distribution G. Let $m_k(G) = \int \theta^k dG$ be the kth order moment of θ, and denote the Hermite polynomials of Y as

$$H_k(y) = (-1)^k \exp(y^2/2)\left[\frac{d^k}{dy^k}\exp(-y^2/2)\right].$$

It can be verified that the Hermite polynomials provide unbiased estimators for the moments $m_k(G)$. For example, we have,

$$\begin{aligned} H_1(y) &= y, & \mathbb{E}[H_1(Y)] &= \mathbb{E}[\theta], \\ H_2(y) &= y^2 - 1, & \mathbb{E}[H_2(Y)] &= \mathbb{E}[\theta^2], \\ H_3(y) &= y^3 - 3y, & \mathbb{E}[H_3(Y)] &= \mathbb{E}[\theta^3]. \end{aligned}$$

If the support of G is compact, then knowing all the moments from $\mathbb{E}[H_k(y)]$ $k = 1, 2, \ldots$ allows us to recover the distribution G. We can also recover the Tweedie formula via the moments since we can represent the marginal density of Y through a series expansion in the Hermite polynomials. In particular,

$$\frac{\phi(y-\theta)}{\phi(y)} = 1 + \sum_{k=1}^{\infty} \frac{1}{k!}\theta^k H_k(y).$$

Since the marginal density of Y is, $f_G(y) = \int \phi(y-\theta)dG$, this implies

$$f_G(y) = \phi(y)\left\{1 + \sum_{k=1}^{\infty} \frac{1}{k!} m_k(G) H_k(y)\right\}.$$

Taking logarithms and differentiating with respect to y, the Tweedie formula becomes

$$\begin{aligned} \mathbb{E}[\theta|y] &= \frac{d}{dy}\log f_G(y) - \frac{d}{dy}\log\phi(y) \\ &= \frac{d}{dy}\log\left\{1 + \sum_{k=1}^{\infty}\frac{1}{k!} m_k(G) H_k(y)\right\} \\ &= \frac{\sum_{k=1}^{\infty}\frac{1}{k!} m_k(G)\frac{d}{dy}H_k(y)}{1 + \sum_{k=1}^{\infty}\frac{1}{k!} m_k(G) H_k(y)}. \end{aligned}$$

For infinite mixtures, having to estimate all the moments of G from the expectation of the Hermite polynomials is daunting. However, for finite mixtures, this approach may yield a viable estimation strategy as originally suggested by Lindsay (1989) and further developed by Wu and Yang (2020).

In the k-component Gaussian sequence model, with $\theta \sim G = \sum_{\ell=1}^{k} w_\ell \delta_{a_\ell}$, if k is known, we need to learn only $2k-1$ parameters, the weights and locations of the mass points of G. Learning the first $2k-1$ raw moments of G provides enough constraints to identify the $2k-1$ parameters. This can be formalized in the following lemma.

Lemma 3.5. *Let G and G' be two discrete distribution with k mass points; then $G = G'$ if and only if $m_i(G) = m_i(G')$ for $i = 1, 2, \ldots, 2k-1$, provided both sides exist.*

Proof: One direction is trivial: If $G = G'$ then its first $2k - 1$ moments will match. For the other direction, denote the location of the mass points for G and G' as $a_1, \ldots, a_k$ and $a_1', \ldots, a_k'$ respectively. Let the set S collect distinct the values of $\{a_1, \ldots, a_k\} \cup \{a_1', \ldots, a_k'\}$. We would like to show that for any $t \in \mathbb{R}$,

$$G(t) = \mathbb{E}_G[1\{\theta \leq t\}] = \mathbb{E}_{G'}[1\{\theta \leq t\}] = G'(t).$$

Since G and G' only have mass points from S, it suffices to consider the step function $\theta \to 1\{\theta \leq t\}$ on the set S. The cardinality of S is at most $2k$. By the polynomial interpolation theorem, there exists a polynomial P of degree at most $2k - 1$ that interpolates the step function on S, that is,

$$P(\theta) = 1\{\theta \leq t\} \text{ for all } \theta \in S,$$

where $P(\theta)$ is a polynomial function of θ up to degree $2k - 1$. Since P is of degree at most $2k - 1$, it follows that $\mathbb{E}_G[P(\theta)] = \mathbb{E}_{G'}[P(\theta)]$, since the first $2k - 1$ moments of G and G' match. ■

There are several possible estimation methods for discrete problems like this. Maximum likelihood is problematic because in the finite-mixture setting the likelihood is nonconvex; the set of k-atomic discrete measures is no longer convex. An alternative approach is to optimize the method of moments criteria,

$$\min_{\boldsymbol{\zeta}} (\hat{\boldsymbol{m}}_n - \boldsymbol{m}(\boldsymbol{\zeta}))^\top W (\hat{\boldsymbol{m}}_n - \boldsymbol{m}(\boldsymbol{\zeta})),$$

where W is a weighting matrix, the jth entry of $\boldsymbol{m}(\boldsymbol{\zeta})$ is

$$[\boldsymbol{m}(\boldsymbol{\zeta})]_j = \sum_{\ell=1}^{k} w_\ell a_\ell^j,$$

and the jth entry of $\hat{\boldsymbol{m}}_n$ is

$$[\hat{\boldsymbol{m}}_n]_j = n^{-1} \sum_{i=1}^{n} H_j(y_i),$$

for $j = 1, \ldots, 2k - 1$. This problem is again nonconvex in $\boldsymbol{\zeta} = (w_1, \ldots, w_k, a_1, \ldots, a_k)$. However, a suggestion of Wu and Yang (2020) yields an attractive algorithm. Their first step is to de-noise the sample moment vectors $\hat{\boldsymbol{m}}_n$. This is done by projecting $\hat{\boldsymbol{m}}_n$ onto the moment space

$$\mathcal{M}(\mathcal{K})_r = \Big\{\boldsymbol{m} \in \mathbb{R}^r : [\boldsymbol{m}]_j = \int x^j dG(x), \text{ with } G \text{ as a distribution supported on } \mathcal{K}\Big\},$$

which is the convex hull of $\{(x, x^2, \ldots, x^r) : x \in \mathcal{K}\}$ with $\mathcal{K} \subseteq \mathbb{R}$. If the projection distance is Euclidean, then it is equivalent to the GMM criteria with an identity weighting matrix, except that we do not optimize with respect to $\boldsymbol{\zeta}$ but rather optimize over $\boldsymbol{m} \in \mathcal{M}(\mathcal{K})_r$ with $r = 2k - 1$. Recall that to recover a k-atomic distribution, we require $2k-1$ moments for identification. In particular, we must solve

$$\widetilde{\boldsymbol{m}} := \underset{\boldsymbol{m} \in \mathcal{M}(\mathcal{K})_{2k-1}}{\text{argmin}} \; (\hat{\boldsymbol{m}}_n - \boldsymbol{m})^\top W (\hat{\boldsymbol{m}}_n - \boldsymbol{m}).$$

When $\mathcal{K} = [a,b]$, the moment space is completely characterized by the following semidefinite matrix constraints:

$$\begin{aligned} &\boldsymbol{M}_{0,r} \succcurlyeq 0, (a+b)\boldsymbol{M}_{1,r-1} \succcurlyeq ab\boldsymbol{M}_{0,r-2} + \boldsymbol{M}_{2,r}, && r \text{ even},\\ &b\boldsymbol{M}_{0,r-1} \succcurlyeq \boldsymbol{M}_{1,r} \succcurlyeq a M_{0,r-1}, && r \text{ odd}, \end{aligned}$$

where $\boldsymbol{M}_{i,j}$ are matrices of the form

$$\boldsymbol{M}_{i,j} = \begin{pmatrix} m_i & m_{i+1} & \cdots & m_{\frac{i+j}{2}} \\ m_{i+1} & m_{i+2} & \cdots & m_{\frac{i+j}{2}+1} \\ \vdots & \vdots & \vdots & \vdots \\ m_{\frac{i+j}{2}} & m_{\frac{i+j}{2}+1} & \cdots & m_j \end{pmatrix}.$$

The m_j denote the elements of the moment vector $\boldsymbol{m}$. Since the constraint conditions that characterize the convex set $\mathcal{M}(\mathcal{K})_r$ all take the form of matrices restricted to be semidefinite, we have a semidefinite programming problem that is convex. See Vandenberghe and Boyd (1996) and Exercise 5 in this chapter. Having obtained an optimizer $\widetilde{\boldsymbol{m}}$ from the semidefinite programming problem, we can take a second key step to produce a k-atomic distribution G that recovers $\widetilde{\boldsymbol{m}}$. For this step, Wu and Yang (2020) propose a Gaussian quadrature method. This is a grid-free way to solve for the k-atomic distribution. They use the fact that for any distribution supported on $[a,b] \subseteq \mathbb{R}$, a k-point Gauss quadrature is a k-atomic distribution $G_k = \sum_{\ell=1}^{k} w_\ell \delta_{a_\ell}$ also supported on $[a,b]$ such that for any polynomial P of degree at most $2k-1$,

$$\mathbb{E}_G[P] = \mathbb{E}_{G_k}[P] = \sum_{\ell=1}^{k} w_\ell P(a_\ell).$$

Gaussian quadrature points always exist and are uniquely determined by the first $2k-1$ moments, $(\tilde{m}_1, \ldots, \tilde{m}_{2k-1})$. Basic quadrature algorithms and many of their variants are available in the literature. We provide further details in Chapter 12.

When the noise variance, σ^2, is known but $\sigma^2 \neq 1$, we can construct

$$\gamma_k(y,\sigma) = \sigma^k H_k(y/\sigma) = k! \sum_{j=0}^{\lfloor k/2 \rfloor} \frac{(-1/2)^j}{j!\,(k-2j)!} \sigma^{2j} y^{k-2j},$$

and it is easy to verify that $\mathbb{E}[\gamma_k(Y,\sigma)] = \mathbb{E}[\theta^k]$ when $Y = \theta + \sigma U$ with $U \sim \mathcal{N}(0,1)$. We can then construct unbiased estimator for $\mathbb{E}[\theta^k]$ from

$$\hat{m}_k = k! \sum_{j=0}^{\lfloor k/2 \rfloor} \frac{(-1/2)^j}{j!\,(k-2j)!} \sigma^{2j} \frac{1}{n} \sum_{i=1}^{n} y_i^{k-2j},$$

and by following the de-noising and Gaussian quadrature steps obtain an estimator for G.

Wu and Yang (2020) establish that the resulting k-atomic distribution estimator achieves the minimax optimal rate of convergence in 1-Wasserstein distance when we know k and the variance of the noise.

When the noise variance is unknown, a remarkable result of Lindsay (1989) establishes that σ^2 is still identifiable for $k-$atomic G.

Theorem 3.6 (Lindsay (1989, lemma 5A)). *For $Y = \theta + \sigma U$ with $U \sim \mathcal{N}(0,1)$ and $\theta \sim G$, which is a distribution with k-atoms, we can identify σ as the smallest non-negative root of $d_k(\sigma) = 0$ where $d_k(\sigma)$ is the determinant of the moment (Hankel) matrix of order k,*

$$\boldsymbol{M}_k(\sigma) := \begin{pmatrix} 1 & m_1(\sigma) & \dots & m_k(\sigma) \\ m_1(\sigma) & m_2(\sigma) & \dots & m_{k+1}(\sigma) \\ & & \vdots & \\ m_k(\sigma) & m_{k+1}(\sigma) & \dots & m_{2k}(\sigma) \end{pmatrix},$$

with $m_k(\sigma) = \mathbb{E}[\gamma_k(Y,\sigma)]$.

Proof: For any $\tilde{\sigma} < \sigma$, we can represent $Y \sim \tilde{G} \star \mathcal{N}(0,\tilde{\sigma}^2)$ as $\tilde{G} = G \star \mathcal{N}(0,\sigma^2 - \tilde{\sigma}^2)$, hence

$$\mathbb{E}[\gamma_k(Y,\tilde{\sigma})] = m_k(\tilde{G}).$$

Let $d_k(\tilde{\sigma})$ be the determinant of the Hankel matrix of order k formed from $\mathbb{E}[\gamma_j(Y,\tilde{\sigma})]$ with $j = 1,2,\dots,2k$. Then theorem 2A(a) of Lindsay (1989) implies that $d_k(\tilde{\sigma}) = 0$ for $\tilde{\sigma} = \sigma$, and $d_k(\tilde{\sigma}) > 0$ for $\tilde{\sigma} < \sigma$, since $\tilde{G}$ is a continuous distribution. Therefore, σ can be identified as the smallest nonzero root of $d_k(\sigma) = 0$. ■

This result then leads to an algorithm described in detail in Chapter 12. Wu and Yang (2020) show that the resulting estimator, $\hat{\sigma}$, is a consistent estimator for σ and is minimax rate optimal.

Surprisingly, infinite-dimensional mixtures can be considerably easier to estimate than finite-dimensional ones as we have already noted, and we will now turn our attention to such models.

Exercises

(1) An analogue of Stein's lemma for the Poisson case: Show that if $Z|\theta \sim Poisson(\theta)$, then for any function $u(z)$ defined for $z = 0, 1, \ldots,$

$$cov(Z, u(Z)) = \mathbb{E}[Z(u(Z) - u(Z-1))].$$

(2) For smoothing equally spaced univariate time series, show that the smoothing spline procedure described in Section 3.6 reduces to choosing the matrix $A(\lambda)$ to compute second differences of the response. In macroeconometrics this procedure has become known as the Hodrick–Prescott filter. It can be implemented in R concisely as:

```
hpfilter <- function(y,lambda=1600){
eye <- diag(length(y))
solve(eye+lambda*crossprod(diff(eye,d=2)),y)
}
```

Try this on a simple example.

(3) Suppose the distribution F has the same first k moments as the standard Gaussian distribution, Φ. Lindsay and Basak (2000) showed that the maximal Kolmogorov discrepancy

$$\sup_x |F(x) - \Phi(x)|$$

can be as large as 0.18 for $k = 20$, and 0.15 for $k = 30$. Portnoy (2015) observes that this bound can be well approximated by $(2/\pi)/\sqrt{k}$, a considerable improvement over the bound given by Uspensky (1937) of $\sqrt{\pi/(2k)}$. What do these extremal F's look like?

(a) A rough answer can be found by solving a linear program that assigns mass to a fine grid of points on an interval, say $[-8, 8]$. Try this with a few hundred grid points.

(b) (Portnoy (2015)) Show that when the number of matched even moments k is even, the optimal choice of support points for the discrete solutions maximizing the Kolmogorov discrepancy are zeros of the Hermite polynomials with mass assigned by classical Gaussian quadrature rules.

(c) Reflect upon the Lindsay and Basak (2000) conclusion that moments are not very informative about the center of the distribution but are mainly influenced by its tail behavior.

(4) For a smoother example of the foregoing, consider the distribution introduced by McCullagh (1994) with density, $f(x) = \varphi(x)(1 + 0.5\sin(2\pi x))$.

(a) Plot the two densities to get a visual impression of their differences.

(b) Show that the cumulant generating functions of this distribution and the standard Gaussian differ by a factor that is bounded in absolute value by 1.34×10^{-9}, so their moments are essentially indistinguishable.

(c) Show that their characteristic functions differ by a purely imaginary component that is negligible except near $\pm 2\pi$.

(5) Consider a simple version of the Wu and Yang (2020) de-noising problem involving only the first three moments of G with support on the interval $[0, 1]$ and set $W = I$. We have sample moments, $\hat{m}_n$, and would like to solve

$$\min_m \|\hat{m}_n - m\|_2^2$$

subject to the positive semidefiniteness of the two Hankel matrices,

$$\begin{pmatrix} 1 - m_1 & m_1 - m_2 \\ m_1 - m_2 & m_2 - m_3 \end{pmatrix} \succcurlyeq 0, \quad \begin{pmatrix} m_1 & m_2 \\ m_2 & m_3 \end{pmatrix} \succcurlyeq 0.$$

Show that this problem can be reformulated as a standard semidefinite programming problem:

$$\min_x \left\{ c^\top x \mid F(x) = F_0 + \sum_{i=1}^p x_i F_i \succcurlyeq 0 \right\},$$

where $F_0, F_1, \ldots, F_p$ are all known symmetric matrices.

CHAPTER 4

Nonparametric Empirical Bayes Methods

The compound decision paradigm of Robbins imagines a family of exchangeable parametric statistical problems,

$$Y_i \sim \varphi(y|\beta, \eta_i), \quad i = 1, \ldots, n.$$

We will refer to β as the structural parameter and the $\eta_i, i = 1, \ldots, n$ as incidental parameters. The problem is nonparametric, or semiparametric insofar as we intend to view η_i as a random variable with an unknown distribution rather than treating them as fixed parameters. The investigator observes independent realizations, $Y_1, \ldots, Y_n$ and is asked either to estimate the entire n-vector, η, subject to some specified loss function, or to predict some configuration of future values of Y. There is always the option of treating the problems individually, but there is usually benefit, as we have seen, in treating them as an ensemble. Parametric prior information about the distribution of the η_i can aid in this, at the risk of imposing too much structure on the decision rule. Nonparametric empirical Bayes offers more flexibility and enhanced performance for many compound decision problems. For sufficiently large n performance is close to that achievable by an oracle with full knowledge of the distribution of the latent η_i's.

4.1 EXPONENTIAL FAMILY MIXTURES AND THE TWEEDIE FORMULA

We will begin by considering a special, albeit large, class of compound decision problems in which φ takes the form of an exponential family density with natural parameter η, that is, the support of $\varphi(y|\eta)$ is independent of η, and suppressing dependence on the structural parameter, β,

$$\varphi(y|\eta) = m(y)e^{y\eta}h(\eta).$$

Exchangeability of the Y_i implies that we can write their marginal distribution as

$$f_G(y) = \int \varphi(y|\eta)dG(\eta),$$

for some mixing distribution G. Estimating the η_i's subject to quadratic loss

$$L(\hat{\eta}, \eta) = n^{-1} \sum (\hat{\eta}_i - \eta_i)^2$$

yields the following result for known G.

Theorem 4.1 (Tweedie). *Under the foregoing conditions the optimal (Bayes) decision rule is the conditional mean*

$$\delta(y) \equiv \mathbb{E}(\eta | Y = y) = \frac{d}{dy} \log(f_G(y)/m(y)),$$

and the decision rule δ is monotone in y.

Proof: Straightforward computations as in van Houwelingen and Stijnen (1983) give

$$\begin{aligned}
\delta(y) &= \mathbb{E}[\eta | Y = y] \\
&= \int \eta \varphi(y|\eta) dG \Big/ \int \varphi(y|\eta) dG \\
&= \int \eta e^{y\eta} h(\eta) dG \Big/ \int e^{y\eta} h(\eta) dG \\
&= \frac{d}{dy} \log \left(\int e^{y\eta} h(\eta) dG \right) \\
&= \frac{d}{dy} \log(f_G(y)/m(y)).
\end{aligned}$$

Differentiating again,

$$\begin{aligned}
\delta'(y) &= \frac{d}{dy} \left[\frac{\int \eta \varphi dG}{\int \varphi dG} \right] \\
&= \frac{\int \eta^2 \varphi dG}{\int \varphi dG} - \left(\frac{\int \eta \varphi dG}{\int \varphi dG} \right)^2 \\
&= \mathbb{E}[\eta^2 | Y = y] - (\mathbb{E}[\eta | Y = y])^2 \\
&= \mathbb{V}[\eta | Y = y] \geq 0,
\end{aligned}$$

which implies that δ must be monotone. ∎

The Gaussian case is particularly simple and attractive.

Corollary 4.2 When φ is Gaussian, so $Y|\theta \sim \mathcal{N}(\theta, \sigma^2)$ with known variance σ^2, then

$$\delta(y) \equiv \mathbb{E}(\theta | Y = y) = y + \sigma^2 f_G'(y)/f_G(y).$$

Proof: In the Gaussian case the natural parameter for the exponential family is $\eta = \theta/\sigma^2$, and $m(y) = (2\pi\sigma^2)^{-1/2} \exp(-y^2/2\sigma^2)$ so $\mathbb{E}(\eta|y) = y/\sigma^2 + f_G'(y)/f_G(y)$, and the result follows from the fact that $\eta\sigma^2 = \theta$. ∎

Robbins (1956) attributes the general exponential family result to M.C.K. Tweedie, although the eponym came into common usage only following Efron (2011). The Gaussian version appears earlier in Dyson (1926), attributed there to the astronomer Arthur Eddington. Stein (1986) credits Brown (1971) for closely related results. The striking feature of the Tweedie formula in its various forms is that the shrinkage term depends only on the marginal density of the observed response. Thus, if interest focuses on estimation of posterior means as it naturally would under quadratic loss, then nonparametric decision rules apparently require only estimation of $f_G(y)$, the marginal density. Efron (2019) has termed this f-modeling and contrasts it with G-modeling that directly tackles the estimation of the mixing distribution, G for nonparametric compound decision making. This will be a major theme of the remainder of this chapter. In the Gaussian setting f-modeling led Brown and Greenshtein (2009) to propose plug-in Bayes rules based on kernel density estimation of f_G.

A deficiency of the kernel estimate of f_G is that it is difficult to ensure that the resulting Bayes rule for the posterior mean is monotone as required from Theorem 4.1. This led to the momentous question Larry Brown asked one of us on that fateful morning in 2011, "Is there a shape-constrained density estimator for f_G that would ensure monotonicity of the Bayes rule?" The answer proved to be surprisingly simple. Penalized maximum likelihood of the density subject to the convex cone constraint that the function

$$K_f(y) = \frac{1}{2}y^2 + \log f(y)$$

is convex suffices. The resulting optimization problem is easily seen to be convex and closely related to extensive recent work on log concave density estimation. See Koenker and Mizera (2014) and Exercise 5 for further details. Viewed as a plug-in estimator for the posterior mean, this estimator can be seen as an f-modeling strategy. It does not fully exploit the maximum likelihood deconvolution structure of the Kiefer–Wolfowitz NPMLE, but it performs quite well in the simulation exercises of Koenker and Mizera (2014).

For p-dimensional multivariate Gaussians, with known, common covariance matrix, $Y_i \sim \mathcal{N}_p(\theta_i, \Sigma)$, there is an analogous Tweedie formula,

$$\hat{\theta}_i = \delta(y) = y + \Sigma \frac{\nabla f_{G,\Sigma}(y)}{f_{G,\Sigma}}.$$

Soloff et al. (2025) extend this result to heteroscedastic covariance matrices and provide extensive discussion of both statistical and computational aspects of the NPMLE for multivariate Gaussian mixture problems. Liu et al. (2020) extend this f-modeling approach to the dynamic panel data setting.

4.1.1 The Gaussian Sequence Model: A Simulation Bake-Off

In the Robbins Ur problem we had a relatively simple Gaussian, $\mathcal{N}(\theta, 1)$ setting in which θ took only one of two known values. Before turning to nonparametric empirical Bayes procedures in this chapter, we would like to explore various extensions of this simple setting. To this end we will consider another highly stylized setting in which we again have only two possible values for the unknown parameters, $\theta_1, \ldots, \theta_n$, but we aren't privy to these values, nor do we know the amount of mass assigned to each. This simple setting, quite similar in design to the experiment described in Section 3.6.2 and again motivated by the Johnstone minimax procedure described in Section 2.1.2, is a special case of what we refer to as the Gaussian sequence model. It has been extensively used in simulation experiments. More explicitly, suppose we see $Y_i \sim \mathcal{N}(\theta_i, 1)$ for $i = 1, \ldots, n$. The parameters, θ_i, take the value zero with probability γ, or with probability $1 - \gamma$ they take Δ. The presumption is that γ is near one, so in the terminology of Johnstone and Silverman (2004) and Castillo and van der Vaart (2012) we are looking for "needles in haystacks." When Δ is well separated from zero, one might guess that the problem would be relatively easy.

We consider the simulation setting of Castillo and van der Vaart (2012), which is quite similar to that of Johnstone and Silverman (2004). The sample size is $n = 500$, of which the number of nonzeros, denoted s, is either 25, 50 or 100. All the nonzeros take only one of the three values 3, 4 or 5. A naive benchmark for this experiment would be to use the maximum likelihood estimator $\hat{\theta}_i = Y_i$ for each realization; this would achieve scaled mean squared error of 500. Table 4.1 compares the performance of 10 other estimators. The first eight rows of this table are taken directly from Table 1 of Castillo and van der Vaart (2012) and reflect performance of various Bayesian and empirical Bayesian procedures described and compared there. All of these estimators share the feature that observed Y_i's are shrunk toward zero. The HT and HTO estimators are variants of the hard thresholding minimax procedures described earlier in Section 2.1.2, see Castillo and van der Vaart (2012) for details. The ninth row of the table reports MSE for the posterior mean estimator, labeled NPMLE, based on the Kiefer–Wolfowitz nonparametric maximum likelihood estimator, $\hat{G}$. The last row of the table reports MSE

Table 4.1. *MSE based on 100 replications.*

	$s = 25$			$s = 50$			$s = 100$		
	3	4	5	3	4	5	3	4	5
PM1	111	96	94	176	165	154	267	302	307
PM2	106	92	82	169	165	152	269	280	274
EBM	103	96	93	166	177	174	271	312	319
PMed1	129	83	73	205	149	130	255	279	283
PMed2	125	86	68	187	148	129	273	254	245
EBMed	110	81	72	162	148	142	255	294	300
HT	175	142	70	339	284	135	676	564	252
HTO	136	92	84	206	159	139	306	261	245
NPMLE	79	55	28	121	83	40	170	106	47
Oracle	73	48	21	115	77	33	163	100	41

for the infeasible oracle estimator based on the empirical distribution of the θ_i's, G_n.

Clearly the nonparametric empirical Bayes procedure, NPMLE, does substantially better than any of procedures considered by Castillo and van der Vaart. Why? All of the first eight estimators have the advantage that they know that there is substantial mass associated with the event, $\theta_i = 0$. What they don't "know" is that all of the nonzero θ_i's are piled up at only one other point. The NPMLE doesn't have any preconceptions about where mass is located, or how it is allocated. It doesn't know about the special status of the null value $\theta_i = 0$, nor does it know that there are only two possible values that θ_i can take on in these experiments. And yet it performs nearly as well as the oracle procedure that knows both the location of the atoms and their relative frequency. The explanation for this apparently magical performance is quite simple: When the two mass points of the G_n distribution are well separated, the NPMLE delivers a very precise estimate of G_n. This estimate becomes more and more precise as the separation increases. It should be stressed, however, that the excellent performance of the NPMLE $\hat{G}$ in such discrete settings for G is quite exceptional, and minimax rates of convergence for smooth deconvolution problems are known to be as slow as $\mathcal{O}(1/\log n)$. For this reason, $\hat{G}$ estimates should generally be understood as a means to an end, not an end in themselves. The discrete G settings of the Castillo and van der Vaart experiments are particularly favorable for the NPMLE in this respect.

In a similar simulation setting Abadie and Kasy (2019) compare ridge and lasso estimators with penalty parameters selected by Stein's unbiased risk estimator (SURE) and cross-validation criteria with NPMLE posterior means. They conclude that except for relatively small sample sizes and high dispersion of the true mean parameters the NPMLE performs extremely well. It is worth noting that the computational cost of the NPMLE is also attractive, because it requires no tuning parameter selection. Abadie and Kasy (2019) make additional comparisons in several empirical settings that help to visualize the differences in the shrinkage rules corresponding to the various procedures. We can interpret all of the hard and soft thresholding procedures as parametric empirical Bayes methods with tuning parameters chosen by some optimization method.

To further assist the visualization of the shrinkage effect of the NPMLE posterior mean estimator, Figure 4.1 illustrates a histogram based on 1,000 observations generated from the Gaussian location mixture model $Y \sim \frac{3}{4}\mathcal{N}(0,1) + \frac{1}{4}\mathcal{N}(3,1)$. Superimposed on the histogram is the $\hat{G}$ solution of the Kiefer–Wolfowitz NPMLE. It is remarkably accurate with a mass of 0.755 located at 0.06 and mass 0.245 at 3.02. The Bayes rule, or posterior mean, used to predict θ_i based on the realization y_i is given by the Tweedie formula,

$$\hat{\theta}_i = y_i + f'_{\hat{G}}(y_i)/f_{\hat{G}}(y_i),$$

where $f_{\hat{G}}$ is the marginal density, $f_{\hat{G}}(y) = \int \phi(y-\theta)d\hat{G}(\theta)$. The nonlinear Tweedie shrinkage is depicted in Figure 4.2. The posterior must have the same

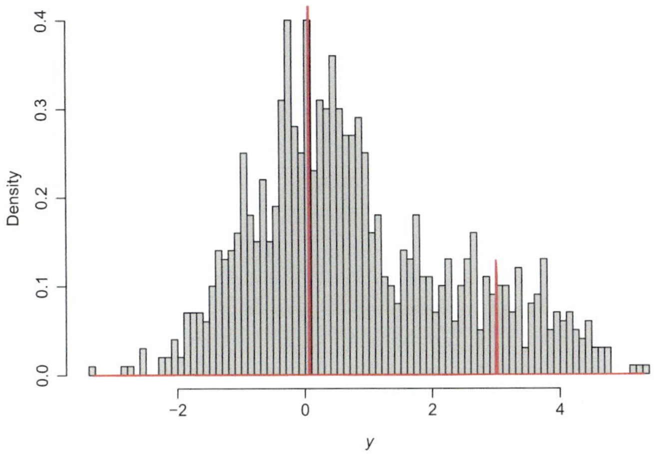

Figure 4.1. Histogram of 1,000 observations from a Gaussian mixture model with density $f(z) = \frac{3}{4}\phi(z-0) + \frac{1}{4}\phi(z-3)$ and NPMLE $\hat{G}$ superimposed.

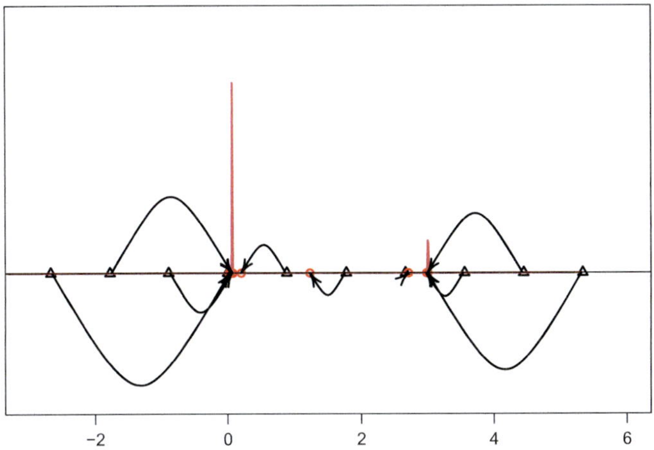

Figure 4.2. Nonlinear shrinkage of the Tweedie posterior mean for the Gaussian mixture model shown in Figure 4.1. Black triangular observations are transformed to the red circles.

support as the estimated prior, $\hat{G}$, which may seem to be a bug since $\hat{G}$ has only two points of support. But it is really a feature. Observations below the lower point of support 0.06 are dragged all the way up to this value. Similarly, points above the upper support point of 3.02 are dragged back to that value. For intermediate points, the posterior mean must recognize that posterior mass is attracted from both directions, so for our example the black triangle midway between the two mass points is moved somewhat to the left attracted more strongly by the larger mass near zero. The black triangle closer to zero is moved almost all the way to the posterior mode. We should stress that all of this shrinkage is location equivariant. If we were to shift all of the observations to the right by an amount a, then all the predictions would shift by a as well. See Proposition 12.3. This is in sharp contrast to most other shrinkage proposals such as those considered by Castillo and van der Vaart (2012) that prioritize shrinkage to a fixed value, usually zero.

We defer further computational details to Chapter 12. In Chapter 6 we will describe several variants of the Gaussian sequence model and consider applications to heteroscedastic and longitudinal data. We now consider another common compound decision model that is often used for the analysis of count data.

4.2 POISSON MIXTURE MODELS

Poisson mixture models appear in many settings from ecology to insurance. Montiel Olea et al. (2021) analyze Poisson variation in police departments' use of deadly force from an empirical Bayes perspective.

Suppose we observe, $Y_1, \ldots, Y_n$ with $Y_i \sim \text{Pois}(\lambda_i)$, so $\mathbb{P}(Y_i = y|\lambda_i) = \varphi(y|\lambda_i) = e^{-\lambda_i}\lambda_i^y/y!$, and we assume $\lambda_i \sim G$. Again, if we are averse to the Bayesian interpretation of G, we may simply conjure up an oracle who happens to know the empirical distribution of the λ_i for our problem. The marginal distribution of the Y_i's is now

$$f_G(y) = \int \varphi(y|\lambda)dG(\lambda),$$

and the posterior mean of $\lambda_i|Y_i = y$ is

$$\delta(y) = \frac{\int \lambda\varphi(y|\lambda)dG(\lambda)}{\int \varphi(y|\lambda)dG(\lambda)} = \frac{(y+1)f_G(y+1)}{f_G(y)}.$$

Robbins (1956) proposed estimating this quantity by simply plugging in the observed sample frequencies $\hat{f}_G(y) = n^{-1}\sum \mathbb{1}(Y_i = y)$ for $y = 0, 1, \ldots$. This is an f-modeling strategy since it depends only on the estimation of the marginal distribution of the response, Y. Several other estimators are considered in Brown et al. (2013). Various G-modeling approaches may also be considered. They have the advantage that they automatically impose monotonicity on the decision rule $\delta(y)$, which need not be the case for the Robbins estimator.

Let $\hat{\lambda}_G(Y)$ denote the oracle Bayes rule based on full knowledge of G, and denote the Bayes risk of this estimator as

$$B(\hat{\lambda}_G(Y), G) = \mathbb{E}_G(\hat{\lambda}_G(Y) - \theta)^2.$$

How well can we hope to do relative to this infeasible benchmark? Define the total regret over a class of priors $G \in \mathcal{G}$ as

$$\text{TotRegret}(\mathcal{G}) = \inf_{\hat{\lambda}_n} \sup_{G \in \mathcal{G}} \left\{ \mathbb{E}_G \left[\|\hat{\lambda}_n - \lambda\|^2 \right] - nB(\hat{\lambda}_G(Y), G) \right\}.$$

Table 4.2. *Root mean squared error based on 1,000 replications.*

	$(\alpha, \beta) = (2, 1)$				$(\alpha, \beta) = (5, 1)$			
	Robbins	NPMLE	PMLE	Oracle	Robbins	NPMLE	PMLE	Oracle
n = 100	2.226	1.777	1.721	1.718	4.307	2.799	2.721	2.723
n = 1,000	1.903	1.745	1.733	1.732	3.134	2.745	2.730	2.733
n = 10,000	1.768	1.734	1.732	1.732	2.821	2.742	2.740	2.739

This is the price one pays for ignorance of G. Ignoring the compound decision structure of the problem implies that regret grows linearly with sample size. However, the infimum above is taken over all estimators $\hat{\lambda}_n = \hat{\lambda}_n(Y_1, \ldots, Y_n)$. Robbins demonstrated that his proposed estimator for the Poisson model achieved sublinear total regret, that is, the total regret grows at a rate slower than n.

Polyanskiy and Wu (2021) have recently shown that for $\mathcal{G}$ with bounded support, total regret scales like $\mathcal{O}((\log n / \log \log n)^2)$, while for $\mathcal{G}$ with sub-exponential tail behavior it scales like $\mathcal{O}(\log^3 n)$. In both cases, these rates are attained by the original estimator proposed by Robbins, fully justifying earlier claims of its "near optimality."

To provide some further evidence on the relative performance of nonparametric versus parametric empirical Bayes methods we report results of a small simulation experiment in Table 4.2. Poisson mixtures with Gamma mixing distribution, $G = Gamma(\alpha, \beta)$, are considered with three sample sizes. Gamma mixing is convenient because there is a closed form for the resulting mixture distribution and its associated posterior mean Bayes rules. We consider four estimators for the n-vector of λ parameters: The original Robbins (1956) proposal, the NPMLE procedure, a parametric empirical Bayes procedure, PMLE, that employs a plug-in maximum likelihood estimate of the parameters of the Gamma distribution and an oracle Bayes rule that "knows" the precise parametric form of G. Loss is measured by root mean squared error of the estimates of the λ_i's for the four procedures. Robbins's nonparametric estimator is somewhat noisier than the other methods, especially in the right tail. This is most apparent when the sample size is modest and may be attributed to the fact that the Robbins estimator does not enforce the monotonicity constraint that the other methods do. This has prompted various proposals to smooth and/or monotonize it, see for example, Brown et al. (2013). Not surprisingly the parametric empirical Bayes estimator shows excellent performance, but the nonparametric G-modeling estimator is nearly as good even though it is totally ignorant about the form of the true mixing distribution.

4.2.1 Missing Species and Shakespeare's Vocabulary

A classical problem in ecology involves estimating the number of *unseen* species based on the frequencies of observed species seen in large field studies.

Table 4.3. *Observed frequencies of Corbet's species.*

Frequency	1	2	3	4	5	6	7	8	9	10	11	12	13	14	15	16	17	18	19	20	21	22	23	24
Species	118	74	44	24	29	22	20	19	20	15	12	14	6	12	6	9	9	6	10	10	11	5	3	3

The first systematic statistical investigation of this problem was reported in Fisher et al. (1943). It should be noted that Good (1953, 1976) has pointed out that Alan Turing developed similar empirical Bayes methods at Bletchley Park during World War II.

The English naturalist A.S. Corbet had collected a large sample of Malayan butterflies and asked Fisher's help in analyzing the resulting data. Corbet's data is shown in Table 4.3; 118 species were observed only once, 74 only twice and so forth. In all there were 501 species represented in the sample with 3,306 individual specimens. Very common species observed more than 24 times were deemed irrelevant to the main question: How many species were missed by the collection survey?

In order to address this question, Fisher resorted to his favorite tool – the method of maximum likelihood. It was clear that a simple Poisson model would be inadequate. Instead he opted for a Gamma mixture with parameters (α, β) of Poissons. Conditioning on $n_1 = 118$, the number of species in the sample occurring only once, and using the negative binomial representation of the Gamma mixture, the likelihood of the other counts can be written as, $\ell(\alpha, \beta) = \sum_{j=2}^{24} \log p(n_j, n_1 \lambda_j(\alpha, \beta))$, where

$$\lambda_j(\alpha, \beta) = \frac{\Gamma(\alpha + j)\gamma^{j-1}}{j!\,\Gamma(\alpha + 1)},$$

where $\gamma = \beta/(1 + \beta)$ and $p(n, \lambda)$ denotes the Poisson density. Maximizing this log likelihood yields a fit shown in Figure 4.3 to the observed counts. The NPMLE fit for the same data is also plotted in the same figure and seems to fit somewhat better. The linear extrapolation of both fitted models, shown by the dashed lines in the figure, can be used to estimate the number of unseen species, $\eta_0 = \mathbb{E} n_0$. This seems to be a dangerous, but irresistible exercise. Extrapolation of the Fisher estimate gives $\hat{\eta}_0 \approx 134$, while the NPMLE extrapolation yields 237.

A closely related application that has received considerable statistical attention is the estimation of size of authors' vocabularies based on a corpus of written material. Efron and Thisted (1976) and Thisted and Efron (1987) explore this question for Shakespeare in considerable detail including an application to attribution of authorship of a recently discovered poem. Koenker and Gu (2019) contrast several methods of estimation for the Shakespeare data, including a more formal Bayesian Dirichlet procedure. It should be remarked that inference for such quantities can be very challenging due to the discrete nature of the support and other irregularity of the likelihood. Some of the latest progress has been made in Mao and Lindsay (2004) and Mao and Lindsay (2007).

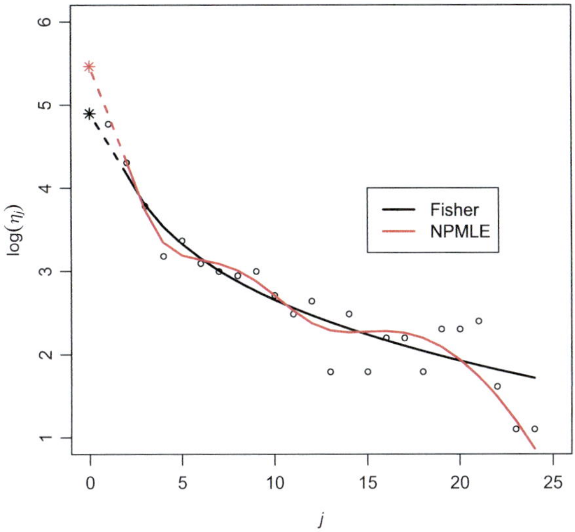

Figure 4.3. Raw Corbet frequencies (in logarithms) with two estimated models: The smoother curve represents Fisher's Gamma mixture of Poissons; the more undulating curve depicts the NPMLE estimate of the expected counts. Linear extrapolations to estimate the number of unseen species are shown as the dashed portions of the two estimated curves.

4.2.2 Prediction in the Poisson Model

From a practical decision making perspective, posterior mean estimates of λ may not be as relevant as predictions of future occurrences. Robbins (1977) considers a hypothetical setting in which we observe the number of accidents, $X_1, \ldots, X_n$, experienced by individuals in a baseline period and we would like to predict their experience $Y_1, \ldots, Y_n$ in a subsequent period. For example, we might like to predict the total number of new claims filed by those with fewer than k accidents in the initial period,

$$S_n(k) = \sum_{i=1}^{n} Y_i \mathbb{1}(X_i < k).$$

To illustrate, imagine an insurance company interested in predicting the total number of claims by policy holders who had no claims in the previous period, for example, $k = 1$. Clearly, it makes little sense to assume that they will all remain accident free in the forecast period. Instead, Robbins (1977) proposed to estimate $S_n(1)$ by the observed frequency,

$$\hat{S}_n(1) = \sum_{i=1}^{n} \mathbb{1}(X_i \le 1),$$

so, in particular the number of claims in the forecast period by those filing no claim in the prior period is estimated to be the number filing one claim in the prior period. Prediction intervals for such estimates are also proposed. Given λ_i, X_i and Y_i are assumed to be independent draws from the density $\mathrm{Pois}(\cdot|\lambda_i)$, so policy holders have a stable "accident proneness" λ_i that persists over the two periods.

Theorem 4.3 (Robbins (1977)). *Given the independence condition, define the random variables:* $V_i = \mathbb{1}(X_i < k)$, $U_i = \mathbb{1}(X_i \le k)$ *and* $W = V_i Y_i$. *Then,*

$$\sqrt{n}\left(\frac{\hat{S}_n(k)}{N_n(k)} - \frac{S_n(k)}{N_n(k)}\right) = \frac{n^{-1/2}\sum_{i=1}^n (U_i - W_i)^2}{n^{-1}\sum_{i=1}^n V_i} \rightsquigarrow \mathcal{N}(0, A_k^2),$$

where $N_n(k) = \sum_{i=1}^n V_i$, *and* $A_k^2 = \mathbb{E}(U - W)^2/\mathbb{E}V^2$. *The asymptotic variance* A_k^2 *is consistently estimable as* $\hat{A}_k^2 = (c_{k+1} - c_k + 3b_k - b_{k+1})/a_k^2$, *where* $\hat{f}_n(j) = n^{-1}\sum_{i=1}^n \mathbb{1}(X_i = j)$, *and*

$$a_k = \sum_{j=1}^{k-1} \hat{f}_n(j), \quad b_k = \sum_{j=1}^{k} j\hat{f}_n(j), \quad c_k = \sum_{j=1}^{k} j^2 \hat{f}_n(j).$$

Thus, a $1 - 2\alpha$ prediction interval for $S_n(k)$ can be expressed as $\hat{S}_n(k) \pm z_\alpha a_k \hat{A}_k \sqrt{n}$, where z_α denotes the α quantile of the standard Gaussian distribution.

In Tables 4.4–4.7 we compare the coverage and length of these intervals for $k = 2$ with those constructed using the raw frequencies, $\hat{f}_n(j)$, labelled as Robbins, versus the frequencies estimated based on the NPMLE estimates of G, labeled as NPMLE $\hat{G}$. The latter can be viewed as a projection of the raw frequencies to the model-restricted frequencies. Lambert and Tierney (1984) show that the Poisson NPMLE projects raw frequencies into the model space and that these projected frequencies have the same asymptotic behavior as the raw frequencies themselves.

The simulation confirms that the asymptotic approximation is extremely accurate even for the moderate, $n = 100$, sample size. In the simulation we assume G to be Gamma with the shape parameter, α, taking values 2 and 5, and the scale parameter set to 1. There is close agreement between the raw frequency counts and those estimated by the G-modeling of the NPMLE. Further smoothing or isotonization of the original Robbins proposal

Table 4.4. *Coverage with nominal size* 0.50.

	Robbins		**NPMLE $\hat{G}$**	
	$\alpha = 2$	$\alpha = 5$	$\alpha = 2$	$\alpha = 5$
$n = 100$	0.499	0.507	0.498	0.505
$n = 1{,}000$	0.468	0.485	0.467	0.486
$n = 10{,}000$	0.507	0.523	0.506	0.523

Table 4.5. *Coverage with nominal size* 0.95.

	Robbins		**NPMLE $\hat{G}$**	
	$\alpha = 2$	$\alpha = 5$	$\alpha = 2$	$\alpha = 5$
$n = 100$	0.953	0.952	0.951	0.945
$n = 1{,}000$	0.952	0.965	0.951	0.965
$n = 10{,}000$	0.959	0.948	0.959	0.948

Table 4.6. *Length of C.I. with nominal coverage* 0.5.

	Robbins		**NPMLE $\hat{G}$**	
	$\alpha = 2$	$\alpha = 5$	$\alpha = 2$	$\alpha = 5$
$n = 100$	19.1	16.2	19.1	16.1
$n = 1{,}000$	60.4	51.2	60.4	51.3
$n = 10{,}000$	190.8	162.2	190.8	162.2

Table 4.7. *Length of C.I. with nominal coverage* 0.95.

	Robbins		**NPMLE $\hat{G}$**	
	$\alpha = 2$	$\alpha = 5$	$\alpha = 2$	$\alpha = 5$
$n = 100$	55.4	47.1	55.3	46.8
$n = 1{,}000$	175.3	149.3	175.4	149.3
$n = 10{,}000$	554.0	471.2	553.9	471.3

as suggested by Brown et al. (2013) seems hardly worth the additional effort. The NPMLE intervals do impose monotonicity, but this doesn't lead to any appreciable improvement in performance.

4.2.3 Occupational Premiums for Life Insurance

To illustrate application of the Poisson mixture model we consider an application to life insurance premiums based on Norwegian data originally reported in Norberg (1989) and subsequently reanalyzed by Haastrup (2000). The data consists of 1,125 contracts aggregated in 72 occupational categories reporting the number of deaths, Y_i, and the number of years exposed to risk, X_i, for each occupational group. Following Norberg we assume a Poisson model for Y_i, so conditional on λ_i,

$$Y_i \sim \text{Pois}(\lambda_i X_i).$$

Exposures are renormalized as in Haastrup (2000) so they can be interpreted as the expected number of claims in a contract period. The multiplicative factor,

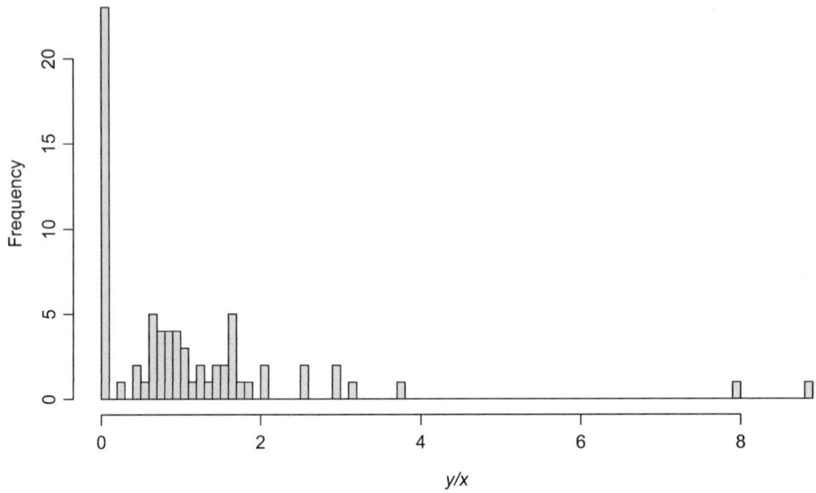

Figure 4.4. Histogram of claims per exposure for 72 occupation groups.

λ_i, accounts for the plausible variability in risk across occupational groups. In actuarial science where mixture models are commonplace, mixing distributions are typically parametric; see Bühlmann and Gisler (2005) for an authoritative exposition. In the Poisson case, assuming G is Gamma, with density

$$g(\lambda) = \frac{\beta^\alpha}{\Gamma(\alpha)} \lambda^{\alpha-1} \exp(-\beta\lambda)$$

is particularly convenient since the resulting marginal (mixture) distribution can be found in closed form as a negative binomial,

$$\begin{aligned} f(y|x) &= \int \frac{(\lambda x)^y \exp(-\lambda x)}{x!} \frac{\beta^\alpha}{\Gamma(\alpha)} \lambda^{\alpha-1} \exp(-\beta\lambda) d\lambda \\ &= \binom{x+\alpha-1}{y} \left(\frac{\beta}{x+\beta}\right)^\alpha \left(\frac{x}{x+\beta}\right)^y . \end{aligned}$$

The parameters α and β of the Gamma distribution can be estimated by maximum likelihood, giving a simple plug-in parametric empirical Bayes strategy. The posterior mean risk per exposure is

$$\hat{\lambda}_i = \delta_i y_i / x_i + (1 - \delta_i)\mathbb{E}(\lambda) = \frac{y_i + \alpha}{x_i + \beta},$$

with $\mathbb{E}(\lambda) = \int \lambda dG(\lambda) = \alpha/\beta$ and $\delta_i = \frac{\mathbb{V}(\lambda)}{\mathbb{V}(\lambda) + \mathbb{E}(\lambda)/x_i}$ with $\mathbb{V}(\lambda) = \alpha/\beta^2$. The Gamma assumption on G, however convenient, may not accurately represent the underlying mixing distribution, and resulting premium calculations based on it may be questionable. For this reason it seems prudent to explore nonparametric estimation of the Poisson mixture model.

Figure 4.5 contrasts the NPMLE estimator of G with the corresponding parametric estimates assuming that G is Gamma. Maximum likelihood of the

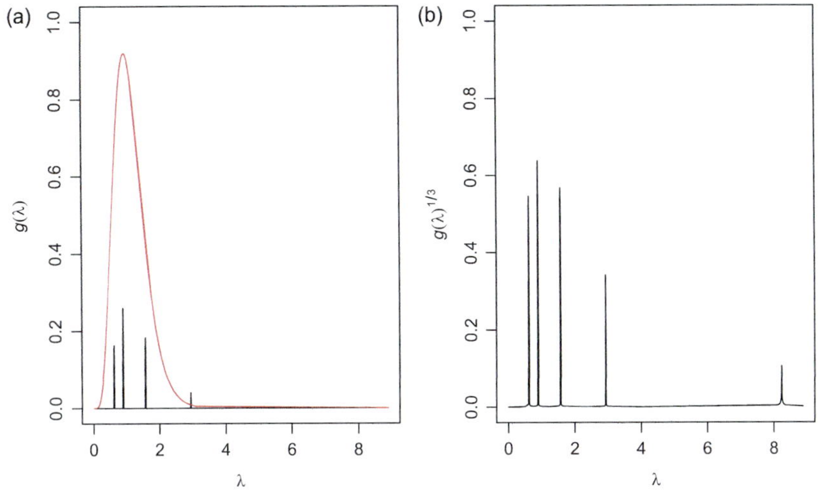

Figure 4.5. Estimated mixing distributions G for the group insurance data. Panel (a) depicts the Kiefer–Wolfowitz NPMLE estimator $\hat{G}$ for G in black. Panel (b) plots the cube root of the mass associated with support points in $\hat{G}$ to accentuate the mass of the estimated atom near 8. The smooth red curve superimposed in panel (a) corresponds to the estimated G for the parametric Gamma–Poisson model. The Gamma shape and rate parameters are estimated by maximum likelihood.

Gamma parameters from the negative binomial model yields quite precise estimates: $\hat{\alpha} = 6.02$ and $\hat{\beta} = 5.25$ with standard errors of 2.00 and 1.82, respectively. We see that although the majority of the NPMLE support points seem to be comfortably situated under the "umbrella" of the estimated Gamma density, the Gamma distribution fails to detect the two outliers, Group 13 and Group 53, with y/x ratios equal to 8.89 and 7.98, respectively, that are apparent in the histogram in Figure 4.4. In panel (b) of Figure 4.5, we plot the cube root of the estimated mixing distribution to magnify the very small yet important mass point of the NPMLE near 8. One might argue that these two occupational groups could be viewed as outliers and hence should not be allowed to influence our views about the distribution of the unobserved risk factor λ. However, an insurance company would ignore them at its peril.

Figure 4.6 contrasts the posterior means $\hat{\lambda}_i$ based on the parametric Poisson–Gamma empirical Bayes estimator and those based on the nonparametric Poisson mixture model. We can see that for most of the occupational groups, the two estimators agree closely except for the two most extreme cases of Group 13 and 53 that have the largest y/x ratios. The nonparametric empirical Bayes procedure, based on the small mass associated with its much larger support point, produces substantially higher estimates for these "riskier" groups, thereby presumably justifying a higher premium.

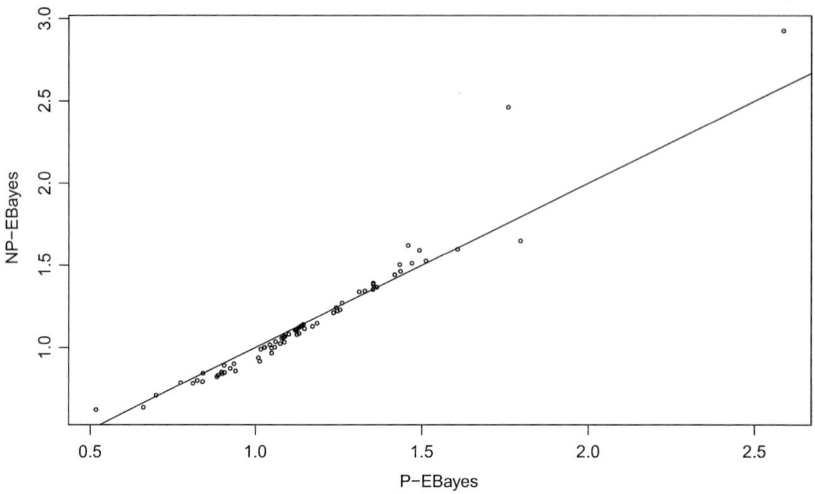

Figure 4.6. Comparison of the parametric and the nonparametric empirical Bayes estimates of λ_i for 72 occupation groups. As indicated by the 45-degree line there is good agreement between the parametric and nonparametric Bayes rules except for the two groups appearing in the upper right corner of the plot.

4.3 RISK AND REGRET OF NONPARAMETRIC EMPIRICAL BAYES RULES

In this section we will very briefly review the current state of the art on performance guarantees for nonparametric empirical Bayes rules in the Gaussian and Poisson compound decision problems. As we have seen, estimation of sparse Gaussian mixture models has attracted a large literature dealing with various forms of hard and soft thresholding rules and assorted parametric Bayes priors. The seminal papers of Zhang (2009) and Jiang and Zhang (2009) on nonparametric empirical Bayes methods represented a drastic shift away from these parametric methods toward Robbins's original proposal to estimate mixing distributions nonparametrically.

In the standard Gaussian sequence model, $Y_i \sim \mathcal{N}(\theta_i, 1)$, $i = 1, \ldots, n$, with θ_i's drawn iidly from the distribution, G, the Bayes risk of a decision rule δ under quadratic loss,

$$B_n(\delta, G) = n^{-1}\mathbb{E}_G\left\{\sum_{i=1}^{n}(\delta(Y_i) - \theta_i)^2\right\},$$

is minimized by the posterior mean given by the Tweedie formula,

$$\delta_G^*(y) = y + f_G'(y)/f_G(y).$$

Maximum regret, defined as the difference between the Bayes risk of a decision rule, δ, and what would be achievable with $\delta_G^*(y)$, for the least favorable $G \in \mathcal{G}$, the class of all distribution functions,

$$\mathcal{R}_n(\delta, \mathcal{G}) = \sup_{G \in \mathcal{G}} \left\{ B_n(\delta, G) - B_n(\delta_G^*, G) \right\},$$

has been thoroughly investigated in Zhang (2009) and Jiang and Zhang (2009) for the plug-in decision rule, $\delta_{\hat{G}_n}$ based on the Kiefer–Wolfowitz NPMLE,

$$\hat{G}_n = \operatorname{argmax}_{G \in \mathcal{G}} \left\{ \sum_{i=1}^{n} \log f_G(y_i) \mid f_G(y) = \int \phi(y - \theta) dG(\theta) \right\},$$

and its associated estimate of the marginal density of the observations, $Y_1, Y_2, \ldots, Y_n$,

$$f_{\hat{G}_n}(y) = \int \phi(y - \theta) d\hat{G}_n(\theta).$$

The first step in this effort is an exponential inequality for the Hellinger distance,

$$H(f_{\hat{G}_n}, f_{G_n}) = \left(\int \left(\sqrt{f_{\hat{G}_n}} - \sqrt{f_G} \right)^2 \right)^{1/2}.$$

Theorem 1 of Zhang (2009) classifies rates of Hellinger convergence according to the tail behavior of G. Light-tailed G – either those with bounded support or those with sub-Gaussian tails denoted $\mathcal{G}_\infty$ – make it relatively easy to estimate the marginal density. Heavier-tailed G satisfying the moment condition, in the class $\mathcal{G}_p = \{G : \int |u|^p dG(u) = \mathcal{O}(1)\}$, make it more difficult. More explicitly,[1]

$$\sup_{G \in \mathcal{G}} \mathbb{E} H^2(f_{\hat{G}_n}, f_G) \lesssim \begin{cases} n^{-1} (\log n)^2 & \text{if } \mathcal{G} = \mathcal{G}_\infty, \\ n^{-p/(1+p)} (\log n)^{\frac{2+3p}{2+2p}} & \text{if } \mathcal{G} = \mathcal{G}_p \text{ for some fixed } p. \end{cases}$$

By $A \lesssim B$ we mean that $A \leq CB$ for some constant C depending only on p. Regret for $\delta_{\hat{G}_n}$ is then established in theorem 5 of Jiang and Zhang (2009) to satisfy

$$\mathcal{R}_n(\delta_{\hat{G}_n}, \mathcal{G}) \lesssim \begin{cases} n^{-1} (\log n)^5 & \text{if } \mathcal{G} = \mathcal{G}_\infty, \\ n^{-p/(1+p)} (\log n)^{\frac{8+9p}{2+2p}} & \text{if } \mathcal{G} = \mathcal{G}_p \text{ for some fixed } p. \end{cases}$$

Theorem 1 of Polyanskiy and Wu (2021) establishes that these regret bounds are minimax rate optimal up to logarithmic factors.

[1] In the following discussion we have suppressed some technical conditions involving regularization of the NPMLE, $\hat{G}_n$. The interested reader is urged to consult the original sources for further details. Similar results also hold for compound decision settings where the $\theta_1, \ldots, \theta_n$ are a sequence of fixed parameters. In that case we may simply replace G by the empirical distribution of the θ_i's.

Saha and Guntuboyina (2020) consider regret for classes $\mathcal{G}_K$ of atomic G with at most K atoms and show that

$$\mathcal{R}_n(\delta_{\hat{G}_n}, \mathcal{G}_K) \lesssim \frac{K}{n}(\log n)^5.$$

The foregoing results are quite remarkable. We know that the NPMLE, $\hat{G}_n$, is self-regularizing, yielding a discrete distribution with a modest number of mass points with automatic selection of their location and associated mass without the intervention of any tuning parameters. When G is itself discrete, Bayes regret shrinks at almost the parametric rate, up to the log factor. It is also established that no other estimator can achieve a better rate for this relative risk measure than K/n, so the NPMLE is minimax rate optimal: up to logarithmic factor in this discrete setting.

Corresponding results for Poisson mixtures have been recently derived in Jana et al. (2022) and Shen and Wu (2022). Mixing distributions, G, are now supported on the positive half line, and bounded support classes, $\mathcal{G}_h = \{G : G([0,h]) = 1\}$, and sub-exponential classes, $\mathcal{G}_s = \{G : \int e^{cu} dG(u) \leq 1,\ c > 0\}$, are distinguished. Moment classes are modified to explicitly specify bounds, $\mathcal{G}_p(M_p) = \{G : \int_0^\infty u^p dG(u) \leq M_p\}$. The oracle Bayes rule for the Poisson compound decision problem is given by

$$\delta_G(y) = (y+1)\frac{f_G(y+1)}{f_G} = (y+1)\left(\frac{\Delta f_G(y)}{f_G} + 1\right),$$

where $\Delta f_G(y) = f_G(y+1) - f_G(y)$, which Robbins (1956) famously proposed approximating by

$$\hat{\delta}_n(y) = (y+1)\frac{N_n(y+1)}{N_n(y)},$$

where $N_n(y) = \sum_{i=1}^n \mathbb{1}\{Y_i = y\}$. The plug-in NPMLE decision rule, in contrast, is

$$\delta_{\hat{G}_n}(y) = (y+1)\frac{f_{\hat{G}_n}(y+1)}{f_{\hat{G}_n}} = (y+1)\left(\frac{\Delta f_{\hat{G}_n}(y)}{f_{\hat{G}_n}} + 1\right).$$

Combining results from Polyanskiy and Wu (2021) and Shen and Wu (2022), rates of Hellinger convergence for the nonparametric maximum likelihood estimator of the (marginal) mixture distribution are given by

$$\sup_{G \in \mathcal{G}} \mathbb{E} H^2(\hat{f}_{\hat{G}_n}, f_G) \lesssim \begin{cases} n^{-1} \frac{\log n}{\log\log n} & \text{if } \mathcal{G} = \mathcal{G}_h, \\ n^{-1} \log n & \text{if } \mathcal{G} = \mathcal{G}_s, \\ n^{\frac{-2p}{1+2p}} M_p^{\frac{1}{1+2p}} (\log n)^{\frac{3p+6}{1+2p}} & \text{if } \mathcal{G} = \mathcal{G}_p(M_p) \text{ for some fixed } p, \end{cases}$$

where $H^2(f,g) = \sum_{y=0}^\infty (\sqrt{f(y)} - \sqrt{g(y)})^2$. Regret for the NPMLE decision rule satisfies

$$\mathcal{R}_n(\delta_{\hat{G}_n}, \mathcal{G}) \lesssim \begin{cases} n^{-1}\left(\frac{\log n}{\log\log n}\right)^2 & \text{if } \mathcal{G} = \mathcal{G}_h, \\ n^{-1}(\log n)^3 & \text{if } \mathcal{G} = \mathcal{G}_s, \\ n^{\frac{-2(p-1)}{1+2p}} M_p^{\frac{3}{1+2p}} (\log n)^6 & \text{if } \mathcal{G} = \mathcal{G}_p(M_p) \text{ for some fixed } p. \end{cases}$$

Shen and Wu (2022) prove that these rates are minimax optimal up to logarithmic factors.

Since the Tweedie formula for both the Gaussian and Poisson compound decision problems involve only the marginal, f_G, it is tempting to try to circumvent estimation of the mixing distribution, G, altogether and focus instead on some ad-hoc estimator of f_G. The foregoing results suggest that such f-modeling strategies are misguided. In the Poisson case especially it is known that the original Robbins proposal can be highly variable in the upper tail, whereas G-modeling rules such as those based on the NPMLE are much more stable. This can be attributed in part to the fact that the Tweedie formula based on $f_{\hat{G}_n}$ is assured to be monotone, whereas alternatives like the Robbins estimator for the Poisson or the kernel density methods of Brown and Greenshtein (2009) for the Gaussian compound decision problem need not be. Indeed, in the heavier-tailed moment-constrained class, Shen and Wu (2022) show that the NPMLE decision rule improves upon the Robbins rule by a polynomial factor.

4.4 BAYES RULES, SELECTION BIAS AND THE WINNER'S CURSE

Suppose we observe noisy measurements, $Y_1, \ldots, Y_n$, of latent ability with $Y_i \sim \mathcal{N}(\theta_i, \sigma^2)$. You would like to select the individual, i, with the largest θ_i. Naturally, one is inclined to choose the i with the largest Y_i, but a moment's reflection raises doubts about this choice. Perhaps Y_i is largest merely because it happened to get a large draw of the measurement error. This skepticism is often referred to as the winner's curse. It is closely related to Galton's famous regression to mediocrity observation. Of course the likelihood that the largest Y_i comes from the largest θ_i is bound up with the tail behavior of the distribution of θ_i's, and perhaps also with the plausibility of the assumed-to-be-homoscedastic Gaussian noise. The discussion by Galton (1892) of scores on the Cambridge mathematical (Tripos) exam suggests that Senior Wranglers with scores exceeding 5000 were clearly superior to the bulk of examinees with scores below 2000, and yet one is still entitled to be skeptical about whether such a test instrument provided an accurate assessment of mathematical prowess. Often such selection problems arise with heterogeneous measures of precision attached; this poses some new challenges that will be addressed in more detail in Chapter 6.

Empirical Bayes methods provide valuable tools for decision making in such settings. Both parametric and nonparametric shrinkage methods can help to improve estimation and inference about latent parameters. From a formal Bayesian perspective, the selection problem and the winner's curse are completely innocuous. Given a firmly held subjective prior, G, for the distribution of the θ_i's, Tweedie's formula gives us an explicit Bayes rule for the posterior means of each of the θ_i's, as well as the uncertainty surrounding the posterior means. The difficulty of course is to find this G. When the courage of our convictions weakens we must resort to external evidence. Imagine for instance that we were to adopt the much maligned uniform, noninformative prior for G, then posterior mean estimates would be $\hat{\theta}_i = Y_i$, and colleagues would be justified in regaling us with their stories of the winner's curse. Likewise, if G is believed to be Gaussian, say $\mathcal{N}(\theta_0, \sigma_0^2)$, then we might confidently proceed to compute the appropriate linear-shrinkage Stein rule,

$$\delta(y) = \theta_0 + \left(1 - \frac{\sigma^2}{\sigma^2 + \sigma_0^2}\right)(y - \theta_0).$$

And this may again engender criticism from colleagues who wonder about the plausibility of linear shrinkage and its sensitivity to unverified features of the prior.

Dawid (1994) stresses that posterior inference based on conventional priors, while formally justified, can produce estimators and inference procedures that suffer from the same defects as classical frequentist methods. Nonparametric empirical Bayes methods offer a less dogmatic approach that provides more flexibility about prior specifications based on empirical evidence. Efron (2011) makes a strong, yet balanced, case for nonparametric empirical Bayes, and Tweedie's formula in particular, as a way to ameliorate the effects of selection bias and the winner's curse. See also Senn (2008) and Andrews et al. (2024), and the further discussion in Section 11.5.

4.5 EMPIRICAL BAYES ESTIMATION OF A SCALAR TREATMENT PARAMETER

As we noted at the end of Chapter 2, Robbinns's view of empirical Bayes methods extended far beyond the realm of compound decisions. In this section we describe an application to estimating a scalar treatment effect in a model with biased allocation of treatment. This line of inquiry was developed in a series of papers, Robbins and Zhang (1988, 1989, 1991), and foreshadowed in earlier work of Robbins (1982, 1988).

To study the effectiveness of a new drug for hypertension, suppose a large group of patients have been screened to obtain initial blood pressure measurements, $X_i, i = 1, \ldots, n$. For ethical or other reasons it is decided that the drug should be administered only to "risky" patients with $X_i \geq a$. Let $d(x) = \mathbb{1}\{x \geq a\}$ denote the treatment rule, and assume, following Robbins and Zhang (1988), that $X_i \sim \mathcal{N}(\theta_i, 1)$ and that after treatment a subsequent measurement, Z_i would be $Z_i \sim \mathcal{N}(\theta_i + \tau, 1)$. If all patients were given the drug, to estimate the treatment effect, τ, we could simply average the quantities, $Z_i - X_i$ over the entire sample; however we have observed only $Y_i = d(X_i)Z_i$, and this biased allocation of treatment requires some adjustment.

The likelihood of the observed pairs (X_i, Y_i) is again of mixture form with typical element

$$f_{\tau,G}(x, y) = \int f_{\tau,\theta}(x, y) dG(\theta).$$

G denotes the unknown distribution of the latent θ_i's, and

$$f_{\tau,\theta}(x,y) = (2\pi)^{-(1+d(x))/2}\exp[-(x-\theta)^2/2 - d(x)(y-\tau-\theta)^2/2].$$

If G were known, the efficient score function for τ would be

$$\dot{\ell}_{\tau,G}(x,y) = \nabla_\tau \log f_{\tau,G}(x,y).$$

When G is unknown, the semi-parametric efficient score function becomes

$$\psi_{\tau,G}(x,y) = \dot{\ell}_{\tau,G} - \mathbb{E}[\dot{\ell}_{\tau,G}|S_\tau(X,Y) = s_\tau(x,y)],$$

where $S_\tau(X,Y)$ is the sufficient statistic for θ. See Section 5.4 for other examples. If the second adjustment term is zero, then we are in the fully adaptive case, implying that ignorance of G does not entail an efficiency loss. The first term of the efficient score can be written as

$$\begin{aligned}\dot{\ell}_{\tau,G}(x,y) &= \frac{\int [d(x)(y-\tau-\theta)] f_{\tau,\theta}(x,y)dG(\theta)}{\int f_{\tau,\theta}(x,y)dG(\theta)}\\ &= d(x)(y-\tau) - \frac{\int \theta d(x) f_{\tau,\theta}(x,y)dG(\theta)}{\int f_{\tau,\theta}(x,y)dG(\theta)}.\end{aligned}$$

The sufficient statistic for θ_i is $S_\tau(X_i,Y_i) = (S_1(X_i,Y_i), S_2(X_i,Y_i)) = (d(X_i), X_i + d(X_i)(Y_i - \tau))$, so factoring the likelihood,

$$f_{\tau,\theta}(X,Y) = f(X,Y|S_\tau(X,Y),\tau) f(S_\tau(X,Y)|\theta,\tau),$$

implies that the second adjustment term in $\dot{\ell}_{\tau,G}(x,y)$ can be rewritten as

$$\begin{aligned}\frac{\int \theta d(x) f_{\tau,\theta}(x,y)dG(\theta)}{\int f_{\tau,\theta}(x,y)dG(\theta)} &= \frac{\int \theta d(x) f(S_\tau(x,y)|\theta,\tau)dG(\theta)}{\int f(S_\tau(x,y)|\theta,\tau)dG(\theta)}\\ &= \mathbb{E}[\theta d(X)|S_\tau(X,Y) = s_\tau(x,y)].\end{aligned}$$

So the semi-parametric efficient score takes the form

$$\begin{aligned}\psi_{\tau,G}(x,y) &= \Big(d(x)(y-\tau) - \mathbb{E}[d(X)(Y-\tau)|S_\tau(X,Y) = s_\tau(x,y)]\Big)\\ &\quad - \Big\{\Big(d(x) - \mathbb{E}[d(X)|S_\tau(X,Y) = s_\tau(x,y)]\Big)\mathbb{E}[\theta|S_\tau(X,Y) = s_\tau(x,y)]\Big\}.\end{aligned}$$

Further simplification is achieved by exploiting the Gaussian distribution of the measurement error.

Lemma 4.4. *Under the Gaussian measurement error condition,*

$$\begin{aligned}&\mathbb{E}[d(X)(Y-\tau)|d(X) = s_1, X+Y-\tau = s_2]\\ &= s_1\left[\frac{s_2}{2} - \frac{1}{\sqrt{2}}\frac{\varphi(\sqrt{2}(s_2/2-a)}{\Phi(\sqrt{2}(s_2/2-a))}\right].\end{aligned}$$

Proof: Since the first element of the sufficient statistic only takes the values 0 and 1, if we condition on $d(X) = 0$ and $X + Y - \tau = s_2$, the conditional expectation will be zero, so it suffices to consider the conditional for $d(X) = 1$. With $d(X) = 1$, we have $X + Y - \tau = X + Z - \tau$. Then,

$$\begin{pmatrix} X \\ X + Z - \tau \end{pmatrix} \sim \mathcal{N}_2\left(\begin{pmatrix} \theta \\ 2\theta \end{pmatrix}, \begin{pmatrix} 1 & 1 \\ 1 & 2 \end{pmatrix}\right),$$

and $W \stackrel{d}{=} (X|X + Z - \tau = s_2) \sim \mathcal{N}(s_2/2, 1/2)$. Therefore, $(X, Z - \tau|X + Z - \tau = s_2) \sim (W, s_2 - W)$, and

$$\begin{aligned}
&\mathbb{E}[d(X)(Y - \tau)|d(X) = 1, X + Y - \tau = s_2] \\
&\quad = d(X)\mathbb{E}[Z - \tau|W \geq a, X + Z - \tau = s_2] \\
&\quad = d(X)\mathbb{E}[(s_2 - W)1\{W \geq a\}]/\mathbb{P}(W \geq a) \\
&\quad = d(X)[s_2 - \mathbb{E}[W|W \geq a]] \\
&\quad = d(X)\left[\frac{s_2}{2} - \frac{1}{\sqrt{2}}\frac{\phi\left(\sqrt{2}(a - s_2/2)\right)}{1 - \Phi\left(\sqrt{2}(a - s_2/2)\right)}\right] \\
&\quad = d(X)\left[\frac{s_2}{2} - \frac{1}{\sqrt{2}}\frac{\phi\left(\sqrt{2}(s_2/2 - a)\right)}{\Phi\left(\sqrt{2}(s_2/2 - a)\right)}\right].
\end{aligned}$$

■

Finally, since $\mathbb{E}[d(X)|d(X) = s_1, X + d(X)(Y - \tau) = s_2] = s_1 = d(X)$, the efficient score function becomes

$$\psi(x, y, \tau) = d(x)\left[(y - \tau - x)/2 + \frac{\phi((x + y - \tau - 2a)/\sqrt{2})}{\sqrt{2}\Phi\left((x + y - \tau - 2a)/\sqrt{2}\right)}\right].$$

The estimating equation,

$$\sum_{i=1}^{n} \psi(X_i, Y_i, \tau) = 0,$$

is monotone in τ and thus yields a unique $\hat{\tau}$. As noted by Robbins and Zhang (1988), it is completely free of any dependence on G and the θ_i's and therefore can be interpreted as a conditional MLE in the sense of Andersen (1970). It is semi-parametrically efficient in the sense of van der Vaart (1996) with

$$\sqrt{n}(\hat{\tau}_n - \tau)/\sigma_n(\psi) \sim \mathcal{N}(0, 1), \quad \sigma_n^2(\psi) = \sum_{i=1}^{n} \mathbb{E}\psi^2(X_i, Y_i, \tau).$$

4.6 TREATMENT EFFECT HETEROGENEITY AND THE PARALLEL TRENDS ASSUMPTION

The constant treatment effect assumption of the previous section is quite strong. Robbins and Zhang (1989) relax this condition while continuing to explore estimation of treatment effects in the biased allocation setting. Again, we have initial screening measurements $X_i, i = 1, \ldots, n$, and we administer the treatment only to "risky" patients with $X_i \geq a$. It is assumed that $X_i \sim \mathcal{N}(\theta_i, \sigma^2)$ and that the expected post treatment response is

$$\mathbb{E}(Y|\theta, X = x) = \theta + c + \mathbb{1}\{X \geq a\}t(\theta, x). \tag{4.1}$$

In potential outcome notation, the treatment response is $Y_i = D_i Y_i(1) + (1 - D_i)Y_i(0)$, where $D_i = \mathbb{1}\{X_i \geq a\}$. It is assumed that $Y_i(0), Y_i(1) \perp\!\!\!\perp X_i|\theta_i$, and condition (4.1) implies that $\mathbb{E}(Y(0)|\theta, X = x) = \theta + c$, while $\mathbb{E}(Y(1)|\theta, X = x) = \theta + c + t(\theta, x)$. Our objective is to estimate the mean treatment effect on the treated,

$$\begin{aligned}\tau &= \mathbb{E}[Y_i(1) - Y_i(0)|D_i = 1] = \mathbb{E}[t(\theta, X)|X \geq a] \\ &= \frac{\mathbb{E}[\mathbb{1}\{X \geq a\}t(\theta, X)]}{\mathbb{P}(X \geq a)}.\end{aligned}$$

Note that in contrast to the previous section, here we observe post-treatment response for both treated and control subjects.

The following lemmas follow from Stein's lemma, recall Lemma 3.2,

Lemma 4.5. *If the function $u(\cdot)$ is of bounded variation and absolutely continuous, and $X|\theta \sim \mathcal{N}(\theta, \sigma^2)$, then*

$$\mathbb{E}[u(X)\theta] = \mathbb{E}[Xu(X)] - \sigma^2\mathbb{E}[u'(X)].$$

Lemma 4.6. *Given condition (4.1), if the function $u_1(\cdot)$ is of bounded variation, absolutely continuous and vanishes when $x \geq a$, then*

$$\mathbb{E}[u_1(X)(Y - X)] + \sigma^2\mathbb{E}[u_1'(X)] = c\mathbb{E}[u_1(X)].$$

Proof: From (4.1), we have

$$\mathbb{E}[u_1(X)Y|\theta, X = x] = u_1(x)[\theta + c + 1\{x \geq a\}t(\theta, x)];$$

using Lemma 4.5,

$$\begin{aligned}&\mathbb{E}[u_1(X)(Y - X)] + \sigma^2\mathbb{E}[u_1'(X)] \\ &\quad = c\mathbb{E}[u_1(X)] + \mathbb{E}[u_1(X)1\{X \geq a\}t(\theta, X)] = c\mathbb{E}[u_1(X)],\end{aligned}$$

since $u_1(x)$ vanishes when $x \geq a$. ■

Lemma 4.6 allows estimation of c when σ^2 is known, taking for example, $u_1(x) = (a - x)\mathbb{1}\{x < a\}$. When σ^2 is unknown we can use $u_2(x) = (a - x)^2\mathbb{1}\{x < a)$ to generate another estimating equation.

Theorem 4.7. *From (4.1) and using Lemma 4.5, and the fact that $\mathbb{E}[X] = \mathbb{E}[\theta]$*

$$\tau = \frac{\mathbb{E}[\mathbb{1}\{X \geq a\}t(\theta, X)]}{\mathbb{P}(X \geq a)} = \frac{\mathbb{E}[Y - X] - c}{\mathbb{P}(X \geq a)}.$$

In contrast with the familiar parallel trends assumption of the difference-in-difference (DiD) literature, Robbins and Zhang (1989) establish that the usual DiD mean treatment effect estimate requires some adjustment.

Theorem 4.8. *Under the foregoing conditions the mean treatment effect, τ, can be expressed as*

$$\tau = \underbrace{\frac{\mathbb{E}[\mathbb{1}\{X \geq a\}(Y - X)]}{\mathbb{P}(X \geq a)} - \frac{\mathbb{E}[\mathbb{1}\{X < a\}(Y - X)]}{\mathbb{P}(X < a)}}_{\textit{difference in difference estimator}} + \frac{\sigma^2 f(a)}{\mathbb{P}(X \geq a)\mathbb{P}(X < a)},$$

where f denotes the marginal density of X.

Proof: Let $u_1(x) = \mathbb{1}\{x < a\}$; then from (4.1) we have

$$\mathbb{E}[u_1(X)Y] = \mathbb{E}[u_1(X)\theta] + c\mathbb{E}[u_1(X)]. \tag{4.2}$$

Because $X|\theta \sim \mathcal{N}(\theta, \sigma^2)$, with conditional density, $\varphi(x|\theta)$,

$$\begin{aligned} \mathrm{Cov}(X - \theta, u_1(X)|\theta) &= \mathbb{E}[(X - \theta)1\{X < a\}|\theta] \\ &= \int_{-\infty}^{a} (x - \theta)\varphi(x|\theta)dx \\ &= -\sigma^2 \int_{-\infty}^{a} d\varphi(x|\theta) \\ &= -\sigma^2\varphi(a|\theta). \end{aligned}$$

Thus,

$$\mathbb{E}[X\mathbb{1}\{X < a\}|\theta] - \theta\mathbb{E}[\mathbb{1}\{X < a\}|\theta] = -\sigma^2\varphi(a|\theta).$$

Integrating with respect to θ, we have

$$\mathbb{E}[X\mathbb{1}\{X < a\}] - \mathbb{E}[\theta\mathbb{1}\{X < a\}] = -\sigma^2 f(a),$$

where $f(\cdot)$ is the marginal density of X. So from (4.2),

$$c = \frac{\mathbb{E}[\mathbb{1}\{X < a\}(Y - X)]}{\mathbb{P}(X < a)} - \frac{\sigma^2 f(a)}{\mathbb{P}(X < a)},$$

and from Theorem 4.7,

$$\begin{aligned}
\tau &= \frac{\mathbb{E}[Y - X]}{\mathbb{P}(X \geq a)} - \frac{c}{\mathbb{P}(X \geq a)} \\
&= \frac{\mathbb{E}[\mathbb{1}\{X \geq a\}(Y - X)]}{\mathbb{P}(X \geq a)} - \frac{\mathbb{E}[\mathbb{1}\{X < a\}(Y - X)]}{\mathbb{P}(X < a)} \\
&\quad + \frac{\mathbb{E}[\mathbb{1}\{X < a\}(Y - X)]}{\mathbb{P}(X \geq a)} + \frac{\mathbb{E}[\mathbb{1}\{X < a\}(Y - X)]}{\mathbb{P}(X < a)} \\
&\quad - \frac{\mathbb{E}[\mathbb{1}\{X < a\}(Y - X)]}{\mathbb{P}(X < a)\mathbb{P}(X \geq a)} + \frac{\sigma^2 f(a)}{\mathbb{P}(X < a)\mathbb{P}(X \geq a)} \\
&= \frac{\mathbb{E}[\mathbb{1}\{X \geq a\}(Y - X)]}{\mathbb{P}(X \geq a)} - \frac{\mathbb{E}[\mathbb{1}\{X < a\}(Y - X)]}{\mathbb{P}(X < a)} \\
&\quad + \frac{\sigma^2 f(a)}{\mathbb{P}(X < a)\mathbb{P}(X \geq a)}.
\end{aligned}$$

■

This result provoked a strong reaction from Paul Holland (Holland, 1990) who asserted in personal correspondence to Robbins that the Gaussian measurement error assumption and role played by the $u(x)$ functions were "unnecessary," effectively arguing for the parallel trends assumption in the nascent potential outcomes framework. Not surprisingly, Robbins (Robbins, 1990) responded with a vigorous defense of his new approach demonstrating that Holland's DiD estimator was inconsistent under the conditions posited in Robbins and Zhang (1989).

To further clarify the need for the adjustment term in Theorem 4.8, suppose instead of making treatment decisions based on the observable X_i, we treat subjects based on their latent effect, θ_i, that is, we modify the condition (4.1) to

$$\mathbb{E}[Y|\theta, X = x] = \theta + c + \mathbb{1}\{\theta \geq a\}t(\theta, x). \tag{4.3}$$

This is the model considered in Ashenfelter and Card (1985). We have normalized the time-fixed effect in the pre-treatment period to be zero so c plays the role of the time-fixed effect in the post-treatment period and θ is the subject's latent fixed effect.

Corollary 4.9 Under Assumption (4.3), the parallel trends assumption holds:

$$\mathbb{E}[Y(0) - X|\theta \geq a] = \mathbb{E}[Y(0) - X|\theta < a].$$

Proof: Note

$$\mathbb{E}[Y(0)|\theta] = \theta + c, \text{and } \mathbb{E}[X|\theta] = \theta.$$

Thus,

$$\mathbb{E}[Y(0) - X|\theta] = c, \text{ a.s.}$$

and therefore,

$$\mathbb{E}[Y(0) - X|\theta \geq a] = c = \mathbb{E}[Y(0) - X|\theta < a].$$

■

Corollary 4.10 Under Assumption (4.3), the difference-in-difference estimator identifies τ.

Proof: We have

$$\tau = \mathbb{E}[Y(1) - Y(0)|\theta \geq a].$$

Note that

$$\mathbb{E}[Y(1)|\theta \geq a] = \mathbb{E}[Y|\theta \geq a].$$

On the other hand,

$$\mathbb{E}[Y(0)|\theta \geq a] = c + \mathbb{E}[X|\theta \geq a].$$

Hence

$$\tau = \mathbb{E}[Y - X|\theta \geq a] - c.$$

And from the proof of Corollary 4.9,

$$c = \mathbb{E}[Y(0) - X|\theta < a] = \mathbb{E}[Y - X|\theta < a].$$

Therefore,

$$\tau = \mathbb{E}[Y - X|\theta \geq a] - \mathbb{E}[Y - X|\theta < a].$$

■

Thus, reliance on familiar difference-in-differences methods may be justified under the Ashenfelter and Card assumption of treatment selection based on the latent θ_i's. But such assumptions may be regarded as heroic in some applications, and the empirical Bayes approach of Robbins and Zhang merits serious reconsideration. In the project evaluation literature the DiD bias introduced by treatment assignment based on the observable X_i's rather than the latent θ_i's has become known as the "Ashenfelter dip" following Ashenfelter (1978). See, for example, Heckman and Smith (1999). It occurs because treatment is assigned to some subjects due to transitory fluctuations in X, subjects who wouldn't be treated based on their latent θ, or conversely. This is yet another insidious form of Galton's regression to mediocrity.

4.7 LOCAL TREATMENT EFFECTS AND REGRESSION DISCONTINUITY

One can interpret the final term in the expression for τ in Theorem 4.7 as a posterior mean adjustment analogous to the shrinkage effect we have already seen from the Tweedie formula. This connection becomes even more apparent if we limit consideration of the treatment effect to the local "regression discontinuity" parameter τ_a. Under the foregoing conditions the local mean treatment effect, τ_a, can be expressed as

$$\tau_a = \mathbb{E}[t(\theta, X)|X = a].$$

Suppose for a moment we let $t(\theta, X) = \tau$, so the treatment effect is homogenous; then we have

$$\mathbb{E}[Y|X = x] = \mathbb{E}[\theta|X = x] + c + \mathbb{1}\{x \geq a\}\tau.$$

Recall in the Gaussian sequence model $X|\theta \sim N(\theta, \sigma^2)$ and $\theta \sim G$. If $G = N(\mu_\theta, \sigma_\theta^2)$, then $\mathbb{E}[\theta|X = x] = (\sigma^2\mu_\theta + \sigma_\theta^2 x)/(\sigma^2 + \sigma_\theta^2)$. This implies

$$\mathbb{E}[Y|X = x] = \begin{cases} \alpha_1 + \beta x & x < a, \\ \alpha_2 + \beta x & x \geq a, \end{cases}$$

with $\tau = \alpha_2 - \alpha_1$ and $\beta = (\sigma_\theta^2)/(\sigma^2 + \sigma_\theta^2)$. However, for G taking any other form, $\mathbb{E}[\theta|X = x]$ would likely be a more flexible nonlinear function of x. The modern regression discontinuity literature would use a locally linear regression to approximate such functions locally around the cutoff, but empirical Bayes methods deliver an alternative without the need of any tuning parameters provided one is willing to believe the model (4.1) with constant treatment effect. In particular, we can construct an estimator for τ as $\mathbb{E}[Y - \hat{g}(X)|X \geq a] - \mathbb{E}[Y - \hat{g}(X)|X < a]$ with $\hat{g}(x)$ as an estimator for $\mathbb{E}[\theta|X = x]$.

In Table 4.8 we report the results of a small simulation experiment designed to compare the Robbins and Zhang (1989) $\hat{\tau}_a$ with more conventional regression discontinuity estimators of the local treatment effect. We consider three models for the distribution of the θ_i as indicated in the table, and three candidate estimators. Data is generated as described above with the pre-treatment measurement, $X \sim \mathcal{N}(\theta, 1)$, and the post treatment measurements as $Y_i \sim \mathcal{N}(\theta + \mathbb{1}\{X_i \geq a\}\tau, 1)$. The treatment threshold is taken to be $a = 1$ and $\tau = -1$. The first two columns of the table report RMSE for the "conventional" and "bias-corrected" RD coefficient estimates from the R package **rdrobust** of Calonico et al. (2023). The third column reports RMSE for a version of the Robbins–Zhang $\hat{\tau}_a$ employing the NPMLE $\hat{G}$ estimate of the θ_i distribution. All three methods produce nearly unbiased estimates of the τ_a treatment effect; however the Robbins–Zhang estimator is clearly more efficient. Default tuning is used for the **rdrobust** methods, while the Robbins–Zhang NPMLE procedure is tuning parameter free.

When treatment effects are heterogeneous, then we have the following result.

Table 4.8. *Root MSE for several estimates of* τ_a.

	Conventional RD	Unbiased RD	Robbins–Zhang RD
$\theta \sim \mathcal{N}(0, 1)$	0.313	0.362	0.122
$\log\theta \sim \mathcal{N}(0, 1)$	0.242	0.281	0.098
$\theta \sim 0.5\delta_1 + 0.5\delta_4$	0.293	0.336	0.105

Theorem 4.11. *With the model specified in (4.1), the mean treatment effect at the cut-off, defined as* τ_a*, is identifiable.*

$$\begin{aligned}\tau_a &= \mathbb{E}[t(\theta,X)|X=a] \\ &= \lim_{x\downarrow a}\Big\{\mathbb{E}[Y|X=x]-\mathbb{E}[\theta|X=x]\Big\} \\ &\quad -\lim_{x\uparrow a}\Big\{\mathbb{E}[Y|X=x]-\mathbb{E}[\theta|X=x]\Big\}.\end{aligned}$$

Proof: Given the model in Assumption (4.1), we have

$$\mathbb{E}[Y|\theta,X=a]=\theta+c+t(\theta,a).$$

Then

$$\mathbb{E}[Y|X=x]=\begin{cases}\mathbb{E}[\theta|X=x]+c+\mathbb{E}[t(\theta,x)|X=x] & x\geq a,\\ \mathbb{E}[\theta|X=x]+c & x<a.\end{cases}$$

■

Assumption (4.1) may be too special for the method to be generally applicable. Further progress is made by Eckles et al. (2025), which makes use of the random noise structure in the running variables but makes minimal assumptions on how the potential outcome depends on the latent variable θ.

Exercises

(1) Suppose we observe, $Y_1,\ldots,Y_n$, exchangeable Poisson random variables with means $\theta_1,\ldots,\theta_n$. We would like to estimate the means subject to the loss function,

$$L(\hat{\theta},\theta)=\sum_{i=1}^{n}\theta_i^{-1}(\hat{\theta}_i-\theta_i)^2.$$

This compound decision problem was posed by Clevenson and Zidek (1975) who suggested the linear shrinkage estimator,

$$\hat{\theta}_i=\left[1-\frac{\beta+n+1}{S_n+\beta+n-1}\right]Y_i,\quad i=1,\ldots,n,$$

where $S_n=\sum Y_i$. They showed that this estimator dominates the naive minimax estimator, $\tilde{\theta}_i=Y_i$, $i=1,\ldots,n$, if $n\geq 2$ and $0\leq\beta\leq n-1$, and it is admissible provided that $\beta>1$. The latter result is established by demonstrating that the estimator is a Bayes rule with respect to an explicit prior for θ. An alternative tactic is to start from the de Finetti observation that we can express the Y_i's as draws from a mixture distribution, with φ denoting the Poisson density,

$$f_G(y)=\int\varphi(y,\theta)dG(\theta),$$

for some choice of the mixing distribution, G. Were G known to the subjective Bayesian, show that the Bayes rule for θ under this rescaled loss is the posterior *harmonic* mean. Suggest an empirical Bayes variant.

(2) Another perspective on the Tweedie formula for Gaussian mixtures appearing in Stein's discussion of the Efron and Morris (1973a) paper is the following. Suppose $Y \sim \mathcal{N}(\theta, I_n)$; show that

$$\mathbb{E}\|Y+\nabla \log f(Y)-\theta\|^2 = n-\mathbb{E}\left\{\|\nabla \log f(Y)\|^2 - \frac{2}{f(Y)}\nabla^2 f(Y)\right\},$$

where ∇ is the vector of first partial derivatives, and ∇^2 is the Laplacian, $\sum \partial^2/\partial y_i^2$.

(3) Simplify the expression in curly brackets in the previous problem to write

$$\mathbb{E}\|Y + \nabla \log f(Y) - \theta\|^2 = n + 4\mathbb{E}\left\{\frac{\nabla^2\sqrt{f(Y)}}{\sqrt{f(Y)}}\right\}.$$

Conclude that if $\sqrt{f}$ is superharmonic, that is, $\nabla^2\sqrt{f} \leq 0$, then the Tweedie estimator, $\delta(Y) = Y + \nabla \log f(Y)$, is minimax.

(4) If a prior density, g, can be expressed as

$$g(\theta) = \int \|\theta - \xi\|^{-(n-2)} d\mu(\xi),$$

for some positive Borel measure, μ, with $n \geq 3$, then g is superharmonic by the Riesz decomposition theorem, see for example, Solomentsev (2020). Show that the corresponding marginal density,

$$f_g(y) = \int \phi(y - \theta)g(\theta)d\theta,$$

is then also superharmonic and consequently that the Bayes rule, $\delta(y) = y + f_g'(y)/f_g(y)$, is minimax.

(5) Show that the shape-constrained maximum likelihood density estimator described in Section 4.1 is a convex optimization problem with a unique solution free of tuning parameters. In the **REBayes** R package an illustrative example of the computation of this estimator is available with `demo(Brown)`.

CHAPTER 5

Mixture Models

This chapter addresses some general aspects of estimation of nonparametric mixture models. We begin with the fundamental question of identification in infinite-dimensional mixture models and then consider profile likelihood methods for structural parameters in the presence of an infinite-dimensional nuisance parameter.

5.1 IDENTIFICATION IN GENERAL MIXTURE SETTINGS

Having violated the basic econometric principle, as formulated for mixture problems by Teicher (1961), "the identifiability question must be settled before one can meaningfully discuss the problem of estimating the mixing [distribution] G on the basis of observations from the mixture F," we now seek to make amends for this oversight.

Definition 5.1 Let $\Phi(x|\theta)$ be a distribution function defined for all $\theta \in \Theta \subset \mathbb{R}$ and G be a distribution function defined on Θ. The mixture

$$F(x) = \int_{\Theta} \Phi(x|\theta) dG(\theta)$$

is identifiable if and only if there is a unique G yielding F.

Teicher (1961) provides a very thorough treatment of identification of mixtures with a scalar mixing parameter. For both location mixtures,

$$F(x) = \int_{-\infty}^{\infty} \Phi(x-\theta) dG(\theta),$$

and scale mixtures,

$$F(x) = \int_{0}^{\infty} \Phi(x\theta) dG(\theta),$$

identification of G follows from the uniqueness of the characteristic function provided that the Fourier transforms of $\Phi(x)$ and of $\Phi(e^x)$, respectively, are not identically zero on some nondegenerate real interval. This result covers all of the applications we have encountered so far.

Location mixtures with heterogeneous scale can be handled similarly. Suppose

$$Y_i = \theta_i + \sigma_i Z_i,$$

with

$$Y_i|\theta_i, \sigma_i^2 \sim \mathcal{N}(\theta_i, \sigma_i^2),\ \theta_i \sim G,\ \sigma_i^2 \sim H,\ Z_i \sim \mathcal{N}(0,1),\ \sigma_i \perp\!\!\!\perp \theta_i,$$

and we observe the σ_i's; then provided that the noise component, σZ has characteristic function $\int \exp(-\frac{1}{2}\sigma^2 t^2) dH(\sigma^2)$ that is not identically zero on a nondegenerate interval, identifiability of the mixing distribution, G, holds.

For multivariate latent parameters like our location-scale mixture model of income dynamics, considered in Section 6.3, Barndorff-Nielsen (1965) considers identifiability of mixtures of the general exponential family densities,

$$d\Psi(x;\theta) = a(\theta)b(x)\exp\left(\sum_{j=1}^{m}\theta_j\psi_j(x)\right)d\mu(x),$$

for some σ-finite measure μ, $x \in \mathbb{R}^n$, $\theta \in \Theta \subset \mathbb{R}^m$, and $a(\theta) > 0$, $b(x) \geq 0$, and $a, b, \psi_j, j = 1, \ldots, m$ all measurable. Identifiability requires that if we consider any two mixing distributions, G_1 and G_2, their corresponding mixture densities,

$$f_k(x) = \frac{dF_{G_k}}{d\mu} = b(x)\int_{\Theta} a(\theta)\exp\left(\sum_{j=1}^{m}\theta_j\psi_j(x)\right)dG_k(\theta),\ \ k=1,2,$$

are distinct. More explicitly, let $X = \{x : f_1(x) = f_2(x) \neq 0\}$, $S = \{s = (\psi_1(x), \ldots, \psi_m(x))$ for $x \in X\}$ and

$$f_k^*(s) = b(x)\int_{\Theta} a(\theta)\exp(\theta^\top s)dG_k(\theta), \quad k = 1,2;$$

then the mixture, F, is identifiable if $f_1^*(s) = f_2^*(s)$ for $s \in S$ implies $G_1 = G_2$. Corollary 3 of Barndorff-Nielsen (1965) establishes that this holds provided that (a) μ is an n-dimensional Lebesgue measure, (b) the functions $\psi_j : j = 1, \ldots, m$ are all continuous and (c) the set $\{s : s = (\psi_1(x), \ldots, \psi_m(x)), b(x) > 0, x \in \mathbb{R}^n\}$ contains a nonempty, open set. It follows by corollary 4 of Barndorff-Nielsen (1965), that in the bivariate Gaussian setting of our income dynamics model, identifiability of the joint mixing distribution of location and scale holds.

Mixtures of Poissons have a long history in statistical applications, and their identification was first considered by Feller (1943). Feller noted that the probability generating function of a Poisson mixture can be represented by the Laplace transformation of the mixing distribution. Poisson mixtures with variable exposures as illustrated in the occupational risk example in Section 4.2.3 can be treated similarly.

Identifiability for mixtures of discrete distributions is considerably more precarious. Teicher (1967) demonstrates that mixtures of binomials,

$$F(x;k,p) = \sum_{j<x} \binom{k}{j} p^j (1-p)^{k-j},$$

are not identifiable for fixed k. To see this, note that any such mixture is a step function with jumps of magnitude,

$$\begin{aligned} h_j &= \int_0^1 \binom{k}{j} p^j (1-p)^{k-j} dG(p) \\ &= \binom{k}{j} \sum_{i=0}^{k-j} (-1)^i \binom{k-j}{i} \int_0^1 p^{i+j} dG(p), \end{aligned}$$

at $j = 0, 1, \ldots, k$. Consequently, any two binomial mixtures with G_1 and G_2 mixing distributions and having identical first k moments will be observationally equivalent. In binomial mixture settings with k large and possibly varying within the sample, characterizing the partially identified set of mixing distributions is a challenging problem as discussed in Section 12.1.1. Barndorff-Nielsen (1965) considers a much broader class of discrete base distributions supported on multivariate lattices of $\mathbb{R}^m$.

5.2 IDENTIFICATION OF BOTH φ AND G FROM REPEATED MEASUREMENTS

When repeated measurements on the response are available for each θ_i, there is an extensive theoretical literature on nonparametric identification of both φ, what we call the base distribution, and the mixing distribution, G. In the linear panel data model, Horowitz and Markatou (1996) show that the characteristic function of φ can be estimated by differencing under a symmetry condition thereby reducing the estimation of G to a conventional deconvolution problem. This approach has been further developed by Li and Vuong (1998) and Bonhomme and Robin (2010).

When observed outcomes Y are discrete and conditionally independent, and the latent signal θ_i also has a discrete distribution with a known number of atoms, nonparametric identification is also possible for both φ and G. Hall and Zhou (2003) consider nonparametric identification for multivariate mixtures with two groups, each with $k \geq 3$ independently distributed components. Earlier work on multiway tables by Kruskal (1976, 1977) extended by Allman et al. (2009) has proven to be essential for these developments. These results are further developed to dynamic models in Kasahara and Shimotsu (2009) and Bonhomme et al. (2016). For continuous Y, the analogous results are developed in Hu and Schennach (2008). Hu (2017) offers an overview of these results. When additional exogenous covariates are available, they can also provide identification power, as demonstrated in Henry et al. (2014), and further examples are surveyed in Compiani and Kitamura (2016).

5.3 ESTIMATION OF FUNCTIONALS OF *G*

It is often tempting to interpret the discrete NPMLE as revealing something intrinsic about a small number of "types" corresponding to the mass points of $\hat{G}$. *This temptation should be resisted.* Polyanskiy and Wu (2020) have shown that if G is continuous with sub-Gaussian tails, the number of mass points of $\hat{G}$ is upper bounded by $\mathcal{O}(\log n)$. At best, we can hope to reliably estimate functionals of G. The obvious prototype for such functionals is the posterior mean,

$$\mathbb{E}[\theta | Y = y] = \frac{\int \theta \varphi(y|\theta) dG(\theta)}{\int \varphi(y|\theta) dG(\theta)},$$

which reduces to computing two linear functionals.

In classical deconvolution problems where we observe a random sample, $Y_1, \ldots, Y_n$, from a Gaussian mixture density,

$$f_G(y) = \int \phi(y - \theta) dG(\theta),$$

we may consider functionals of the form

$$\Psi(y) = \int \psi(\theta) \phi(y - \theta) dG(\theta).$$

For $\psi(\theta) \equiv 1$ this is just the marginal density of Y. For $\psi(\theta) = \theta$ it is the numerator of the posterior mean expression. When $\psi(\theta) = \exp(\gamma\theta)$, it can be shown that

$$\Psi(y) = \int \exp(\gamma\theta) \varphi(y - \theta) dG(\theta) = \exp(\gamma y + \gamma^2/2) f_G(y + \gamma).$$

For polynomial ψ, that is, $\psi(\theta) = \sum_{i=1}^m \beta_i \theta^i$, with known coefficients, β_i, Matias and Taupin (2004) show that $\Psi(y)$ can be estimated at an almost parametric rate, $(\log n)^{\frac{2m+1}{4}} / \sqrt{n}$, for any y in $\mathbb{R}$ under mean-squared risk. For more general functionals minimax rates have also been established by Butucea and Comte (2009) and Pensky (2017). Provided ψ satisfies certain smoothness and boundedness conditions, these results suggest that we can expect parametric convergence rates for functionals up to some logarithmic factor.

In some special cases functionals are estimable from the data without recourse to an intermediate estimate of the mixing distribution, G. Suppose we would like to estimate the mth moment of G. If we can find a function, $h_m(y)$, such that

$$\int \varphi(y|\theta) h_m(y) dy = \theta^m$$

then we have

$$\int \theta^m dG = \int\int \varphi(y|\theta)h_m(y)dydG = \mathbb{E}[h_m(Y)].$$

Hence the mth moment of G is directly estimable from the data.

Example 5.2 For the standard Gaussian sequence model, the form of h_m is the mth Hermite polynomial.

Example 5.3 In a binomial model with $Y \sim \text{Bin}(2, p)$ and $p \sim G$, then the first two moments of G can be directly estimated from linear combinations of the observed frequencies of Y. For example:

$$h_1(y) = 0.5\ \mathbb{1}\{y = 1\} + \mathbb{1}\{y = 2\},$$
$$h_2(y) = \mathbb{1}\{y = 2\}.$$

Then we have $\int pdG = 0.5\mathbb{P}(Y = 1) + \mathbb{P}(Y = 2)$ and $\int p^2 dG = \mathbb{P}(Y = 2)$.

More generally, for base densities belonging to the quadratic variance exponential family as discussed in Morris (1983), unbiased estimators for the moments of G follow directly from a linear combination of the sample moments of Y.

5.4 PROFILE LIKELIHOOD AND SEMIPARAMETRIC EFFICIENCY

As we have already seen, the mixture models that arise naturally in empirical Bayes compound decision problems often involve structural parameters that need to be estimated in conjunction with the distribution of the incidental parameters. In this section we will consider several variants of these semiparametric mixture models and investigate the performance of profile likelihood as a way to estimate them. In some cases estimation of the mixing distribution leads to fully adaptive estimators, as if it imposed no asymptotic cost. In other cases we can explicitly evaluate a loss of efficiency due to the estimation of the mixing distribution. There will also be some cases in which $\sqrt{n}$ estimability of the structural parameters is impossible, but some slower rate of convergence is possible, or as a drastic final possibility, identification fails completely.

There is an extensive literature on semiparametric models with infinite-dimensional incidental parameters. We will restrict our attention to mixture models of the type considered by van der Vaart (1996), and we follow his notation and approach closely. This is the setting of Kiefer and Wolfowitz (1956) who were motivated by the findings of Neyman and Scott (1948). The general form of the models we will consider has the form

$$f_{\theta,G}(y) = \int \varphi(y \mid \theta, \eta)dG(\eta),$$

where G denotes an unknown distribution function for the nuisance parameters, η. Were G known to us we would have the score function for the structural parameters, θ,

$$\dot{\ell}_{\theta,G}(y) = \nabla_\theta \log f_{\theta,G}(y),$$

and we could solve for a root of this function. When G is unknown we must account for this. The semiparametrically efficient score function becomes

$$\tilde{\ell}_{\theta,G}(y) = \dot{\ell}_{\theta,G}(y) - \mathbb{E}[\dot{\ell}_{\theta,G}(Y) \mid S_\theta(Y) = s_\theta(y)],$$

where $S_\theta(Y)$ denotes a sufficient statistic for η for each fixed value of θ. Existence of such sufficient statistics is typically ensured by the exponential family form of φ. If the second piece is identically zero, then the efficient score function coincides with the known G score function, and this is usually called the fully adaptive case. For example, in iid error regression settings with unknown error distribution, slope parameters can be adaptively estimated by M-estimation or L-estimation as shown by Bickel (1982) and Portnoy and Koenker (1989), respectively.

When the second piece of $\tilde{\ell}$ does not vanish, there is no (asymptotic) free lunch, and there is an efficiency cost imposed by our ignorance of G. In some settings, we may solve for a pair, $(\hat{\theta}, \hat{G})$, such that

$$\sum_{i=1}^{n} \tilde{\ell}_{\hat{\theta},\hat{G}}(Y_i) = 0.$$

Expanding formally, we have:

$$0 = \sum_{i=1}^{n} \tilde{\ell}_{\hat{\theta},\hat{G}}(Y_i) = \sum_{i=1}^{n} \tilde{\ell}_{\theta_0,\hat{G}}(Y_i) + (\hat{\theta} - \theta_0) \sum_{i=1}^{n} \nabla_\theta \tilde{\ell}_{\tilde{\theta},\hat{G}}(Y_i),$$

where $\tilde{\theta}$ is between θ_0 and $\hat{\theta}$. Then, under regularity conditions,

$$\sqrt{n}(\hat{\theta} - \theta_0) = \left(n^{-1} \sum_{i=1}^{n} \nabla_\theta \tilde{\ell}_{\tilde{\theta},\hat{G}}(Y_i) \right)^{-1} n^{-1/2} \sum_{i=1}^{n} \tilde{\ell}_{\theta_0,\hat{G}}(Y_i).$$

In particular, provided that the class of functions $\{\tilde{\ell}_{\theta,G} : \|\theta - \theta_0\| < \delta, d(G, G_0) < \delta\}$ is P_{θ_0,G_0}-Donsker for some $\delta > 0$, and that $(\hat{\theta}, \hat{G})$ is consistent for (θ_0, G_0), then van der Vaart (1996) shows that $\hat{\theta}$ achieves the semiparametric efficiency bound. Thus, at least asymptotically their performance is optimal. In the following examples we consider several special cases ranging from a fully adaptive case to situations in which there is an efficiency loss due to estimation of G.

5.4.1 Adaptive Estimation of Location for Gaussian Scale Mixtures

The investigations of Tukey (1960) that foreshadowed the robustness movement in statistics prominently featured distributions that were scale mixtures of Gaussians,

$$f_{\theta,G}(y) = \int_0^\infty \frac{1}{\eta}\phi((y-\theta)/\eta)dG(\eta).$$

This is a convenient class for studying robust estimators of a location or regression parameter since members of the class are symmetric, unimodal and easily simulated. For these reasons such distributions were extensively employed in the influential simulation study of Andrews et al. (1972). See Efron and Olshen (1978) and Andrews and Mallows (1974) for further characterization of Gaussian scale mixtures.

A prototypical robustness problem is the Tukey contaminated Gaussian location model,

$$Y_i = \theta + \eta_i u_i, \quad i = 1, \ldots, n,$$

with u_i iid standard Gaussian and $\eta_i \sim G$. The efficient score function for θ with known G takes the form

$$\dot{\ell}_{\theta,G}(y) = (y-\theta)\frac{\int \eta^{-2}\frac{1}{\eta}\phi((y-\theta)/\eta)dG(\eta)}{\int \frac{1}{\eta}\phi((y-\theta)/\eta)dG(\eta)}.$$

When G is unknown, we have sufficient statistics $S_\theta(Y_i) = (Y_i - \theta)^2$ for each η_i, and the semiparametric efficient score function is

$$\begin{aligned}\tilde{\ell}_{\theta,G}(y) &= \dot{\ell}_{\theta,G}(y) - \mathbb{E}[\dot{\ell}_{\theta,G}(Y) \mid S_\theta(Y) = s_\theta(y)] \\ &= \dot{\ell}_{\theta,G}(y) - \mathbb{E}\left[\left\{\frac{\int \eta^{-2}\frac{1}{\eta}\phi((y-\theta)/\eta)dG(\eta)}{\int \frac{1}{\eta}\phi((y-\theta)/\eta)dG(\eta)}(Y-\theta)\right\}\Big|(Y-\theta)^2 = (y-\theta)^2\right].\end{aligned}$$

But $Y - \theta$ is symmetrically distributed around zero, so the second term vanishes and a fully efficient estimator of θ can be constructed as shown by van der Vaart (1996). This example can be easily extended to regression as in Koenker (2013). Full adaptation as in this example is far from typical, as later examples will illustrate.

5.4.2 Treatment Effect Estimation for Mixtures of Paired Exponentials

Suppose we observe independent random variables, $X_i \sim \exp(\eta_i)$ and $Y_i \sim \exp(\theta\eta_i)$, and we are interested in estimating the treatment effect, θ. Their conditional density is

$$f_\theta(x, y \mid \eta) = \theta\eta^2 e^{-\eta(x+\theta y)},$$

and the marginal density for (X_i, Y_i) evaluated at (x, y) is

$$f_{\theta,G}(x, y) = \int f_\theta(x, y \mid \eta)dG(\eta).$$

The sufficient statistic for η is $S_\theta(X,Y) = X + \theta Y$, and it is easy to see that for given η, $S_\theta(X,Y)$ it follows a Erlang distribution with density

$$f_S(s|\eta) = \eta^2 s e^{-\eta s}.$$

If G were known, the score function for θ would be

$$\dot{\ell}_{\theta,G}(x,y) = \frac{1}{\theta} - \frac{\int \eta y f_\theta(x,y|\eta)dG(\eta)}{\int f_\theta(x,y|\eta)dG(\eta)} = \frac{1}{\theta} - y\mathbb{E}[\eta|S_\theta(X,Y) = x + \theta y].$$

When G is unknown we need an adjustment term

$$\begin{aligned}
&\mathbb{E}[\dot{\ell}_{\theta,G}(X,Y)|S_\theta(X,Y) = x + \theta y] \\
&= \frac{1}{\theta} - E[Y|S_\theta(X,Y) = x + \theta y]\mathbb{E}[\eta|S_\theta(X,Y) = x + \theta y] \\
&= \frac{1}{\theta} - \frac{x + \theta y}{2\theta}\mathbb{E}[\eta|S_\theta(X,Y) = x + \theta y],
\end{aligned}$$

noting that $\mathbb{E}[Y|S_\theta(X,Y) = x + \theta y] = \frac{1}{\theta}E[\theta Y|S_\theta(X,Y) = x + \theta y]$ and $(\theta Y|S_\theta(X,Y) = s) \sim U[0,s]$.

Thus, the efficient score function for θ is

$$\tilde{\ell}_{\theta,G}(x,y) = \frac{x - \theta y}{2\theta}\mathbb{E}[\eta|S_\theta(X,Y) = x + \theta y].$$

And Fisher information for θ can be computed as

$$\begin{aligned}
\mathbb{E}[\tilde{\ell}_{\theta,G}(X,Y)^2] &= \frac{1}{2\theta^2}\mathbb{E}\left[\frac{(S - 2\theta Y)^2}{2}(\mathbb{E}[\eta|S])^2\right] \\
&= \frac{1}{2\theta^2}\mathbb{E}\left[\frac{S^2 - 4\theta Y S + 4\theta^2 Y^2}{2}(\mathbb{E}[\eta^2|S] - \mathbb{V}(\eta|S))\right] \\
&= \frac{1}{2\theta^2}\mathbb{E}\left[\frac{S^2}{6}(\mathbb{E}[\eta^2|S] - \mathbb{V}(\eta|S))\right] \\
&= \frac{1}{2\theta^2}\left[1 - \frac{1}{6}\mathbb{E}[S^2\mathbb{V}(\eta|S)]\right].
\end{aligned}$$

In the third line we have used the fact that $\mathbb{E}[\theta Y|S] = S/2$ and $\mathbb{E}[\theta^2 Y^2|S] = \mathbb{V}[\theta Y|S] + E[\theta Y|S]^2 = \frac{S^2}{12} + \frac{S^2}{4}$ because $(\theta Y|S = s) \sim U[0,s]$ as noted earlier.

In a model where we treat θ and η as fixed parameters, the information per observation for θ equals $\frac{1}{2\theta^2}$. To see this, note that $\nabla_\theta \log f_{\theta,\eta}(x,y) = \frac{1}{\theta} - \eta y$ and $\nabla_\eta \log f_{\theta,\eta}(x,y) = \frac{2}{\eta} - (x + \theta y)$ with information matrix

$$I = \begin{pmatrix} I_{\theta\theta} & I_{\theta\eta} \\ I_{\theta\eta} & I_{\eta\eta} \end{pmatrix} = \begin{pmatrix} \theta^{-2} & -(\theta\eta)^{-1} \\ -(\theta\eta)^{-1} & 2/\eta^2 \end{pmatrix}.$$

Hence the information for θ is $I_{\theta\theta} - I_{\theta\eta}I_{\eta\eta}^{-1}I_{\theta\eta} = (2\theta^2)^{-1}$.

Thus the fraction $1 - \frac{1}{6}\mathbb{E}[S^2\mathbb{V}(\eta|S)]$ measures the loss of information that results from needing to estimate the mixing distribution G. But how large can this loss of information be? We now show that the semiparametric Fisher information cannot be smaller than $1/(3\theta^2)$. First note that

$$\begin{aligned}
-\nabla_s \mathbb{E}(\eta|S) &= -\nabla_s \frac{\int \eta^3 e^{-\eta s} dG}{\int \eta^2 e^{-\eta s} dG} \\
&= -\left\{ -\frac{\int \eta^4 e^{-\eta s} dG}{\int \eta^2 e^{-\eta s} dG} + \left(\frac{\int \eta^3 e^{-\eta s} dG}{\int \eta e^{-\eta s} dG} \right)^2 \right\} \\
&= \mathbb{E}[\eta^2|S] - (\mathbb{E}(\eta|S))^2 \\
&= \mathbb{V}(\eta|S).
\end{aligned}$$

Conversely, we have

$$\begin{aligned}
-\nabla_s \mathbb{E}(\eta|S) &= -\nabla_s \left[\frac{1}{s} - \nabla_s \log f_S(s) \right] \\
&= \frac{1}{s^2} + \nabla_s^2 \log f_S(s) \\
&= \frac{1}{s^2} + \frac{\nabla_s^2 f_S(s)}{f_S(s)} - \left(\frac{\nabla_s f_S(s)}{f_S(s)} \right)^2.
\end{aligned}$$

Assembling, see Exercise 1, we have

$$\begin{aligned}
1 &- \frac{1}{6} \mathbb{E}[S^2 \mathbb{V}(\eta|S)] \\
&= 1 - \frac{1}{6} \int s^2 \left(\frac{1}{s^2} + \frac{\nabla_s^2 f_S(s)}{f_S(s)} - \left(\frac{\nabla_s f_S(s)}{f_S(s)} \right)^2 \right) f_S(s) ds \\
&= \frac{5}{6} - \frac{1}{6} \int s^2 \nabla_s^2 f_S(s) ds + \frac{1}{6} \int s^2 \left(\frac{\nabla_s f_S(s)}{f_S(s)} \right)^2 f_S(s) ds \\
&\geq \frac{2}{3}.
\end{aligned}$$

Thus, the cost incurred by estimating G increases the asymptotic variance from $2\theta^2$ to, at most, $3\theta^2$.

As another point of comparison, we can consider the maximal invariant statistic, $M(X, Y) = Y/X$, which has a density

$$f_M(m \mid \theta) = \frac{\theta}{(m\theta + 1)^2} \mathbb{1}\{m \geq 0\}.$$

To see this, note that $Z = X/\theta Y$ has a density $f_Z(z) = 1/(z+1)^2$, and make the change of variable from Z to M. The information about θ based on M is

$$\mathbb{E}\left[\left(\frac{1}{\theta} - \frac{2m}{\theta m + 1} \right)^2 \right] = \frac{1}{\theta^2} \int_0^{+\infty} \frac{(1 - \theta m)^2}{(1 + \theta m)^2} \frac{\theta}{(m\theta + 1)^2} dm = \frac{1}{3\theta^2}.$$

Thus, the semiparametric Fisher information is at least as great as the information about θ achieved by relying on the maximal invariant. This example first appeared in Lindsay (1980).

How do we exploit this efficiency gain? Note that the key component in the efficient score function depending on the distribution G is

$$\mathbb{E}[\eta|S=s] = \frac{\int \eta f_S(s|\eta)dG(\eta)}{\int f_S(s|\eta)dG(\eta)} = \frac{1}{s} - \nabla_s \log f_S(s),$$

with $f_S(s) = \int f_S(s|\eta)dG(\eta)$. This is the "Tweedie" formula for the Erlang mixture model. Thus, for each fixed value of θ, we can construct $S_\theta(X,Y) = X + \theta Y$ and estimate the marginal distribution of $S_\theta(X,Y)$. This may be interpreted as an f-modeling strategy in the terminology of Efron (2019) to construct the efficient score function. Alternatively, we can also proceed by estimating G directly from $S_\theta(X,Y)$, and estimate θ by profile likelihood. This is the G-modeling approach.

5.4.3 Dynamic Linear Panel Model with Individual Specific Effects

Consider the dynamic panel data model,

$$y_{it} = \rho y_{it-1} + \alpha_i + u_{it},\ u_{it} \sim \mathcal{N}(0,\theta),\ t=1,\ldots,T,\ i=1,\ldots,n.$$

Suppose the α_i's are independent with conditional distribution $G(\cdot \mid y_{i0})$. For convenience we will assume $y_{i0} = 0$ and that θ is known. The likelihood for each $y_i = \{y_{i1},\ldots,y_{iT}\}$ can be factored as

$$L_i = \underbrace{\frac{1}{\sqrt{T}}\left(\frac{1}{\sqrt{2\pi\theta}}\right)^{T-1} \exp(-v_i^\top Q v_i/2\theta)}_{L_{1i}}$$
$$\times \underbrace{\int \frac{1}{\sqrt{2\pi\theta/T}} \exp\left(-\frac{(\bar{v}_i - \alpha_i)^2}{2\theta/T}\right) dG(\alpha \mid y_{i0})}_{L_{2i}},$$

where $v_i = y_i - \rho y_{i,-1}$ is a T-vector with entries $y_{it} - \rho y_{it-1}$, the matrix $Q = I_T - 1_T 1_T^\top/T$ and $\bar{v}_i = T^{-1}\sum_t v_{it}$.

If we ignore the second factor of the likelihood, the contribution to the score function for ρ is

$$\nabla_\rho \log L_{1i} = \frac{v_i' Q y_{i,-1}}{\theta}.$$

However, it can be shown that $\mathbb{E}[v_i' Q y_{i,-1}/\theta] = -h_T(\rho) \neq 0$ where $h_T(\rho) = \frac{1}{1-\rho}\left[1 - \frac{1}{T}\left(\frac{1-\rho^T}{1-\rho}\right)\right]$, so using this score function as an estimating equation results in a biased estimator of ρ. Instead, Lancaster (2002) suggests an integrated likelihood estimator that is consistent for fixed T. The basic idea is to find a reparameterization of the incidental parameters such that there is information orthogonality between the reparameterized incidental parameters and the structural parameter, ρ. In this AR(1) model this leads to $\tilde{\alpha}_i = \alpha_i \exp(-b_T(\rho))$ where $\nabla_\rho b_T(\rho) = h_T(\rho)$. Integrating out $\tilde{\alpha}_i$ with respect to a uniform prior yields a concentrated likelihood from which we obtain the Lancaster estimating equation,

$$\dot{\ell}^L(\rho) = \sum_{i=1}^{n} v_i' Q y_{i,-1}/\theta + h_T(\rho).$$

Although Lancaster's proposal is effective in removing the bias, some loss of efficiency can be anticipated due to neglecting the second term in the likelihood.

Moreira (2009) has proposed an alternative estimator based on the maximal invariant statistic $M(Y) = Y^\top Y$, where Y denotes the $n \times T$ matrix with typical element y_{it}. Since $y_{i0} = 0$, we can represent Y by

$$Y = \alpha(B1_T)^\top + [u_1, \dots, u_T]B^\top,$$

where 1_T denotes a T vector of ones, and

$$B = \begin{pmatrix} 1 & \dots & 0 \\ \rho & \dots & 0 \\ \dots & \dots & \dots \\ \rho^{T-1} & \dots & 1 \end{pmatrix}.$$

Each row of Y follows a T-variate multivariate normal distribution with mean $\alpha_i(B1_T)^\top$ and covariance matrix $V = \theta BB^\top$. Thus, $M(Y)$ follows a non-central Wishart distribution of dimension T, degrees of freedom n, covariance matrix $\theta BB^\top$ and noncentrality parameter $B\mathbb{1}_T\alpha^\top\alpha(B\mathbb{1}_T)^\top$. The distribution only depends on the incidental parameters α_i through its sum of squares; hence the likelihood of $M(Y)$ no longer suffers from the incidental parameter problem. Maximizing the likelihood constructed from the distribution of this maximal invariant, we arrive at the estimator of Moreira (2009).

Finally, consider the semiparametric score function based on the entire likelihood as we did in the previous example. We have

$$\begin{aligned}\dot{\ell}_i &= \nabla_\rho \log L_i = v_i^\top Q y_{i,-1}/\theta \\ &\quad + \bar{y}_{i,-1} \frac{\int \frac{\bar{v}_i-\alpha_i}{\theta/T} \frac{1}{\sqrt{2\pi\theta/T}} \exp\left(-\frac{(\bar{v}_i-\alpha_i)^2}{2\theta/T}\right) dG(\alpha_i|y_{i0})}{\int \frac{1}{\sqrt{2\pi\theta/T}} \exp\left(-\frac{(\bar{v}_i-\alpha_i)^2}{2\theta/T}\right) dG(\alpha_i|y_{i0})} \\ &= v_i^\top Q y_{i,-1}/\theta + \bar{y}_{i,-1}\mathbb{E}\left[\frac{\bar{v}_i - \alpha_i}{\theta/T}|\bar{v}_i\right].\end{aligned}$$

Since $\bar{v}_i$ is a sufficient statistic for α_i, the adjustment for the fact that we do not know G takes the form

$$\mathbb{E}[\dot{\ell}_{i,\rho}|\bar{v}_i] = -h_T(\rho) + h_T(\rho)\bar{v}_i\mathbb{E}\left[\frac{\bar{v}_i - \alpha_i}{\theta/T}|\bar{v}_i\right],$$

and the semiparametric efficient score is

$$\tilde{\ell}_i = v_i^\top Q y_{i,-1}/\theta + h_T(\rho) + [\bar{y}_{i,-1} - h_T(\rho)\bar{v}_i]\mathbb{E}\left[\frac{\bar{v}_i - \alpha_i}{\theta/T}|\bar{v}_i\right].$$

Note that if we take G to be the improper prior, $G(\alpha) = \alpha$ so α is distributed uniformly on the entire real line, then $\mathbb{E}[\alpha_i|\bar{v}_i] = \bar{v}_i$, the last term is zero and $\tilde{\ell}_i$ collapses to the Lancaster score function. The general form of the semiparametric efficient score again has the feature that it depends only on G through the weights

$$w_i = \mathbb{E}\left[\frac{\bar{v}_i - \alpha|\bar{v}_i}{\theta/T}\right],$$

which is a posterior mean. Since $\bar{v}_i$ is normally distributed conditional on α_i, this term again leads back to the (Gaussian) Tweedie formula.

In Table 5.1 we compare several estimators for ρ for the AR(1) model in simulations. We generate α_i either as iid from the standard Gaussian, labeled DGP(1), or from a discrete distribution with only two mass points, $\alpha_i \sim 0.5\delta_{-1} + 0.5\delta_2$, labeled DGP(2). In addition to the estimators proposed

Table 5.1. *RMSE performance for several profile estimators of the AR(1) parameter. Based on 500 replications.*

n	T	AR1(ρ)	DGP	Lancaster	MILE	P-KW	P-Efron	ES-KW	ES-Efron
100	5	0.5	1	0.055	0.054	0.056	0.053	0.054	0.054
500	5	0.5	1	0.022	0.022	0.022	0.022	0.022	0.022
1,000	5	0.5	1	0.016	0.016	0.017	0.016	0.016	0.016
100	10	0.5	1	0.032	0.032	0.034	0.032	0.033	0.033
500	10	0.5	1	0.014	0.014	0.014	0.014	0.014	0.014
1,000	10	0.5	1	0.010	0.010	0.010	0.010	0.010	0.010
100	5	0.5	2	0.038	0.037	0.038	0.042	0.036	0.037
500	5	0.5	2	0.017	0.017	0.017	0.023	0.017	0.017
1,000	5	0.5	2	0.012	0.012	0.012	0.018	0.011	0.011
100	10	0.5	2	0.025	0.025	0.026	0.031	0.025	0.025
500	10	0.5	2	0.011	0.011	0.011	0.016	0.011	0.011
1,000	10	0.5	2	0.008	0.008	0.008	0.012	0.008	0.008
100	5	0.8	1	0.044	0.043	0.045	0.043	0.043	0.043
500	5	0.8	1	0.017	0.017	0.018	0.017	0.017	0.017
1,000	5	0.8	1	0.013	0.013	0.013	0.013	0.013	0.013
100	10	0.8	1	0.021	0.021	0.023	0.021	0.021	0.021
500	10	0.8	1	0.009	0.009	0.010	0.009	0.009	0.009
1,000	10	0.8	1	0.007	0.007	0.007	0.007	0.007	0.007
100	5	0.8	2	0.027	0.027	0.027	0.030	0.026	0.026
500	5	0.8	2	0.012	0.012	0.012	0.016	0.012	0.012
1,000	5	0.8	2	0.008	0.008	0.008	0.013	0.008	0.008
100	10	0.8	2	0.014	0.014	0.014	0.016	0.013	0.013
500	10	0.8	2	0.006	0.006	0.006	0.009	0.006	0.006
1,000	10	0.8	2	0.004	0.004	0.005	0.007	0.004	0.004

by Lancaster (2002) and Moreira (2009), we consider the profile likelihood estimators whose distribution for α_i is estimated by the Kiefer–Wolfowitz NPMLE or the Efron log spline procedure with degrees of freedom 5 and penalty parameter 0.50. These are denoted as P-KW and P-Efron in the table. We also consider two efficient score estimating equation methods that solve for a root of the estimating equation. These methods are designated as ES-KW and ES-Efron respectively, depending upon how the score function is constructed.

It is evident from the table that there are only minor differences in the performance of the six estimators. The invariance methods of Lancaster and Moreira, referred to in the table as "Lancaster" and "MILE" respectively, are as good, if not better, than the NPMLE profiling methods, so there is little gain to be squeezed out of learning more about the distributional form of the incidental parameters in this setting.

5.4.4 Estimation of the Weibull Shape Parameter

As we have seen, profile likelihood estimation of structural parameters can be a powerful tool in many empirical Bayes settings, but it can also be highly problematic. The cautionary side of the profile likelihood story is well illustrated by its behavior in certain survival analysis models. Consider the Heckman and Singer (1984) model of unemployment durations. Individuals with observed covariates, X, and latent frailty parameter, θ, have durations that are conditionally Weibull. Observed durations, T, arise from a Weibull frailty model with mixture density

$$f(t|x) = \int \alpha t^{\alpha-1} \exp(\theta + x^\top \beta) \exp(-t^\alpha \exp(\theta + x^\top \beta)) dG(\theta|x).$$

Provided we are willing to assume independence of θ and X, so $G(\theta|x) = G(\theta)$, estimation of the structural parameter, β, is relatively benign as we will see in Chapter 8, so in this section we will focus our attention on the simplified model,

$$f(t) = \int \alpha t^{\alpha-1} \exp(\theta) \exp(-t^\alpha \exp(\theta)) dG(\theta) \tag{5.1}$$

involving only the structural Weibull shape parameter, α.

Without any further restrictions on the set $\mathcal{G}$ of admissible G, as shown by Ishwaran (1996) the pair (α, G) is not point identified. However, Heckman and Singer (1984) show that by imposing further integrability conditions on, $\mathcal{G}$ point identification can be restored.

Theorem 5.4. *If the distributions $\mathcal{G}$ in the Weibull model (5.1) satisfy the condition $\int \exp(\theta) dG < \infty$, then the pair (α, G) is point identified.*

Proof: Consider two pairs (α_1, G_1) and (α_2, G_2). Denote the marginal density as $f_j(t) = \int \alpha_j t^{\alpha_j - 1} \exp(\theta) \exp(-t^{\alpha_j} e^\theta) dG_j(\theta)$. To establish point identification of (α, G), it suffices to prove that $f_1(t) = f_2(t)$ for all $t \geq 0$ if and only if $(\alpha_1, G_1) = (\alpha_2, G_2)$. We have,

$$\frac{f_1(t)}{f_2(t)} = \frac{\alpha_1}{\alpha_2} t^{\alpha_1 - \alpha_2} \frac{\int e^{\theta} e^{-t^{\alpha_1} e^{\theta}} dG_1}{\int e^{\theta} e^{-t^{\alpha_2} e^{\theta}} dG_2}.$$

As $t \to 0$, provided $\int e^{\theta} dG_1 < \infty$ and $\int e^{\theta} dG_2 < \infty$, the right-hand side converges to 0 if $\alpha_1 > \alpha_2$, or converges to infinity if $\alpha_1 < \alpha_2$, so $f_1(t)/f_2(t) \neq 1$ unless $\alpha_1 = \alpha_2$. This proves identification of α. Identification of G follows from the uniqueness of Laplace transforms. ■

As we illustrate in Figure 8.12 for a model of medfly mortality, the profile log likelihood,

$$\ell_{\hat{G}(\alpha)}(\alpha) = \sum_{i=1}^{n} \log f_{\hat{G}(\alpha)}(t_i),$$

tends to nicely increase quadratically over a range of small values of the shape parameter α, but rather than turning back down it continues to increase linearly. This linear increase is accompanied by a gradual increase in the number of mass points of the NPMLE $\hat{G}(\alpha)$. Imposing some form of roughness penalty as, for example, is accomplished by the Efron logspline estimator may help to restore a meaningful maximum of the profile log likelihood function. Similar sieve strategies have been suggested by Chen et al. (2011) and Chen and Liao (2014), although in our experience it is difficult to adjust tuning parameters to achieve stable solutions. An alternative approach proposed by Honoré (1990) involves using only a few of the lowest duration-order statistics to produce an estimate of the shape parameter. For the lowest k durations we can approximate the Weibull hazard function as

$$\log h(t_{(i)}) \approx \log \alpha + (\alpha - 1) \log t_{(i)} \quad i = 1, \ldots, k,$$

and we can recover an estimate of α from the regression of $\log h(t_{(i)})$ on $\log t_{(i)}$ based on the smallest k order statistics. This strategy is closely related to the Hill (1975) estimator of the Pareto tail exponent. We illustrate its use in the analysis of medfly mortality in Chapter 8.

Exercises

(1) To justify the semiparametric efficiency bound in Section 5.4.2, for the paired exponential model, show that:

(a) $\int s^2 \nabla_s^2 f_S(s) ds = 2$.
(b) $\int s^2 (\nabla_s f_S(s)/f_S(s))^2 f_S(s) ds \geq 1$.

(2) To derive the efficient semiparametric score function for the AR(1) model of Section 5.4.3, show that:

(a) $y_{it} = \rho^t y_{i0} + [1 + \rho + \cdots + \rho^{t-1}]\alpha_i + \sum_{s=1}^{t} \rho^{t-s} u_{is}$.

(b) $\bar{y}_{i,-1}|\alpha_i$ and $\bar{v}_i|\alpha_i$ are jointly Gaussian with respective means: $\frac{1}{T}\frac{1-\rho^T}{1-\rho}y_{i0} + h_T(\rho)\alpha_i$ and α_i, respective variances, $\frac{\theta}{T^2}\left[\frac{(1-\rho^{T-1})^2}{(1-\rho)^2} + \frac{(1-\rho^{T-2})^2}{(1-\rho)^2} + \cdots + 1\right]$, and $\frac{\theta}{T}$ and covariance $h_T(\rho)\frac{\theta}{T}$.

(c) $\mathbb{E}[\bar{y}_{i,-1}|\bar{v}_i] = \frac{1}{T}\frac{1-\rho^T}{1-\rho}y_{i0} + h_T(\rho)\bar{v}_i$.

(d) $\mathbb{E}[v_i' Q y_{i,-1}/\theta] = -h_T(\rho) \neq 0$.

CHAPTER 6

Heteroscedastic Gaussian Mixture Models and Longitudinal Data

In this chapter we consider important extensions of the simple Gaussian sequence model to accommodate variability in the precision of the observed data and then to consider longitudinal (panel) data.

6.1 HETEROSCEDASTIC GAUSSIAN PROBLEMS

In many applications researchers are faced with plausibly Gaussian observations that arrive with an associated measure of variability that requires special attention. This is the case, for example, in the classical empirical Bayes analysis of baseball batting averages. Binomial batting averages are typically transformed to approximately Gaussian observations with associated variances that depend on the number of "at bats" experienced by the player over the sample period. This heteroscedasticity can be addressed in several different ways. We will begin by considering the simplest case in which we are willing to condition on the observed variances as if they were exogenously fixed and assume that latent θ_i's are drawn iidly from a distribution G_θ and are independent from the variances. This is sometimes plausible, for instance, when variances depend upon an exogenous sample size, but even in the baseball setting one can easily imagine baseball managers influencing the number of "at bats" of various players based on perceived batting "ability." See Gu and Koenker (2017a) for further details.

The first systematic study of such situations was work by Efron and Morris (1973b) who sought to extend Stein rules to account for this additional source of heterogeneity. They noted that a Bayesian observing iid $Y_i|\theta_i \sim \mathcal{N}(\theta_i, \sigma_i^2)$, $i = 1, \ldots, n$ with mutually independent priors, $\theta_i \sim \mathcal{N}(0, A)$, $i = 1, \ldots, n$, and focused exclusively on the estimation of a single coordinate, say θ_k, would simply compute the posterior, $\theta_k|y_k \sim \mathcal{N}((1 - B_k)y_k, \sigma_k^2(1 - B_k))$ where $B_k = \sigma_k^2/(A + \sigma_k^2)$, and proceed accordingly. But suppose instead, the analyst was unsure about the prior and faced a compound decision problem involving all of the θ_i's; what then? A naive approach that they dismiss immediately is to rescale the responses, so $\tilde{y}_i = y_i/\sigma_i$, and the parameters, so $\mu_i = \theta_i/\sigma_i$, and apply the classical Stein rule to the transformed data,

$$\hat{\mu}_i = \left(1 - \frac{n-2}{\sum_{j=1}^n y_j^2/\sigma_j^2}\right)\tilde{y}_i.$$

To get back the estimator for the unscaled effect θ_i, we multiply by σ_i and hence

$$\hat{\theta}_i = \left(1 - \frac{n-2}{\sum_{j=1}^n y_j^2/\sigma_j^2}\right)y_i.$$

They find this "unappealing" since all observations are shrunk by the same factor even though the univariate case already suggests that shrinkage should be greater when the observations are less precise. The resolution of this quandary would seem to be to find a way to *estimate* the A appearing in the hypothetical prior.

To this end Efron and Morris (1973b) propose a fixed point iteration scheme that reduces to the original Stein rule in the case that the σ_i^2 are all identical. They begin by noting that $S_i = Y_i^2 \sim (A + \sigma_i^2)\chi_1^2$, and hence $E_i = (S_i - \sigma_i^2)$ is a minimum variance unbiased estimator for A with variance, $1/\mathcal{I}_i(A)$ where

$$\mathcal{I}_i(A) = 1/(2(A + \sigma_i^2)^2).$$

The maximum likelihood estimator of A is given by the solution to the equation

$$\hat{A} = \sum_i E_i \mathcal{I}(\hat{A}) / \sum_i \mathcal{I}_i(\hat{A}),$$

and the resulting empirical Bayes estimator would take the form

$$\delta_i(Y_i) = \left(1 - \frac{\sigma_i^2}{\hat{A} + \sigma_i^2}\right)Y_i.$$

However, this does not reduce to the James–Stein estimator when $\sigma_i^2 = \sigma^2$. Efron and Morris (1973b) then propose a variant of the estimation of A, for which we define $E_i = (S_i - d_i\sigma_i^2)/d_i$ and

$$\mathcal{I}_i(A) = d_i/(2(A + \sigma_i^2)^2).$$

And the estimator for A is given by solutions to the equation

$$\hat{A} = \sum_{i=1}^n E_i \mathcal{I}_i(\hat{A}) / \sum_{i=1}^n \mathcal{I}_i(\hat{A}).$$

Rather than employing this scalar estimate of A, they solve this equation for individual $\hat{A}_i$, with $d_i = 3$ and $d_j = 1, j \neq i$. Finally, defining

$$d_i^* = 2(\hat{A}_i + \sigma_i^2)^2 \sum_{j=1}^n \frac{d_j}{2(\hat{A}_j + \sigma_j^2)^2},$$

they propose the shrinkage factor

$$\hat{B}_i = \frac{d_i^* - 4}{d_i^*} \frac{\sigma_i^2}{\hat{A}_i + \sigma_i^2},$$

so the final estimator is $\delta_i(Y_i) = (1 - \hat{B}_i)Y_i$. An appeal of this procedure is that when $\sigma_i^2 = \sigma^2$ for all i, it collapses to the original James–Stein rule. It is, we should caution, still reliant on the Gaussian prior assumption on the θ_i's.

To explore the relative performance of these estimators, we consider a simple simulation setting in which $Y_i|\theta_i \sim \mathcal{N}(\theta_i, \sigma_i^2)$, $\theta_i \sim G$, where G is the Gamma distribution with shape parameter 2 and scale 1, and $\sigma_i^2 \sim \chi_3^2$ and independent of θ_i. We compare performance of five estimators:

(1) The MLE $\delta(y_i) = y_i$,
(2) The original James–Stein estimator $\delta(y_i) = (1 - (n-2)/S)y_i$, with $S = \sum y_i^2$,
(3) The weighted James–Stein estimator $\delta(y_i) = (1 - (n-2)/S_w)y_i$, with $S_w = \sum y_i^2/\sigma_i^2$,
(4) The Efron and Morris (1973b) estimator,
(5) A nonparametric posterior mean estimator based on the NPMLE of G.

Table 6.1 reports root mean squared errors for the five estimators and three sample sizes. As expected the first three estimators are dominated by the Efron–Morris procedure, but there is a substantial additional improvement achieved by the NPMLE G-modeling estimator. Perhaps this is not so surprising since the Efron–Morris estimator is still targeted at Gaussian prior settings, whereas the NPMLE is better able to adapt to the non-Gaussian nature of the "prior" of the simulation environment. For the estimation of G in the heteroscedastic model, see further details in Chapter 12.

6.1.1 Scale Transformations of the Response

Suppose we proceed nonparametrically with the transformed data, $\tilde{y}_i = y_i/\sigma_i$, maintaining the assumption that $\theta_i \sim G$ and $\theta_i \perp\!\!\!\perp \sigma_i$. We can construct a nonparametric estimator corresponding to the James–Stein estimator for the weighted observations,

$$\tilde{Y}_i = Y_i/\sigma_i = \mu_i + \epsilon_i.$$

Table 6.1. *Root mean squared error for five estimators in heteroscedastic Gaussian sequence model: Based on 1,000 replications.*

	MLE	JS	WJS	EM	NPMLE
$n = 100$	1.729	1.564	1.503	1.326	1.025
$n = 500$	1.731	1.564	1.516	1.328	0.990
$n = 1{,}000$	1.732	1.563	1.519	1.324	0.981

Now, ϵ_i follows a standard normal distribution. The Tweedie estimator for μ_i takes the form

$$\mathbb{E}[\mu_i|\tilde{Y}_i = \tilde{y}] = \tilde{y} + \frac{f'_{\tilde{Y}}(\tilde{y})}{f_{\tilde{Y}}(\tilde{y})}.$$

However, we are still interested in $\mathbb{E}[\theta_i|Y_i = y, \sigma_i = \sigma]$, which equals $\mathbb{E}[\sigma_i\mu_i|\tilde{Y}_i = \tilde{y}, \sigma_i = \sigma]$; this is typically different than $\sigma_i\mathbb{E}[\mu_i|\tilde{Y}_i = \tilde{y}]$. To obtain the former quantity, we require knowledge of the conditional density of μ_i given $\sigma_i = \sigma$, which takes the form

$$\nabla_a\mathbb{P}(\mu_i \le a|\sigma_i = \sigma) = \nabla_a\mathbb{P}(\theta_i \le a\sigma|\sigma_i = \sigma) = \nabla_a G(a\sigma),$$

where the last equality makes use of the independence assumption between σ_i and θ_i. This requires knowledge of G, but using the model on the transformed data does not seem to provide a straightforward path to the recovery of the distribution of G.

An alternative way of modeling such heteroscedasticity is to assume that the transformed effects, $\mu_i = \theta_i/\sigma_i$ are independent of σ_i. In this case, we would first identify the distribution H_μ (with density h_μ) of μ_i from the model

$$\tilde{Y}_i \equiv Y_i/\sigma_i = \mu_i + \epsilon_i.$$

Then we can express the distribution function G of θ_i as

$$G(a) = \mathbb{P}(\theta_i \le a) = \mathbb{P}(\mu_i\sigma_i \le a) = \int H_\mu(a/\sigma)dH_\sigma(\sigma),$$

where H_σ is the distribution of the standard deviation σ_i. The density of θ_i takes the form

$$g(a) = \nabla_a G(a) = \int h_\mu\left(\frac{a}{\sigma}\right)\frac{1}{\sigma}dH_\sigma(\sigma).$$

The conditional density of θ given σ now takes the form

$$g_{\theta|\sigma}(a|\sigma) = h_\mu(a/\sigma)/\sigma,$$

so the posterior mean of θ_i is

$$\begin{aligned}\mathbb{E}[\theta_i|Y_i = y, \sigma_i^2 = \sigma^2] &= \frac{\int \theta\phi((y-\theta)/\sigma)/\sigma g_{\theta|\sigma}(\theta|\sigma)d\theta}{\int \phi((y-\theta)/\sigma)/\sigma g_{\theta|\sigma}(\theta|\sigma)d\theta} \\ &= \frac{\int \theta\phi((y-\theta)/\sigma)h_\mu(\theta/\sigma)/\sigma^2 d\theta}{\int \phi((y-\theta)/\sigma)h_\mu(\theta/\sigma)/\sigma^2 d\theta}.\end{aligned}$$

Independence of μ_i and σ_i^2 implies a specific dependence structure between θ_i and σ_i^2. For example, $\mathbb{E}[\theta_i|\sigma_i^2] = \mathbb{E}[\mu_i\sigma_i|\sigma_i^2] = \mathbb{E}[\mu_i]\sigma_i$. If $\mathbb{E}[\mu_i] = \bar{\mu} > 0$, then θ_i tends to increase with σ_i on average. Whether this is reasonable is obviously subject to the specific considerations of the application at hand. A slight generalization is considered by Stephens (2017), who proposes assuming independence between θ_i/σ_i^a and σ_i, for some $a \in [0, 1]$. Again, the defensibility of this assumption depends upon the context of the application.

One can assess the plausibility of this independence assumption by investigating dependence between $\tilde{Y}_i$ and σ_i^2, or by estimating H_μ for different bins of values of σ_i^2's provided that they can be reasonably binned in the data. See Kline et al. (2022) for further details in the context of their application to evaluating applicant job discrimination. In their context, θ_i is interpreted as the causal effect of race on contact rates at jobs in firm i, Y_i is the White/Black differential in mean contact rates at firm i among J_i jobs and σ_i^2 is an estimate of the variance; the $\tilde{Y}_i$ correspond to the sample Z-score. They provide evidence that the independence assumption between μ_i and σ_i^2 is reasonable in this context.

6.2 COMPOUND DECISIONS WITH HETEROGENEOUS VARIANCES

In the compound decision framework, if we adopt the Efron–Morris model $Y_i|\theta_i \sim \mathcal{N}(\theta_i, \sigma_i^2)$ with $\theta_1, \ldots, \theta_n$ viewed as fixed parameters and $\sigma_1^2, \ldots, \sigma_n^2$ as known variances, simple decision rules of the form, $d_i(y_1, \ldots, y_n) = d(y_i)$ have compound risk

$$R_n(d,\theta) = n^{-1} \sum_{i=1}^{n} \int L(d(y), \theta_i) \varphi(y|\theta_i, \sigma_i^2) dy.$$

Due to the heterogeneity of the σ_i^2, this compound risk can no longer be reduced to a single copy of representative Bayes risk by the fundamental theorem of compound decisions; exchangeability is broken.

In the closely related longitudinal setting, $Y_{ij}|\theta_i \sim \mathcal{N}(\theta_i, \sigma_i^2)$, we can take the sample mean and sample variance of the Y_{ij}'s as sufficient statistics for the pair (θ_i, σ_i^2) with both elements now regarded as unknown parameters. Exchangeability can be restored by considering mixture models requiring the joint distribution of these pairs. This setting will be considered in Section 6.3.

Without longitudinal data, we can restore exchangeability by allowing the simple decision rule to depend on the pair (y_i, σ_i); in this case, the compound risk is

$$R_n(d,\theta) = n^{-1} \sum_{i=1}^{n} \int \int L(d(y,\sigma), \theta_i) f(y, \sigma|\theta_i) dy d\sigma.$$

Viewing the data associated with θ_i as (y_i, σ_i^2), we can again reduce the compound problem to a single copy of the representative Bayes problem.

With only one observation Y_i and known variance σ_i^2, one can consider Bayesian settings in which each θ_i is assumed to be drawn independently of σ_i^2 from a prior distribution G. This is the approach taken by Efron and Morris (1973b).

There are several ways to relax the independence assumption between θ_i and σ_i^2 and we will consider several such proposals. Xie et al. (2012) introduced

Table 6.2. *Root mean squared error for several estimators of a heteroscedastic Gaussian sequence model.*

	DGP1	DGP2	DGP3	DGP4	DGP5
MLE	0.234	0.234	0.234	0.111	0.173
SG	0.229	0.189	0.178	0.067	0.172
EJS	0.229	0.190	0.188	0.064	0.172
GL	0.228	0.187	0.147	0.054	0.168
WGLV	0.233	0.179	0.138	0.045	0.170

several new estimators designed to accommodate heteroscedastic variances and motivated by the Stein unbiased risk principle. Weinstein et al. (2018) emphasize the need to consider dependence of θ_i and σ_i^2 and suggest a grouped, linear estimator that can partially account for such dependence. Chen (2025) suggests an alternative way to model dependence, in which θ_i is assumed to have nonparametric mean function, $m_0(\sigma_i^2)$, and variance function, $s_0^2(\sigma_i^2)$ such that $(\theta_i - m_0(\sigma_i^2))/s_0(\sigma_i^2)$ is iid with distribution G. Table 6.2 compares several estimators in various heteroscedastic Gaussian linear model settings adapted from Weinstein et al. (2018):

(1) $\sigma_i^2 \sim U[0.1, 1]$, $\theta_i \sim \mathcal{N}(0, 1)$,
(2) $\sigma_i^2 \sim U[0.1, 1]$, $\theta_i \sim U[0, 1]$,
(3) $\sigma_i^2 \sim U[0.1, 1]$, $\theta_i = \sigma_i^2$,
(4) $\sigma_i^2 \sim \chi_{10}^{-2}$, $\theta_i = \sigma_i^2$,
(5) $D_i \sim 0.5\delta_{0.1} + 0.5\delta_{0.5}$, $\theta_i \sim \mathbb{1}\{\sigma_i^2 = 0.5\}\mathcal{N}(2, 0.1) + \mathbb{1}\{\sigma_i^2 = 0.1\}\mathcal{N}(0, 0.5)$.

In each case, the models have a longitudinal structure with $Y_{ij} \sim \mathcal{N}(\theta_i, \sigma_i^2)$, $j = 1, \dots, m, i = 1, \dots, n$. The first two of these DGPs is a vanilla Gaussian mixture model with no dependence between mean and variances, for which we might expect that linear shrinkage would perform well. The remaining DGPs impose strong dependence between mean and variance parameters and are therefore more challenging. It should be stressed that although DGPs (3) and (4) both set $\theta_i = \sigma_i^2$, the simulation assumes that the investigator is unaware of this fact. The competing estimators comprise:

MLE: $\hat{\theta}_i = m^{-1} \sum_{j=1}^m Y_{ij}$
SG: $\hat{\theta}_i$ = Xie et al. (2012) monotonized SURE G estimator
EJS: $\hat{\theta}_i$ = Weinstein et al. (2018) extended James–Stein estimator
GL: $\hat{\theta}_i$ = Weinstein et al. (2018) group linear estimator
WGLV: $\hat{\theta}_i$ = `WGLVmix` estimator

Each of the SG, EJS, M and GL procedures are evaluated at the n vectors, $\hat{Y} = (\hat{Y}_i) = m^{-1} \sum_{j=1}^m Y_{ij}$ and $\hat{\sigma}^2 = (\hat{\sigma}_i^2) = m^{-1} \sum_{j=1}^m (Y_{ij} - \hat{Y}_i)^2$. Sample size is $n = 1{,}000$ with $m = 10$ and 100 replications for each DGP.

The last WGLV estimator based on the `WGLVmix` function in the **REBayes** package (Koenker and Gu, 2015–2024) requires some further exposition since it involves estimation of the joint distribution of the pairs, (θ_i, σ_i^2). This leads us naturally into the longitudinal mixture models described in Section 6.3.

6.3 EMPIRICAL BAYES FOR GAUSSIAN LONGITUDINAL MODELS

Consider the location-scale Gaussian mixture model,

$$y_{it} = \theta_i + \sqrt{\eta_i} u_{it}, \quad t = 1, \ldots, m_i, \quad i = 1, \ldots, n,$$

with $u_{it} \sim \mathcal{N}(0, 1)$. We need not interpret the t subscript temporally, as we have seen above, but it is often natural to do so. We will provisionally assume that $\theta_i \sim G_\theta$ and $\eta_i \sim G_\eta$ are independent. We then have sufficient statistics:

$$\bar{y}_i | \theta_i, \eta_i \sim \mathcal{N}(\theta_i, \eta_i / m_i)$$

and

$$S_i | r_i, \eta_i \sim \gamma(s | r_i, \eta_i / r_i),$$

where $r_i = (m_i - 1)/2$, $S_i = (m_i - 1)^{-1} \sum_{t=1}^{m_i} (y_{it} - \bar{y}_i)^2$, and $\gamma(s|a, b)$ is the density of the Gamma distribution with parameters, (a, b). The log likelihood becomes

$$\ell(G_\theta, G_\eta | y) = K(y) + \sum_{i=1}^{n} \log \int\int \gamma(S_i | r_i, \eta / r_i) \sqrt{m_i} \\ \times \phi\left(\sqrt{m_i}(\bar{y}_i - \theta_i) / \sqrt{\eta}\right) / \sqrt{\eta} dG_\theta(\theta) dG_\eta(\eta).$$

Since the scale component of the log likelihood is additively separable from the location component, we can solve for $\hat{G}_\eta$ in a preliminary step and then solve for the $\hat{G}_\theta$ distribution. In fact, under the independent prior assumption, we can re-express the Gaussian component of the likelihood as Student-t and thereby eliminate the dependence on η in the Kiefer–Wolfowitz problem for estimating G_θ. An implementation is available in the function `WTLVmix` of **REBayes**. Gu and Koenker (2017a) describe an application to predicting baseball batting averages in which, following Brown (2008), batting averages are transformed to normality, and the η's reflect either under or over dispersion relative to the standard binomial model. Profile likelihood can be used to explore covariate effects embedded in this model of heterogeneity. In particular we study the age profile for batting prowess as a quadratic effect and estimate that batting "ability" peaks at age 27. Comparing predictive performance for this model we find that the independent prior NPMLE performs considerably better than its more naive competitors that ignore heterogeneity in scale.

It is also possible to relax the independence assumption on the location and scale effects completely. In Gu and Koenker (2017b) we use longitudinal data on 938 individuals from the Panel Study on Income Dynamics (PSID) to study models of income dynamics with an arbitrary joint distribution of location and scale heterogeneity. This is the approach used for the WGLV estimator in Table 6.2. The implementation employs the function `WGLVmix` from the **REBayes** package. In the income dynamics application we find a distinct *negative* dependence between the θ (location) and η scale effects indicating that low "ability" individuals also tend to have higher income variability. In this application temporal dependence in the income process is specified as a simple AR(1) process whose coefficient, ρ is estimated by profile likelihood. We find a rather mild transitory $\rho \approx 0.5$ effect in contrast to the very persistent unit root process often assumed in prior literature. The Bayesian formulation of these models offers the significant additional advantage that it provides a convenient environment for forecasting future income trajectories.

To make this more explicit, we consider the model

$$\begin{aligned} y_{it} &= \theta_i + \beta_i x_{it} + v_{it}, \\ v_{it} &= \rho v_{it-1} + \sqrt{\eta_i}\epsilon_{it}, \quad \epsilon_{it} \sim \mathcal{N}(0, \sigma_\epsilon^2). \end{aligned}$$

Assuming that initial conditions, y_{i0}, are drawn from the stationary distribution $\mathcal{N}(\theta_i, \sigma_\epsilon^2 \eta_i/(1-\rho^2))$ is a convenient option and yields an efficient estimator for ρ provided that the assumption holds. One could also consider less restrictive specifications for y_{i0} at the cost of introducing additional parameters as in Arellano (2003). However it seems simpler to consider Chamberlainian dependence of the latent effects on covariates while trying to maintain a nonparametric perspective, a topic we defer to future research. More complex short-run dynamics could be introduced via state space representations and Kalman filter formulations of the likelihood, as illustrated in Koenker and Gu (2024), but our strategy is to proceed parsimoniously trying to understand at each stage the consequences of expanding the flexibility of the model.

Following standard practice in the literature, we removed dependence on the covariates, x_{it}, by a preliminary least squares projection, so y_{it} can be interpreted as residuals from this projection. This leaves ρ, the AR(1) coefficient, as the only parameter requiring profile likelihood treatment.[1]

Under the restrictions that $\beta_i \equiv 0$ and $\eta_i \equiv 1$, we can rewrite the model as

$$y_{it} = \rho y_{it-1} + (1-\rho)\theta_i + \epsilon_{it}.$$

This is a textbook dynamic panel model; in such models of earnings dynamics, estimates of ρ are typically very close to one. In contrast to Meghir and Pistaferri (2004), who postulate a permanent component of earnings with a unit root, Browning et al. (2010) – using the same data – find no unit root after introducing further heterogeneity in the covariance structure of the model.

[1] A natural question would be: Why not permit ρ to be random as well as θ_i and η_i? Introducing a third dimension for the latent parameter structure of the model not only complicates the gridding of the NPMLE problem but would also disrupt the convenient sufficient statistic feature. These drawbacks, in our view, outweigh the potential benefits of introducing heterogeneous ρ.

In Figure 6.1, we present some preliminary evidence that helps to explain why the persistence of innovations may be reduced by introducing conditional heterogeneity, for example, by relaxing the restrictions of a homogeneous variance of ϵ_{it} across individuals.

The QQ plots of Figure 6.1 confirm earlier evidence of Horowitz and Markatou (1996) and Guvenen et al. (2022) based on more extensive CPS and Social Security data respectively that earnings innovations are considerably heavier-tailed than our usual Gaussian assumptions would imply. There are a variety of possible treatments for this disease: One option would be to abandon the Gaussian assumption entirely, but this would lead us into realm of choosing a non-Gaussian likelihood model that would, inevitably, be rather arbitrary. It is known that heavy-tailed distributions can be very flexibly modeled as scale mixtures of Gaussians, as documented in the extensive discussion in Andrews et al. (1972), and we have already seen in Section 5.4.1 that it is relatively straightforward to estimate these mixture models. Further details appear in Chapter 12.

To provide a further visual impression of the degree of individual heterogeneity we present in Figure 6.2 scatter plots of the individual specific sample means, $\bar{y}$, and log variances, S, for the partially differenced y_{it} data for several ρ's. In addition to confirming that there is substantial heterogeneity in these quantities, the figure also reveals that more moderate values of ρ yield a more elliptical scatter that would be favored by a Gaussian/Gamma location-scale mixture model.

Fixing ρ and σ_ϵ^2, and setting $z_{it} = y_{it} - \rho y_{it-1}$, our model can be expressed as

$$z_{it} = (1-\rho)\theta_i + \sqrt{\eta_i}\epsilon_{it}.$$

And for Gaussian ϵ_{it}, sufficient statistics for θ_i and η_i are respectively the sample mean and sample variance:

$$\bar{y}_i = \frac{1}{m_i}\sum_{t=1}^{m_i} z_{it},$$

$$S_i = \frac{1}{m_i - 1}\sum_{t=1}^{m_i}((z_{it} - \bar{y}_i)/\sigma_\epsilon)^2.$$

Furthermore, we have, $\bar{y}_i \mid \theta_i, \eta_i \sim \mathcal{N}((1-\rho)\theta_i, \eta_i\sigma_\epsilon^2/m_i)$ and $(m_i - 1)S_i/\eta_i \mid \eta_i \sim \chi^2_{m_i-1}$. Assuming the pairs (θ_i, η_i) are iid with joint distribution function H, we can discretize H on a two-dimensional grid and write the likelihood of observing $(z_{i1}, \ldots, z_{i,m_i})$ as a function of H, ρ and σ_ϵ^2, and compute the NPMLE for the distribution H. Profile likelihood can then be employed to estimate the parameter ρ.

Various special cases of this model have previously been considered in the literature. For example, the random effects model of Alvarez and Arellano (2003) assumes η_i to be degenerate taking value 1 while $\theta_i \sim \mathcal{N}(\psi y_{i0}, \sigma_h^2)$.

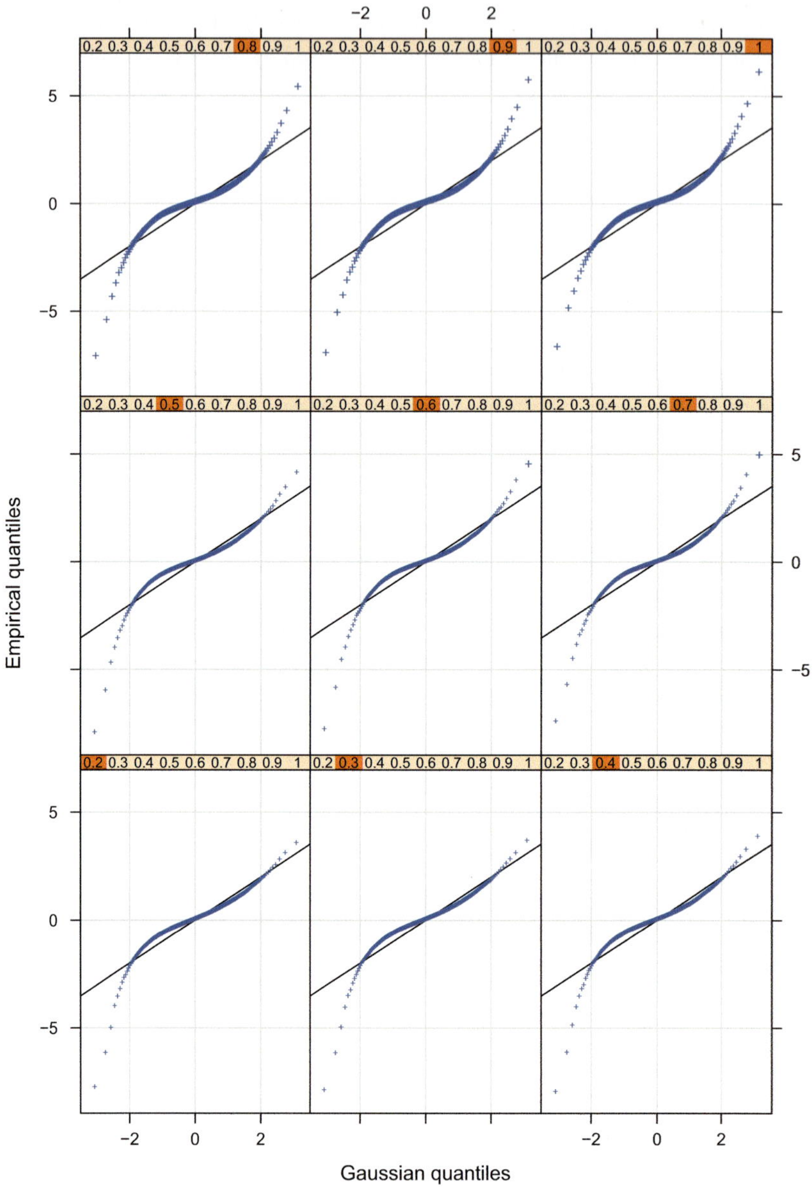

Figure 6.1. Normal QQ plots of partially differenced earnings for various ρ: For $\rho \in \{0.2, 0.3, \ldots, 1.0\}$ we plot empirical quantiles of the partial differences $y_{it} - \rho y_{it-1}$ standardized by their empirical standard deviation, against the corresponding Gaussian quantiles. The ρ's are indicated in the thin strip at the top of each panel; the solid line in each plot is the 45 degree line indicating conformity to the Gaussian hypothesis. It is apparent from the plot that the observed quantiles are far too leptokurtic to be Gaussian, that is much too peaked near the median and exhibiting much heavier tails than the Gaussian. For small ρ there is also some left skewness in innovations that becomes less pronounced for larger ρ.

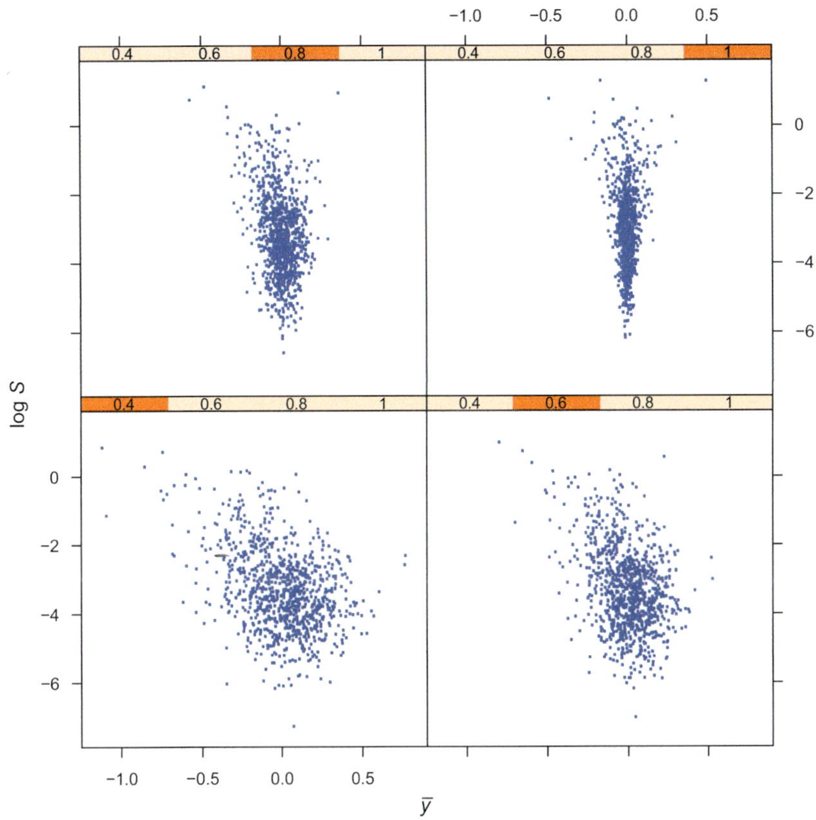

Figure 6.2. Scatterplot of individual specific mean and log variance effects for Various ρ: For $\rho \in \{0.4, 0.6, 0.8, 1.0\}$ we plot sample means, $\bar{y}$, and log variances, S, of the partial differences $y_{it} - \rho y_{it-1}$. The ρ's are indicated in the thin strip at the top of each panel. The more elliptical shape of the scatter for smaller ρ may suggest that it could be more parsimoniously fitted by the Gaussian/Gamma location-scale mixture model.

This leads to a marginal density for the $\bar{y}_i$ conditional on y_{i0} as $\bar{y}_i \sim \mathcal{N}(\psi y_{i0}, \sigma_\theta^2)$ with $\sigma_\theta^2 = \sigma_\epsilon^2/m_i + \sigma_h^2$ as a free parameter. The parameters $(\rho, \psi, \sigma_h^2, \sigma_\theta^2)$ can then be estimated by maximizing the likelihood conditional on y_{i0}. The Gaussian assumption on the θ_i is very convenient and very commonly employed, notably in Chamberlain (1980) and Chamberlain and Hirano (1999) among others. However, the normality assumption on the θ_i may be hard to justify. As we have seen in Figure 6.2, there is also considerable heterogeneity in the η_i, and it seems plausible that there may be some dependence between θ_i and η_i. These considerations motivate a nonparametric maximum likelihood framework allowing estimation of the nonparametric mixing distribution $H(\theta, \eta)$ conditional on some structural parameters like ρ, that can, in turn, be estimated by maximizing a profile likelihood.

Without loss of generality, we can set $\sigma_\epsilon^2 = 1$, since it is not identified once we allow individual specific η_i unless we make further moment restrictions on η_i. We have the following NPMLE problem:

$$\hat{H}_\rho := \underset{H \in \mathcal{H}}{\operatorname{argmax}} \prod_{i=1}^{n} \int \int f(\bar{y}_i \mid \theta, \eta) g(S_i \mid \eta) dH(\theta, \eta),$$

where $\mathcal{H}$ is the space of all bivariate distribution functions on the domain of $\mathbb{R} \times \mathbb{R}_+$. Here, f is the conditional normal density of $\bar{y}_i$ and g is the conditional Gamma density for S_i. The NPMLE for H is indexed by ρ because both $\bar{y}_i$ and S_i involve ρ, a dependence that we have suppressed in the notation, but can be estimated by maximizing the profile log likelihood,

$$\ell(\rho, \hat{H}_\rho) = \sum_{i=1}^{n} K(\bar{y}_i, S_i) + \log \int \int f(\bar{y}_i \mid \theta, \eta) g(S_i \mid \eta) d\hat{H}_\rho(\theta, \eta).$$

Allowing heterogeneous individual variances in earnings innovations is not new. Geweke and Keane (2000) contend that variance heterogeneity is crucial to account for non-Gaussian features of the innovation distribution and use a parametric three-component mixture formulation. Hirano (2002) adopts a more flexible Dirichlet prior specification for similar reasons. Browning et al. (2010) also find significant evidence that the variance of innovations varies across individuals. Their model posits eight latent factors all of which are constrained to obey parametric marginals. They comment, "Nowhere in the literature is there any indication of how to specify a general joint distribution for these parameters, nor is there any hope of identifying the joint distribution nonparametrically." In contrast, our approach allows only two latent factors but has the advantage that it does permit nonparametric estimation of their joint distribution.

What if $\hat{\rho} \approx 1$? Our joint distribution for (θ_i, η_i) would then be meaningless, since the θ_i's would be annihilated. Panel (a) of Figure 6.3 plots the profile likelihood for ρ, which (fortunately) peaks at 0.48. The shaded region indicates a 0.95 confidence interval for ρ as determined by the classical Wilks inversion procedure, see, for example, Murphy and van der Vaart (2000), and Fan et al. (2001). Our estimate of ρ is close to the estimate of Hospido (2012) who also allows an individual specific variance component in a ARCH effect variance. She adopts a fixed effect specification for (θ_i, η_i) and uses a bias corrected estimator for ρ to account for the asymptotic bias introduced by estimating all the incidental parameters $(\theta_i, \eta_i), i = 1, \ldots, n$.

Panel (b) of Figure 6.3 plots the two-dimensional nonparametric estimate of $\hat{H}_{\hat{\rho}}(\theta, \eta)$ on a 60×60 grid. Mass points of the estimated distribution are indicated by shaded hexagons, with darker shading indicating more mass. The support of $\hat{H}$ is determined by the support of the observed $(\bar{y}_i, S_i)$. The mixing distribution shows some negative dependence between θ and η, especially for $\theta < 0$. So a low draw for θ is more likely to be accompanied by a more risky

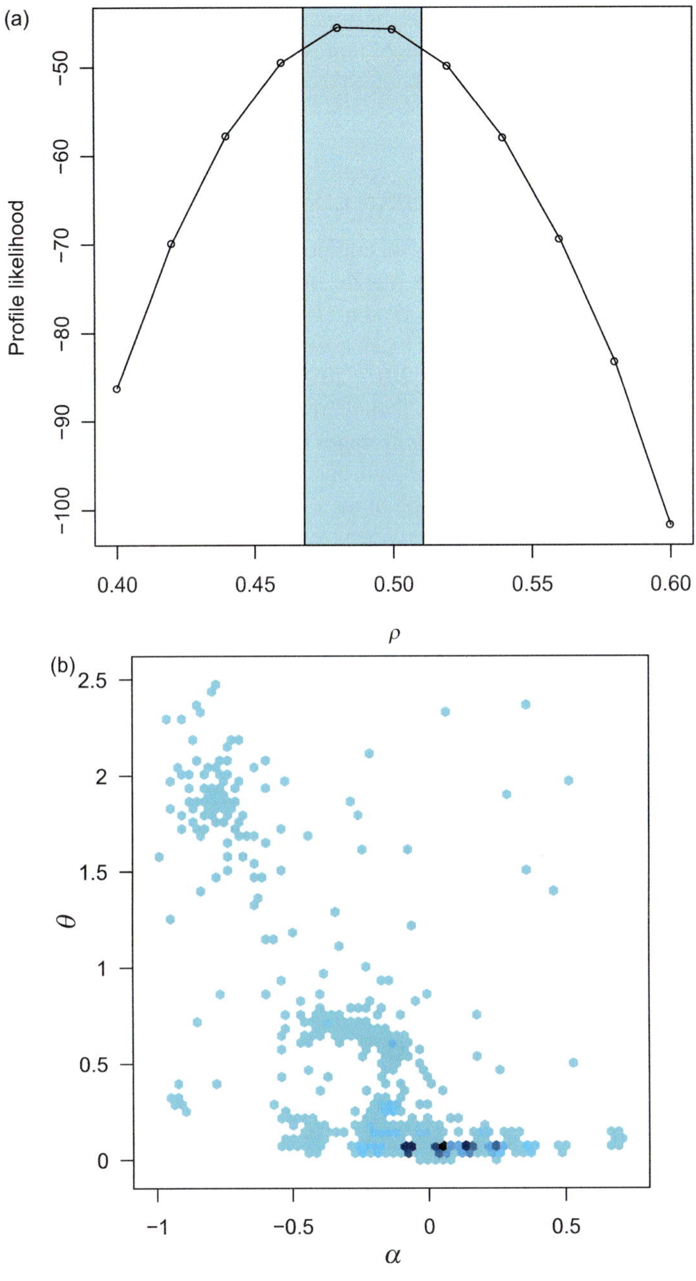

Figure 6.3. Profile likelihood for the ρ parameter and heterogeneity distribution $H(\theta, \eta)$: In panel (a) we plot the Kiefer–Wolfowitz profile likelihood as a function of ρ. The shaded region represents a 0.95 confidence interval for ρ based on the usual Wilks inversion procedure. In panel (b) we plot the estimated joint heterogeneity distribution, evaluated at the optimal $\hat{\rho}$, $\hat{H}_{\hat{\rho}}(\theta, \eta)$. Darker hexagons indicate greater mass, lighter ones less mass and white regions contain no mass.

(higher) η. Most of the mass of $\hat{H}_{\hat{\rho}}$ is concentrated at very low levels of η, but it is not at all obvious how one might represent this estimated heterogeneity by a conventional parametric model.

6.4 PREDICTION IN GAUSSIAN LONGITUDINAL MODELS

In Gaussian settings the most basic compound decision problem is simply to denoise the existing sample. This was the objective of the earliest astronomical use of the Tweedie formula, in Dyson (1926) for the posterior mean. More recently, this technique has been extensively used in genomic studies exemplified by the work of Efron (2011, 2016, 2019) and others.

But there are bigger fish to fry than merely denoising a single sample: There are next season's baseball batting averages to be predicted. This is the acid test of the empirical Bayes endeavor and has been ever since Efron and Morris (1973b). It is an irresistible problem as a glance at Jiang and Zhang (2009), Brown and Greenshtein (2009) or Koenker and Mizera (2014) confirms.

Batting performance is notoriously difficult to predict. Maybe this is what makes it so irresistible. For something so probabilistically simple, after all we have just a vector of binomials, there are quite a few choices to make. The first is whether to make a variance-stabilizing transformation to normality, and if so which one? The second is whether the number "at bats" is informative about the probability of a successful hit? Third, we might, after deciding to make a variance stabilizing transformation, consider a joint distribution of latent mean batting ability, and latent batting consistency represented by over or under dispersion relative to what is predictable by the strict binomial model. These agonizing choices are all carefully considered in Gu and Koenker (2017a). Rather than revisiting these choices, we will instead describe a more typically econometric Gaussian forecasting problem based on the model of income dynamics introduced in Section 6.3.

In Section 6.3 we described a simple model of income dynamics that involved latent location and scale individual effects. The estimated joint distribution of these latent effects suggested that individuals with highly variable income trajectories were also likely to have relatively low mean income. See Figure 6.3.

We would like to adapt the univariate empirical Bayes rules described earlier to compound decision problems for these longitudinal data models. This objective is closely aligned with the objectives of Chamberlain and Hirano (1999), although our computational methods, and perhaps our philosophical outlook, may be quite distinct. Given an initial trajectory for an individual's earnings, we would like to predict the remainder of the trajectory based not only on the prior history for the given individual but also on the observed experience of a large sample of similar individuals. Chamberlain and Hirano motivate this prediction problem as one facing a typical financial advisor. Similar problems present themselves in biomedical settings where diagnosis is based on reference growth charts or some measures of the progression of disease.

Given a trajectory $\mathcal{Y}_0 = \{y_t : t = 1, \ldots, T_0\}$ for a hypothetical individual, we can easily determine a posterior, $p(\theta, \eta|\mathcal{Y}_0)$, based on our estimated mixture model. This NPMLE posterior is necessarily discrete, but one is entitled to draw from the estimated model for simulation purposes. The following simulation strategy can be employed to construct an ensemble of completed trajectories:

(1) Draw (θ, η) from $p(\theta, \eta|\mathcal{Y}_0)$,
(2) Simulate $\mathcal{Y}_1 = \{y_t : t = T_0 + 1, \ldots, T\}$ as,

$$y_{T_0+s} = \theta + \hat{\rho} y_{T_0+s-1} + \sqrt{\eta} u_s, \; s = 1, \ldots, T - T_0, \text{ and } u_s \sim \mathcal{N}(0, 1),$$

to obtain m paths, $\mathcal{Y}_1$, then
(3) Repeat steps 1 and 2, M times.

This procedure yields mM trajectories from which it is easy to construct pointwise and/or uniform prediction bands.

From a formal Bayesian perspective the foregoing procedure may seem rather heretical. We began with a perfectly legitimate likelihood formulation: Data was assumed to be generated from a very conventional Gaussian model, but individuals had idiosyncratic (θ, η) parameters whose joint distribution, H, could be viewed as a prior. If this H were delivered on a silver platter by some local oracle, we could proceed just as we have described. Bayes's rule would allow us to update H in the light of the observed initial trajectory, $\mathcal{Y}_0$, for each individual, and we would use these updated, individual-specific $\tilde{H}_i$'s to construct an ensemble of forecast paths. Various functionals of these forecast paths could then be presented. However, lacking a local oracle, we have relied instead on the NPMLE and the PSID data to produce an $\hat{H}$. Not only H, but also ρ and potentially other model parameters are estimated by maximum likelihood. Remarkably, no further regularization is required, and profile likelihood delivers an asymptotically efficient estimator of these structural, that is, "homogeneous," parameters. Admittedly, we have "sinned" – we've peeked at the data when we shouldn't have peeked – but our peeking has revealed a much more plausible H than we could have otherwise been expected to produce by pure introspection. This is the charm of the empirical Bayes approach. Discussion of a more formal inference procedure that accounts for the fact that H has been estimated is deferred to Chapter 11.

Our prediction exercise takes $T_0 = 9$, so the first nine years of observed earnings have been used as $\mathcal{Y}_0$ to construct individual-specific $\tilde{H}_i$ that are then used to construct pointwise confidence bands for earnings in subsequent years. We have selected two pairs of individuals to illustrate the variety of earnings predictions generated by our model. In Figure 6.4 we contrast predictions for an individual with relatively large mean, that is, high θ, and large variance, high η, with an individual with large variance, but lower mean. The "fan plot" depicts pointwise quantile prediction bands from 0.05 to 0.95 based on the

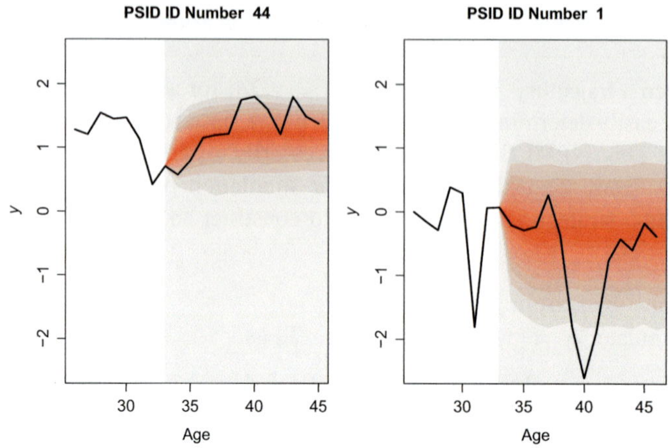

Figure 6.4. Fan plot of earnings forecasts for two individuals: Based on the initial nine years' earnings, pointwise prediction bands are shown with graduated shading indicating bands from the 0.05 to 0.95 quantiles with the actual realizations superimposed as the black lines.

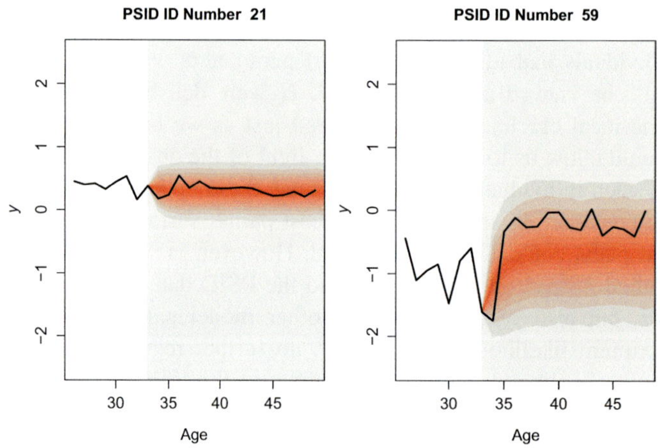

Figure 6.5. Fan plot of earnings forecasts for two individuals: Based on the initial nine years' earnings, pointwise prediction bands are shown with graduated shading indicating bands from the 0.05 to 0.95 quantiles.

simulated trajectories described above. For the high-mean individual, the bands are relatively narrow reflecting the fact that the "prior" assigns little mass to high-η individuals. In contrast, for the lower-mean individual the bands are much wider; indeed the upper portion of the band overlaps with the lower portion of the band for the higher-θ individual. Nevertheless, we see that the lower 0.05 quantile of the prediction band is exceeded. Our uniform band (not shown) for this individual just barely covers this excursion.

In Figure 6.5 we contrast a high-mean, low-variance individual with a low-mean, high-variance one. The prediction band is very narrow for the former individual and much wider for the latter. Other features are also apparent from these figures: Individuals who begin the forecast period below their pre-forecast mean, like PSID 59, are predicted to come back toward their mean, and some asymmetry is visible, for example in PSID 44, whose lower tail is somewhat wider than the upper one. Note that asymmetry requires some asymmetry in the location component of the mixture distribution $\hat{H}$, since pure scale mixtures of Gaussians are necessarily symmetric.

6.5 TESTING MANY MEANS

The Gaussian longitudinal model is also widely used in genomics and high-throughput biology. The goal is to screen for associations across many genes or proteins. In the Gaussian sequence model with repeated independent observations,

$$y_{ij} \sim \mathcal{N}(\theta_i, \sigma_i^2), \quad i = 1, \ldots, n, \; j = 1, \ldots, J.$$

With sufficient statistics, $\hat{\theta}_i = J^{-1} \sum_j y_{ij}$ and $\hat{\sigma}_i^2 = (J-1)^{-1} \sum_j (y_{ij} - \hat{\theta}_i)^2$. A common practice is to take the estimated location parameters $\hat{\theta}_i$ at face value and only the $\hat{\sigma}_i^2$ are subjected to the indignity of shrinkage. In the parametric empirical Bayes implementation, as we have mentioned in Section 3.5, the limma procedure assumes the prior takes the form

$$\sigma_i^{-2} \sim (v_0 s_0^2)^{-1} \chi^2_{v_0} \quad i = 1, \ldots, n,$$

and the degrees of freedom, v_0, and scale, s_0, parameters are estimated either by the method of moments or maximum likelihood. Tests of the n hypotheses, $H_0 \colon \mu_i = 0$ are then based on the p-values,

$$p_i = 2(1 - F_{t, v_0 + v}(|\tilde{t}_i|)),$$

where $\tilde{t}_i = \hat{\mu}_i / \tilde{s}_i$, $\tilde{s}_i^2 = (v_0 s_0^2 + v \hat{\sigma}_i^2)/(v_0 + v)$ with $v = J - 1$, and $F_{t,v}$ is the distribution function of a Student t random variable with v degrees of freedom. With these p-values in hand one can consider selection of units with non-null effects and account for multiple testing error by the Benjamini and Hochberg (1995) procedure or some variant of it.

Ignatiadis and Sen (2025a) have recently proposed replacing the inverse-gamma prior of the limma procedure with an NPMLE estimate of a more flexible prior for the σ_i^2. More explicitly they consider the mixture model,

$$\hat{\sigma}_i^2 \mid \sigma_i^2 \sim \frac{\sigma_i^2}{v} \chi^2_v, \quad i = 1, \ldots, n,$$

with the σ_i^2 drawn iidly from an unknown distribution, G. An earlier proposal by Lu and Stephens (2016) also considered more flexible priors but restricted the class of prior distributions, G, to be unimodal.

6.6 NONPARAMETRIC MODELING OF φ WITH LONGITUDINAL DATA

Up to this point we have relied on parametric specifications of the "base distribution," φ, to anchor the estimation of our mixture models, be they Gaussian, Poisson, Gamma, or binomial. With longitudinal data, the question arises: Can we relax this parametric specification and rely on the data itself to guide the form of the density φ? An affirmative answer to this question is proposed in Ignatiadis et al. (2021). When φ is assumed to be Gaussian, with known variance, we are immediately led to collapse the observations, $Y = (Y_1, \ldots, Y_m)$, into their sample mean as a sufficient statistic for the location parameter, θ. However, suppose we have the location model

$$Y_{ij} = \theta_i + U_{ij}, \quad i = 1, \ldots, n, \quad j = 1, \ldots, m,$$

with U_{ij} iid with common, but unknown, density φ; we can express the conditional mean of θ_i given $(Y_{i1}, \ldots, Y_{im})$ in terms of the expectation of any one of elements of this vector given the remaining elements,

$$\mathbb{E}[\theta_i | Y_{i1}, \ldots, Y_{im-1}] = \mathbb{E}[Y_{im} | Y_{i1}, \ldots, Y_{im-1}].$$

Ignatiadis et al. (2021) propose a regression formulation,

$$\mathbb{E}[Y_{im} | Y_{i1}, \ldots, Y_{im-1}] = \beta_0 + \sum_{j=1}^{m-1} \beta_j Y_{i,(j)}, \tag{6.1}$$

where $Y_{i,(1)} < Y_{i,(2)} < \cdots < Y_{i,(m-1)}$ denote the order statistics of $Y_{i1}, \ldots, Y_{im-1}$. The regression coefficients, $\beta \in \mathbb{R}^m$, may be interpreted as L-statistic weights as discussed, for example, in Serfling (1980).

Suppose that φ is really standard Gaussian although we don't happen to be aware of this, and that $G = \mathcal{N}(\mu, \sigma_\theta^2)$, then

$$\begin{aligned}
\mathbb{E}[\theta_i | Y_{i1}, \ldots, Y_{im-1}] &= \mathbb{E}[Y_{im} | Y_{i1}, \ldots, Y_{im-1}] \\
&= \mu + \frac{\sigma_\theta^2}{1 + \sigma_\theta^2} \left(\frac{1}{m-1} \sum_{j=1}^{m-1} (Y_{ij} - \mu) \right) \\
&= \frac{1}{1 + \sigma_\theta^2} \mu + \sum_{j=1}^{m-1} \frac{\sigma_\theta^2}{1 + \sigma_\theta^2} \frac{1}{m-1} Y_{i,(j)},
\end{aligned}$$

which falls into this class of estimators (6.1) with the first term playing the role of the intercept, and the remaining terms representing the slope parameters in the order statistic regression. When φ is Gaussian the optimal slope parameters are all identical so we recover an optimal L-estimator, in this case the sample mean, for each θ_i with shrinkage of the James–Stein type. Rather than rely only on the model for the last, Y_{im}, the authors suggest including all the leave-one-out conditional expectations in the regression estimator.

In contrast, suppose that φ is Laplace with mean zero and unit variance. The efficient estimator for θ_i is now the conditional median. Again the regression procedure recovers coefficients of the order statistic regression that mimic the optimal L-estimator, which puts most of its weight on the central order statistics. The approach, which has an earlier antecedent in a neglected paper of Johns (1986), is remarkable in that it offers an adaptive way to be agnostic about the base distribution of the mixture specification. The linear regression formulation in (6.1) yields linear estimators that presume a Gaussian prior distribution for G, but this too can be relaxed by considering nonlinear regression alternatives.

Exercises

(1) Consider a scale mixture of Gamma random variables, $Y_1, \ldots, Y_n$, with densities

$$\varphi(y_i|\theta_i) = \frac{1}{\Gamma(r)(\theta_i/r)^r} y_i^{r-1} \exp(-y_i r/\theta_i),$$

where r and θ_i/r are shape and scale parameters, respectively and we assume $\theta_i \sim G$. Show that Bayes's rule under quadratic loss for estimating the θ_i's is given by

$$\delta(y) = r y^{r-1} \int_y^{\infty} x^{1-r} f(x) dx / f(y),$$

where f denotes the marginal (mixture) density of the Y_i's.

(2) Generate a sample from the foregoing model with $n = 400$, $Y_i = (m-1)^{-1} \sum_{j=1}^{m} (X_{ij} - \bar{X}_i)^2$, $X_{ij} \sim \mathcal{N}(0, \theta_i)$, $m = 11$ and θ_i drawn iidly from the discrete distribution $G = \frac{2}{3}\delta_{1.5} + \frac{1}{3}\delta_3$. Compare the NPMLE estimates of G, f and $\delta(y)$ with those in figure 3 of Gu and Koenker (2017b).

(3) Reproduce Figure 6.3.

CHAPTER 7

Ranking and Selection as Compound Decisions

This chapter addresses some practical problems arising from empirical Bayes decision making. In contrast to much of our earlier discussion that focused on decision rules for posterior means, in this chapter we will consider discrete decision problems, where the decision maker must choose among a finite set of actions. We will begin with an illustrative application to binary selection and then turn to a more general formulation of the ranking and selection problem. Adapting formal decision theory to realistic applied settings is inevitably very challenging. Conventional loss functions have been carefully chosen to make this seem easy, but with greater realism concerning loss functions come greater difficulties. Nevertheless, we believe that the framework developed in Robbins's prescient compound decision theory offers a valuable starting point for a wide variety of practical decision problems.

7.1 BINARY SELECTION

It is common in applications to have heterogeneous latent effects, $\theta_i \in \mathbb{R}$, from among which we would like to select a subset of the most consequential. Such problems are obviously closely related to multiple testing problems and classification. Early consideration of such problems from an empirical Bayes perspective may be found in Johns and Van Ryzin (1971, 1972).

Suppose that we observe a random sample $Y_1, \ldots, Y_n$, each has density $\varphi(\cdot|\theta_i)$, and the parameters θ_i are assumed to be drawn iidly from G. Our objective is to select a subset of observations whose θ_i exceeds a threshold, say c, that is to choose a decision rule, $\delta(y) \in \{0, 1\}$ subject to loss

$$L(\delta(y_i), \theta_i) = \{a_1 + b_1(\theta_i - c)\}(1 - \delta(y_i))\mathbb{1}\{\theta_i > c\} \\ + \{a_2 + b_2(c - \theta_i)\}\delta(y_i)\mathbb{1}\{\theta_i \leq c\}.$$

When $b_1 = b_2 = 0$ this represents standard classification loss with potentially asymmetric costs of false positives and false negatives. In this case we can normalize $a_1 = 1$, and the optimal rule is given by

$$\delta(y_i) = \mathbb{1}\left\{v(y_i) \geq \frac{a_2}{1+a_2}\right\},$$

where $v(y_i) = \mathbb{P}(\theta_i \geq c|Y_i = y_i)$. Nonzero values of b_1 and b_2 penalize decisions that are far from the threshold, c. For instance, with $b_1 = b_2 = 1$ and $a_1 = a_2 = 0$, the optimal Bayes rule is given by

$$\delta(y_i) = \mathbb{1}\{E[\theta_i|y_i] \geq c\}.$$

This rule first appears in Johns (1957); see Exercises 1 and 2.

7.1.1 Connection to Multiple Testing

The binary selection problem with $b_1 = b_2 = 0$ resembles the typical setting of multiple testing problems with many independent individual hypotheses. Let $H_i = \mathbb{1}\{\theta_i \notin A\}$ where the set A characterizes the null hypothesis. For instance, in the example above we have $A = (-\infty, c]$, and it corresponds to the usual one-sided test with cutoff value c for each hypothesis. The binary decision $\delta(y_i)$ takes the value one if we reject the ith hypothesis. Suppose $\theta_i \sim G$, then $1 - \omega = \mathbb{P}(H_i = 0) = \int_A dG(\theta)$ characterizes the null proportion. Given this setting, we can view (Y_i, H_i) as iid random variables, and furthermore,

$$Y_i|H_i \sim (1 - H_i)F_0 + H_i F_1,$$

where F_0 and F_1 have densities

$$f_0(y) = (1-\omega)^{-1}\int_A \varphi(y|\theta)dG(\theta)$$

and

$$f_1(y) = \omega^{-1}\int_{A^c} \varphi(y|\theta)dG(\theta).$$

The marginal density for Y_i can then be written as $f(y) = (1-\omega)f_0(y) + \omega f_1(y)$, and we can write

$$\begin{aligned} t(y_i) &\equiv 1 - v(y_i) = \mathbb{P}(\theta_i \leq c|Y_i = y_i) \\ &= \frac{\int_A \varphi(y|\theta)dG(\theta)}{\int \varphi(y|\theta)dG(\theta)} = \frac{(1-\omega)f_0(y_i)}{f(y_i)}. \end{aligned} \tag{7.1}$$

The quantity $t(y)$ can be recognized as the local false discovery rate of Efron et al. (2001) and Storey (2002). It is interpreted as the posterior probability of θ_i belonging to the null set given y_i. The link to binary classification suggests that we are ranking individual hypotheses according to the local false discovery rate and rejecting those that fall below our threshold. The cut-off value a_2 in the classification loss can be linked to the marginal false discovery rate, as a multiple testing analogue of Type I error in classical hypothesis testing.

Table 7.1. *Errors in multiple hypothesis testing.*

	Accept ($\delta_i = 0$)	Reject ($\delta_i = 1$)	Total
Null case ($H_i = 0$)	U	V	n_0
Non-null case ($H_i = 1$)	T	S	$n - n_0$
	$n - R$	R	n

In multiple testing problems there are several error control criteria regarding false rejections as shown in Table 7.1. The most strict criterion is the family-wise error rate (FWER), which aims to control $\mathbb{P}(V \geq 1)$. The classical procedure that controls for FWER applies the Bonferroni bound on individual p-values. The step-wise procedure of Holm (1979) improves power in comparison to the Bonferroni correction but can still be quite conservative, and further improvements have been proposed by Romano and Wolf (2005). An alternative criterion, false discovery rate (FDR) control, introduced by Benjamini and Hochberg (1995), relies upon

$$FDR = \mathbb{E}\left[\frac{V}{R}|R > 0\right]\mathbb{P}(R > 0)$$

for controlling the FDR by selecting a proportion of p-values below a preselected value, say α.

In the Bayesian framework it is more convenient to consider two slightly modified quantities: the positive false discovery rate,

$$pFDR = \mathbb{E}\left[\frac{V}{R}|R > 0\right],$$

defined in Storey (2003), and the marginal false discovery rate,

$$mFDR = \mathbb{E}[V]/\mathbb{E}[R].$$

As Storey (2003) showed, in the iid setting, for the same rejection region implied by the rule δ and given thresholding value, we have

$$pFDR = mFDR = \mathbb{P}(H_i = 0|\delta_i = 1).$$

Furthermore, as $n \to \infty$, $FDR = pFDR + O(n^{-1/2})$ as shown by Genovese and Wasserman (2002) and Storey (2002). This immediately provides a link between the choice of a_2 in our classification loss function and the false discovery rate. Setting $\lambda = 1/(1 + a_2)$,

$$\delta(y_i) = \mathbb{1}\left\{v(y_i) \geq \frac{a_2}{1 + a_2}\right\} = \mathbb{1}\{t(y_i) \leq \lambda\},$$

and for any given λ:

$$\begin{aligned} mFDR(\lambda) &= \mathbb{P}(H_i = 0|\delta_i = 1) = \mathbb{P}(\theta_i \in A|t(Y_i) \leq \lambda) \\ &= \frac{\int \mathbb{1}\{t(y) \leq \lambda\}t(y)f(y)dy}{\int \mathbb{1}\{t(y) \leq \lambda\}f(y)dy}. \end{aligned}$$

See Exercise 3.

It is easy to show that when φ is the normal density, the mFDR is a monotone function of λ; hence there is a unique a_2 that corresponds to any specified α as control of the false discovery rate of the procedure that thresholds $t(y)$. Given the loss function, the local false discovery rate $t(y_i)$ yields the best ranking of individual hypotheses. Once we construct a reasonable estimator $\hat{t}(y_i)$, the mFDR can be estimated by the plug-in estimator:

$$\widehat{mFDR}(\lambda) = \frac{\sum_i \mathbb{1}\{\hat{t}(y_i) \leq \lambda\}\hat{t}(y_i)}{\sum_i \mathbb{1}\{\hat{t}(y_i) \leq \lambda\}}.$$

Estimating the local false discovery rate $t(y_i) = 1 - v(y_i)$ as in (7.1) requires three components: ω and the two densities, $f_0(y)$ and $f_1(y)$. In the special case that the set A is a degenerate point, for example, $H_{0i}: \theta_i = 0$ and $H_{ai}: \theta_i \neq 0$, we have $A = \{0\}$, so f_0 is nothing but $(1-\omega)^{-1}\varphi(y|0)$, and $f(y)$ is the marginal density of the observed Y_i's, which can be identified directly from the data, leaving us only with the task of estimating ω. When the set A is not a singleton, we also need to estimate the component density f_0. Several kernel-based methods have been proposed in conjunction with estimation of ω, see, for example, Sun and Cai (2007) and Sun and McLain (2012). The latter paper also considers settings with heterogeneous variances, which we will discuss later in the context of an application.

An alternative G-modeling approach notes that $t(y)$ can be viewed as a functional of G; hence from an estimator of G, we can construct an estimator $\hat{t}(y)$. If G happens to have a mass point at our hypothetical threshold, however, we are faced with a more subtle identification issue, as we discuss next.

7.1.2 Estimating the Null Proportion

To explore estimation of this proportion, consider the two-component mixture model with a mass point at some fixed value, say zero, as is usually the case, and with the remaining mass distributed according to some non-null distribution, G_1,

$$G(\theta) = (1-\omega)\delta_0(\theta) + \omega G_1(\theta).$$

Parametric models of this type are often used in empirical Bayes applications with G_1 taken to be Laplace or Cauchy centered at zero with a free scale parameter as we have discussed in Chapter 3. The null proportion, $(1-\omega)$, and the scale parameter can be jointly estimated by maximum likelihood or some other method. This approach offers some flexibility but has some obvious limitations, for instance it presumes that the non-null effects are symmetrically distributed about zero.

Nonparametric estimation of G_1 poses an identification problem since one can always write

$$G(\theta) = (1-\omega-\gamma)\delta_0 + (\omega+\gamma)\left(\frac{\omega}{\omega+\gamma}G_1(\theta) + \frac{\gamma}{\omega+\gamma}\delta_0\right)$$

with $0 \leq \gamma \leq 1 - \omega$. Unless we can assume that $G_1(\theta)$ does not have a discontinuity point at zero, ω and G_1 are not point identified. In practice even if G_1 does not have a mass point at zero, mass can be placed arbitrarily near zero, rendering the estimation of ω challenging. A precise definition of sparsity in settings like this may be found in McCullagh and Polson (2018).

Under further conditions, a consistent estimator for ω based on empirical characteristic function methods has been proposed by Jin (2008). In the context of the Gaussian sequence model, Gu and Shen (2018) use the Jin estimator in conjunction with the NPMLE for G_1 to construct a consistent estimator for a general two-component model. Various forms of profiling can also be considered for this model. For any fixed ω we can define $F_\omega(y)$ as the distribution function with density $f_\omega(y) = \int \phi(y - \theta)dG_\omega(\theta)$ and $G_\omega = (1 - \omega)\delta_0 + \omega G_1(\theta)$. Then the Kolmogorov discrepancy between F_ω and the empirical distribution function of the observed, Y_i's,

$$D_n(\omega) = \sup_y |F_\omega(y) - \hat{F}_n(y)|,$$

can be used to estimate ω as

$$\hat{\omega}_n = \inf_{\omega \in (0,1)} \{D_n(\omega) \leq c_n/\sqrt{n}\}.$$

Provided that $c_n/\sqrt{n} \to 0$ and $c_n \to \infty$, a consistent estimate of ω can be made. This approach may be viewed as a form of F-localization discussed in more detail in Chapter 11. It can also be used to construct a finite sample lower confidence bound with coverage $1 - \alpha$,

$$\mathbb{P}(\omega \geq \underline{\hat{\omega}}_n) \geq 1 - \alpha,$$

using results of Massart (1990),

$$\underline{\hat{\omega}}_n = \inf_{\omega \in (0,1)} \left\{D_n(\omega) \leq \sqrt{\log(2/\alpha)/2n}\right\}.$$

Alternative distances can also be used, for instance the L_2 construction in Patra and Sen (2016) on a related problem or Kullback–Leibler as in Xue and Wang (2023).

Decision problems with binary actions of this type have many applications in economics and other fields. It should be noted that there is nothing special about the null value of zero. Any *known* value may be substituted; however compound decision problems with an endogenous choice of the null threshold introduce some new difficulties that we address in the next section. Before doing so, however, we will describe an application of the simpler two-component model with a zero null value taken from Gu and Shen (2018). The objective is to evaluate school performance based on a regression discontinuity design. The data is taken from Pop-Eleches and Urquiola (2013) who study the effect of attending a more selective high school as determined by having crossed a performance threshold on a national exam in Romania.

7.1.3 Romanian High School Performance Evaluation

Treatment effects are estimated based on a regression discontinuity design as in Gu and Shen (2018). Let θ_i represent the treatment effect of attending a more selective high school i. In Pop-Eleches and Urquiola (2013) a mean treatment effect is estimated by pooling all schools together. In contrast, we focus on treatment effect heterogeneity. Each school has its own entrance cut-off values, which generates a regression discontinuity design for individual school treatment effects. As in Gu and Shen (2018), we consider two outcomes at the school level: the proportion of students taking the baccalaureate exam, and the average baccalaureate exam grade. A satisfactory grade on the baccalaureate exam at the conclusion of high school is a prerequisite for admission to university. We will denote by Y_i an estimator for the school effect θ_i. Since school sizes differ, each Y_i has an associated standard error denoted as σ_i, which puts us in a heterogeneous variance setting discussed in Chapter 6 with

$$Y_i|\theta_i, \sigma_i \sim \mathcal{N}(\theta_i, \sigma_i^2).$$

Naturally, we would like to select schools that have positive θ_i; hence we have $A = (-\infty, 0]$ as the null set. One way to proceed is to assume independence between θ_i and σ_i and construct the local false discovery rate as

$$t(y_i, \sigma_i) = \mathbb{P}(\theta_i \leq 0 | y_i, \sigma_i) = \frac{\int_A \varphi(y|\theta, \sigma_i) dG(\theta)}{\int \varphi(y|\theta, \sigma_i) dG(\theta)},$$

and then apply a thresholding rule that controls the false discovery rate at a targeted level. However, if the independence assumption is misspecified, simulations in Gu and Shen (2018) show that the false discovery rate can be inflated.

When the independence between θ_i and σ_i is implausible, we can exploit the fact that the cut-off value for the null set A is zero, and hence a scale transformation of y_i scales the effect θ_i but does not change its sign. We assume

$$S_i = Y_i / \sigma_i \sim \mathcal{N}(\mu_i, 1)$$

with $\mu_i = \theta_i / \sigma_i$. After this standardization, we can apply the binary classification compound decision framework.

Figure 7.1 shows evidence of effect heterogeneity for both the likelihood of taking the baccalaureate exam and the exam score among 503 schools. Assuming there is a mass point at zero, Gu and Shen (2018) propose a hybrid estimator for the distribution G of the latent scaled effects μ. Using the hybrid estimates for G to construct the local false discovery rate, Table 7.2 compares the selected set among various procedures that aim to control FDR at the 1%, 5% and 10% level. The first row is the multiple testing procedure applied on the scaled effects where we use the hybrid NPMLE approach to estimate local false discovery rate. The selection outcome suggests that there is stronger evidence that a more selective high school improves the average exam score but has less of an effect on the probability of taking the exam. In comparison, the Benjamini

Table 7.2. *Comparison of the size of the selected set for several procedures designed to control false discovery.*

	Take baccalaureate exam			Baccalaureate exam score		
	FDR 1%	FDR 5%	FDR 10%	FDR 1%	FDR 5%	FDR 10%
Hybrid NPMLE	9	19	29	53	87	115
Sun and McLain	23	49	78	109	239	340
Benjamini–Hochberg	11	17	22	45	70	88
ALL	502	502	502	502	502	502

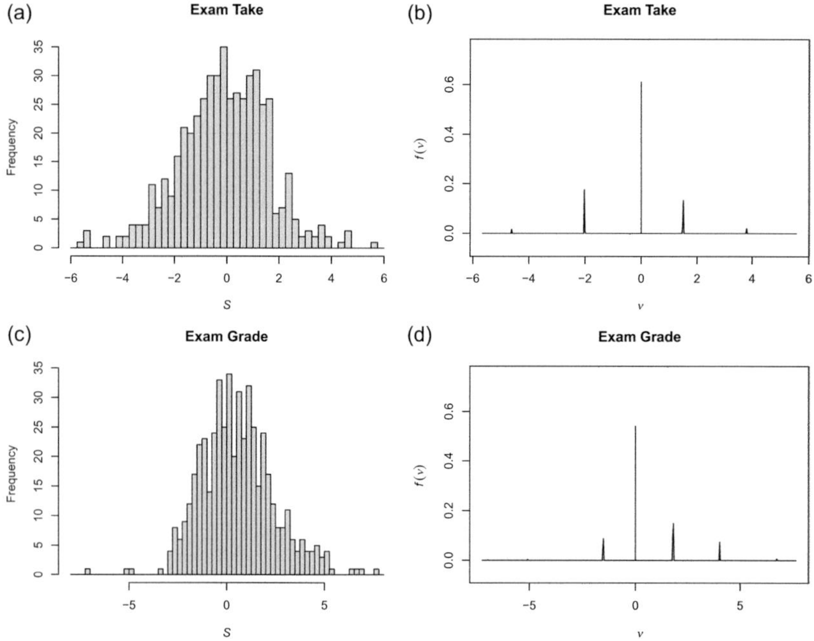

Figure 7.1. The histograms (panels (a) and (c)) are the scaled effects estimates S_i and panels (b) and (d) are the hybrid NPMLE of the distribution G. The non-null proportion in $\hat{G}$ is estimated using the procedure of Jin (2008). The estimated mass $\hat{\omega}$ at zero is indicated by the vertical gray line. Data are from Pop-Eleches and Urquiola (2013).

and Hochberg (1995) procedure tends to select fewer schools. Recall that the Benjamini–Hochberg procedure controls FDR at level $(n_0/n)\alpha$ and hence can be more conservative. The ratio n_0/n corresponds to the null proportion, which is estimated to be around 0.6 for the first outcome and 0.54 for the second outcome in this application. In comparison, the procedure of Sun and McLain (2012) assumes independence between θ_i and σ_i, which may be violated in this application. It tends to select many more schools than the other procedures.

7.2 RANKING AND SELECTION DECISIONS

In binary action models like selecting Romanian schools, the focus was on selecting a subset of schools that had a positive impact on the proportion of students taking the baccalaureate exam or on the exam scores of those who did take the exam. A related question immediately arises: How would we go about ranking schools according to their latent effects or select the top performers? These questions appear in many disparate settings: school or teacher evaluations and many other "league table" constructions. In this section we take a somewhat broader perspective.

Suppose you are given real-valued measurements, $y_i : i = 1, 2, \ldots, n$, of some attribute like test score performance for students or their teachers, survival rates for hospital surgical procedures, etc., and are told that the measurements are exchangeable and approximately Gaussian with unknown means θ_i and known variances σ^2. Your task, should you decide to accept it, is to choose a group of size not to exceed αn of the elements with the largest θ_i's. One's first inclination might be to view each y_i as the maximum likelihood estimate for the corresponding θ_i, and select the αn largest observed values, but the compound decision framework suggests that it might be better to treat the problems as an ensemble, borrowing strength from the entire sample to improve each coordinate. A second natural inclination might be to compute posterior means of the θ's with some linear or nonlinear shrinkage rule, rank them and select the αn best, but we will see that this too may be questionable. See Gu and Koenker (2023) and the associated comments for further discussion of the methods described in this section.

7.2.1 Posterior Tail Probability

A natural alternative to ranking by posterior means is to rank by posterior tail probabilities. We have already seen in Section 7.1 that with classification error loss, the optimal Bayes rule ranks individuals by the posterior probability of the null hypothesis. What distinguishes our current setting is that the ranking and selection task requires us to pick a cut-off value that is data driven. Let $\theta_\alpha = G^{-1}(1 - \alpha)$, and define $v_\alpha(y) := \mathbb{P}(\theta \geq \theta_\alpha | Y = y)$; then ranking by posterior tail probability gives the decision rule

$$\delta(y) = \mathbb{1}\{v_\alpha(y) \geq \lambda_\alpha\},$$

where the threshold λ_α is chosen so that $\mathbb{P}(v_\alpha(Y) \geq \lambda_\alpha) = \alpha$ to reflect the fact that our task is to select the upper α proportion of the effects θ_i. This ranking criterion has been proposed by Henderson and Newton (2016), motivated as a ranking device for a fixed quantile level α. It can be interpreted in multiple testing terms as we have seen in the previous section: $1 - v_\alpha(y)$ is the local false discovery rate, for testing the hypothesis $H_0 : \theta < \theta_\alpha$ vs. $H_A : \theta \geq \theta_\alpha$. To see this, we focus on the Gaussian sequence model setting for our discussion below. Let h_i be a binary random variable $h_i = \mathbb{1}\{\theta_i \geq \theta_\alpha\}$. The loss function for observation i is

$$L(\delta_i, \theta_i) = \lambda \mathbb{1}\{h_i = 0, \delta_i = 1\} + \mathbb{1}\{h_i = 1, \delta_i = 0\},$$

for a generic Lagrange multiplier, λ. The compound risk, which due to the fundamental theorem of compound decisions coincides with the Bayes risk, takes the form

$$\alpha + \int \delta(y)[(1-\alpha)\lambda f_0(y) - \alpha f_1(y)]dy,$$

where $f_0(y) = (1-\alpha)^{-1} \int_{-\infty}^{\theta_\alpha} \varphi(y|\theta, \sigma^2) dG(\theta)$, and $f_1(y) = \alpha^{-1} \int_{\theta_\alpha}^{+\infty} \varphi(y|\theta, \sigma^2) dG(\theta)$, with $\varphi(y|\theta, \sigma^2) = \phi((y-\theta)/\sigma)/\sigma$. The Bayes rule for a fixed λ is

$$\delta_\alpha(y_i) = \mathbb{1}\left\{v_\alpha(y_i) \geq \frac{\lambda}{1+\lambda}\right\},$$

where $v_\alpha(y) = \alpha f_1(y)/f(y) = \mathbb{P}(\theta \geq \theta_\alpha | Y = y)$, with $f(y) = (1-\alpha) f_0(y) + \alpha f_1(y)$. Provided that $v_\alpha(y)$ is monotone in y, a unique λ^* can be found such that $\mathbb{P}(\delta_\alpha(Y) = 1) = \mathbb{P}(v_\alpha(Y) \geq \lambda^*/(1+\lambda^*)) = \alpha$. The following lemma provides a sufficient condition for nestedness of the selected sets. Proofs of all the results in this section appear in Gu and Koenker (2023).

Lemma 7.1. *For fixed α, assuming $\mathbb{E}_{\theta|Y}[\nabla_y \log \varphi(y|\theta, \sigma^2)|Y] < \infty$, $v_\alpha(y)$ is monotone in y and the sets $\Omega_\alpha := \{Y : v_\alpha(Y) \geq \lambda_\alpha/(1+\lambda_\alpha)\}$ have a nested structure, that is if $\alpha_1 > \alpha_2$, then $\Omega_{\alpha_2} \subseteq \Omega_{\alpha_1}$.*

Any implementation of such a Bayes rule requires an estimate of the mixing distribution, G, that would enable us to compute the local false discovery rates $v_\alpha(y)$ and the cut-off θ_α. The NPMLE, or perhaps a smoothed version of it, will provide a natural $\hat{G}$ for this task.

7.2.2 False Discovery and the α-Level

Although our loss functions yield distinct criteria for ranking, their decision rules lead to the same selections when the precision of the measurements is homogeneous as the next lemma establishes.

Lemma 7.2. *For fixed α and homogeneous variance, posterior mean, posterior tail probability and posterior tail expectation all yield the same ranking and therefore the same selection.*

To evaluate the performance of such selection rules it is natural to consider both types of potential errors: the false discovery rate as discussed in the previous section as well as the false nondiscovery rate. The marginal false discovery rate for the selection rule, $\delta_\alpha(y) = \mathbb{1}(y \geq \eta_\alpha)$, in our Gaussian mixture setting is

$$mFDR = \mathbb{P}(\theta < \theta_\alpha | \delta_\alpha(Y) = 1) = \alpha^{-1} \int_{-\infty}^{\theta_\alpha} \Phi((\theta - \eta_\alpha)/\sigma) dG(\theta).$$

The marginal false nondiscovery rate is

$$mFNR = \mathbb{P}(\theta \geq \theta_\alpha | \delta_\alpha(Y) = 0) = (1-\alpha)^{-1} \int_{\theta_\alpha}^{\infty} \Phi((\eta_\alpha - \theta)/\sigma) dG(\theta).$$

Figure 7.2 shows the false discovery rate and false nondiscovery rate for a range of capacity constraints, α, when the mixing distribution, G, is standard Gaussian and $\sigma^2 = 1$. In this low signal-to-noise ratio case, the cut-off value η_α is the $(1 - \alpha)$ quantile of $\mathcal{N}(0, 2)$, and it is very difficult to distinguish the meritorious from the merely lucky. For selecting individuals at the top α quantile, the false discovery rate is alarmingly high, especially for smaller α, implying that the selected set may consist of a very high proportion of false discoveries. When $\alpha = 0.10$ the proportion of selected observations with θ below the threshold θ_α is slightly greater than 50%.

When the variance of the θ's, the signal-to-noise ratio, increases from 1 to 5, the selection problem becomes somewhat easier. This is reflected not only by the false discovery rate decreasing from above one-half to about a third, but is also reflected in results in Table 7.3 that show that the wrongly selected individuals have their true values of θ clustered closer to the thresholding value θ_α measured in terms of standard deviation.

When $\sigma^2 = 1$, we have about 50% falsely selected, and the θ's among the correctly selected and the wrongly selected individuals are roughly symmetrically distributed around the thresholding value. In such a case, even oracle decision rules that incorporate complete knowledge of the precise distributional features of the problem may not be able to achieve better than about even odds that selected individuals have latent ability above the selection thresholds when measurement error is comparable in magnitude to Gaussian variability in latent ability.

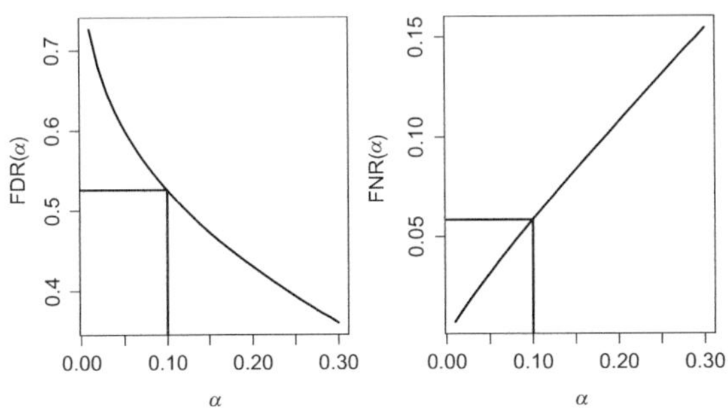

Figure 7.2. False discovery rates and false nondiscovery rates for a standard Gaussian mixing distribution.

Table 7.3. *FDR improves as the signal becomes more dispersed. In settings with standard Gaussian measurement error and Gaussian distribution, G, for the θ's, the variance of G can be interpreted as a signal-to-noise ratio. As the variance of G increases selection becomes easier and FDR is reduced. The wrongly selected units become more concentrated near the selection threshold. Columns 2–6 of the table report quantiles of the wrongly selected units measured in standard deviations from the threshold. Columns 7–11 report corresponding quantiles for the correctly selected units.*

	FDR	**Wrongly selected**					**Correctly selected**				
		20%	40%	50%	60%	80%	20%	40%	50%	60%	80%
$\sigma_\theta^2 = 1$	0.526	0.205	0.414	0.531	0.658	0.990	0.188	0.391	0.504	0.632	0.966
$\sigma_\theta^2 = 2$	0.421	0.146	0.302	0.391	0.486	0.743	0.197	0.394	0.503	0.625	0.951
$\sigma_\theta^2 = 3$	0.361	0.120	0.248	0.320	0.402	0.620	0.197	0.393	0.500	0.618	0.931
$\sigma_\theta^2 = 4$	0.319	0.103	0.212	0.275	0.347	0.540	0.198	0.392	0.495	0.609	0.915
$\sigma_\theta^2 = 5$	0.296	0.093	0.192	0.247	0.313	0.487	0.196	0.383	0.484	0.596	0.897

It is perhaps worth stressing that at the margin, near the decision boundary, it will always be difficult to distinguish true from false discoveries, but FDR measures the proportion of all selections that are incorrect, not just those near the threshold. Other loss functions that penalize in a more continuous way may be considered to reflect the information in Table 7.3. For example, losses that weight the classification error by the magnitude of the discrepancy between the latent effect and the threshold could be considered. Such losses, however, make it more difficult to incorporate conventional forms of error control.

Thus far we have implicitly assumed that the size of the selected set is predetermined by the parameter α. Having established a ranking based on a particular loss function, we simply select a subset of size $\lceil \alpha n \rceil$ consisting of the highest ranked observations. In the next subsection we begin to consider modifying this strategy by constraining the probability of false discoveries. This will allow the size of the selected set to adapt to the difficulty of the selection task.

7.2.3 Guarding against False Discovery

Recognizing the risk of false discoveries among those selected, we can consider an expanded loss function,

$$L(\boldsymbol{\delta}, \boldsymbol{\theta}) = \sum_{i=1}^{n} h_i(1-\delta_i) + \tau_1 \left(\sum_{i=1}^{n} \left\{ (1-h_i)\delta_i - \gamma\delta_i \right\} \right) + \tau_2 \left(\sum_{i=1}^{n} \delta_i - \alpha n \right), \tag{7.2}$$

where $h_i = \mathbb{1}\{\theta_i \geq \theta_\alpha\}$. If we set τ_1 to zero, then minimizing the expected loss leads to the Bayes rule discussed in Section 7.2.1. Conversely, if we set τ_2 to zero, then minimizing expected loss leads to a decision rule that is equivalent to a multiple testing problem with null hypothesis $H_{0i}: \theta_i < \theta_\alpha$; the goal is to minimize the expected number of overlooked discoveries subject to the constraint that the marginal FDR rate is controlled at level γ, that is, $\mathbb{E}[\sum_{i=1}^{n}(1-h_i)\delta_i]/\mathbb{E}[\sum_{i=1}^{n}\delta_i] \leq \gamma$. When $\tau_1 = 0$, the aggregated risk can be expressed as

$$\mathbb{E}_{\boldsymbol{Y}}\left[\mathbb{E}_{\boldsymbol{\theta}|\boldsymbol{Y}}\left[L(\boldsymbol{\delta}, \boldsymbol{\theta})\right]\right] = \mathbb{E}\left[\sum_{i=1}^{n}(1-\delta_i)v_\alpha(Y_i) + \tau_2\left(\sum_{i=1}^{n}\delta_i - \alpha n\right)\right],$$

where $v_\alpha(y_i) = \mathbb{P}(\theta_i \geq \theta_\alpha | Y_i = y_i)$. Minimizing over both $\boldsymbol{\delta}$ and τ_2 leads to the decision rule

$$\delta_i^* = \begin{cases} 1, & \text{if } v_\alpha(y_i) \geq \tau_2^*; \\ 0, & \text{if } v_\alpha(y_i) < \tau_2^*. \end{cases}$$

The Lagrange multiplier is chosen so that the constraint $\mathbb{P}(\delta_i = 1) \leq \alpha$ holds with equality:

$$\tau_2^* = \min\{\tau_2 \colon \mathbb{P}(v_\alpha(y_i) \geq \tau_2) \leq \alpha\}.$$

Each selection improves the objective function by $v_\alpha(y_i)$ but incurs a cost of τ_2. Since all selections incur the same cost, we may rank according to $v_\alpha(y_i)$, selecting units until the capacity constraint αn is achieved. Selection of the last unit may need to be randomized to exactly satisfy the constraint, as we note below.

When $\tau_2 = 0$ the focus shifts to the marginal FDR – the ratio of the expected number of false discoveries – to the expected number of selections. Our objective becomes

$$\mathbb{E}_{\boldsymbol{Y}}\Big[\mathbb{E}_{\boldsymbol{\theta}|\boldsymbol{Y}}\Big[L(\boldsymbol{\delta},\boldsymbol{\theta})\Big]\Big]$$
$$= \mathbb{E}\left[\sum_{i=1}^{n}(1-\delta_i)v_\alpha(Y_i) + \tau_1\left(\sum_{i=1}^{n}\{\delta_i(1-v_\alpha(Y_i)) - \gamma\delta_i\}\right)\right].$$

Again minimizing over both $\boldsymbol{\delta}$ and τ_1 yields

$$\delta_i^* = \begin{cases} 1, & \text{if } v_\alpha(y_i) > \tau_1^*(1 - v_\alpha(y_i) - \gamma); \\ 0, & \text{if } v_\alpha(y_i) \le \tau_1^*(1 - v_\alpha(y_i) - \gamma), \end{cases}$$

and the Lagrange multiplier takes a value τ_1^* to make the marginal FDR constraint hold with equality.

When both constraints are incorporated we must balance the power gain from more selections and the cost that occurs from both the capacity constraint and FDR control. The Bayes rule solves

$$\min_{\delta} \mathbb{E}\left[\sum_{i=1}^{n}(1-\delta_i)v_\alpha(y_i)\right] + \tau_1\left(\mathbb{E}\left[\sum_{i=1}^{n}\{(1-v_\alpha(y_i))\delta_i - \gamma\delta_i\}\right]\right)$$
$$+ \tau_2\left(\mathbb{E}\left[\sum_{i=1}^{n}\delta_i\right] - \alpha n\right).$$

Given the discrete nature of the decision function, this problem appears to take the form of a classical knapsack problem; however following the approach of Basu et al. (2018) we will consider a relaxed version of the problem in which units are selected sequentially until one or the other constraint would be violated, with the final selection randomized to satisfy the constraint exactly.

Given the Lagrangian form of our loss function, it is natural to consider an optimization perspective for the selection problem. Minimizing the expectation of the loss defined in (7.2) is equivalent to minimizing $\mathbb{P}[\delta_i = 0, \theta_i \ge \theta_\alpha]$ subject to the constraint that $\mathbb{P}[\delta_i = 1, \theta_i < \theta_\alpha]/\mathbb{P}[\delta_i = 1] \le \gamma$ and $\mathbb{P}[\delta_i = 1] \le \alpha$. So we are looking for a thresholding rule that minimizes the expected number of missed discoveries subject to the capacity constraint and the constraint that the marginal FDR rate of the decision rule is below level γ. This minimization problem is also easily seen, from a testing perspective, to be equivalent to maximizing the power of the decision rule δ, $\mathbb{P}[\delta_i = 1|\theta_i \ge \theta_\alpha]$, subject to the same two constraints.

Proposition 7.3 For any pair, (α, γ) such that $\gamma < 1 - \alpha$, the optimal Bayes rule takes the form $\delta_i^* = \mathbb{1}\{v_\alpha(y_i) \geq \lambda^*(\alpha, \gamma)\}$, where $\lambda^*(\alpha, \gamma) = v_\alpha(t^*)$ with $t^* = \max\{t_1^*, t_2^*\}$:

$$t_1^* = \min\left\{t : \frac{\int_{-\infty}^{\theta_\alpha} \tilde{\Phi}((t-\theta)/\sigma)dG(\theta)}{\int_{-\infty}^{+\infty} \tilde{\Phi}((t-\theta)/\sigma)dG(\theta)} - \gamma \leq 0\right\},$$

$$t_2^* = \min\left\{t : \int_{-\infty}^{+\infty} \tilde{\Phi}((t-\theta)/\sigma)dG(\theta) - \alpha \leq 0\right\},$$

and $\tilde{\Phi}$ denoting the survival function of a standard normal random variable.

The optimal cutoff t^* depends on the data generating process and also on the choice of α and γ. When the data is noisy, the FDR control constraint may be binding before the capacity constraint is reached, and consequently the selected set may be strictly smaller than the prespecified α proportion. Conversely, when the signal is strong, the FDR control constraint is unlikely to bind before the capacity constraint is reached.

We have seen that when variances are homogeneous, the optimal selection rule thresholds on Y, so it is clear then that any ranking that is based on a monotone transformation of Y will lead to an equivalent selected set. We should also stress that we have focused on a null hypothesis that depends on α, while the multiple testing literature, for example Efron et al. (2001), Sun and Cai (2007) and Basu et al. (2018), typically focuses on the null hypothesis of $H_{0i} : \theta_i = 0$. When variances are homogeneous, it doesn't matter whether we use an α-dependent null or the conventional zero null, because the transformation based on the conventional null, $\mathbb{P}(\theta > 0 | Y = y)$, is also a monotone function of Y and therefore yields an equivalent decision rule. However, when variances are heterogeneous, this invariance no longer holds: Different transformations of the pair (y, σ) lead to distinct decision rules that lead to distinct performance, and using the conventional null hypothesis is no longer advisable for the ranking and selection problem as we will show in the next section.

7.2.4 Heterogeneous Known Variances

The homogeneous variance assumption of the preceding section is unsustainable in most applications. Batting averages are accompanied by a number of "at bats," and mean test score performances for schools or teachers are accompanied by student sample sizes. In this section we will consider the expanded model,

$$Y_i \sim \mathcal{N}(\theta_i, \sigma_i^2), \quad \text{and} \quad \theta_i \sim G, \quad \sigma_i \sim H, \quad \sigma_i \perp\!\!\!\perp \theta_i.$$

We will assume provisionally that we observe the σ_i, an assumption that will be relaxed in the next section. With the same alternative hypothesis for each individual as $H_{ai} : \theta_i \geq \theta_\alpha$, it is natural to consider the posterior tail probability again, now as a function of the pair, (y_i, σ_i):

$$v_\alpha(y_i,\sigma_i) = \mathbb{P}(\theta_i \geq \theta_\alpha | y_i,\sigma_i) = \frac{\int_{\theta_\alpha}^{+\infty} \varphi(y_i|\theta,\sigma_i^2)dG(\theta)}{\int_{-\infty}^{+\infty} \varphi(y_i|\theta,\sigma_i^2)dG(\theta)}. \tag{7.3}$$

Solving the same decision problem with the loss function specified in (7.2), we have conditional risk

$$\mathbb{E}_{\boldsymbol{\theta}|\boldsymbol{Y},\boldsymbol{\sigma}}\Big[L(\boldsymbol{\delta},\boldsymbol{\theta})\Big] = \sum_{i=1}^{n}(1-\delta_i)v_\alpha(Y_i,\sigma_i) + \tau_1\left(\sum_{i=1}^{n}\{\delta_i(1-v_\alpha(Y_i,\sigma_i)) - \gamma\delta_i\}\right) + \tau_2\left(\sum_{i=1}^{n}\delta_i - \alpha n\right).$$

Taking another expectation with respect to the joint distribution of the (Y_i,σ_i)'s, the Bayes rule solves

$$\min_{\boldsymbol{\delta}} \mathbb{E}\left[\sum_{i=1}^{n}(1-\delta_i)v_\alpha(y_i,\sigma_i)\right] + \tau_1\left(\mathbb{E}\left[\sum_{i=1}^{n}\{(1-v_\alpha(y_i,\sigma_i))\delta_i - \gamma\delta_i\}\right]\right) + \tau_2\left(\mathbb{E}\left[\sum_{i=1}^{n}\delta_i\right] - \alpha n\right).$$

The optimal selection rule can again be characterized as a thresholding rule, now on $v_\alpha(y_i,\sigma_i)$.

Proposition 7.4 For a prespecified pair (α,γ) such that $\gamma < 1-\alpha$, the Bayes rule takes the form $\delta^*(y,\sigma) = \mathbb{1}\{v_\alpha(y,\sigma) \geq \lambda^*(\alpha,\gamma)\}$, where $\lambda^*(\alpha,\gamma) = \max\{\lambda_1^*(\alpha,\gamma),\lambda_2^*(\alpha)\}$,

$$\lambda_1^*(\alpha,\gamma) = \min\left\{\lambda : \frac{\int\int_{-\infty}^{\theta_\alpha}\tilde{\Phi}((t_\alpha(\lambda,\sigma)-\theta)/\sigma)dG(\theta)dH(\sigma)}{\int\int_{-\infty}^{+\infty}\tilde{\Phi}((t_\alpha(\lambda,\sigma)-\theta)/\sigma)dG(\theta)dH(\sigma)} - \gamma \leq 0\right\},$$

$$\lambda_2^*(\alpha) = \min\left\{\lambda : \int\int_{-\infty}^{+\infty}\tilde{\Phi}((t_\alpha(\lambda,\sigma)-\theta)/\sigma)dG(\theta)dH(\sigma) - \alpha \leq 0\right\},$$

and $t_\alpha(\lambda,\sigma)$ defined as $v_\alpha(t_\alpha(\lambda,\sigma),\sigma) = \lambda$ for all $\lambda \in [0,1]$.

Note that although the thresholding value λ^* does not depend on the value of σ, the ranking does depend on σ. One way to see this is that since $v_\alpha(y,\sigma)$ is monotone in y for all $\sigma > 0$, the optimal rule is equivalent to $\mathbb{1}\{y_i > t_\alpha(\lambda^*,\sigma)\}$, where $t_\alpha(\lambda,\sigma)$ is a function of σ. For a fixed value of λ^*, the selection region for Y depends on σ in a nonlinear way. Comparing individuals i and j, it may be the case that $y_i > y_j$, but y_j belongs to the selection region while y_i does not. An example to illustrate this appears below. It should also be emphasized that when variances are heterogeneous, different ranking criteria need not lead to equivalent selections.

The posterior tail probability criterion is motivated by viewing the ranking and selection problems as hypothesis testing while allowing the null hypothesis to be α dependent. The particular construction of the null hypothesis turns out to be critical for the ranking exercise. In this subsection we present a simple example to illustrate that tail probability based on the conventional null hypothesis of zero effect does not lead to a powerful ranking device. Consider data generated from a three-component normal mixture model,

$$Y_i|\sigma_i \sim 0.85\mathcal{N}(-1,\sigma_i^2) + 0.1\mathcal{N}(0.5,\sigma_i^2) + 0.05\mathcal{N}(5,\sigma_i^2), \quad \sigma_i \sim U[0.5,4]. \tag{7.4}$$

Instead of transforming the data by v_α as in (7.3), we consider the transformation

$$\mathrm{T}(y_i,\sigma_i^2) = \mathbb{P}(\theta_i > 0|y_i,\sigma_i^2) = \frac{\int_0^{+\infty} \varphi(y_i|\theta,\sigma_i^2)dG(\theta)}{\int_{-\infty}^{+\infty} \varphi(y_i|\theta,\sigma_i^2)dG(\theta)} \tag{7.5}$$

and rank individuals accordingly. This transformation corresponds to the procedure proposed in Sun and McLain (2012) and is motivated for multiple testing problems under the conventional null hypothesis $H_0\colon \theta \leq 0$. The decision rule $\delta_i^{\mathrm{T}} = \mathbb{1}\{\mathrm{T}(y_i,\sigma_i) \geq \lambda\}$ then chooses the cutoff value λ that respects both the capacity constraint and the FDR control constraint for selecting the top α proportion.

Figure 7.3 compares the selection region for the two ranking procedures with $\alpha = 5\%$ and marginal FDR control at level 10%. The small black highlighted area below the blue selection boundary corresponds to a region where the ranking method based on T will select but the ranking method based on v_α does not. In contrast, the larger blue highlighted area corresponds to a region selected by v_α but not by T. The transformation T ranks those in the

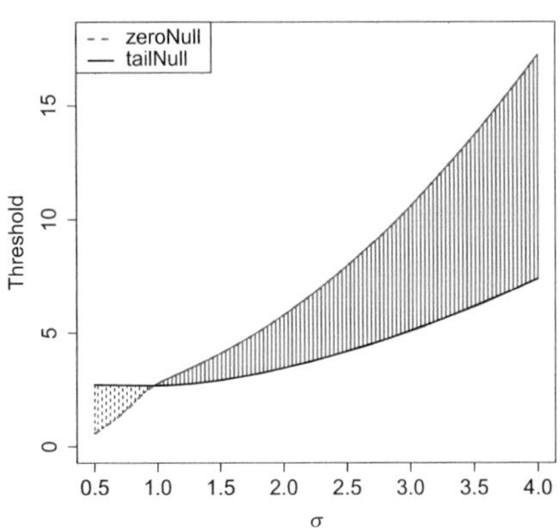

Figure 7.3. Selection boundaries based on the model (7.4) with $\alpha = 0.05$ and $\gamma = 0.1$. The solid black curve corresponds to the boundary of the selection region based on transformation v_α. The dashed red curve corresponds to the boundary of the selection region based on transformation T in (7.5). Density of σ is assumed to be uniform on the interval $[0.5,4]$.

black region higher than those in the blue region because although they have a relatively smaller mean effect y, their associated variances are also smaller indicating stronger evidence that such individuals have a more positive θ than those located in the blue area. However, our task is to find individuals with true effects, θ_i, in the upper tail. For $\alpha = 5\%$, we aim to select all individuals with $\theta = 5$; individuals in the black region present strong evidence that their true effect *can not* be too large because their observed effect y is small and their associated variance is also small, while those in the blue region, although their observed mean effects are associated with larger variances offer reasonable evidence that their associated true effect θ may be large. This evidence is not apparent in the transformation $\mathtt{T}$ but is captured in the transformation v_α.

Indeed, the average power of ranking based on the two different transformations v_α and $\mathtt{T}$ differ significantly. Defining the power of the selection rule as $\beta(\delta) = \mathbb{P}(\theta_i \geq \theta_\alpha, \delta_i = 1)/\mathbb{P}(\theta_i \geq \theta_\alpha)$, the proportion of true top α cases selected based on decision rule $\boldsymbol{\delta}$ is then $\beta(\boldsymbol{\delta}^{\mathtt{T}}) = 39\%$ for the $\mathtt{T}$-based method and $\beta(\boldsymbol{\delta}^*) = 69\%$ for the method based on v_α. Thus, although much of the literature relies on ranking and selection rules based on some form of posterior means and the conventional hypothesis testing apparatus, we would caution that such methods can be quite misleading and inefficient for ranking and selection problems.

7.2.5 Nestedness Property of the Selection

If we were to relax the capacity constraint to allow a larger proportion, $\alpha_1 > \alpha_0$, to be selected while maintaining our initial false discovery control, we would expect that members selected under the more stringent capacity constraint should remain selected under the relaxed constraint. We now discuss sufficient conditions under which we obtain this nestedness of the selection sets when using the posterior tail probability rule. This is a natural condition in applications like our analysis of ranking and selection of dialysis centers, Gu and Koenker (2023), especially because we might eventually like to assign "letter grades" to several subgroups of the centers.

The optimal Bayes rule defines the selection set for each pair of (α, γ) as

$$\Omega_{\alpha,\gamma} := \{(y,\sigma) : v_\alpha(y,\sigma) \geq \lambda^*(\alpha,\gamma)\},$$

and when σ is known, $v_\alpha(y,\sigma)$ is monotone in y as shown in Lemma 7.2 for each fixed σ; hence the selection set can also be represented as

$$\Omega_{\alpha,\gamma} = \{(y,\sigma) : y \geq t_\alpha(\lambda^*(\alpha,\gamma),\sigma)\},$$

where $t_\alpha(\lambda,\sigma)$ is defined as $v_\alpha(t_\alpha(\lambda,\sigma),\sigma) = \lambda$ for all $\lambda \in [0,1]$. It is also convenient for later discussion to define

$$\Omega^{FDR}_{\alpha,\gamma} := \{(y,\sigma) : v_\alpha(y,\sigma) \geq \lambda_1^*(\alpha,\gamma)\} = \{(y,\sigma) : y \geq t_\alpha(\lambda_1^*(\alpha,\gamma),\sigma)\},$$
$$\Omega^{C}_{\alpha} := \{(y,\sigma) : v_\alpha(y,\sigma) \geq \lambda_2^*(\alpha)\} = \{(y,\sigma) : y \geq t_\alpha(\lambda_2^*(\alpha),\sigma)\},$$

which are respectively the selection sets when the false discovery rate constraint or the capacity constraint is binding. It is easy to see that $\Omega_{\alpha,\gamma} = \Omega_{\alpha,\gamma}^{FDR} \cap \Omega_{\alpha}^{C}$.

Lemma 7.5. *Let the density function of $v_\alpha(y_i, \sigma_i)$ be denoted as $f_v(v;\alpha)$ and let*

$$\lambda_1^*(\alpha,\gamma) = \min\left\{\lambda : \frac{\int\int_{-\infty}^{\theta_\alpha} \tilde{\Phi}((t_\alpha(\lambda,\sigma)-\theta)/\sigma) dG(\theta) dH(\sigma)}{\int\int_{-\infty}^{+\infty} \tilde{\Phi}((t_\alpha(\lambda,\sigma)-\theta)/\sigma) dG(\theta) dH(\sigma)} - \gamma \leq 0\right\}$$

with $t_\alpha(\lambda,\sigma)$ defined as $v_\alpha(t_\alpha(\lambda,\sigma),\sigma) = \lambda$ and $\tilde{\Phi}$ the survival function of the standard normal random variable. If $\nabla_\alpha \log f_v(v;\alpha)$ is nondecreasing in v, then for fixed γ, if $\alpha_1 > \alpha_2$, we have $\lambda_1^*(\alpha_1,\gamma) \leq \lambda_1^*(\alpha_2,\gamma)$.

The density function $f_v(v;\alpha)$ can be viewed as a function of v indexed by the parameter α. An explicit form for $f_v(v;\alpha)$ is given below for the normal–normal model. The condition imposed in Lemma 7.5 is equivalent to a monotone likelihood ratio condition, that is that the likelihood ratio $f_v(v;\alpha_1)/f_v(v;\alpha_2)$ is nondecreasing in v if $\alpha_1 > \alpha_2$.

Corollary 7.6 If the condition in Lemma 7.5 holds, then $\Omega_{\alpha_2,\gamma}^{FDR} \subseteq \Omega_{\alpha_1,\gamma}^{FDR}$ for any $\alpha_1 > \alpha_2$.

The condition in Lemma 7.5 is sufficient but not necessary for nestedness of $\Omega_{\alpha,\gamma}^{FDR}$. Even when $\lambda_1^*(\alpha_1,\gamma) > \lambda_1^*(\alpha_2,\gamma)$, we can still have $t_{\alpha_1}(\lambda_1^*(\alpha_1,\gamma),\sigma) < t_{\alpha_2}(\lambda_1^*(\alpha_2,\gamma),\sigma)$ because the function $v_\alpha(Y,\sigma)$ depends on α, as does its inverse function t_α.

Lemma 7.7. *Let $\lambda_2^*(\alpha)$ be defined as in Proposition 7.4. If for any $\alpha_1 > \alpha_2$, $t_{\alpha_1}(\lambda_2^*(\alpha_1),\sigma) \leq t_{\alpha_2}(\lambda_2^*(\alpha_2),\sigma)$ for each σ, then $\Omega_{\alpha_2}^{C} \subseteq \Omega_{\alpha_1}^{C}$.*

The monotonicity here coincides with the condition in theorem 3 of Henderson and Newton (2016), who demonstrate that it holds when G is Gaussian. However, it need not hold more generally as shown in our counterexample in Online Appendix B of Gu and Koenker (2023).

Lemma 7.8. *If $\nabla_\alpha \log f_v(v;\alpha)$ is nondecreasing in v and the condition in Lemma 7.7 holds, then for a fixed γ, the selection region has a nested structure: If $\alpha_1 > \alpha_2$ then $\Omega_{\alpha_2,\gamma} \subseteq \Omega_{\alpha_1,\gamma}$.*

7.2.6 Rating US Dialysis Centers

To illustrate these ranking and selection methods we briefly reprise the analysis of Gu and Koenker (2023) evaluating the relative performance of US kidney dialysis centers. Longitudinal data on 3,230 centers over the period 2004–2018 is taken from Michigan Kidney Epidemiology and Cost Center (2018).

We focus on a primary measure of performance: the annual standardized mortality rate (SMR) for each center, the ratio of observed deaths to expected deaths for center patients. Since the mix of patients varies considerably from center to center, a Cox proportional hazard model estimated by the Michigan Center is employed to estimate expected deaths to account for this heterogeneity. Observed deaths, z_{it} for center i in year t, are modeled as a Poisson,

$$z_{it} \sim \text{Pois}(\rho_i \mu_{it}),$$

where μ_{it} is center i's expected deaths as predicted by the Cox model in year t and ρ_i is center i's idiosyncratic, latent mortality rate. The classical variance-stabilizing transformation of the Poisson brings us back to an approximately Gaussian model,

$$y_{it} = \sqrt{z_{it}/\mu_{it}} \sim \mathcal{N}(\theta_i, 1/w_{it}),$$

where $\theta_i = \sqrt{\rho_i}$ and $w_{it} = 4\mu_{it}$. For the sake of simplicity we will assume that the reported estimates of expected mortality, μ_{it}, are sufficiently accurate that we can treat w_{it} as known and independent of the θ_i. Over short time horizons, say three years, we assume that centers have a stable draw of θ_i from the distribution, G, so we can consider sufficient statistics,

$$T_i = \sum_t w_{it} y_{it}/w_i \sim \mathcal{N}(\theta_i, 1/w_i),$$

where $w_i = \sum_t w_{it}$.

Our objective is then to select centers based on the posterior distributions of their θ_i's. The posterior tail probability of center i is given by

$$v_\alpha(t_i, w_i) = \mathbb{P}(\theta_i \geq \theta_\alpha | t_i, w_i) = \frac{\int_{\theta_\alpha}^{+\infty} \varphi(t_i|\theta, w_i) dG(\theta)}{\int_{-\infty}^{+\infty} \varphi(t_i|\theta, w_i) dG(\theta)},$$

where φ is the density function of T_i conditional on θ_i and w_i. The capacity constraint requires choosing a thresholding value $\lambda_2^*(\alpha)$ such that

$$\alpha = \int\int \mathbb{1}\{v_\alpha(t, w) \geq \lambda_2^*(\alpha)\} \varphi(t|\theta, w) dG(\theta) dH(w),$$

which can be approximated by $\frac{1}{n}\sum_i \mathbb{1}\{v_\alpha(t_i, w_i) \geq \lambda_2^*(\alpha)\}$ and inverted to obtain the threshold. Capacity and FDR constraints can be imposed accordingly, see Exercises 5 and 6. In contrast, posterior mean ranking and selection is based on

$$\delta(t_i, w_i) = \mathbb{E}[\theta_i | t_i, w_i] = \int \theta \varphi(t_i|\theta, w_i) dG(\theta),$$

with suitably modified capacity and FDR constraints, see Exercise 6.

In Gu and Koenker (2023, Table 8.1) we contrast the estimated FDR rates at various capacity levels for the tail probability and posterior mean with several other parametric empirical Bayes criteria. The discrete nature of the NPMLE,

$\hat{G}$, makes it difficult to choose thresholds for this exercise, so we resort to smoothing $\hat{G}$ by convolution with a biweight density. It is of considerable interest to see conflicts among the selection criteria in which centers are selected. Figure 8.1 of Gu and Koenker (2023) explores conflicts between the tail probability criterion and James–Stein shrinkage and a naive p-value rule based on the unshrunken MLE. Combination of capacity and FDR control in conjunction with the NPMLE empirical Bayes does seem to offer a more prudent approach to these challenging decision problems.

7.3 TREATMENT ASSIGNMENT

In an influential series of recent papers, Manski (2004), Stoye (2012) and Manski and Tetenov (2016) have criticized the use of the Neyman–Pearson paradigm of testing for decision making based on clinical trials and other public policy experiments. This seems not entirely fair since the reification of the Type I α-level at 0.05 occurred long after it was originally motivated more flexibly by the relative costs of Type I and Type II errors. Nevertheless, the critique of current practice stands, and the objective of improving the design, analysis and decision making from randomized trials is admirable. In this section we would like to briefly suggest some ways that empirical Bayes methods might aid this effort.

Adopting the framework of Manski and Tetenov (2016), we have K treatments, $t_1, \ldots, t_K$. Individuals have observable covariates, x, with discrete support $\xi_1, \ldots, \xi_J$ and potential outcomes $U_j(t_k)$ when assigned to the kth treatment. Covariates follow distribution P_s, and the uncertainty is incorporated by allowing s to take different values from a set S. Experimental treatments are assigned randomly, with sample sizes n_{jk} for the jth covariate group receiving the kth treatment. From this experiment, we observe a statistic, $\psi \in \Psi$, consisting, for example, of the sample means of the outcomes for each treatment–covariate stratum of the experiment. Given the outcome of this experiment it is proposed to adopt the minimax regret decision rule $\delta \in \Delta$ that assigns subsequent treatment to minimize the maximum regret. The maximum regret for a decision rule δ is

$$\max_s \{U^*(P_s) - W(\delta, P_s, Q_s)\},$$

where the Q_s denote the distribution of the outcome of the experiment,

$$W(\delta, P_s, Q_s) = \sum_j P_s(X = \xi_j) \sum_k \mathbb{E}_s(\delta(t_k, \xi_j, \psi))\mu_{jsk},$$

and

$$U^*(P_s) = \sum_j P_s(X = \xi_j)\mu_{sj}^*,$$

with $\mu_{sjk} = \mathbb{E}_s[U_j(t_k)]$ and $\mu_{sj}^* = \max_k \mu_{sjk}$. Optimal mean treatment assignment would achieve $U^*(P_s)$, and $W(\delta, P_s, Q_s)$ measures what would be actually achieved, in expectation, using the decision rule δ. The difference of these two quantities is regret, and the proposed procedure for choosing δ is to minimize the maximal regret over all possible states, s.

Manski and Tetenov (2016) focus on "empirical success" rules that assign all subjects in each covariate stratum, ξ_j, to the treatment t_k that has the largest sample average outcome. When the outcomes, $U_j(t_k)$, are bounded, classical large deviation results can be used to establish ϵ-optimality of such rules: Maximal regret can be controlled to be less than any specified ϵ by choosing the experimental sample sizes, n_{jk}, sufficiently large. Of course, the use of raw sample means offers considerable scope for empirical Bayes refinements of the type described above. Particularly when there may be heterogeneous variability in treatment response, treatment assignment should presumably be designed to account for this possibility. In discrete covariate settings with moderate J, it would be prudent to consider the distribution of the observed $U_j(t_k)$, or at least its dispersion, since prospective patients may be reluctant to adopt treatments that have highly variable outcomes.

Stoye (2009) shows that the minimax regret criterion can be extremely pessimistic especially when sample information is conditioned on continuously measured covariates. His results are reminiscent of the Robbins (1951) Ur compound decision problem discussed in Chapter 1. The least favorable prior dictated by the minimax procedure yields decision rules that view each covariate setting in isolation from all the others. Stoye (2012) suggests some ways to avoid this pathology.

The empirical Bayes perspective, rather than relying entirely on observable covariates, naturally focuses on latent heterogeneity. To illustrate this contrasting view we will sketch a toy model of treatment assignment from the empirical Bayes perspective.

Treatments are "actions" in the Wald schema; suppose that there are K of them $a_1, \ldots, a_K$. For each of the K treatments suppose we have a model for treatment response Y described by a density $\tau_k(y|\theta)$ with $\theta \in \mathbb{R}$. For each new subject the decision maker receives an independent signal, say Z, that offers some information about θ expressed by the conditional density $\varphi(z|\theta)$. These signals are exchangeable with mixing distribution G, so a posterior for θ, say $H(\theta|Z = z)$, can be constructed for each subject. These posterior functions serve as a prior for evaluating the treatment response for each subject and each treatment. The efficacy of treatment k for a patient with signal $Z = z$ can be expressed as

$$W_k(z) = \int U(y)\tau_k(y|\theta)dH(\theta|Z = z),$$

where $U(\cdot)$ denotes a utility function that transforms responses, y, to utilities. Optimal treatment assignment for a subject of type z simply selects t_k as the treatment with the largest value of $W_k(z)\colon\ k = 1, \ldots, K$. This selection obviously depends upon the prior, $H(\theta|Z = z)$, and therefore may differ from patient to patient. This may seem impossibly vague; in order to make it at all practical one would have to specify how θ was related to observable covariates and how one might implement estimation of the τ_k densities and the mixing distribution G. We leave further development to the future.

7.4 A/B TESTING

Similar concerns arise in the application of large scale A/B testing protocols in marketing and industry. Berman and van den Bulte (2022) survey this domain focusing primarily on conventional multiple testing concerns but conceding that in many applications of this sort the relative costs of Type I and Type II errors are similar and consequently "empirical success" rules that effectively set $\alpha = 0.50$ are appropriate. When costs are asymmetric, however, closer attention should be paid to the false discovery rate, and empirical Bayes methods can be more useful. Coey and Hung (2022) consider the compound decision problem of selecting the "best" m out of n treatments in a Gaussian setting comparable to that discussed in Section 7.2.

Azevedo et al. (2020) describe a large scale A/B testing procedure at Microsoft Bing. Evidence is presented showing that the innovations under test exhibited a heavy right tail. The model adopted is the classical Gaussian sequence model. An observed signal, Y_i of the value of a proposed innovation, θ_i has conditional distribution

$$Y_i|\theta_i, n_i \sim \mathcal{N}(\theta_i, \sigma_i/n_i), \quad \theta_i \perp\!\!\!\perp \sigma_i,\ \theta_i \sim G,$$

where n_i denotes the sample size of the ith test, and the σ_i are treated as known constants. A parametric prior for G is taken to be Student with location parameter, μ, scale parameter, τ, and degrees of freedom, υ. Maximum likelihood estimation of these prior parameters produces a degrees of freedom estimate of $\hat{\upsilon} = 1.31$ for their preferred data configuration, thereby vindicating their assertion of heavy-tailed innovations.

The decision problem facing the firm is to choose a vector of sample sizes $\boldsymbol{n} = (n_1, \ldots, n_m)$ and a vector of binary indicators $\boldsymbol{s} = (s_i, \ldots, s_m)$ denoting innovations to be implemented. The expected payoff is given by

$$\Pi(\boldsymbol{n}, \boldsymbol{s}) = \mathbb{E} \sum_{i=1}^{m} s_i \theta_i - c \sum_{i=1}^{m} n_i.$$

Since for any $n > 0$, $\mathbb{E}[\theta_i|Y_i, n]$ is monotone in Y_i, there exists an optimal threshold $\theta_i^*(n)$ such that $\mathbb{E}[\theta_i|Y_i = \theta_i^*(n), n] = 0$, and the optimal decision rule can be expressed as

$$s_i^* = \mathbb{1}\{Y_i > \theta_i^*(n)\}.$$

This is the decision rule investigated in Johns (1957) and mentioned above in Section 7.1. Optimization with respect to the sample size, n, can be carried out explicitly in the Gaussian case as shown by Azevedo et al. (2020). The posterior mean of θ as a function of the observed signal, y, is depicted in Figure 7.4 by the solid blue curve. It is determined entirely by the estimated parameters of the

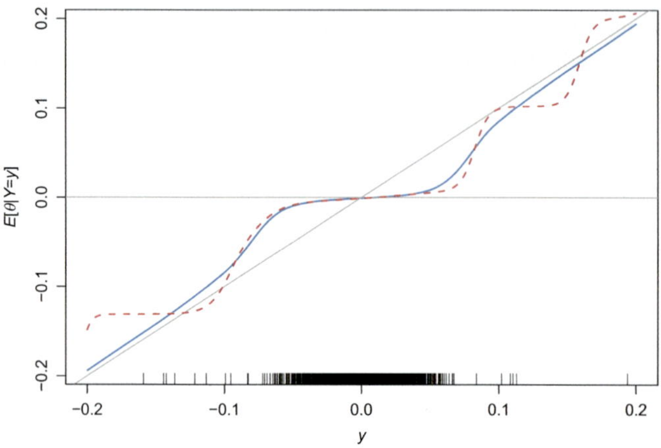

Figure 7.4. Posterior mean estimates from a Gaussian sequence model with a heavy-tailed prior distribution. The solid blue curve depicts the posterior mean function based on the estimated parametric prior for the A/B testing data of Azevedo et al. (2020). The dashed red curve shows the NPMLE estimate of the posterior mean based on a sample of 2,000 observations from the parametric model. The rug plot on the y axis indicates the distribution of the observed sample.

Student specification of the prior and a fixed value for the scale of the Gaussian noise, $\sigma/n = 0.022$. Because the scale of the estimated prior is quite small, $\tau = 0.00296$, so the prior is quite concentrated around its mean, $\mu = 0.00946$, it exerts a strong shrinkage effect on observed signals near zero: Anything in the interval $[-0.5, 0.5]$ is pulled back almost to zero. However, observed signals outside the interval $[-0.1, 0.1]$ are regarded as anomalous, unlikely to be attributable to the Gaussian noise, and the estimated prior regards them as plausible draws from its heavy tails. This is consistent with a sample of 2,000 observations from the estimated prior model depicted in the "rug" plot along the y axis of the figure: Only 10 of the 2,000 observations lie outside this interval.

Superimposed in Figure 7.4 is a red dashed curve showing the estimated posterior mean function based on the NPMLE $\hat{G}$ for a sample of 2,000 observations drawn from the estimated parametric prior of Azevedo et al. (2020), and with the same scale for the Gaussian noise employed there. The NPMLE posterior mean tracks the parametric estimate quite well in the central region of the plot; only in the far tails does it deviate in a somewhat oscillatory fashion. This is an inevitable consequence of the sparsity of the data in this region. Of course, from the binary decision rule perspective such departures are entirely harmless. Unfortunately, the Microsoft data underlying the parametric prior estimate is not publicly accessible, so we are unable to investigate posterior mean estimates based on NPMLE $\hat{G}$ for the original data, but it may not be unreasonable to suggest some skepticism about the symmetry assumption underlying the Student model. One might also have some concern about the independence assumption on the σ_i's, as we have discussed in Chapter 6. Finally, it would be interesting to explore issues of false discovery in the context of A/B testing, thereby expanding the scope of potential loss functions and decision rules.

In treatment assignment and other experimental settings it is increasingly clear that there is a need to balance the process of learning about the effectiveness of treatments with the immediate goal of implementing them. Robbins's early research on sequential methods has been at the forefront of this effort. Multi-arm bandit problems and related challenges make this an exciting new research frontier.

Exercises

(1) If $a_1 = 1$ and $b_1 = b_2 = 0$, in the loss function of Section 7.1 show that the Bayes rule minimizing $B(\delta, G)$ takes the form

$$\delta(y_i) = \mathbb{1}\{a_2(1-v(y_i))-v(y_i) \leq 0\} = \mathbb{1}\{v(y_i) \geq a_2/(1+a_2)\}.$$

(2) If $a_1 = a_2 = 0$ and $b_1 = b_2 = 1$, show that the Bayes rule is given by the sign of the posterior mean of θ_i conditional on observing $Y_i = y_i$:

$$\delta(y_i) = \mathbb{1}\{\mathbb{E}[\theta_i | Y_i = y_i] > c\}.$$

(3) Prove

$$\mathbb{P}(\theta_i \in A | t(Y_i) \leq \lambda) = \frac{\int \mathbb{1}\{t(y) \leq \lambda\} t(y) f(y) dy}{\int \mathbb{1}\{t(y) \leq \lambda\} f(y) dy}.$$

(4) Consider the setting in Gu and Shen (2018), as discussed in 7.1.3,

$$Y_i | \theta_i, \sigma_i^2 \sim N(\theta_i, \sigma_i^2),$$

and we transform it to

$$S_i = Y_i / \sigma_i \sim N(\mu_i, 1), \mu_i \overset{iid}{\sim} G.$$

Suppose the distribution of μ_i is

$$G(\mu) = (1 - \omega)\delta_0(\mu) + \omega G_1(\mu)$$

with known ω, and $\delta_0(\mu)$ represents a mass point at $\mu = 0$. Propose a NPMLE estimator for G.

(5) Show that the capacity constraint for the tail probability criterion requires a thresholding value $\lambda_2^*(\alpha)$ such that

$$\alpha = \int \int \mathbb{1}\{v_\alpha(t, \sigma) \geq \lambda_2^*(\alpha)\} \varphi(t | \theta, \sigma) dG(\theta) dH(\sigma),$$

which can be approximated by $\frac{1}{n} \sum_i \mathbb{1}\{v_\alpha(t_i, \sigma_i) \geq \lambda_2^*(\alpha)\}$ and inverted to obtain the threshold.

(6) Show that the FDR constraint requires a thresholding value, $\lambda_1^*(\alpha,\gamma)$,

$$\gamma = \frac{\int\int \mathbb{1}\{v_\alpha(t,\sigma) \geq \lambda_1^*(\alpha,\gamma)\}(1 - v_\alpha(t,\sigma))\varphi(t|\theta,\sigma)dG(\theta)dH(\sigma)}{\int\int \mathbb{1}\{v_\alpha(t,\sigma) \geq \lambda_1^*(\alpha,\gamma)\}\varphi(t|\theta,\sigma)dG(\theta)dH(\sigma)},$$

where H is the marginal distribution of the observed portion of the variance effect. The numerator can be approximated by $\frac{1}{n}\sum_i(1 - v_\alpha(t_i,\sigma_i))\mathbb{1}\{v_\alpha(t_i,\sigma_i) \geq \lambda_1^*(\alpha,\gamma)\}$, and the denominator can be approximated by, $\frac{1}{n}\sum_i \mathbb{1}\{v_\alpha(t_i,\sigma_i) \geq \lambda_1^*(\alpha,\gamma)\}$.

(7) Explore the conflict between the ranking and selection criterion for the dialysis center data. Hint: Download the supplementary material for Gu and Koenker (2023) from the Econometric Society Data Archive and read the tutorial included in the zip file.

(8) Given a binary medical treatment with response $Y \in [0,1]$ measured in utils, let Y_0 denote the potential outcome under the control (placebo) regime and Y_1 denote the potential outcome under treatment. Suppose $Y_0 = Y_{-1} + V$, where Y_{-1} denotes an initial state of health, and $V \sim U[-\epsilon,\epsilon]$, and $Y_1 = \mathbb{1}(V \geq 0)$ with independent $V \sim U[-\epsilon,\epsilon]$. Compare optimal treatment decisions for patients based on maximizing expected health status, Y, with the minimax regret decision.

(9) A medical treatment depends upon a diagnosis, $\theta \in \{-1,1\}$, but physicians see only a noisy signal $Y = \theta + U$, with $U \sim \mathcal{N}(0,1)$ for each patient. Show (Robbins, 1951) that the minimax treatment assignment, subject to the compound loss, $\sum_{i=1}^n L(\hat{\theta}_i,\theta_i) = \sum_{i=1}^n |\hat{\theta}_i - \theta_i|$ is to choose the treatment appropriate for $\hat{\theta}_i = \text{sgn}(Y_i)$ for each patient. Suggest a way to improve upon these decisions when n is moderately large.

(10) Generalize the previous exercise to a setting in which the physician observes repeated measurements, Y_{ij} $j = 1,\ldots,m$, for each individual patient and it is believed that there may be heterogeneity in the probabilities $p = \mathbb{P}(\theta_i = 1)$.

(11) Show that whatever the sampling cost, c, in the A/B testing context of Section 7.4, the selection decision rule takes the same form.

CHAPTER 8

Empirical Bayes Methods for Survival Analysis

The notion of frailty to describe unobserved heterogeneity of population risks has been a familiar feature of demographic analysis since Vaupel et al. (1979) and has gradually spread to other statistical domains. A valuable early exposition of the impact of frailty in models of treatment evaluation is provided by Shepard and Zeckhauser (1980). Often, as in the aforementioned sources, parametric models are posited for the frailty effects, but it is usually difficult to justify such assumptions given the unobserved nature of the frailty components. The seminal work of Heckman and Singer (1984) introduced the Kiefer–Wolfowitz NPMLE as a more flexible alternative to these parametric models for survival and duration modeling.

Perhaps because frailty has been a fixture of survival modeling for so long, there seems to be no tradition of regarding mixture models as inherently Bayesian even though the basic structure of the mixture model makes the frailty distribution look very much like the prior mixing distribution we have described earlier for Poisson and Gaussian mixture models. The Bayesian paradigm with its sharp distinction between likelihood and prior is elided in a way that makes joint estimation of maximum likelihood estimation of parametric frailty models perfectly Fisherian. Extending this attitude to nonparametric frailty models again raises the rhetorical question: What is Bayesian about empirical Bayesianism?

8.1 PARAMETRIC MODELS OF FRAILTY

Before turning to nonparametric frailty we should review some basic features of some common parametric models of frailty in survival analysis. A natural starting point is the proportional hazard model,

$$h(t|\theta) = \theta\alpha(t),$$

where $\alpha(t)$ denotes a baseline hazard model and θ is a positive random variable representing individual specific frailty. Observable covariate effects can easily be introduced with a multiplicative term $\exp(x^\top \beta)$, but we will suppress this dependence for the moment. The conditional probability of survival up to time t is given by

$$\mathbb{P}(T \geq t|\theta) = S(t|\theta) = \exp(-\theta A(t)),$$

where $A(t) = \int_0^t \alpha(s)ds$ is the baseline cumulative hazard function. Thus, we can express the population survival function as

$$S(t) = \mathbb{E}e^{-\theta A(t)} = \mathcal{L}(A(t)),$$

where $\mathcal{L}(s) = \mathbb{E}e^{-s\theta} = \int_0^\infty e^{-s\theta} dG(\theta)$ is the Laplace transform of $\theta \sim G$, and the population hazard function is

$$h(t) = -(\log S(t))' = \alpha(t)\frac{\mathcal{L}'(A(t))}{\mathcal{L}(A(t))}.$$

Example 8.1 Gamma frailty is convenient since its Laplace transform $\mathcal{L}(s) = (\nu/(\nu + s))^\eta$, where ν and η are respectively the rate and shape parameter, is relatively simple. Normalizing mean frailty to be one, so $\nu = \eta$ and setting $\delta = 1/\nu$, the variance of the frailty distribution, simplifies the Laplace transform further to $\mathcal{L}(s) = (1 + \delta s)^{-1/\delta}$. Thus, $S(t) = (1 + \delta A(t))^{-1/\delta}$, and $h(t) = \alpha(t)/(1 + \delta A(t))$. Even when the baseline hazard is rapidly increasing, for example, $\alpha(t) = t^2$, the frailty effect moderates the hazard as seen in Figure 8.1 for several values of δ. The unimodal shape of the population hazard is typical of many economic settings with initially increasing risk followed by a gradual decline in risk.

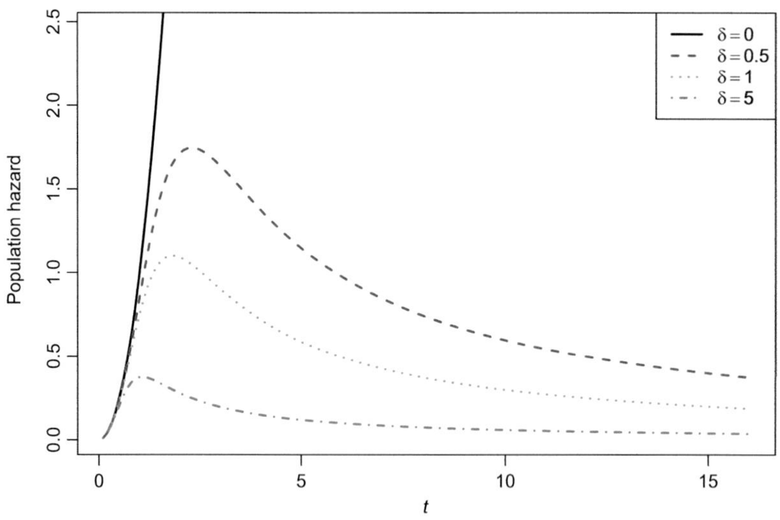

Figure 8.1. Population hazards for several different gamma frailty distributions with mean 1 and variance δ.

Example 8.2 A larger parametric family with a tractable Laplace transform is the class of power variance distributions (Hougaard, 1986; Aalen, 1988; Aalen et al., 2008) with Laplace transform

$$\mathcal{L}(s,\rho,\nu,\eta) = \exp\Big\{-\rho\Big[1-\Big(\frac{\nu}{\nu+s}\Big)^{\eta}\Big]\Big\},$$

with $\nu > 0$, $\eta > -1$ and $\eta\rho > 0$. This family nests a wide variety of other prominent parametric frailty models:

Gamma: Letting $\rho \to \infty$, $\eta \to 0$ so $\eta\rho \to \eta_0$ yields Gamma frailty.

Compound Poisson: When $\eta > 0$ frailty is the sum of Gammas with scale, ν and shape parameter η. The number of summands is Poisson with mean ρ. Frailty in this case has the feature that there is a positive mass of $e^{-\rho}$ at zero. Aalen et al. (2008) interpret this as a "cumulative damage" model: units incur a Poisson number of gamma "insults" whose cumulative damage determines frailty.

Inverse Gaussian: When $\eta = -1/2$ and $\rho < 0$ yields inverse Gaussian frailty that can be interpreted as a first passage time of a Brownian motion with drift.

Stable: If $\eta \in (-1,0)$, $\nu \to 0$ and $\rho \to -\infty$ with $\nu^{\eta}\rho \to a > 0$, then $\mathcal{L}(s,\eta,a) = \exp(-as^{-\eta})$, the Laplace transform of a skewed stable distribution.

Poisson: Letting $m \to \infty$, $\nu \to \infty$ so $\eta/\nu \to 1$ yields Poisson frailty with mean ρ.

Gaussian: If $\rho \to \pm\infty$ and $\nu \to \infty$ so that $\rho/\nu \to a$ then frailty is Gaussian with mean $a\eta$ and variance $a\eta(\eta+1)/\nu$.

Aalen (1992) has studied the compound Poisson variant of the power variance family, which he reparameterizes in terms of moments as $\gamma = \mathbb{E}\theta = \rho\eta/\nu$, $\delta = \mathbb{V}\theta/\mathbb{E}\theta^2 = (\eta+1)/(\eta\rho)$ and $\alpha = \eta + 1$. He shows that the form of the frailty distribution is preserved over time, that is, survivors at time $t > 0$ have Laplace transform

$$\mathcal{L}_t(s) = \mathbb{E}(e^{-sZ}|T > t) = \frac{\mathcal{L}(s+\Lambda(t))}{\mathcal{L}(\Lambda(t))},$$

which has the same form as the original $\mathcal{L}(t)$ at time zero, but with new parameters:

$$\alpha_t = \alpha,\ \gamma_t = \gamma\left(1+\frac{\delta\gamma}{\alpha}\Lambda(t)\right)^{-\alpha},\ \delta_t = \delta\left(1+\frac{\delta\gamma}{\alpha}\Lambda(t)\right)^{-\alpha-1}.$$

Parametric frailty distributions when combined with a convenient parametric baseline survival distributions like the Weibull produce a quite flexible family of survival models. Alternatively, one may achieve more flexibility by adopting a semiparametric specification with nonparametric baseline survival as suggested by Murphy (1995), who imposes gamma frailty in a proportional hazard framework, a choice partially justified by the limiting results of Abbring and van der Berg (2007).

In single-spell duration models, baseline hazard and frailty are intertwined in such a way that it is difficult to untangle them. This makes comparisons of hazards for distinguishable groups also difficult. Aalen et al. (2008) illustrate this with a comparison of relative mortality rates for Norwegian males in 1901–5 versus 1991. At younger ages, as expected, the ratio of mortality rates in the earlier period to the later one is substantially greater than one, but this differential vanishes at more advanced ages. This is attributed to a selection effect due to frailty: Those reaching age, say 80, in the earlier period are presumed to be considerably more robust, less frail, than the much larger proportion of men reaching 80 in 1991. Similar difficulties arise in the comparison of mortality rates across countries. An interesting perspective on these issues is provided in Vaupel (2005).

8.2 NONPARAMETRIC IDENTIFICATION IN FRAILTY MODELS OF DURATION

Unlike the Poisson and Gaussian mixture models we have considered so far, modeling duration and survival data offers no firm foundation for choosing $\varphi(t|\theta)$ that might serve as a plausible candidate as a parametric base distribution. Heckman and Singer (1983) observed that this implies a fundamental lack of identification for the specification of mixture, or frailty, models of duration.

To illustrate this they note that the general mixture model of survival,

$$\mathbb{P}(T \geq t) = S(t) = \int_0^\infty \varphi(t,\theta)dG(\theta),$$

with $\varphi(t,\theta) = 1 - e^{-t\theta}$ and $dG(\theta) = \delta_\eta(\theta)$ is observationally indistinguishable from a model in which

$$\varphi(t,\theta) = 1 - \frac{2}{\sqrt{2\pi}}\int_c^\infty e^{-s^2/2}ds,$$

with $c = t/\sqrt{2\theta}$ and $dG(\theta) = \eta^2 e^{-\eta^2\theta}d\theta$. That is, both models have the same marginal survival distribution, $S(t) = 1 - e^{-\eta t}$, though they have quite different interpretations.

There are many variations on this theme. Focusing on the canonical proportional hazard model of Cox (1972), Rodriguez (2005) observes that the constant hazard model,

$$\lambda(t,x) = \exp(\alpha + x^\top\beta),$$

is indistinguishable from a frailty model in which

$$\lambda(t,x,\theta) = \theta\exp\{\alpha + x^\top\beta + \sigma^2 t\exp(\alpha + x^\top\beta)\}$$

when θ has a gamma distribution with mean one and any fixed variance. Alternatively, suppose

$$\lambda(t,x,\theta) = \theta \exp\{\alpha + x^\top \beta\}(1 + \sigma^2 t \exp\{\alpha + x^\top \beta\}),$$

and θ has an inverse Gaussian distribution with mean one and variance σ^2; then the population hazard is again identical to the original constant hazard model. Horowitz (1999) has proposed a deconvolution estimator for the proportional hazard model with unknown baseline hazard and frailty distribution that exploits smoothness conditions. An elegant paper of Elbers and Ridder (1982) shows that frailty and baseline hazard *are* distinguishable in proportional hazard models when observable covariates are present to shift the baseline hazard. Unfortunately, this identifiability result does not produce a consistent estimator for single spell duration data. Instead, they suggest adopting parametric forms for the baseline hazard and the covariate effects and focusing attention on nonparametric estimation of the frailty distribution. This is the strategy of Heckman and Singer (1984), and it is also what we would advocate.

It may be disconcerting that we can't untangle these competing models, but on further reflection it should not be surprising. Unless we see repeated measurements, spells of unemployment for the same individuals or all the proverbial nine lives of cats, we can't expect to discern frailty from the form of the base distribution. We might compare this predicament to a more familiar situation in which we observe one measurement from each of n individuals but can't distinguish whether they come iidly from a standard Cauchy distribution or from standard Gaussians that happen to each be scaled by independent $1/\sqrt{\chi_1^2}$ variates. Faced with this dilemma, it is natural to adopt a firm stance regarding the base distribution and try to be as flexible as possible about the form of the frailty distribution. This is the approach taken by Heckman and Singer (1984), who opted for the Weibull model with log hazard function,

$$\log h(t|\theta,x) = \theta + x^\top \beta + (\alpha - 1)\log t,$$

treating the scale parameter, θ, as the source of the unobserved heterogeneity. Observable heterogeneity is captured by the covariates, x, and Weibull shape parameter, α. In the simplest case, with known α and no covariates, the mixing distribution, G, of θ can be estimated by maximum likelihood following the same protocol we have described earlier for the NPMLE. This is the visionary strategy advocated by Heckman and Singer (1984), armed only with the nascent EM algorithm of Laird (1978) for computational assistance. Recent developments in convex optimization have considerably reduced the computational burden of this approach and open the door to many future developments.

8.3 REAPPRAISING MEDFLY MORTALITY

We will illustrate some features of this approach using a reanalysis of the influential Carey et al. (1992) study of medfly mortality based on prior work of Koenker and Geling (2001) and Koenker and Gu (2013). The Mediterranean fruit fly, or medfly, is an agricultural pest especially virulent periodically in California citrus orchards. One effective treatment for infestations has been the release of infertile males into the wild population. For this purpose facilities were built to raise large quantities of medflies. One of these facilities was subsequently repurposed to study the demography of this species. In the largest of the three experiments reported in Carey et al. (1992), 1.2 million medflies (*Ceratitis Capitata*) were raised in a large facility in Mexico,

> ...Pupae were sorted into one of five size classes using a pupal sorter. This enabled size dimorphism to be eliminated as a potential source of sex-specific mortality differences. Approximately, 7,200 medflies (both sexes) of a given size class were maintained in each of 167 mesh covered, 15 cm by 60 cm by 90 cm aluminum cages. Adults were given a diet of sugar and water, ad libitum, and each day dead flies were removed, counted and their sex determined ...

The primary objective of the experiment was to study the upper tail of the mortality distribution, an endeavor that revealed several surprising features. Prior to this experiment it was an article of faith throughout biology that within-species mortality (hazard) rates were monotonically increasing with age. Indeed it was commonly suggested that each species had a species specific upper bound for age, rendering the whole notion of investigating the "tail behavior" of the mortality distribution pointless. In Figure 8.2 we plot raw daily mortality rates from the experiment and superimpose a smoothed, geometric moving average curve. More explicitly, let y_t denote the number of flies alive (at risk) at the beginning of day t; then the raw mortality rates plotted in Figure 8.2 are $r_t = 1 - y_{t+1}/y_t$, and the smoothed (geometric) weekly moving average is given by

$$\tilde{r}_t = 1 - \left(\prod_{s=t-3}^{s=t+3} (1 - r_s) \right)^{1/7}.$$

Contrary to the received wisdom, mortality rates actually declined after about age 60!

This finding provoked an extensive reappraisal of the biology of aging. The observed decline in mortality offered no consolation to the 99.8 percent of the flies that were already dead by age 60, but to the remaining more than 2,000 less frail flies, it offered some hope of a prolonged retirement. The oldest flies in the experiment expired on day 172.

How should we interpret this remarkably long tail? One explanation, suggested by Vaupel and Carey (1998), is that the population under study was really a mixture of several subpopulations of varying frailties. Rather than assume a particular parametric form for the frailty distribution, Vaupel and Carey adopted a nonparametric mixture model. While their two-page note in *Science* precluded a detailed description of their computational methods, we have attempted to "reverse engineer" an approach that closely resembles the results reported in their Figure 1.

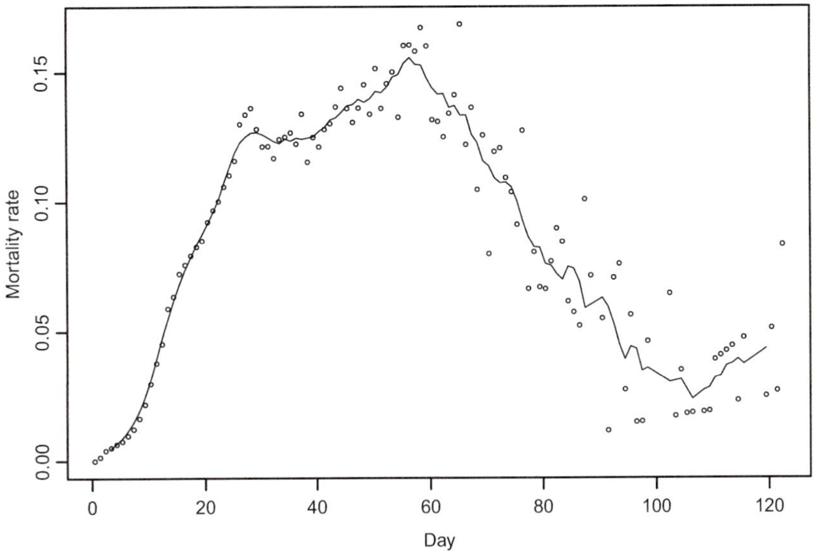

Figure 8.2. Raw daily medfly mortality rates and moving average smooth.

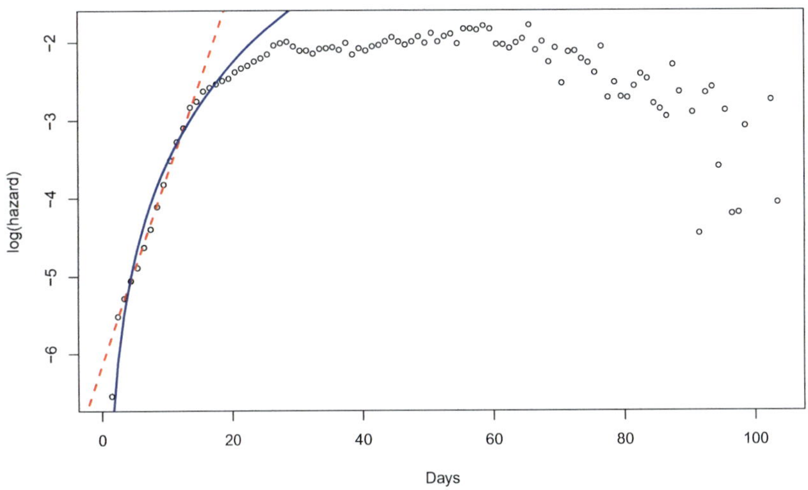

Figure 8.3. Estimated baseline Gompertz and Weibull hazard models: Linear (Gompertz) and log linear (Weibull) fits to the initial k observations of raw daily log mortality rates.

The first question is: What are we mixing? Here we follow Vaupel and Carey and consider both Gompertz and Weibull mixtures. The Gompertz model assumes that log hazard is linear in age, while the Weibull model assumes that log hazard is linear in log age. Figure 8.3 illustrates raw log-hazard rates plotted against age, and superimposed are two estimates of the baseline model.

The dashed red line represents the estimated baseline Gompertz model fitted to the data for the first 15 days of the experiment by weighted least squares with weights given by the relative frequencies of the daily counts.

It appears that the first day is an outlier in this plot. However, since few flies died on the first day it exerts little influence on the fitted relationship. The solid curve represents the baseline Weibull fit based on the first 20 days of the experiment. How many observations to use to estimate the parameters of the baseline model is obviously somewhat debatable. In this respect the problem is somewhat similar to the notorious controversies over how to choose k in the Hill estimator (Hill, 1975) of the Pareto tail exponent. We won't indulge in further speculation about these choices, but simply remark that our $k = 20$ selection yields baseline Gompertz hazard of $h(t) = 0.0045\exp(0.17t)$, while Vaupel and Carey use $h(t) = 0.003\exp(0.3t)$, and for the Weibull model we obtain $h(t) = 0.0004t^{1.85}$, against Vaupel and Carey's $h(t) = 0.001t^2$. The intercept in these models is not crucial: Since the estimated mixture distribution is scale equivariant it simply fixes a normalization. The shape parameter is more challenging, as we have already discussed in Section 5.4. Our approach of fitting the left tail of the distribution yields rather similar estimates to those employed by Vaupel and Carey. It is closely related to the more formal proposals of Honoré (1990, 1997).

Given our estimated baseline model we can now address the problem of estimating the mixing, or frailty, distribution. The NPMLE problem of estimating the mixing distribution, G, can be formulated as we have previously done for the Poisson and Gaussian mixtures except that the base distribution is now Gompertz or Weibull.

In Figure 8.4 we plot the two mixing distributions estimated by the Kiefer–Wolfowitz maximum likelihood procedure. Note that the vertical axis in these plots is the cube root of the density chosen to exaggerate the smaller mass points that are nearly invisible on the original $dG(\theta)$ scale. The Weibull model is considerably more parsimonious in this respect with only six distinct points of support. The implied hazard functions for the two estimated mixture densities are shown in Figure 8.5, superimposed over the raw mortality rates. Fewer mass points in the Weibull model translates to much smoother behavior of the hazard function, but this is ultimately traceable back to the forms of the base density, the Gompertz being more sharply peaked and consequently generating a rougher mixture.

8.3.1 Gender Crossover in Mortality Rates for Medflies

An obvious source of *observed* heterogeneity is gender differences. Again, the Carey et al. experiment revealed some surprising new facts. When we repeat our prior exercise fitting separate baseline Weibull models for males and females we obtain the results appearing in Figure 8.6. The Weibull model fits considerably better in both of these plots than in the previous aggregated plot, and considerably better than the corresponding Gompertz plots, so we will

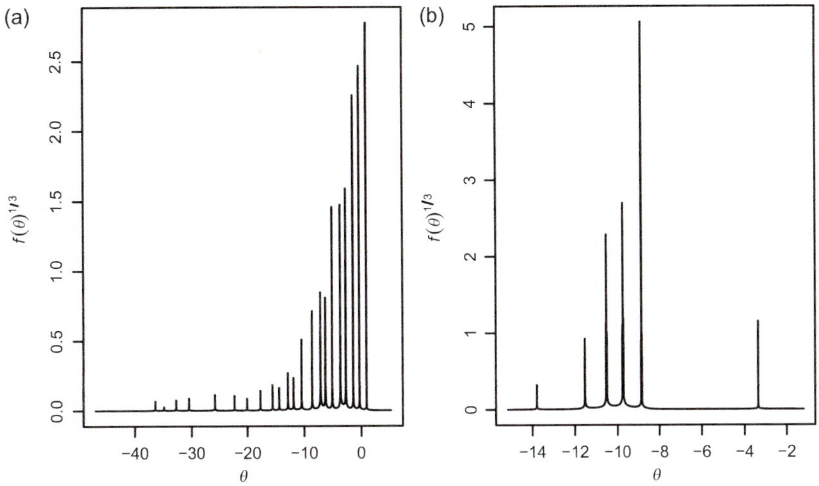

Figure 8.4. Estimated mixing distributions for the Gompertz (a) and Weibull (b) models.

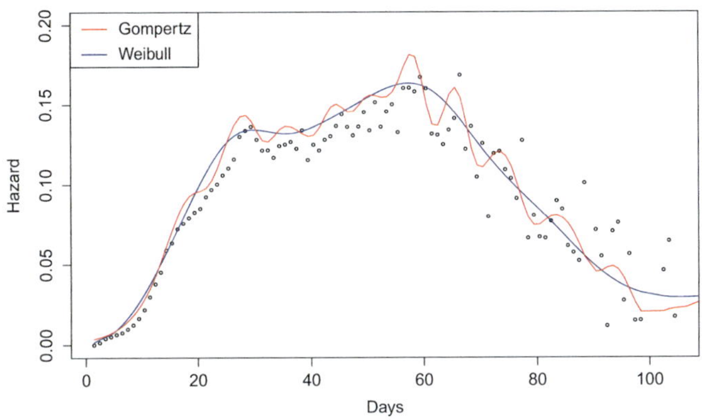

Figure 8.5. Hazard functions for the estimated Gompertz and Weibull models.

restrict attention henceforth to the Weibull model. Given the baseline models, the Kiefer–Wolfowitz estimates of the mixture model yield the gender-specific hazard functions of Figure 8.7. Several features of this plot are worth noting. Until about age 20 female mortality is higher than that of males, but after age 20 female mortality is substantially below male mortality. This crossover of the hazard functions clearly contradicts the proportional hazard assumption that is frequently made in survival analysis. The second crossover of the estimated hazard curves at about age 75 probably shouldn't be taken too seriously, since hazard estimation at advanced ages is itself rather hazardous, but the initial crossing is quite precisely estimated and induces a crossing of the estimated

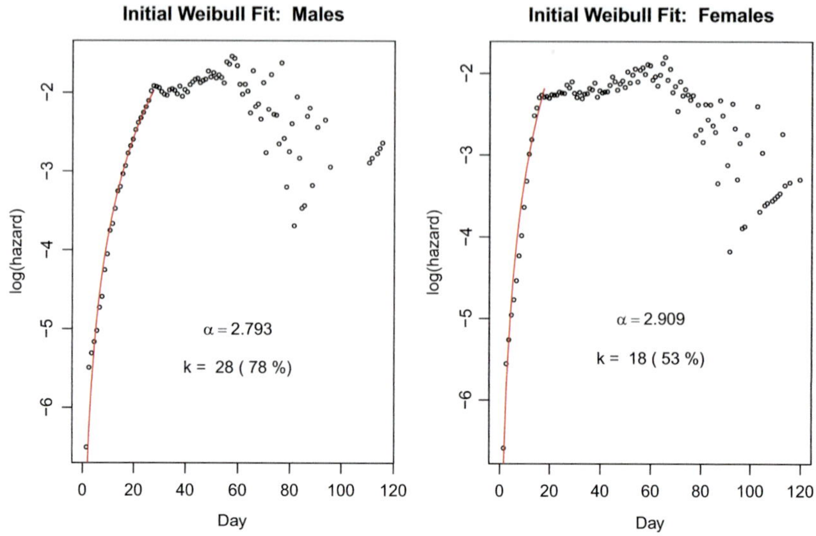

Figure 8.6. Gender-specific baseline Weibull models: Weighted least squares fitting of the initial k observations on daily mortality rates. The percentage of the sample population dead by day k is given in parentheses. The estimated shape parameter of the baseline Weibull model is α.

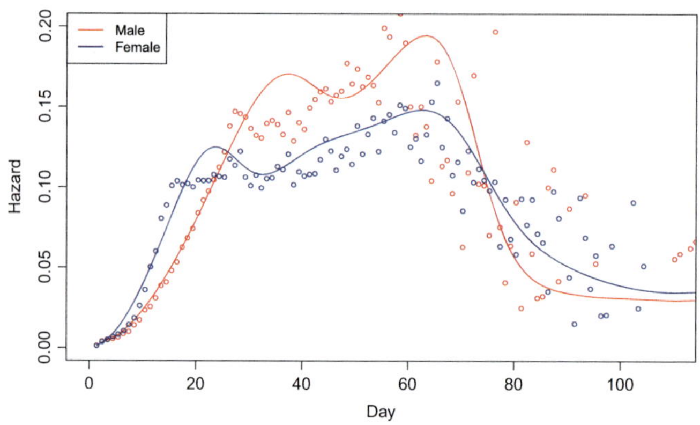

Figure 8.7. Gender-specific hazard functions for the Weibull mixture model: Raw daily mortality rates are plotted in black for males and gray for females; superimposed are the estimated hazard functions for the Weibull mixture models using the baseline models shown in Figure 8.6.

gender-specific survival functions at about age 36. It is impossible to resist noting that this pattern reverses the typical finding for human populations for which males are more frail than females with a possible crossover only at very advanced ages.

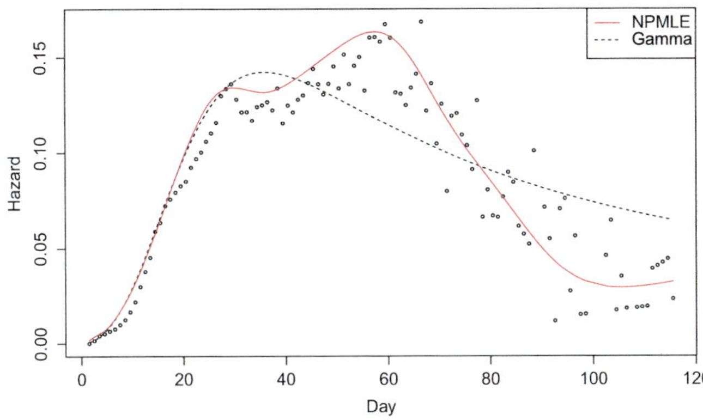

Figure 8.8. The NPMLE offers a more flexible specification compared to more traditional parametric models that assume gamma frailty.

8.3.2 Fly-by-Nite Insurance by Medlife

The most common parametric specification of unobserved heterogeneity for the Weibull survival model is the gamma scale model, so it is worthwhile comparing estimated hazard functions obtained with the NPMLE to those for the gamma model. Figure 8.8 illustrates this comparison. Frailty as viewed through the lens of the gamma specification does decline gradually, but the NPMLE mortality rate declines more sharply in accordance with the scatter plots that appear above. Given the NPMLE estimate of G for the full sample it is straightforward to compute conditional distributions $G(\theta|Y > y)$ for subpopulations at various ages; this is illustrated in Figure 8.9. From these conditional distributions one can easily compute the risk of death in the next 10 days and thus design fair insurance premiums at various ages for 10 day term life insurance as illustrated in Figure 8.10. These premiums for both gamma and NPMLE G inherit the general shape of their respective hazard functions. See Koenker and Gu (2017) for further details.

8.3.3 Profile Likelihood for Covariate Effects in Survival Models

If nonparametric maximum likelihood estimation of frailty effects were restricted to univariate survival models it would still be a very valuable addition to the statistical toolkit, but it would be much more useful if it could be extended to semiparametric applications that included covariate effects. Of course we already have the Cox proportional hazard model for this purpose; however frailty offers another valuable perspective. Factorization of the likelihood makes the proportional hazard assumption especially convenient from a computational viewpoint. The Weibull mixture model has no comparable factorization; nevertheless it is possible to employ a profile likelihood formulation to elaborate the model to include covariate effects. We will illustrate this approach to further explore the medfly mortality data.

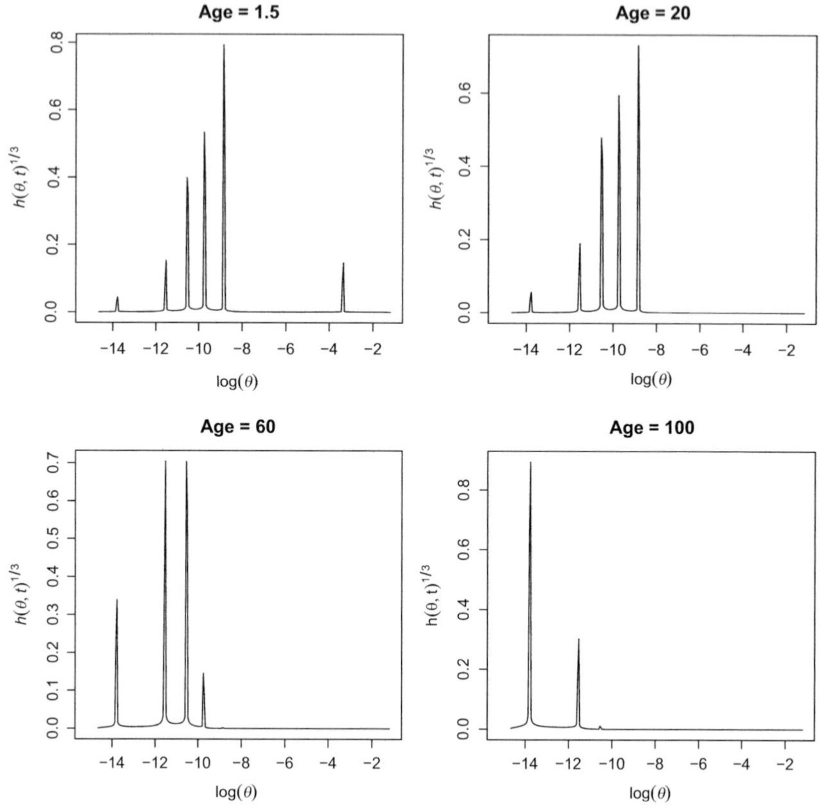

Figure 8.9. Conditioning on age we obtain different frailty distributions. Note the we have plotted the cube root of the density to accentuate smaller masses.

From the beginning a controversial aspect of the Carey experiments was the effect of cage density. Critics claimed that flies raised in more crowded cages would be more likely to die earlier. Carey et al. (1993) responded that the cage density was quite low after 60 days. Only 16 flies per cage, on average, survived beyond this age, so it seemed difficult to attribute differences in mortality rates in elderly medflies to differences in crowding when they were younger. To investigate whether differences in initial cage density had a significant impact on mortality we considered a model in which it entered as a linear multiplicative scale shift in the Weibull model, that is, the baseline Weibull scale becomes $\theta \exp(d_i \beta)$, where d_i denotes initial cage density. To estimate the density effect parameter, β, we simply evaluated the profiled likelihood on a grid of values on the interval $[-1, 1]$, yielding Figure 8.11. This exercise yields a point estimate of about $\hat{\beta} = -0.5$ that is quite precise, at least if we are to believe the confidence bounds implied by the classical Wilks, $2 \log \lambda \rightsquigarrow \chi_1^2$, theorem. Leaving the reliability of such intervals to future investigation, we

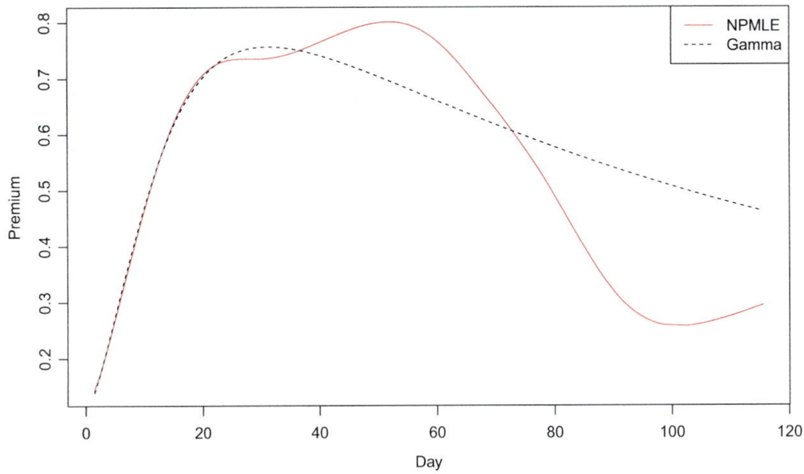

Figure 8.10. Life insurance rates for 10-day policies written for flies by their age, comparing the NPMLE and the parametric gamma solutions.

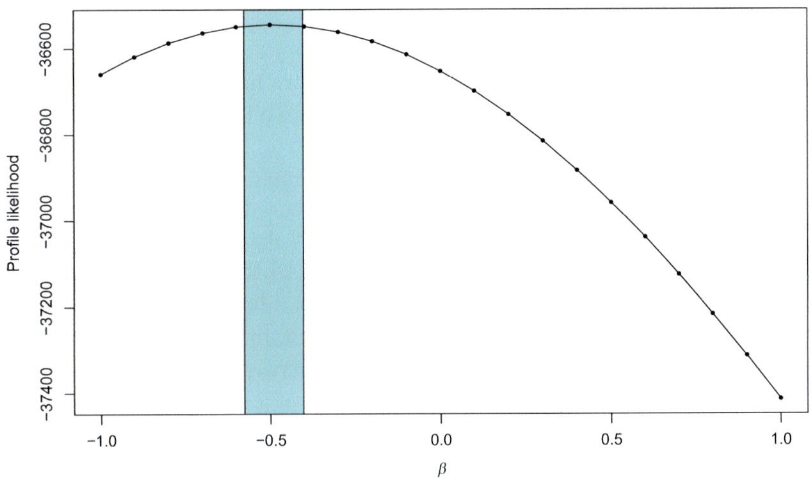

Figure 8.11. Profile likelihood for the initial cage density effect in the Weibull mixture model.

conclude simply that the negative estimated coefficient implies that higher density shifts the survival distribution to the right, thus prolonging lifetimes, and directly contradicting the conjecture of the Carey critics. This finding is confirmed by other methods, see for example Koenker and Geling (2001) where similar results are reported for both the Cox model and several quantile regression models.

The success of profile likelihood in a few cases prompts one to wonder how far similar methods can be extended to other semiparametric mixture settings.

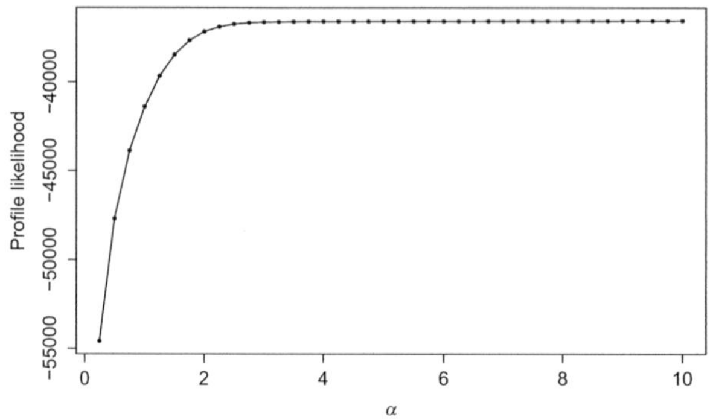

Figure 8.12. Profile likelihood for the Weibull shape parameter, α.

There is a considerable literature on this topic, pioneered by Lindsay. When profiling leads to fully adaptive estimation of structural parameters, not only do we get efficient estimates of those parameters, but as a by-product we also get valid inference from the profiled likelihood ratio statistic, see Murphy and van der Vaart (2000). The latter bonus is sometimes referred to as the Wilks phenomenon, see, for example, Fan et al. (2001).

But profiling is not always so perceptive, as we have seen in Section 5.4; sometimes it can lead the unwary toward disaster. To illustrate this less benign side of profile likelihood for frailty models we would like to briefly reconsider estimation of the Weibull shape parameter, α, based on the medfly data. In Figure 8.12 we show the profile likelihood for α based on the full medfly data. Based on our earlier results we know that $\alpha \approx 2.8$ fits the initial portion of the log hazard plot quite well. What does the profile likelihood have to say about it? The message is a bit confusing: The profile likelihood increases sharply up to about $\alpha = 2.8$ and then dramatically flattens out. In fact, closer examination reveals that the profile likelihood continues to increase beyond this value, but very, very gradually. Indeed, as $\alpha \to \infty$, the profile likelihood also tends to infinity. To understand this better it is helpful to consider how the estimated mixture distribution responds to changes in α. For small α, the estimated mixture distribution has only a single mass point, and this single mass point persists for a while; by the time we get to α between 2.5 and 3.0 though, we have five or six mass points as in Figure 8.4. As α becomes larger we get more and more mass points, eventually yielding positive mass corresponding to virtually all the distinct observed values. This is reminiscent of the familiar Dirac catastrophe produced by kernel density bandwidths chosen by maximum likelihood. Indeed, the situation is quite similar: As α becomes large the effective bandwidth of the baseline Weibull model becomes narrower, and more mass points are needed in the mixture distribution to mimic the density of the observed data.

So profile likelihood has failed us. Now what? There is a familiar litany of circumstances in which naive adherence to the principle of maximum likelihood leads to absurd results: various Gaussian examples in which driving variance parameters to zero yields unbounded likelihood at unlikely places in parameter space, estimation of the threshold parameter of the three parameter lognormal distribution, and many others. One approach that has proven successful in such situations is the maximum product spacing methods introduced by Cheng and Amin (1983) and Ranneby (1984). Roeder (1990) describes an application of this approach in astronomy that, although based on Gaussian assumptions, is qualitatively quite similar to our Weibull problem.

Log-product-spacing optimization can be viewed as a discretization of classical maximum likelihood. Let $G(x, \theta)$ denote the distribution function of a parametric model for a scalar random variable, X. Given a sample, $X_1, \ldots, X_n$ of identical copies of X, let

$$\Delta G_i(\theta) = G(X_{(i)}, \theta) - G(X_{(i-1)}, \theta),$$

for $i = 1, \ldots, n+1$ with $X_{(0)} = -\infty$ and $X_{(n+1)} = +\infty$ and $X_{(i)} : \; i = 1, \ldots, n$ denoting the order statistics of the original sample. Since $G(X, \theta_0)$ is uniform when evaluated at the true parameter θ_0 of the model, the $\Delta G_i(\theta_0)$ constitute a sample of uniform spacings for which there is an extensive theory. Considering

$$R_n(\theta) = \frac{1}{\sqrt{n+1}} \sum_{i=1}^{n+1} (\log(\Delta G_i(\theta)(n+1)) + \gamma)/(\pi^2/6 - 1)^{1/2}$$

with $\gamma \approx 0.577216$, the Euler constant, we have a normalized sum that satisfies a central limit theorem with a standard normal limiting distribution. Maximizing $R_n(\theta)$ with respect to θ requires computing the Kiefer–Wolfowitz mixture distribution, $\hat{G}(x, \theta)$, at each θ to obtain the profile log product spacing objective function. The function $R_n(\theta)$ behaves like the usual log-likelihood; this is to be expected since the summands can be viewed as difference quotient approximations of $g(\tilde{x}_i, \theta)$ for $\tilde{x}_i \in (X_{(i-1)}, X_{(i)})$. However, by avoiding the direct evaluation of densities we circumvent the pathological behavior of the log likelihood.

An important feature of the maximum product spacing method noted by Roeder (1990) is that for given θ, it selects a $\hat{G}(x, \theta)$ that is asymptotically equivalent to the mixture distribution estimated by nonparametric maximum likelihood that we have focused on thus far. For θ taking various values, we get a profiled objective function similar to the profiled nonparametric likelihood. Yet unlike the problematic profiled likelihood, the limiting form of $R_n(\theta)$ yields an estimating function centered at zero for the true parameter and a simple confidence interval construction for the structural parameter. Further details regarding the maximum product spacing method can be found in Section 12.4.

We have seen already that an α parameter that fits the left tail of the survival distribution can be estimated well by a simple regression of log hazards on log event times using data from the first few days of the experiment. This assumes that flies that only survive for the first k days are all from a nearly homogeneous parametric survival model. When we move on to the semiparametric mixture model using all the observations, a natural question becomes how reasonable it is to assume a global value for α while allowing scale heterogeneity with frailty. We employ a first-order form of the log-product-spacing method and find that the test strongly rejects the mixture models with $\alpha = 2.85$. However, when we use only the observations surviving up to 50 days, a subsample that actually contains 99.5% of the full sample, we obtain a test statistic of only 0.33 and the model is not rejected. Similar conclusions are drawn when we estimate gender-specific models. The message seems to be that the Weibull semiparametric mixture model fits the majority of the data quite well but fails to perform adequately for the extreme right tail.

This conclusion may simply reassert that estimating a fixed shape parameter in the Weibull mixture model is an extremely difficult task; this is indeed the impression one gets from the prior literature. Hahn (1994) shows that the information matrix is singular for the mixed Weibull proportional hazard model. When there are no covariates, the score function for α is identically zero, hence also the Fisher information. This means that the Weibull shape parameter cannot be estimated at a root-n rate. Various estimation strategies for α are nevertheless available, for example Honoré (1990), Honoré (1997) and Ishwaran (1996). We would like to highlight what seems to be a somewhat neglected paper by Ishwaran (1999) discussing the information loss phenomenon for a class of semiparametric mixture models. Ishwaran shows that for the Weibull mixture model, there is information loss for α's bigger than the true value α_0, so that with $\alpha > \alpha_0$, one can find a mixing distribution that produces a model that is arbitrarily close to the true model in the sense of Hellinger distance. This corresponds to the nearly flat region in our profile likelihood. Conversely, as he notes, it is curious that the same information loss phenomenon does not occur for α's that are smaller than α_0.

8.4 UNEMPLOYMENT DURATIONS WITH CENSORING

The medfly survival application is unusual in the sense that there is no censoring; we have 1.2 million complete survival times. In this section we return to more familiar economic territory and consider a model of unemployment durations similar to that of Heckman and Singer (1984). The data is taken from McCall (1996) and has been reanalyzed extensively in Cameron and Trivedi (2005). It is derived from the US Current Population Survey of Displaced Workers Supplement for the years 1986, 1988, 1990 and 1992. Individuals between the ages of 20 and 61 who were displaced from nonagricultural jobs due to plant closure, slack work or abolished positions are included in the sample. Of the 3,343 individuals, 1,073 are eventually reemployed in a full-time job. The remaining individuals will be considered right censored although some returned to part-time employment over the sample period.

We will retain our Weibull specification of the baseline hazard,

$$h(t|\theta) = \theta \exp\{-x^\top \beta\} t^{\alpha-1}, \quad \theta \sim G,$$

with a nonparametric frailty effect, θ. The proportional hazard covariate effect will be limited to an indicator of whether the individual applied for unemployment compensation at the outset of the unemployment spell. Thus, we have a scalar, β, parameter and the scalar shape parameter, α, of the Weibull distribution that we would like to estimate by maximum likelihood. Profile likelihood estimation of β is not really a problem since for any fixed α we obtain a nice quadratic shape for the log-likelihood as seen in panel (a) of 8.13. However, attempts to estimate α by profiling produce something like panel (b) of this figure. Log-likelihood increases quadratically for a while, but then, rather than behaving sensibly by turning back down, the log likelihood begins to increase linearly and continues to do so indefinitely. The resulting estimator, $\hat{\alpha} = +\infty$, is clearly nonsensical, but the question is: Can we salvage anything useful from this picture? We have conjectured in Section 5.4 that a point estimate and perhaps even a one-sided confidence interval may be rescued from this likelihood fiasco simply by identifying the change-point at which the log-likelihood makes its transition from being quadratic to being linear.

Fortunately, independent censoring is easily accounted for in such applications. When we have complete spell data, the log likelihood is

$$\ell(G) = \sum \log f_G(y_i),$$

where $f_G(y|\theta) = \int \varphi(y|\theta) dG(\theta)$ and $\varphi(y|\theta)$ is the baseline Weibull density. Denoting the censoring indicator by, δ_i, with censoring we have instead

$$\ell(G) = \sum \delta_i \log f_G(y_i) + (1 - \delta_i) S_G(y_i),$$

where S_G denotes the corresponding survival distribution of the Weibull. Dependent censoring raises difficult new issues as one might anticipate. The basic formulation of the NPMLE for Weibull mixtures is available in the `Weibullmix` function of the **REBayes** R package. The estimates shown in Figure 8.13 by the vertical lines were selected by iterating back and forth from β to α profiling out the frailty distribution G and estimating the change-point in the α plot based on the numerical first-order derivative of the profile log-likelihood. At this solution the frailty distribution is shown in Figure 8.14: There are four distinct mass points and a large mass point on the far left that corresponds to individuals who never attain full time employment within the sample period. It is of interest to know how $\hat{G}$ changes as one increases α beyond the change point we have estimated in Figure 8.13. Careful examination of the marginal density reveals that larger α can be compensated for by rescaling the location and number of mass points of $\hat{G}$. In particular, in our unemployment application the number of mass points of $\hat{G}$ grows slowly with α, and this produces a slow linear growth in the log likelihood. Thus, choosing

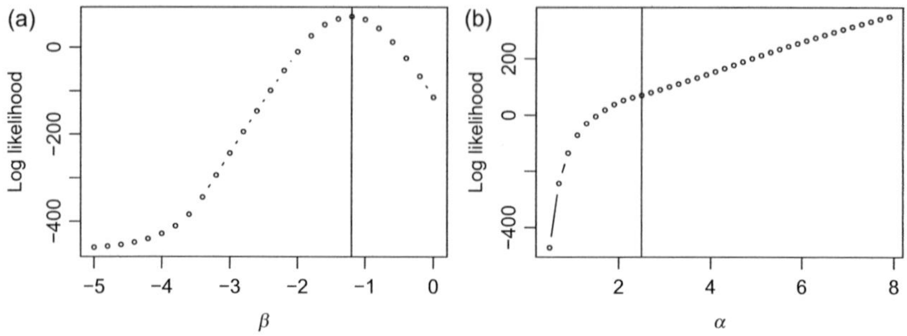

Figure 8.13. Profile log likelihood for unemployment compensation effect (a) and Weibull shape parameter (b).

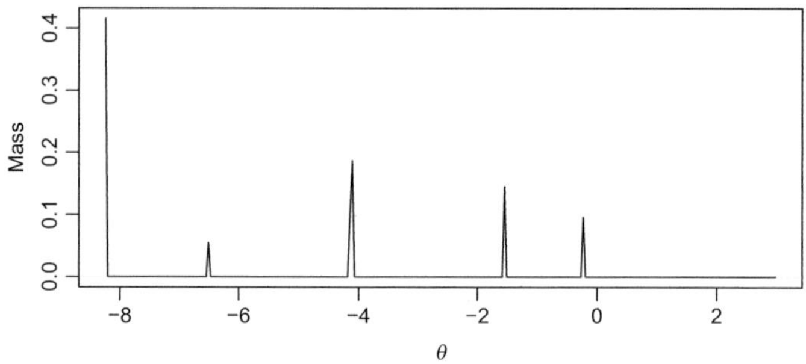

Figure 8.14. NPMLE frailty distribution $\hat{G}$.

$\hat{\alpha}$ as the change point can be viewed as an attempt to choose the solution with the most parsimonious, sparse $\hat{G}$.

Exercises

(1) Verify the observational equivalence of the Heckman–Singer identification example. Hint: If the integrals prove to be too taxing for paper and pencil, try Mathematica.

(2) Fixing the shape parameter estimate, $\hat{\alpha}$, compute a (Wilks) 95% confidence internal for the β coefficient for the unemployment spell data in Section 8.4. Provide an economic interpretation of the interval.

CHAPTER 9

Mixture Models for Categorical Data

Categorical data offers a rich source of empirical Bayes problems. In this chapter we will consider a few of these problems beginning with two classical logistic regression settings and then turning to models for binomial mixtures.

9.1 SEMIPARAMETRIC MIXTURE MODELS FOR BINARY RESPONSE

Generalized linear models figure prominently in many facets of applied statistics. Having already considered Poisson and Gaussian families of these models, we now turn our attention to binomial mixture models involving binary response. We will focus on the canonical logistic link function with the understanding that alternative link functions may be better adapted to some particular applications.

9.1.1 Bradley–Terry Ranking Models

Competitive play among pairs of individuals or teams naturally leads to attempts to construct ratings and rankings of players. The most common statistical model for rating and rankings based on paired comparison data is the Bradley and Terry (1952) model anticipated by Zermelo (1929) as a proposed method for rating chess players. Given $p + 1$ players of unknown "abilities," $\theta_0, \ldots, \theta_p$, it is postulated that the probability of player i defeating player j is given by

$$\pi_{ij} = \theta_i/(\theta_i + \theta_j),$$

and with a sufficiently rich history of competition, player ratings can be estimated by maximum likelihood. It is convenient to reparameterize abilities so $\theta_i = \log \theta_i$, and π_{ij} becomes

$$\pi_{ij} = \frac{1}{1 + \exp(-(\theta_i - \theta_j))}.$$

The log likelihood for n binary outcomes, $y_1, y_2, \ldots, y_n$, can be written with $h_\theta(x_k) = 1/(1 + \exp(-\theta^\top x_k))$, as

$$\ell(\theta|y) = \sum_{k=1}^{n} y_k \log(h_\theta(x_k)) + (1 - y_k)\log(1 - h_\theta(y_k)),$$

where for match k between i and j, x_k is a p vector with ith element 1, jth element -1, and other elements 0. Without loss of generality, we can set $\theta_0 = 0$. When there are multiple meetings between a given pair, (i, j), binary outcomes can be aggregated to write the likelihood in terms of the corresponding binomial outcomes. In this case the log likelihood can be expressed in terms of the θ_i's as

$$\ell(\theta|y) = K + \sum_{i=1}^{p} w_i \log\theta_i - \sum_{i<j} n_{ij} \log(\theta_i + \theta_j),$$

where w_i denotes the total number of "wins" of player i against all other competitors, and n_{ij} is the total number of matches between players i and j. From this it may be concluded that w_i, the Borda count, for each player is a sufficient statistic provided that n_{ij} is the same for all pairs (i, j). Borda ranking is a classical social choice mechanism usually attributed to the 18th century French mathematician Jean-Charles Borda. This observation has played an important role in recent literature on the analysis of paired comparisons in machine learning where A/B experiments constitute an important data structure, see for example Shah and Wainwright (2018). However, this sufficiency result holds if and only if the n_{ij} are uninformative about the ratings. This is plausible if matching is generated at random or by some balanced tournament design, but it certainly cannot be expected to hold if, for example, players are more likely to be matched with players of similar ability. In such cases one must resort to the MLE, which offers protection against such variability in "strength of schedule." Just counting wins is insufficient in designs like this when the n_{ij} are informative too.

In some applications the number of competing players, p, can be large relative to the number of matches, n, so some regularization may be beneficial. In Gu and Koenker (2022b) we have compared several regularization methods that we will briefly review here.

In some ranking problems it is plausible that there are only a few equivalence classes of ability, groups of players that are indistinguishable in terms of their proficiency. For the Bradley–Terry model this suggests a parametric form of penalization of the MLE that would shrink pairwise differences of the rating parameters toward zero. This is conveniently accomplished by solving

$$\min\{-\ell(\theta|y) + \lambda\|D\theta\|_1\},$$

where $\|D\theta\|_1 = \sum_{i<j} |\theta_i - \theta_j|$. This penalty has been proposed by Hocking et al. (2011) and employed by Varin et al. (2016), who refer to it as a ranking lasso penalty, to study journal rating and ranking. As λ is increased the θ

parameters are pulled together into fewer and fewer groups. This is somewhat analogous to total variation regularization for nonparametric smoothing where piecewise linear fitting selects only a few places at which the derivative of the estimated function jumps. The problem is convex and efficiently solved by interior point methods for moderate sample sizes.

Another approach to regularization is to treat the unconstrained logistic estimates, $\hat{\theta}$, as approximately independent draws from a Gaussian sequence model. When the problem design is unbalanced so the numbers of matched pairs are not equal, the MLE point estimates will have different precision, and off-diagonal elements of their covariance matrix are also more heterogeneous. We will ignore the latter aspect and treat the estimated maximum likelihood rating parameters as a sample from a Gaussian sequence model with heterogeneous scale parameters, arising from the mixture density

$$f_G(\hat{\theta}_i|\hat{\sigma}_i) = \int \varphi_{\hat{\sigma}_i}(\theta - \hat{\theta}_i)dG(\theta),$$

where φ_σ denotes the Gaussian density with mean zero and variance σ^2. The mixing distribution G can be estimated by nonparametric maximum likelihood as suggested earlier. Given a $\hat{G}$ we can compute posterior means for each θ_i, and from these ratings, rankings may be constructed.

Alternatively, one can use estimated ratings to construct ranks based on pairwise comparisons of the ratings,

$$R_i = \sum_{j \neq i} \mathbb{1}\{\theta_i \geq \theta_j\}.$$

When the θ_i's are iidly Gaussian, Laird and Louis (1989) have considered the quadratic loss, $\sum_{i=1}^n (\hat{R}_i - R_i)^2$, which by Bayes rule yields the posterior mean rank. We can approximate this by

$$\begin{aligned}\hat{R}_i &= \sum_{j \neq i} \mathbb{P}(\theta_i \geq \theta_j \mid \hat{\theta}_1, \ldots, \hat{\theta}_n) \\ &= \sum_{j \neq i} \frac{\int_{\theta_i \geq \theta_j} \varphi_{ij}((\hat{\theta}_i, \hat{\theta}_j))d\hat{G}(\theta_i)d\hat{G}(\theta_j)}{\int \varphi_{ij}((\hat{\theta}_i, \hat{\theta}_j))d\hat{G}(\theta_i)d\hat{G}(\theta_j)},\end{aligned}$$

where $\varphi_{ij}(z)$ is a bivariate Gaussian density with mean, $\mu = (\theta_i, \theta_j)$ and covariance matrix $\Sigma(i, j)$, estimated from the Hessian of the MLE.

Gu and Koenker (2022b) describe a small simulation experiment to compare the performance of these ranking methods. As expected when players meet equally often, or simply randomly, the Borda ranking performs decently as measured by their Kendall correlation with the true ranks. However when players are assigned to have dissimilar abilities the Borda rankings fail miserably. With 100 players the NPMLE empirical Bayes methods perform similarly, with a slight advantage to the posterior mean rank method. The parametric group lasso method is competitive only at the largest sample sizes considered.

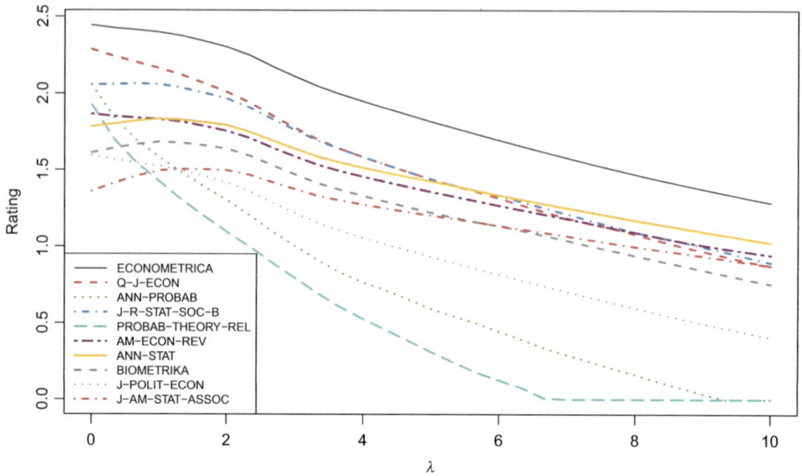

Figure 9.1. Grouped lasso shrinkage plot.

Stigler et al. (1995) and Stigler (1994) have proposed a bilateral trade model of journal influence and ranking based on pairwise citation counts. Citations in journal j of papers appearing in journal i are viewed as a measure of the influence of journal i on journal j. Ratings of journal influence are then formulated as a Bradley–Terry model, and rankings can be evaluated from estimated ratings. We consider pairwise citation counts for 86 journals spanning the econometrics/statistics fields over the decade 2010–2019 as reported in Clarivate Journal Citation Reports. Self-citations, that is, citations by a journal to papers that appeared in the same journal, while perhaps interesting in other contexts, are ignored in the subsequent analysis.

Figure 9.1 illustrates the shrinkage effects of the ranking lasso procedure for the top 10 journals according to the unconstrained maximum likelihood estimates. *Econometrica* is the most highly rated journal and remains so over the whole range of $\lambda \in [0, 10]$. The *Quarterly Journal of Economics* appears to be a strong second place finisher, but careful inspection of the figure actually reveals that the unconstrained MLE very slightly favors the *Annals of Probability*. It may seem surprising that both probability journals are so highly rated, but a little reflection reveals that although they are rarely cited by the other journals they almost never cite these journals; this is the hallmark of an influential journal. Once shrinkage is applied the probability journals fade into obscurity, and more mainstream journals acquire more prominence. This can be attributed to the relatively poor precision of the probability journal ratings. It raises the inevitable question: How should one choose λ? This is always controversial. If we adopt the Schwarz (1978) BIC criterion that penalizes parametric dimension, we obtain a λ around 1 implying a very modest amount of shrinkage. This is reflected in Table 9.1 where we compare rankings of the top 10 journals based on several procedures. The last column of this table,

Table 9.1. *Comparison of top 10 journal influence rankings for five methods.*

	MLE	RMLE	KWPM	Borda	WBorda
ECONOMETRICA	1	1	1	4	1
Q-J-ECON	2	2	2	5	3
ANN-PROBAB	3	3	4	13	7
J-R-STAT-SOC-B	4	4	3	7	2
PROBAB-THEORY-REL	5	5	5	19	9
AM-ECON-REV	6	6	6	1	6
ANN-STAT	7	7	7	3	4
BIOMETRIKA	8	8	8	6	5
J-POLIT-ECON	9	9	9	9	10
J-AM-STAT-ASSOC	10	10	10	2	8

labeled WBorda, uses a weighted form of Borda scores, weighted by the total number of times the individual journal is citing or cited.

As anticipated the ranking lasso regularization doesn't alter the MLE ranking, and the Kiefer–Wolfowitz posterior mean ranking only flips the rankings of the *Annals of Probability* and *JRSS(B)*. The Borda rankings deprecate both probability journals and elevate *JASA* and *JRSS(B)*, which publish more papers. The desire to rank performance of individuals and institutions is deeply ingrained in the human psyche but very challenging from a formal decision theory perspective, as we have seen in Section 7.2.

9.1.2 Rasch Models for Item Response Analysis

The design and analysis of psychological and educational tests has produced a rich literature for studying models of binary response. Intensely studied within this literature is the Rasch (1960) model, which serves as a prototype for a wide variety of longitudinal models of binary choice that have evolved within econometrics and other fields. In its simplest form the Rasch model considers a test administered to a group of individuals. It is assumed that the probability that person i responds correctly, $y_{ij} = 1$, or incorrectly, $y_{ij} = 0$, to question j is given by

$$f(y_{ij} \mid \theta_i, \beta_j) = \frac{\exp(y_{ij}(\theta_i - \beta_j))}{1 + \exp(\theta_i - \beta_j)} \qquad i = 1, \ldots, n, \quad j = 1, \ldots, m.$$

The parameter θ_i represents the putative "ability" of person i, and the parameter β_j represents the difficulty of question j. It is further assumed that responses are independent over individuals, and over questions for a given individual. Without loss of generality it can be assumed that $\beta_1 = 0$. Denoting $\boldsymbol{y}_i = (y_{i1}, \ldots, y_{im})$ and the "raw" scores for each individual by $s_i = \sum_{j=1}^{m} y_{ij}$, the likelihood can be factored as

$$L(\boldsymbol{\theta}, \boldsymbol{\beta}) = \prod_{i=1}^{n} f(\boldsymbol{y}_i \mid \boldsymbol{\theta}, \boldsymbol{\beta}) = \prod_{i=1}^{n} h(\boldsymbol{y}_i \mid s_i, \boldsymbol{\beta}) \varphi(s_i \mid \boldsymbol{\beta}, \theta_i).$$

The score, s_i is a complete sufficient statistic for θ_i. From Andersen (1970) it follows that the difficulty parameter, $\boldsymbol{\beta}$, can be consistently estimated by maximizing the conditional likelihood,

$$\tilde{L}(\boldsymbol{\beta}) = \prod_{i=1}^{n} h(\boldsymbol{y}_i \mid s_i, \boldsymbol{\beta}) = \prod_{i=1}^{n} \exp(\boldsymbol{\beta}^\top \boldsymbol{y}_i - \kappa(\boldsymbol{\beta}, s_i)),$$

where $\kappa(\cdot,\cdot)$ denotes the normalizing constant of the canonical exponential family. Strasser (2012) describes $\mathcal{O}(m^{-2})$ refinements of the asymptotic covariance matrix of the Gaussian approximation of the limiting behavior of this conditional maximum likelihood estimator of $\boldsymbol{\beta}$.

The item difficulty parameters are of considerable interest, if only because their heterogeneity is likely to reveal shortcomings of raw scores in reflecting ability. As in other incidental parameter problems maximum likelihood estimation based on the joint likelihood can yield inconsistent estimators for θ. It is thus natural following Lindsay et al. (1991) to consider mixture models in which we seek to estimate the distribution of the $\boldsymbol{\theta}$ parameters. This suggests a mixture likelihood of the form

$$L(\boldsymbol{\beta}, G) = \prod_{i=1}^{n} \int f(\boldsymbol{y}_i \mid \theta, \boldsymbol{\beta}) dG(\theta).$$

If there are only a few test items, m, this mixture approach raises some delicate issues of identification. See appendix A of Lindsay et al. (1991) for a detailed treatment of the $m = 2$ case. When m is large so the $\boldsymbol{\beta}$ parameters can be reasonably reliably estimated, the typical phenomenon is that the sample frequency of the outcome $\boldsymbol{y}_i$ falls outside of the model space due to sampling errors, which then implies that the maximum likelihood estimator for G together with the estimated $\boldsymbol{\beta}$ implies a vector of frequency that is closest to the sample frequency in the Kullback–Leibler distance. We now compare this strategy with the fixed effect estimator for the abilities.

Fixing the estimated $\boldsymbol{\beta}$ parameters, maximum likelihood estimation of the ability parameters is separable and can be computed by solving the nonlinear equations

$$0 = \nabla_\theta \sum_j \log \frac{\exp(y_{ij}(\theta_i - \hat{\beta}_j))}{1 + \exp(\theta_i - \hat{\beta}_j)}.$$

Simplifying, we have

$$s_i = \sum_j \frac{\exp(\theta_i - \hat{\beta}_j)}{1 + \exp(\theta_i - \hat{\beta}_j)},$$

and since s_i can take at most $m + 1$ distinct values, denoted as $\{s_0, \ldots, s_m\}$, the MLE for $(\theta_1, \ldots, \theta_n)$ can take at most $m + 1$ distinct values, denoted by t_k as solutions to

$$s_k = \sum_j \frac{\exp(t_k - \hat{\beta}_j)}{1 + \exp(t_k - \hat{\beta}_j)}, \qquad k = 0, \ldots, m.$$

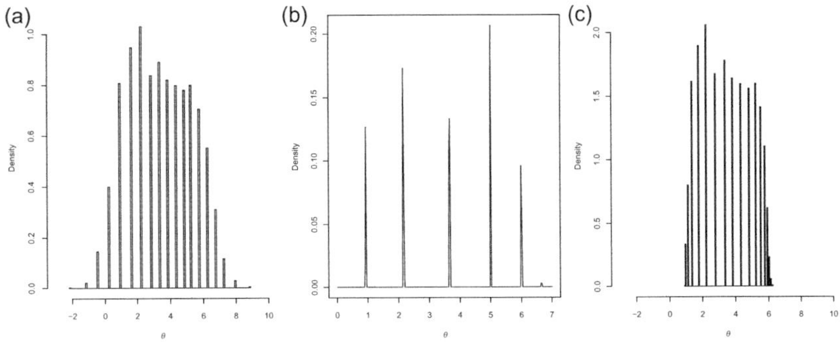

Figure 9.2. Comparison of maximum likelihood and empirical Bayes estimates of ability in the Rasch model: Panel (a) shows a histogram of the maximum likelihood estimates of the 5,000 ability parameters. Panel (b) depicts the NPMLE of the mixing distribution, $\hat{G}$ of the Rasch model, and panel (c) shows a histogram of the posterior means of the ability parameters based on the estimated $\hat{G}$.

These equations can be solved one by one for unique values $\hat{t}_k$ since the right side is monotone in t_k. All subjects with the score s_k receive the same ability estimate, t_k.

To illustrate, we will consider a test with $m = 20$ items and $n = 5{,}000$ subjects. Item difficulty is equally likely to be an integer from 1 to 10, and ability is again uniformly distributed on the integers from 1 to 6. A histogram of the maximum likelihood estimates of the ability parameters is shown in panel (a) of Figure 9.2. There are 19 distinct values for the total scores s_i, somewhat more spread out than the true ability parameters that vary only from one to six. With the same data we can now consider the empirical Bayes estimation of the ability parameters. Again conditioning on the conditional maximum likelihood estimates of the difficulty parameters, panel (b) of Figure 9.2 depicts the estimated mixing distribution, $\hat{G}(\theta)$. It is astonishingly accurate, with mass points quite near each of the integers from one to six, except for an estimated mass point between three and four and the small mass point between six and seven. Given this estimated prior, we can compute posterior mean ability for subjects with each of the possible scores as illustrated in the histogram in panel (c) of Figure 9.2. Comparing panels (a) and (b) of Figure 9.2 it is clear that the empirical Bayes nonparametric shrinkage produces a much more accurate picture of the ability distribution for this example.

Suppose we were to focus on $\mathbb{E}(e^{\theta}|s)$, instead of $\mathbb{E}(\theta|s)$. We will still have only $m+1$ distinct values, but remarkably these values can be identified directly from the data without any explicit knowledge of G, that is, we have a Tweedie type formula,

$$\mathbb{E}[\exp(\theta)|S = s] = \frac{\mathbb{P}(S = s + 1)}{\mathbb{P}(S = s)} h(s, \boldsymbol{\beta})$$

with

$$h(s,\boldsymbol{\beta}) = \sum_{\boldsymbol{y}_i:1^\top \boldsymbol{y}_i=s} \exp(-\boldsymbol{\beta}^\top \boldsymbol{y}_i) \Big/ \sum_{\boldsymbol{y}_i:1^\top \boldsymbol{y}_i=s+1} \exp(-\boldsymbol{\beta}^\top \boldsymbol{y}_i).$$

For any value of $s < m$, this quantity can be point identified from the data despite the fact that G is not point identified. We can view $h(s,\boldsymbol{\beta})$ as an estimator for e^θ. Recall that the MLE of θ, and hence the MLE of e^θ, is also a function that depends only on s and $\boldsymbol{\beta}$. We can verify that $h(s,\boldsymbol{\beta})$ is not the MLE e^θ but relates to the MLE in the sense that

$$h(s,\hat{\boldsymbol{\beta}}) = \exp(\hat{\theta}) \frac{\mathbb{P}(S = s|\hat{\theta},\hat{\boldsymbol{\beta}})}{\mathbb{P}(S = s+1|\hat{\theta},\hat{\boldsymbol{\beta}})},$$

where $(\hat{\theta},\hat{\boldsymbol{\beta}})$ are the maximum likelihood estimators of the parameters of the Rasch model, and

$$\mathbb{P}(S = s|\hat{\theta},\hat{\boldsymbol{\beta}}) = \frac{\exp(s\hat{\theta}) \sum_{\boldsymbol{y}_i:1'\boldsymbol{y}_i=s} \exp(-\boldsymbol{\beta}'\boldsymbol{y}_i)}{\prod_j (1+\exp(\hat{\theta}-\hat{\beta}_j))}$$

is the estimated probability of a total score being s for given $(\hat{\theta},\hat{\boldsymbol{\beta}})$. The posterior mean $\mathbb{E}[e^\theta|S=s]$ can thus be viewed as a shrinkage estimator based upon the preliminary estimator $h(s,\boldsymbol{\beta})$ with the shrinkage factor $\mathbb{P}(S=s+1)/\mathbb{P}(S=s)$. This is closely related to the Tweedie formula proposed by Robbins (1956) for the Poisson. There, when $Y|\lambda \sim \text{Pois}(\lambda)$ and $\lambda \sim G$, we have the Tweedie formula

$$\mathbb{E}[\lambda|Y=y] = (y+1)\frac{\mathbb{P}(Y=y+1)}{\mathbb{P}(Y=y)},$$

so we can view $y+1$ as a preliminary estimator for λ and $\mathbb{P}(Y=y+1)/\mathbb{P}(Y=y)$ as a shrinkage factor.

9.2 BINOMIAL MIXTURE MODELS

To illustrate the binomial mixture model we reconsider an experiment of Beckett and Diaconis (1994), who describe it as follows:

> The example involves repeated rolls of a common thumbtack. A one was recorded if the tack landed point up and a zero was recorded if the tack landed point down. All tacks started point down. Each tack was flicked or hit with the fingers from where it last rested. A fixed tack was flicked 9 times. The data are recorded in Table 1. There are 320 9-tuples. These arose from 16 different tacks, 2 "flickers," and 10 surfaces. The tacks vary considerably in shape and in proportion of ones. The surfaces varied from rugs through tablecloths through bathroom floors.

Given the heterogeneity of the experimental conditions, and following Liu (1996), we treat the data as though it arose from a mixture of binomials with $k=9$ and 320 independent realizations with mixture density

$$f_G(y) = \mathbb{P}(Y=y) = \int \binom{k}{y} p^y (1-p)^{k-y} dG(p).$$

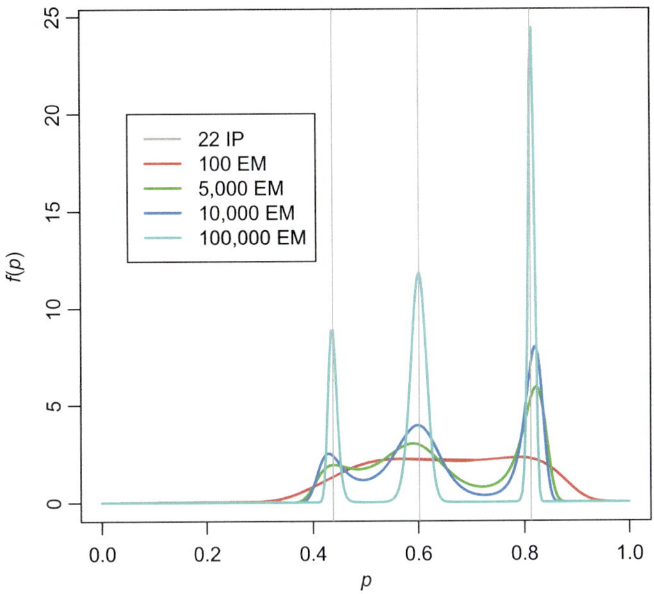

Figure 9.3. Several NPMLE estimates of the binomial mixture model of tack flicking: Smooth curves depict NPMLE estimates based on the EM algorithm with several limits on the number of iterations as indicated in the legend. The vertical gray lines represent the location of the point masses estimated by the interior point solution to the same problem.

In Figure 9.3 we compare several estimates of the mixing density, dG, produced by the EM algorithm with varying numbers of iterations. Even after 100,000 iterations the EM estimates are quite dispersed, but it is clear that EM is tending to the discrete solution represented in the figure by the three vertical gray lines found by interior point convex optimization.

Discrete settings like this one pose some special identification problems. Only k distinct frequencies, $f_G = \{f_{G,1}, \ldots, f_{G,k}\}$, are determined by observations from this binomial model, and they are uniquely determined by the moments $m_{G,j} = \int p^j dG(p)$ of the latent random variable p. For instance, with $k = 3$ we have

$$\begin{aligned} f_{G,1} &= 3m_{G,1} - 6m_{G,2} + 3m_{G,3}, \\ f_{G,2} &= 3m_{G,2} - 3m_{G,3}, \\ f_{G,3} &= m_{G,3}. \end{aligned}$$

Thus, distributions of the random variable p supported on $[0,1]$ that have the same first k raw moments are observationally equivalent. Let $\mathcal{S}_k$ be the unit simplex of dimension k, and $\mathcal{F}$ denote the set of $f \in \mathcal{S}_k$ with elements

$$f_j = \int \binom{k}{j} p^j (1-p)^{k-j} dG(p), \; j = 0, \ldots, k,$$

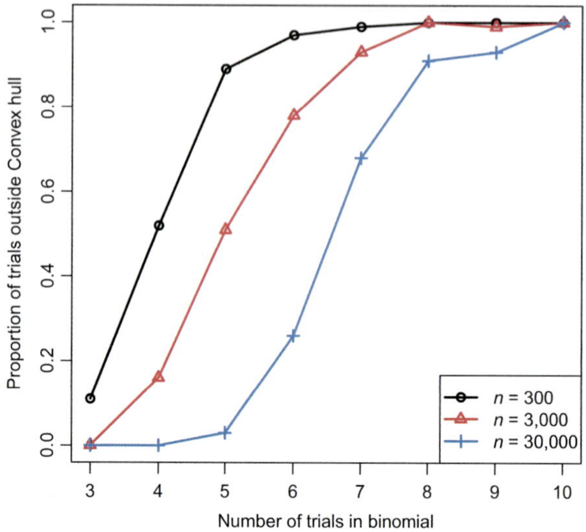

Figure 9.4. Proportion of realized $\hat{f}_n \notin \mathcal{F}$ for binomial problems for three sample sizes. Simulation is based on 100 replications.

for some distribution, G. Point identification of G is only possible in the limit as $k \to \infty$. In finite samples, observed frequencies, $\hat{f}_n$, need not lie in $\mathcal{F}$; indeed the relative volume of $\mathcal{F}$ to $\mathcal{S}_k$ declines dramatically from 0.6 at $k = 2$ to about 2×10^{-8} at $k = 10$, as shown by Wood (1992).

In Figure 9.4 we plot the proportion of realized $\hat{f}_n \notin \mathcal{F}$ for binomial problems with various k and three different sample sizes n. When $k < 5$ the probability is appreciable that $\hat{f}_n$ will lie in $\mathcal{F}$, but for larger k it is quite unlikely, so estimation involves projection into this set.

When $\hat{f}_n \in \mathcal{F}$, unless it is on the boundary, we may find multiple distributions G all leading to the same frequency $\hat{f}_n$. On the contrary when $\hat{f}_n \notin \mathcal{F}$, there are a variety of ways one might go about projecting $\hat{f}_n$ onto $\mathcal{F}$. In our tack-flicking example the NPMLE chooses the nearest Kullback–Leibler point that is unique by the strict convexity of the objective function displayed below:

$$\hat{G} = \underset{G \in \mathcal{G}}{\text{argmin}} \sum_{j=0}^{k} \hat{f}_{j,n} \log f_{G,j},$$

where $f_{G,j} = \int \binom{k}{j} p^j (1-p)^{k-j} dG(p)$. Alternatively, one can consider a method of moments implementation: Let

$$\tilde{G} = \text{argmin}_{G \in \mathcal{G}} (\hat{f}_n - f_G)^\top W (\hat{f}_n - f_G),$$

where W is a weighting matrix. Provided that the matrix W is positive semidefinite, the method of moments estimator solves a convex quadratic programming problem.

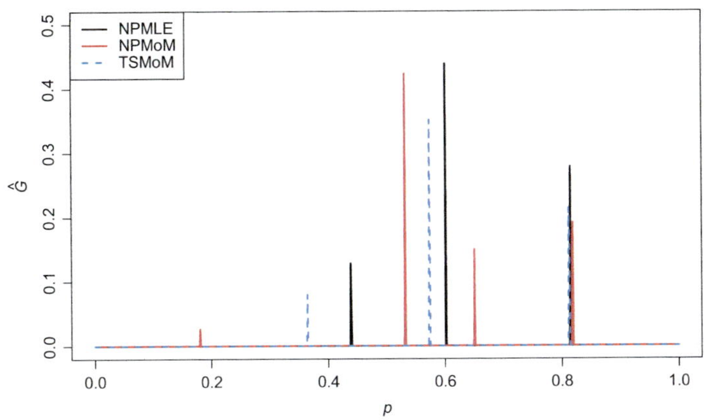

Figure 9.5. Comparison of the NPMLE and NPMoM estimates of G for the Beckett and Diaconis (1994) tack data.

In either case numerical computations proceed by taking a fine grid of points $0 < u_1 < u_2 \cdots < u_m < 1$ as potential mass points of G, with associated masses $g_1, \cdots, g_m$, so the constraint $\hat{f} \in \mathcal{F}$ may be written as

$$\hat{f}_j = \sum_{i=1}^{m} \binom{k}{j} h_i^j (1 - h_i)^{k-j} g_i,$$

where the g_i are constrained to be nonnegative and sum to one. Sparsity of the solutions with either projection is ensured by the Carathéodory theorem. When k varies within the binomial samples it is straightforward to extend the foregoing methods provided that we are willing to condition on the k_i's and assume that the mixing distribution G is common to each realization of the experiment. It should be stressed that despite such projections producing a unique $\hat{G}$, the fundamental identification problem persists. With only a finite number of moments of G available we cannot construct a consistent estimator, and G remains partially identified.

To illustrate the potential difference between the NPMLE and the nonparametric method of moments estimators of the mixing distribution G, we return to the Beckett and Diaconis (1994) tack flipping data and in Figure 9.5 contrast the NPMLE estimate in black with the NPMoM estimate in red based on an identity weighing matrix. The TSMoM is a two-step MoM estimator: In the first step we obtain NPMoM and calculate the implied $f_{\tilde{G}}$; then we construct $W = \text{diag}(f_{\tilde{G}}) - f_{\tilde{G}} f_{\tilde{G}}^\top$. Both estimates are discrete and very sparse. It would be interesting to know why the NPMoM estimate is somewhat more dispersed than the NPMLE.

9.3 DIRICHLET PRIORS AND THE NONPARAMETRIC BAYESIAN ABYSS

From a formal Bayesian perspective nonparametric estimation of probability distributions or densities by maximum likelihood is a forbidden activity since it comes with no associated posterior distribution to assess its precision. For this reason there was an obvious need for a more general strategy for constructing priors for nonparametric Bayesian problems. Ferguson (1973) first proposed using the Dirichlet process as a prior distribution for estimating an unknown probability measure. Antoniak (1974) and Ferguson (1983) extended the Dirichlet process idea to mixtures of Dirichlet processes.

Let $Y_1, \ldots, Y_n$ be independent random variables with respective Gaussian densities $\varphi(y|\theta_i) \sim \mathcal{N}(\mu_i, V_i)$, and assume that the $\theta_i = (\mu_i, V_i)$ parameters are independently distributed with distribution G. A Dirichlet process prior, $G \sim \mathcal{D}(\alpha G_0)$, where $\alpha > 0$ is a real scalar, and G_0 is a distribution function on the support of the θ_i's; G_0 is the expectation of G. This implies that the random prior probability, $G(\theta)$, has a beta distribution with parameters $\alpha G_0(\theta)$ and $\alpha(1 - G_0(\theta))$, and any vector of prior probabilities, $(G(\theta_1), \ldots, G(\theta_K))$, has a Dirichlet distribution. The concentration parameter α controls the precision of the prior, or how concentrated the prior is about its expectation G_0.

Following Escobar and West (1994) we will describe some basic features of this formulation that relate it to the compound decision framework of Robbins. Taking $(\theta_1, \ldots, \theta_n)$ as given, the conditional distribution of a future draw, θ_{n+1}, is

$$\theta_{n+1}|\theta_1, \ldots, \theta_n \sim \theta a_n G_0(\theta) + a_n \sum_{i=1}^{n} \delta_{\theta_i}(\theta),$$

where $a_n = 1/(\theta + n)$. This is only fanciful since it relies on knowledge of the θ_i's, but it is analogous to the oracle procedures we have encountered earlier, except that the usual empirical distribution function of the θ_i's is augmented by the prior, G_0 contribution. As noted by Antoniak (1974) the mixture of Dirichlet processes produces quite sparse models for the θ_i's. This is especially clear when α is small. Given a few θ_i's it is likely that the next draw will be one of those already drawn rather than a draw from G_0, so the natural evolution of the process produces clumps of realizations located at the values drawn early in the process. For $\alpha = 1$, a typical initial value for precision, it can be shown that the number of these groups grows like $\log n$. Of course, the mass associated with these values depends upon the shape of the G_0 choice, but this is another reflection of the fact that only a few discrete mass points are sufficient to characterize an informative prior.

Let $\theta_k^*, k = 1, \ldots, K < n$ denote the points of accumulation of the θ_i's with associated mass n_k; we can write the posterior distribution of the next, θ_{n+1},

$$\theta_{n+1}|\theta_1, \ldots, \theta_n \sim \alpha a_n G_0(\theta) + a_n \sum_{k=1}^{K} n_k \delta_{\theta_k^*}(\theta),$$

which is also often referred to as the predictive distribution. This is obviously also useless unless we can find a way to remove the reliance on knowing the unobservable θ_i's. For this we need to venture into the realm of Markov chain Monte Carlo.

For density estimation Escobar and West (1994) suggest choosing G_0, the mean of G as Gaussian/inverse-gamma, that is, $\mu_k|V_k \sim \mathcal{N}(\mu_0, \tau V_k)$ for some mean μ_0 and scale factor τ, and $V_k^{-1} \sim \text{inv}\Gamma(s/2, S/2)$, with scale and shape parameters $s/2$ and $S/2$, respectively. Given hyperparameters μ_0, τ, s, S, we can express the predictive distribution of Y_{n+1} given the data, $D_n = (Y_1, \ldots, Y_n)$, as

$$\mathbb{P}(Y_{n+1}|D_n, \theta_1, \ldots, \theta_n) = \int \mathbb{P}(Y_{n+1}|\theta_{n+1}) d\mathbb{P}(\theta_{n+1}|\theta_1, \ldots, \theta_n),$$

with

$$Y_{n+1}|\theta_{n+1} \sim \alpha a_n T_s(m, M) + a_n \sum_{k=1}^{K} n_k \mathcal{N}(\mu_k^*, V_k^*),$$

where $T_s(m, M)$ is Student's t distribution with s degrees of freedom, center m and scale $\sqrt{M}$ with $M = (1+\tau)S/s$. This formulation has close connections to conventional kernel density estimation with a Gaussian kernel and bandwidth h, where $Y_{n+1}|D_n \sim n^{-1} \sum_{i=1}^{n} \mathcal{N}(y_i, h)$, except that the observed y_i are shrunken toward their means, and the entire density is shrunken toward the prior, $T_s(m, M)$. Escobar and West (1994) describe two MCMC Gibbs sampling algorithms to simulate the posterior for this problem. We will discuss these in more detail in the context of binomial mixtures.

9.3.1 Dirichlet Priors for Binomial Mixture Models

A natural prior for binomial mixtures is Dirichlet, $\mathcal{D}(\alpha G_0(\theta))$, with G_0 chosen to be conjugate as Beta$(1, 1)$. In Figure 9.6 we show two estimates of the posterior density of θ corresponding to two values of α on the tack data: a typical "noninformative" choice would be $\alpha = 1$ that produces the smoother blue density, and the even more noninformative choice, $\alpha = 0.01$ that gives the black density that further accentuates the mass around $\theta = 0.5$ and $\theta = 0.8$. Dirichlet priors have broad applicability to many nonparametric statistical problems. In this section we will briefly describe their application to estimating binomial mixture problems.

Early expositions of empirical Bayes methods including the influential paper of Efron and Morris (1977) consider prediction of baseball batting averages. Emulating this tradition, in Gu and Koenker (2017a) we compared predictions of several methods with predictions based on empirical Bayes nonparametric maximum likelihood. In the simplest formulation, we have binomial observations on n players, $Y_{1i} \sim \text{Bin}(k_{1i}, \theta_{1i})$, where k_{1i} is the number of "at bats" of player i in the first half of the season and θ_{1i} is their success probability. We would like to predict batting averages for the second half of the season for each player. Players have different abilities, so it is natural to consider a mixture model in which the $\theta_i|k_i \sim G$. Binomial observations are often transformed to consider Gaussian formulations and Stein rules; however when G is Gaussian this approach yields Bayes rules that shrink all players

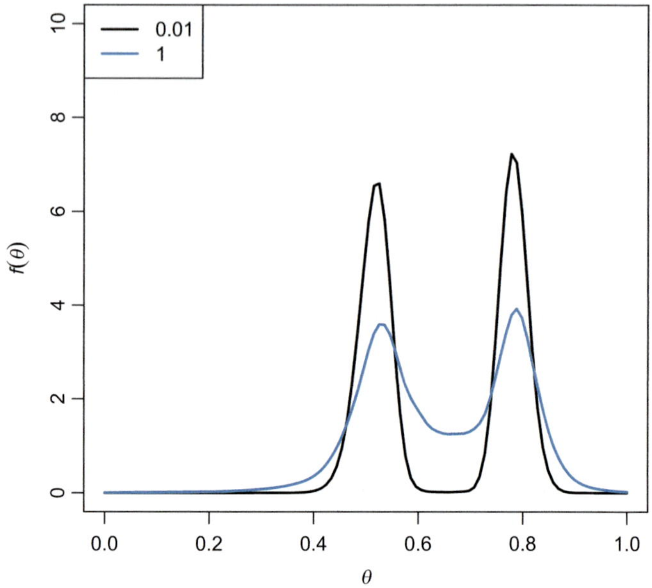

Figure 9.6. Posterior mean predictive densities for binomial mixture model of tack flicking: Two posterior mean densities for weak mixture of Dirichlet process priors. A variant of the Escobar and West (1994) MCMC algorithm as implemented in the function `DPbetabinom` of the **DPpackage** has been used to compute these estimates.

toward a common mean. There have been frequently expressed concerns that particularly good players were overly penalized by such rules. We will describe how the mixture of Dirichlet process prior may be used in a simple version of this binomial model.

We do not observe samples on $\theta_1, \ldots, \theta_n$ directly; instead we would like to find the posterior distribution of θ conditional on observing $y_1, \ldots, y_n$. Antoniak (1974) shows that if $\theta_1, \ldots, \theta_n$ are drawn from a distribution G, with Dirichlet process prior $\mathcal{D}(\alpha G_0)$, and if $Y_1, \ldots, Y_n$ are exchangeable random variables with density $f(y) = \int \varphi(y|\theta) dG(\theta)$, then the posterior distribution of G given $y_1, \ldots, y_n$ is a mixture of Dirichlet processes:

$$p(\theta_1, \ldots, \theta_n | y_1, \ldots, y_n) \sim \int \cdots \int \mathcal{D}\left(\alpha G_0 + \sum_{i=1}^{n} \delta_{\theta_i}\right) dG(\theta_1, \ldots, \theta_n | y_1, \ldots, y_n).$$

The above posterior seems rather intractable; however with the help of the Pólya urn representation of the Dirichlet process by Blackwell and MacQueen (1973), one obtains a simplified form of the posterior distribution, see (Lo, 1984). We will see that this representation opens the way for MCMC sampling from the posterior distribution.

The Pólya urn representation provides the following conditional distribution:

$$\theta_i|\theta_1,\ldots,\theta_{i-1} \sim \frac{\alpha}{\alpha+i-1}G_0(\theta_i) + \frac{1}{\alpha+i-1}\sum_{j=1}^{i-1}\delta_{\theta_j}(\theta_i), \quad (9.1)$$

where δ_{θ_j} denotes the (Dirac) distribution with mass one at point θ_j. In the Pólya urn scheme each new draw θ_i is a random draw from the base distribution G_0 with probability $\frac{\alpha}{\alpha+i-1}$ and otherwise takes the value of one of the previous $i-1$ θ's, each with probability $1/(\alpha+i-1)$. The joint distribution is therefore

$$p(\theta_1,\ldots,\theta_n) = \prod_{i=1}^{n}\frac{\alpha G_0(\theta_i) + \sum_{j=1}^{i-1}\delta_{\theta_j}(\theta_i)}{\alpha+i-1},$$

and the posterior distribution of $(\theta_1,\ldots,\theta_n|y_1,\ldots,y_n)$ can thus be written as

$$p(\theta_1,\ldots,\theta_n|y_1,\ldots,y_n) \propto \prod_{i=1}^{n} f(y_i|\theta_i)\frac{\alpha G_0(\theta_i) + \sum_{j=1}^{i-1}\delta_{\theta_j}(\theta_i)}{\alpha+i-1}. \quad (9.2)$$

At this point we have integrated out the infinite dimensional object G, the distribution for θ.

Our aim is to sample from the above posterior distribution. This can be accomplished by simulating a Markov chain that has the posterior as its stationary distribution. The Gibbs sampling algorithm as described in Escobar and West (1994) provides a simple way to do this. The posterior distribution of θ_i conditional on the remaining parameters $\theta_{(-i)} = (\theta_1,\ldots,\theta_{i-1},\theta_{i+1},\ldots,\theta_n)$ and data $\mathbf{y}$ is such that we only need to track one variable at each step instead of all n of them. A convenient implementation chooses G_0 as the conjugate prior. For the binomial setting, this leads to choosing G_0 as a beta distribution with density denoted $\mathcal{B}(a,b)$. A normal mixture example is provided in Escobar (1994) and Escobar and West (1994).

We can write the posterior distribution as

$$\begin{aligned}
p(\theta_i|\theta_{(-i)},\mathbf{y}) &= \frac{f(y_i|\theta_1,\ldots,\theta_n)\cdot p(\theta_i|\theta_{(-i)})}{\int f(y_i|\theta_1,\ldots,\theta_n)\cdot p(\theta_i|\theta_{(-i)})d\theta_i} \\
&\propto \frac{\alpha}{\alpha+n-1}\mathcal{B}(a,b)f(y_i|\theta_i) + \frac{1}{\alpha+n-1}\sum_{j\neq i} f(y_i|\theta_j)\delta_{\theta_j} \\
&\propto \frac{\alpha}{\alpha+n-1}\frac{B(y_i+a,k_i-y_i+b)}{B(a,b)}\mathcal{B}(y_i+a,k_i-y_i+b) \\
&+ \frac{1}{\alpha+n-1}\sum_{j\neq i}\theta_j^{y_i}(1-\theta_j)^{k_i-y_i}\delta_{\theta_j}, \quad (9.3)
\end{aligned}$$

where $B(\cdot,\cdot)$ denotes the Beta function, and $f(y_i|\theta_i)$ is the binomial density with k_i trials. Note that the posterior distribution only depends on the y_i, because for $j \neq i$, y_j is conditionally independent of θ_i given θ_j's.

Gibbs sampling initiates the Markov chain by sampling $(\theta_1^{(0)}, \ldots, \theta_n^{(0)})$ from $\mathcal{B}(y_i + a, l_i - y_i + b)$ (the posterior obtained by updating the prior G_0 via the likelihood $f(y_i|\theta_i)$ up to a normalization constant). For a more detailed exposition of Gibbs sampling in this context see the appendix of Gu and Koenker (2017a).

9.3.2 Posterior Analysis

Given the posterior distribution (9.3), the posterior mean for θ_i from the mth step of the MCMC scan, is

$$\mathcal{E}_i^{(m)} = \mathbb{E}(\theta_i^{(m)}|y, \theta_{(-i)}^{(m)}) = \int \theta_i\, p(\theta_i|\theta_{(-i)}, y)d\theta_i$$
$$= \frac{\alpha \frac{B(y_i+a+1, l_i-y_i+b)}{B(a,b)} + \sum_{j\neq i}(\theta_j^{(m)})^{y_i+1}(1-\theta_j^{(m)})^{l_i-y_i}}{\alpha \frac{B(y_i+a, l_i-y_i+b)}{B(a,b)} + \sum_{j\neq i}(\theta_j^{(m)})^{y_i}(1-\theta_j^{(m)})^{l_i-y_i}}.$$

The posterior mean of θ_i given data using the entire chain is thus estimated by

$$\frac{1}{M}\sum_{m=1}^{M}\mathcal{E}_i^{(m)},$$

where M is the total number of MCMC scans after initial burn-in. As noted by Gelfand and Smith (1990) this is essentially Rao–Blackwellization. The posterior variance can be found accordingly as

$$\mathbb{V}(\theta_i|y) = \mathbb{E}(\mathbb{V}(\theta_i|\theta^{(-i)}, y)) + \mathbb{V}(\mathbb{E}(\theta_i|\theta^{(-i)}, y)).$$

9.3.3 Predictive Distributions

Nonparametric Bayesian analysis often focuses on the predictive distribution of θ_{n+1} or y_{n+1} for a future experiment. It is also something routinely reported by software packages. As noted by Liu (1996), since G is an infinite-dimensional object, there is no easy way of exploring its full posterior distribution. However, we can look at its posterior mean, $\mathbb{E}(G|y)$, which also turns out to be the predictive distribution of a future θ_{n+1}. The predictive density for a future θ in the mth round of Markov chain simulation, evaluated at grid points on the domain of $(0, 1)$, is

$$p(\theta_{n+1}^{(m)} \mid y, \mathcal{S}^{(m)}, k^{(m)}) = \mathbb{E}(G \mid y_1, \ldots, y_n)$$
$$= \frac{\alpha}{\alpha+n}G_0(\cdot) + \frac{1}{\alpha+n}\sum_{j=1}^{k^{(m)}} n_j^{(m)}\mathcal{B}\Big(\cdot\,; Z_j^{(m)} + a, L_j^{(m)} - Z_j^{(m)} + b\Big)$$

with $Z_j^{(m)} = \sum_{r \in I_j^{(m)}} y_r$ and $L_j^{(m)} = \sum_{r \in I_j^{(m)}} l_r$. The predictive distribution is then obtained as

$$\frac{1}{M} \sum_{m=1}^{M} p\left(\theta_{n+1}^{(m)} \mid y, \mathcal{S}^{(m)}, k^{(m)}\right).$$

It is interesting to compare the two Dirichlet estimates for the tack-flicking data depicted in Figure 9.6 of the posterior density of θ obtained by the nonparametric Dirichlet prior with the estimates one obtains from the nonparametric maximum likelihood method of Kiefer and Wolfowitz (1956). Even for the relatively weak Dirichlet prior with $\alpha = 0.01$, the Dirichlet estimate is quite smooth relative to the EM estimates of the NPMLE in Figure 9.3. Of more concern is the fact that the Dirichlet estimates of the posterior mean are bimodal even when the prior is very weak, while the NPMLE in Figure 9.3 all exhibit trimodal behavior.

This leaves us with a puzzle. In finite-dimensional parametric problems we expect that weak priors will lead us back to posterior means that closely resemble the classical maximum likelihood estimator. This is clearly not what we have seen in our tacky illustrative example. Indeed, even the weakest form of our Dirichlet prior with $\alpha = 0.01$ exerts a strong influence on the posterior mean as revealed by the tail of the Markov chain simulation, while the NPMLE produces something very different.

9.3.4 Model of Employment Discrimination

An interesting extension of the binomial mixture model is the paired binomial setting of Kline and Walters (2021) designed to study discrimination in hiring practices. Multiple job applications were sent to a sample of firms from both apparently Black and White applicants. The number of recalled applicants of each type for the ith firm, denoted (Y_{1i}, Y_{2i}), has distribution

$$\begin{aligned}\mathbb{P}(Y_1 = y_1, Y_2 = y_2) \\ = \int\int \binom{k_1}{y_1}\binom{k_2}{y_2} p_1^{y_1}(1-p_1)^{k_1-y_1} p_2^{y_2}(1-p_2)^{k_2-y_2} dG(p_1, p_2),\end{aligned}$$

where (k_{1i}, k_{2i}) denotes the total number of applications of each type sent to firm i. The difference in the latent propensity for firms to call back Black and White applicants, (p_{1i}, p_{2i}), can then be seen as an indicator of employment discrimination. In the empirical Bayes framework, (p_{1i}, p_{2i}) are random vectors with joint distribution G. If firm i is discriminating, then $D_i = \mathbb{1}\{p_{1i} \neq p_{2i}\} = 1$. Thus, a key parameter that measures evidence of discrimination at the firm level is the posterior probability,

$$\pi(y_1, y_2) = \mathbb{P}(D_i = 1 | Y_{1i} = y_1, Y_{2i} = y_2).$$

Averaging over firms that have a fixed amount of call back $t = y_1 + y_2$, we can also describe the strata posterior probability of discrimination as

$$\begin{aligned}\pi_t(G) &= 1 - \mathbb{P}(D_i = 0 | Y_{1i} + Y_{2i} = t)\\ &= 1 - \frac{\int \mathbb{P}(Y_{1i} + Y_{2i} = t | p_1 = p_2 = p)\mathbb{P}_G(p_1 = p_2 = p)}{\mathbb{P}(Y_{1i} + Y_{2i} = t)}\\ &= 1 - \frac{\binom{K}{t}\int p^t(1-p)^{K-t}dG(p,p)}{\mathbb{P}(Y_{1i} + Y_{2i} = t)},\end{aligned}$$

where the last equality uses the fact that if $Y_{1i} \sim Binom(k_1, p)$, $Y_{2i} \sim Binom(k_2, p)$, and Y_{1i} and Y_{2i} are independent, then $Y_{1i}+Y_{2i} \sim Binom(K, p)$ with $K = k_1 + k_2$. When (k_1, k_2) are small, as in the applications of Kline and Walters (2021) with $k_1 = k_2 = 2$ based on the data from Bertrand and Mullainathan (2004), it is likely that there exist many joint distributions G that exactly fit the sample frequencies: $\hat{\mathbb{P}}_n(y_1, y_2) = \frac{1}{n}\sum_i 1\{Y_{1i} = y_1, Y_{2i} = y_2\}$ for all $(y_1, y_2) \in \{0, 1, 2\}$. In such cases, since π_t is a functional of G that is not point identified, we can bound π_t by $\underline{\pi}_t = \min_{G\in\mathcal{G}^*} \pi_t(G)$ and $\bar{\pi}_t = \max_{G\in\mathcal{G}^*} \pi_t(G)$ with G supported on $[0, 1]^2$,

$$\begin{aligned}\mathcal{G}^* = \Big\{G : &\hat{\mathbb{P}}_n(y_1, y_2)\\ &= \int\int \binom{k_1}{y_1}\binom{k_2}{y_2} p_1^{y_1}(1-p_1)^{k_1-y_1} p_2^{y_2}(1-p_2)^{k_2-y_2} dG(p_1, p_2)\Big\}.\end{aligned}$$

Since $\pi_t(G)$ is a linear functional of G, both the upper and lower bounds can be recovered by solving linear programs.

Using the data of Bertrand and Mullainathan (2004), based on call back data on 1,112 firms, Table 9.2 reports lower and upper bounds for π_t for $t \in \{0, 1, 2, 3, 4\}$ with a 40×40 discretized grid on $[0, 1]^2$. The upper bounds are not informative except at $t = 0$. The lower bounds are quite informative, however. The lower bounds are rationalized by joint distributions G in the set $\mathcal{G}^*$ that allocates as much weight as possible to diagonal grids with $p_1 = p_2$. See Exercise 10 of Chapter 12 for further details on computation in the bivariate binomial setting.

A cautionary remark is warranted when there is no joint distribution G that is capable of exactly fitting the observed frequency vector $\hat{\mathbb{P}}_n$. Since the data is assumed to be generated by a mixture of bivariate binomial distributions, this must be due to sampling error in $\hat{\mathbb{P}}_n$ or failure of the model. In such

Table 9.2. *Bounds on π_t using data from Bertrand and Mullainathan (2004).*

	$t = 0$	$t = 1$	$t = 2$	$t = 3$	$t = 4$
$\underline{\pi}_t$	0.038	0.427	0.444	0.505	0.216
$\bar{\pi}_t$	0.730	0.999	1.000	1.000	1.000

cases, the linear program defined for the lower and upper bounds will be infeasible, and the solution set, $\mathcal{G}^*$, will be empty. One way to proceed is to find a joint distribution G that produces a probability vector $\tilde{\mathbb{P}}(G)$ that makes the model implied probability vector $\tilde{\mathbb{P}}(G)$ and the sample probability vector $\hat{\mathbb{P}}_n$ close. As discussed in the univariate case, we can use either the likelihood criterion to minimize the Kullback–Leibler divergence or a method of moments criterion. In either case we will find a unique joint distribution G that achieves a minimum, and thus leads to a point estimate of π_t. This may be overly optimistic if not outright misleading for the bound of π_t. Kline and Walters (2021) propose to take a two-step approach, first, by initially using a very coarse grid that is more likely to reproduce $\hat{\mathbb{P}}_n$, and then taking a refined grid to solve for the bounds $[\underline{\pi}_t, \bar{\pi}_t]$. Another approach would be to consider a confidence set for the true population probability vector based on $\hat{\mathbb{P}}_n$, and then define a set $\mathcal{G}^*$ based on the set of plausible probability vectors. This approach would more accurately reflect the sampling error.

Exercises

(1) Verify the formula for $\mathbb{E}[\exp(\theta)|S = s]$ and show that

$$\mathbb{E}[\exp(-\theta)|S = s] = \frac{\mathbb{P}(S = s)}{\mathbb{P}(S = s - 1)} q(s, \boldsymbol{\beta})$$

with

$$q(s, \boldsymbol{\beta}) = \sum_{\boldsymbol{y}_i : 1'\boldsymbol{y}_i = s} \exp(-\boldsymbol{\beta}'\boldsymbol{y}_i) \Big/ \sum_{\boldsymbol{y}_i : 1'\boldsymbol{y}_i = s-1} \exp(-\boldsymbol{\beta}'\boldsymbol{y}_i).$$

Then verify that $1/\mathbb{E}[\exp(-\theta)|S = s]$ is the Bayes estimator for loss function $(\exp(\theta_i) - \hat{\delta}_i)^2 / \exp(\theta_i)$ (i.e., the usual $\mathcal{L}_2$ loss normalized by $\exp(\theta)$).

CHAPTER 10

Random Coefficient Models

Random coefficient regression models for both binary and continuous response often employ parametric distributional assumptions that are difficult to justify a priori. In this chapter we explore some nonparametric methods for estimating such models and connections to some related problems in stereology and tomography. As one would expect there are close connections of these random coefficient models to the mixture models that we have considered in previous chapters.

10.1 RANDOM COEFFICIENT BINARY RESPONSE MODELS

Models of binary response are a mainstay of applied statistics. Typically, they take the form

$$Y_i = \mathbb{1}\{x_i^\top \beta + u_i \geq 0\},\ i = 1, \ldots, n,$$

with observed covariates, $x_i \in \mathbb{R}^p$, unknown parameters, β, and random u_i assumed to be either iid logistic or Gaussian. They can be easily estimated by parametric maximum likelihood methods. A few intrepid authors have explored more flexible specifications.

Assuming only that the conditional median $\mathrm{med}(u_i | x_i) = 0$, Manski (1975) proposed estimating β by solving

$$\max_{\|b\|=1} \sum_{i=1}^{n} (2y_i - 1)(2\mathbb{1}\{x_i^\top b \geq 0\} - 1),$$

which finds a β that maximizes the number of correct matches between the observed y_i and the sign of its linear predictor. One can interpret this as a form of median regression equivalent to solving

$$\min_{\|b\|=1} \sum_{i=1}^{n} |y_i - \mathbb{1}\{x_i^\top b \geq 0\}|.$$

Clearly, β is identified only up to scale, so some normalization of its coordinates is necessary. Provided that there is a coordinate known to be nonzero, one can, alternatively, set it equal to either 1 or -1 and estimate the remaining coefficients relative to it.

10.1.1 Univariate Binary Response

Cosslett (1983) proposed an even more ambitious approach that considered the entire vector, β, to be random, and suggested estimation of its distribution by maximum likelihood à la Kiefer and Wolfowitz. This model was subsequently studied by Ichimura and Thompson (1998) and Gautier and Kitamura (2013) among others. In Gu and Koenker (2022a) we elaborated the Cosslett proposal giving it an empirical Bayes twist. There, we consider the general model

$$y_i = \mathbb{1}\{x_i^\top \eta_i + w_i^\top \theta_0 \geq 0\},$$

where we have covariates $x_i \in \mathbb{R}^{d+1}$, $w_i \in \mathbb{R}^p$ and binary response y_i. We assume that the random parameters η_i are independent of the covariates and that the η_i are independent and identically distributed with an unknown distribution G_η.

Before plunging into the multivariate setting, it is worthwhile to consider a special case with only univariate randomness in η, and no θ_0, so,

$$y_i = 1(\eta_i \leq v_i) \quad i = 1, \ldots, n,$$

where v_i is an observable covariate, and our objective is to estimate the distribution of the univariate random variables, η_i. In economic applications, we might take v_i as the price faced by consumer i for an indivisible good, so the survival curve $S(v) = 1 - G_\eta(v)$ can be interpreted as a demand curve, the proportion of the population willing to pay the price v for the good. In biostatistics, this model is referred to as the current status model: Reversing the inequality we interpret v_i as an inspection time and y_i as a binary indicator revealing whether the random event time, η_i, occurred prior to the inspection.

The geometry of maximum likelihood in this univariate setting is quite simple and helps to establish a heuristic for the general multivariate setting. To illustrate the critical role of the intervals between adjacent order statistics of the v_i under the standard convention of the current status model, we can write

$$\mathbb{P}(y = 1|v) = \int 1(\eta \leq v) dG_\eta(\eta).$$

Given a sample $\{(y_i, v_i)\ i = 1, \ldots, n\}$, this relation defines $n + 1$ intervals as illustrated for $n = 10$ in the upper panel of Figure 10.1. Each point defines a half line on $\mathbb{R}$; if $y_i = 1$ then the interval is $R_i = (-\infty, v_i]$, while if $y_i = 0$ the interval is $R_i = (v_i, \infty)$. Neglecting for the moment the possibility of ties, the R_i's form a partition of $n + 1$ intervals of $\mathbb{R}$. We will denote these intervals by I_j, for $j = 1, \ldots, n + 1$; they can be either closed, open or half open. We can now define the associated counts,

$$c_j = \sum_{i=1}^{n} 1\{R_i \cap I_j \neq \emptyset\}$$

$$= \begin{cases} \sum_{i:y_i=0} 1\{v_i < v_{(j)}\} + \sum_{i:y_i=1} 1\{v_i \geq v_{(j)}\} & \text{for } 1 \leq j \leq n, \\ \sum_{i:y_i=0} 1\{v_i \leq v_{(n)}\} & \text{for } j = n+1, \end{cases}$$

where $v_{(j)}$ is the jth-order statistic of the sample $\{v_1, \ldots, v_n\}$. Now suppose we assign probability mass, p_j to each of the intervals I_j, so that $p = \{p_1, \ldots, p_{n+1}\}$ lies in the n dimensional unit simplex, $\mathcal{S}_n$. Then the contribution of the ith data point to the likelihood is $\sum_j p_j 1\{R_i \cap I_j \neq \emptyset\}$. The nonparametric maximum likelihood estimator of G_η has the following essential features:

(1) Since the p_j's are assigned to intervals, it does not matter where mass is located within the intervals, as long as it is assigned to a point inside; in this sense the NPMLE, $\hat{G}_\eta$, is defined only on the σ-algebra of sets formed from the intervals, I_j. By the usual cadlag convention we could assign all the mass to the right end of each interval, but we should remember that this is only a convention. The NPMLE assigns mass to sets, not to points.

(2) Potential nonzero elements of p correspond to intervals I_j with corresponding c_j being a local maximum. Were this not the case, the likelihood could always be increased by transferring mass to adjacent intervals containing larger counts. Figure 10.1 plots values for the vector c. It is

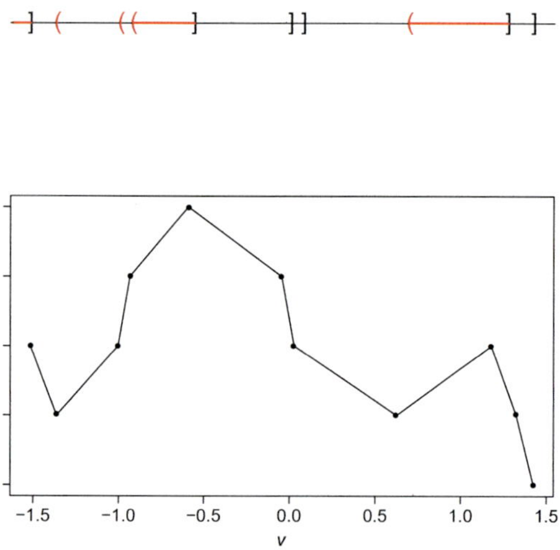

Figure 10.1. Intervals for a sample of 10 observations in the univariate model. Values of v_i corresponding to $y_i = 1$ are marked as] in black and those corresponding to $y_i = 0$ are marked as (in red in the upper panel of the figure. The three intervals demarcated by the heavier (red) segments are local maxima; the number of counts for each interval is illustrated in the lower portion of the figure.

quite efficient to generate the vector c and find these local maxima even when n is very large.

These features suggest a convex optimization strategy for estimation of G_η. Mass needs only to be assigned to the right endpoint of intervals that correspond to local maxima of the counts. Thus, we need only consider the locally maximal intervals; any point within these intervals may be considered as a potential support point for the NPMLE. This serves as a dimension reduction device compared to considering all n original data points. In our experience, the number of potential support points of the distribution G_η identified in this manner still grows linearly with the sample size n, while the number of optimal support points identified by the maximum likelihood estimator grows much more slowly. To determine which of our locally maximal intervals deserves positive mass and if so how much, we must solve

$$\max_{g \in \mathcal{S}_{M-1}} \left\{ \sum_{i=1}^{n} \log f_i \mid Ag = f \right\}, \tag{10.1}$$

where $g = (g_j)$ denotes the mass assigned to the jth-order statistic of our reduced set of potential v of cardinality M. The ith coordinate of Ag equals $\sum_j 1\{v_{(j)} \leq v_i\} g_j$ if $y_i = 1$ and $\sum_j 1\{v_{(j)} > v_i\} g_j$ if $y_i = 0$. As first noted by Cosslett (1983), this problem turns out to be a special instance of the nonparametric maximum likelihood estimator we have described earlier originating in Kiefer and Wolfowitz (1956).

Groeneboom and Jongbloed (2014) stress the characterization of the NPMLE in this setting as a convex minorant, thereby linking it to the celebrated Grenander estimator of a monotone density; the convex optimization formulation given here is equivalent, as established in Groeneboom and Wellner (1992). Noting that the problem is strictly concave in the g_i and subject only to linear equality and inequality constraints, it can be solved very efficiently. When this is carried out one finds that the number of support points of the estimated distribution, $\hat{G}_\eta$, is considerably smaller than the number of local maxima identified as candidates. See Gu and Koenker (2022a) for further details.

10.1.2 Multivariate Random Coefficient Binary Response

To help visualize the geometry of the binary response NPMLE in a more general setting with multivariate random coefficients we will first consider the bivariate case without any auxiliary covariates, w_i, and maintain the small sample focus of the previous section. Now, $x_i = (1, z_i, -v_i)^\top$, where z_i is a scalar and $\eta_i \sim G_\eta$ is bivariate. Our binary response is generated as

$$\mathbb{P}(y_i = 1 | x_i) = \mathbb{P}(\eta_{1i} + z_i \eta_{2i} - v_i \geq 0).$$

To extend our demand analysis interpretation, we could regard v_i as a product price whose coefficient has been normalized to be -1, and z_i might be household income. Were η_{2i} constant and η_{1i} logistic we would be back in a familiar logit setting. Instead, each pair, (z_i, v_i), defines a line that divides $\mathbb{R}^2$ into two half-spaces, an "upper" one corresponding to realizations of $y_i = 1$ and a "lower" one for $y_i = 0$. Let R_i denote these half-spaces and $G_\eta(R_i)$ be the probability assigned to R_i by the distribution G_η. Our objective is to estimate the distribution, G_η. The log likelihood of the observed sample is

$$\ell(G_\eta) = \sum_{i=1}^{n} \log G_\eta(R_i).$$

The R_i partition of the domain of η rather than generating intervals, now consists of polygons formed by intersections of the R_i half-spaces. Adapting our counting method for intervals to these polygons, we seek to identify polygons whose counts are locally maximal. Within these maximal polygons the data is uninformative so again there is some inherent ambiguity about the nature of the NPMLE solutions. As in the one-dimensional case this ambiguity can be resolved by adopting a selection rule for choosing points within each polygon. As long as there is sufficient variability in the pairs (z_i, v_i)'s this ambiguity vanishes as the sample size grows. Figure 10.2 illustrates such a partition with $n = 5$. The data for this example is given in Table 10.1.

The half-spaces $\{R_1, \ldots, R_n\}$ partition $\mathbb{R}^2$ into disjoint polygons $C_1, \ldots, C_M$. Since for each i, it must be that $C_m \cap R_i = \emptyset$ or $C_m \cap R_i = C_m$, we can represent

$$G_\eta(R_i) = \sum_{j=1}^{M} p_j \mathbb{1}\{C_j \subset R_i\},$$

where p_j denotes the probability assigned to C_j, and we can express the log likelihood in terms of these probabilities, $p = (p_j)_{j=1:M}$,

$$\ell(p) = \sum_{i=1}^{n} \log \left(\sum_{j=1}^{M} p_j 1\{C_j \subset R_i\} \right).$$

This log likelihood is strictly concave in the n-vector of half-space probabilities, $q = (G_\eta(R_i))$, which is restricted to lie in a convex set and is, therefore, uniquely determined. Uniqueness of the M vector p is, however,

Table 10.1. *Data for a toy example with $n = 5$.*

	(Intercept)	z_i	v_i	y_i
$i = 1$	1.00	0.41	1.22	1
$i = 2$	1.00	0.40	0.36	0
$i = 3$	1.00	0.17	0.24	1
$i = 4$	1.00	−0.79	0.99	0
$i = 5$	1.00	−0.94	0.55	0

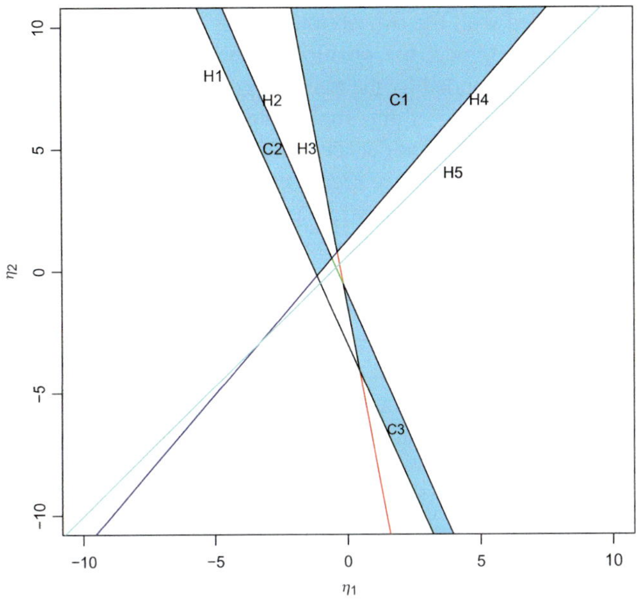

Figure 10.2. The polygons defined by a toy example with $n = 5$.

a more delicate issue. In Appendix B of Gu and Koenker (2022a) we provide a counterexample for which there is a convex set of solutions in p each element of which determines the same vector q. The vector p must lie in the $(M - 1)$-dimensional unit simplex and satisfy $q = Ap$ for the n by M Boolean matrix, $A = (1(C_j \subset R_i))$. When $M > n$ there is the possibility that p may be nonunique as noted earlier by Gentleman and Geyer (1994) and Lindsay (1995). Just as in the univariate setting where we need not consider *all* intervals, only those with locally maximal counts, we now need only consider polygons with locally maximal counts, thereby reducing the dimension, M, of the vector p. Often, this initial step will reduce M to less than n; when it fails to do so the non-negativity constraints on the components of p in the convex optimization of the log likelihood accomplish this.

We now illustrate how to find the maximal polygons for our toy example with $n = 5$. Figure 10.2 shows that there are three maximal polygons, all shaded and denoted as $\{C_1, C_2, C_3\}$. Polygon C_1 is the intersection of $\{R_1, R_3, R_4, R_5\}$, C_2 is the intersection of $\{R_1, R_2, R_4, R_5\}$ and C_3 is the intersection of $\{R_1, R_2, R_3\}$. Each is locally maximal in the sense that they are formed by more intersecting half-spaces than any of their neighbors. The maximum likelihood estimator for p is defined as any maximizer of

$$\max_{p \in \mathcal{S}_2} \Big\{ (p_1 + p_2 + p_3)(p_2 + p_3)(p_1 + p_3)(p_1 + p_2)(p_1 + p_2) \Big\},$$

which leads to the unique solution, $p_1 = p_2 = 1/2$ and $p_3 = 0$, and the optimal log-likelihood of $\log(1/4) = -1.3863$. We should again stress that although the mass associated with the two optimal polygons is uniquely determined by maximizing the likelihood, the position of the mass is ambiguous, confined only to the regions bounded by the two polygons.

As n grows the number of maximal polygons grows rapidly, and finding all of them in the informal manner described above quickly becomes impractical. Fortunately, there is a relatively recent combinatorial geometry literature on "hyperplane arrangements" that offers tractable enumeration methods for the partition induced by any set of n hyperplanes in $\mathbb{R}^d$. Some modest improvements on these earlier proposals are described in Gu and Koenker (2022a), and substantial further improvements are described in Gu et al. (2025).

Cell enumeration produces for each cell an interior, "witness" point and a sign vector that indicates how each of the R_i halfspaces are aligned with respect to the cell. In the simplest implementations these quantities are found by solving a simple linear feasibility problem. Given the cell enumeration, an adjacency matrix A can be created. This is a Boolean matrix of dimension n by M, the number of cells. It incorporates all of the information from the sign vectors of the cells. Column sums of A give the cell counts. Just as in the univariate case we are only interested in maximal cells, those with cell counts greater than any of their neighbors. Neighboring cells have sign vectors that differ by only one element, so it is relatively easy to eliminate cells that are not locally maximal.

At this point it is worth noting that the Manski (1975) maximum score estimator is defined as the cell with the globally maximal cell count. Complete cell enumeration with associated counts is the only really reliable way to find this solution, since local search methods are likely to find themselves marooned at one of the other locally maximal cells.

Having reduced the support of the NPMLE, $\hat{G}$, we are ready to assign mass to the remaining locally maximal cells. Again, we have a pair of primal and dual problems that provide equivalent solutions. In primal form,

$$\min_{p \in \mathcal{S}_{M-1}} \left\{ n^{-1} \sum_{i=1}^{n} \log f_i \mid f = Ap \right\},$$

while the dual is

$$\max_{v} \left\{ n^{-1} \sum_{i=1}^{n} \log v_i \mid A^\top v \leq n 1_M \right\}.$$

Although, these problems appear similar to the NPMLE problems discussed earlier, they are actually somewhat simpler because they are finite dimensional. Once the number of locally maximal cells, M, has been determined by the hyperplane arrangement procedure, the dimensions of both primal and dual problems for the binary response model are fixed; there is no need for any gridding. When covariates with fixed coefficient θ are introduced into the model, estimation of these non-random parameters, θ, can be accommodated by maximizing the profile likelihood.

Conditions for the strong consistency of the NPMLE pair, $(\hat{\theta}_n, \hat{G}_n)$, are discussed in Gu and Koenker (2022a). Crucially, they require that there be sufficient variability of the covariates to ensure that cell volumes in the support of G_η tend to zero with sample size. Software for computation of the NPMLE for the binary response model, including the special case of the current status model, is available in the R package **RCBR**, Gu and Koenker (2019). Some simulation comparisons of this NPMLE approach with the Fourier inversion approach of Gautier and Kitamura (2013) are presented in Gu and Koenker (2022a). When covariates are discrete partial identification persists; these issues are further considered in Gu and Russell (2023) and Gu et al. (2025).

10.1.3 An Application to Commuter Modal Choice

An application to modal choice by urban commuters in Gu and Koenker (2022a) illustrates the role of partial identification in the construction of bounds for marginal effects. The data consists of 842 randomly sampled observations of individuals' transportation choices for their daily journey to work in the Washington DC metro area previously studied by Horowitz (1993). Following Horowitz, we focus on the binary choice of commuting to work by automobile versus public transit.

In addition to the individual mode choice variable, y_i, taking the value 1 if an automobile is used for the journey to work and 0 if public transit is taken, we observe the number of cars owned by the traveler's household (*AUTOS*), the difference in out-of-vehicle (*DOVTT*) and in-vehicle travel time (*DIVTT*). Differences are expressed as public transit time minus automobile time in minutes per trip. The corresponding differences in transportation cost, *DCOST*, public transit fare minus automobile travel cost is measured in cents per trip. We have omitted the variable *DIVTT* from our analysis since it had no significant impact on modal choice in prior work; see table 2 of Horowitz (1993) for estimation results using various parametric and semiparametric models. Although our methodology can accommodate additional x_i variables with random coefficients it becomes considerably more difficult to visualize distributions of random coefficients G_η in higher dimensions. Other control variables in the vector w_i could also be accommodated, but the application doesn't offer obvious candidates.

We consider the following random coefficient binary choice model:

$$\mathbb{P}(y_i = 1 \mid x_i, v_i, AUTOS_i = k) = \int \mathbb{1}\{x_i^\top \eta_i - v_i \geq 0\} dG_{\eta,k},$$

where $x_i = (1, DOVTT_i)$, $v_i = DCOST_i/100$ and $\eta_i = \{\eta_{1i}, \eta_{2i}\}$. We have normalized the coefficient of v_i to be 1, since v_i represents a negative price, transit fare minus automobile cost. Under this normalization, the coefficient η_{2i} has a direct interpretation as the commuter's value of travel time in dollars/minute. The coefficient η_1 has the same units as v_i, and can be interpreted as a threshold – setting a critical value for v_i above which the subject decides to commute by automobile and below which they choose to take public transit, assuming that the time differential is negligible. Auto ownership is a discrete variable, taking values between 0 and 7 in the sample. Sampled households with three cars or more commute exclusively by automobile, so only subjects with fewer than three cars were considered, a subsample containing about 90% of the data. Since car ownership is plausibly an endogenous decision and may act as a proxy for wealth of the household and a potential constraint on the travelers' mode choices, distinct distributions were estimated for the random coefficients of subjects with zero, one and two cars. We focus on the subsample of subjects with one car and refer readers to Gu and Koenker (2022a) for further details.

There are 355 commuters who have 1 automobile of which 302 commute by car. The hyperplane arrangement determined by this subsample of pairs (x_i, v_i) yields a tessellation of $\mathbb{R}^2$ into 55,549 distinct polygons of which there are 1,272 with locally maximal counts. Figure 10.3 displays the estimated mass points of the NPMLE, and the contour plot the Gautier–Kitamura density estimate is displayed in light gray. The NPMLE mass is considerably more dispersed than the Gautier–Kitamura contours. This may be partly attributed to the rather restrictive choice of the tuning parameters, $T = 2$ and $TX = 3$, for the Gautier–Kitamura procedure dictated by the likelihood criterion used to select these tuning parameters. See Gu and Koenker (2022a) for further details on computation and tuning of the Gautier–Kitamura estimates. While most

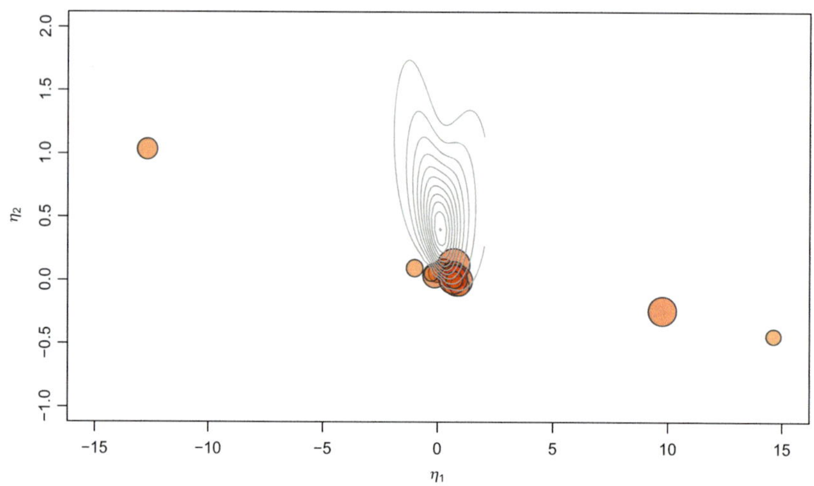

Figure 10.3. Two estimates of the random coefficient distribution G_η based on the subsample of commuters with one automobile: Shaded circles represent the interior points of polygons with positive mass as estimated by the NPMLE. The area inside the circles is proportional to estimated mass. Gray contour lines depict the density contours of the Gautier–Kitamura estimator using Fourier–Laplace tuning parameters $T = 3$ and $TX = 3$ selected by the log-likelihood criterion.

of the NPMLE mass is centered near the origin, there is about 0.10 mass at $(\eta_1, \eta_2) \approx (9.7, -0.24)$ and another, roughly, 0.05 probability with $\eta_1 < -12$. The Gautier–Kitamura contours are much more concentrated around the origin. Not surprisingly, these differences are reflected in substantial alterations in predicted outcomes and estimated marginal effects.

With any discrete choice model, a common parameter of interest is the marginal effect of some control variables. We consider two scenarios for evaluating marginal effects based on estimates of the quantities. Recall that z is the variable DOVTT,

$$\begin{aligned}\Delta_z(z_0, v_0, \Delta z) &= \mathbb{P}(y = 1 \mid v = v_0, z = z_0) \\ &\quad - \mathbb{P}(y = 1 \mid v = v_0, z = z_0 - \Delta z), \\ \Delta_v(z_0, v_0, \Delta v) &= \mathbb{P}(y = 1 \mid v = v_0, z = z_0) \\ &\quad - \mathbb{P}(y = 1 \mid v = v_0 - \Delta v, z = z_0).\end{aligned}$$

The value $\Delta_z(z_0, v_0, \Delta z)$ measures the marginal effect of reducing out-of-vehicle travel time by Δz minutes/trip; the value $\Delta_v(z_0, v_0, \Delta v)$ measures the marginal effect of reducing the transit fare by Δv dollars holding transportation time constant. In each case, we fix the initial values (z_0, v_0) at the 0.75 quantiles for the subsample of individuals who drive to work. Figures 10.4 and 10.5 depict the marginal effect of fare reduction and commute time reduction, respectively, conditional on automobile ownership.

For a fixed n, the NPMLE $\hat{G}_n$ assigns probability mass $\{\hat{p}_j\}_{j=1:M}$ to polytopes $\{C_j\}_{j=1:M}$ that define the partition of the parameter space determined by the hyperplane arrangement, not to specific points. This feature of the NPMLE naturally leads to a set-valued estimator for marginal effects for any finite

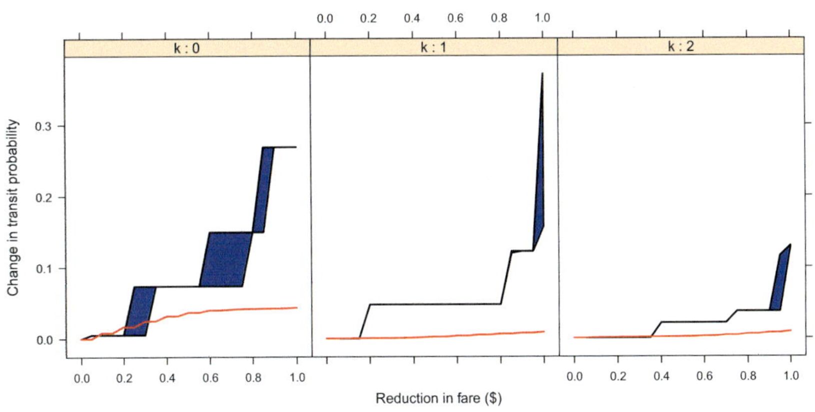

Figure 10.4. Set-valued estimates of marginal effect for transit fare reduction: The shaded solid regions represent the NPMLE set-valued estimates of the marginal effect of reducing the transit fare on the probability of choosing the transit option; the (red) line represents the corresponding estimates from the Gautier–Kitamura fit.

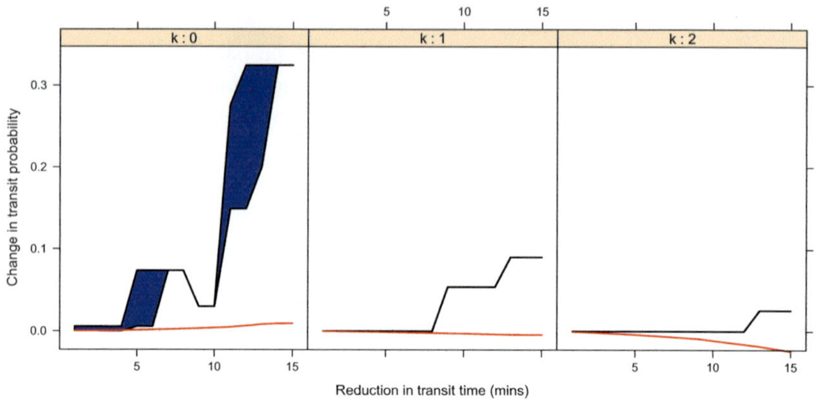

Figure 10.5. Set-valued estimates of marginal effect for transit time reduction: The shaded solid regions represent the NPMLE set-valued estimates of the marginal effect of reducing the transit time in minutes on the probability of choosing the transit option; the (red) line represents the corresponding estimates from the Gautier–Kitamura fit.

sample. Suppose we would like to estimate $\Delta_z(z_0, v_0, \Delta z)$. Denoting the half-space determined by any point, $(1, z, v)$, by $H^+(v, z) := \{(\eta_1, \eta_2) \colon \eta_1 + \eta_2 z - v \geq 0\}$, it is easy to see that the set estimator for $\mathbb{P}(y = 1 \mid v = v_0, z = z_0)$ can be expressed as

$$\mathbb{P}_{\hat{G}_n}(H^+(v_0, z_0)) \in [\hat{L}_n(v_0, z_0), \hat{U}_n(v_0, z_0)]$$

with

$$\hat{L}_n(v_0, z_0) = \sum_{j=1}^{M} \mathbb{1}\{C_j \subseteq H^+(v_0, z_0)\}\hat{p}_j$$

and

$$\hat{U}_n(v_0, z_0) = \sum_{j=1}^{M} \mathbb{1}\{C_j \subseteq H^+(v_0, z_0)\}\hat{p}_j + \sum_{j=1}^{M} \mathbb{1}\{C_j \nsubseteq H^+(v_0, z_0), C_j \cap H^+(v_0, z_0) \neq \emptyset\}\hat{p}_j.$$

These bounds are constructed by finding the corresponding polygons crossed by the new hyperplane $H(v_0, z_0)$. The lower bound sums all nonzero probability masses $\hat{p}_j$ allocated to the polygons that are completely contained in the half-space $H^+(v_0, z_0)$, while the upper bound adds in the additional nonzero probability masses that are allocated to polygons that are crossed by $H(v_0, z_0)$.

The set valued estimator for the marginal effect is therefore

$$\hat{\Delta}_z(z_0, v_0, \Delta z) \in [\hat{L}_n(z_0, v_0) - \hat{U}_n(z_0 - \Delta z, v_0), \hat{U}_n(z_0, v_0) - \hat{L}_n(z_0 - \Delta z, v_0)].$$

Figures 10.4 and 10.5 report these bounds for different values of Δz and Δv. The corresponding marginal effects for the Gautier–Kitamura estimates are depicted as the dotted red curves in this figure. The concentration of the Gautier–Kitamura $\hat{G}_\eta$ near the origin implies marginal effects that are considerably smaller than those implied by the NPMLE results for both the fare and transit time effects. Car ownership is clearly an important influence especially on the marginal effects of time savings for commuters without a car, while there is essentially no marginal effect for commuters with two cars.

As a final comparison, we reconsider several alternative single-index models where the parameter η_2 is treated as fixed and there is only a random intercept effect,

$$\mathbb{P}(y_i = 1 \mid x_i, v_i, AUTOS_i = k) = \int \mathbb{1}\{\eta_{1i} + z_i\eta_2 - v_i \geq 0\} dG_{\eta_1,k}.$$

We consider two semiparametric estimators that make no distributional assumption on $G_{\eta_1,k}$ as well as the parametric probit estimator that presumes that $G_{\eta_1,k}$ is standard Gaussian. Since we can only identify $G_{\eta_{1,k}}$ up to scale, we again normalize the coefficient for v_i to be 1. We consider the kernel-smoothing based estimator proposed by Klein and Spady (1993) and the score estimator proposed in Groeneboom and Hendrickx (2018) based on the nonparametric maximum likelihood estimator of $G_{\eta_1,k}$ as in Cosslett (1983). The former estimator requires a choice of a bandwidth for the kernel estimate, whereas the latter is free of tuning parameters. The Klein–Spady estimates are based on the implementation in the R package **np** of Hayfield and Racine (2008) using a Gaussian kernel. The bandwidth is chosen automatically via a likelihood-based cross-validation criterion. The estimation results are reported in Table 10.2 together with the probit model estimates. For comparison, we also include in the last column the log-likelihood of the random coefficient model where η_2 is allowed to be heterogeneous across individuals.

A virtue of the single index representation is that it is possible to estimate standard errors for the fixed parameter estimate $\hat{\eta}_2$, which appear in the table in parentheses under their coefficients. However, as is clear from the foregoing figures and the log likelihood values of Table 10.2, these standard errors require a willing suspension of disbelief in view of the apparent heterogeneity of the NPMLE estimates of the bivariate model.

10.2 TOMATOES, TOMOGRAPHY AND ECOLOGICAL INFERENCE

In this section we encounter several new/old geometric settings that extend the range of applicability of NPMLE empirical Bayes methods and point the way toward new approaches to the random coefficient regression model.

Table 10.2. *Estimates for η_2 of the single index model for households having different numbers of vehicles. The semiparametric and parametric probit estimates normalize the coefficient of v to be 1. The last column reports the log-likelihood of the NPMLE for the bivariate model in which η_2 is allowed to be individual specific. The Klein–Spady estimator is implemented with the* `npindexbw` *and* `npindex` *functions of the* `np` *package. We use a Gaussian kernel, and the bandwidth is chosen based on optimizing the likelihood criteria for both parameters and the bandwidth through leave-one-out cross validation. The BFGS method was used for optimization with 20 randomly chosen starting initial values. The Groeneboom–Hendrickx results were computed with the* `GH` *function from the R package* `RCBR`.

Cars	Groeneboom–Hendrickx		Klein–Spady		Probit		NPMLE(η_1, η_2)
	$\hat{\eta}_2$	logL	$\hat{\eta}_2$	logL	$\hat{\eta}_2$	logL	logL
0	0.026 (0.022)	−32.87	−0.396 (0.026)	−37.60	0.034 (0.021)	−37.420	−29.55
1	0.018 (0.006)	−121.71	0.034 (0.007)	−131.71	0.028 (0.010)	−130.84	−112.32
2	0.030 (0.009)	−47.33	0.003 (0.003)	−51.85	0.048 (0.019)	−51.80	−46.13

10.2.1 The Tomato Salad Problem

A fundamental problem in stereology initially considered by Wicksell (1925) involves estimating the distribution of spherical radii, denoted as R, from a sample of cross-sectional radii, denoted as r. The problem may be viewed as an idealization of a microscopy setting in which opaque spherical objects embedded in a translucent medium are observable only from two-dimensional slices, or more mundanely as inferring the distribution of the radii of some idealized, spherical tomatoes from a sample of tomato slices.

Assuming tomatoes are sampled proportionally according to their radii R, Wicksell showed that the relationship between the density of the radii of the slices, $q(r)$, and the distribution of the radii of the tomatoes, $Q(R)$, is given by

$$q(r) = C_q \int_r^{\infty} r(R^2 - r^2)^{-1/2} dQ(R).$$

To make our tomato problem look more like a conventional mixture, we can rewrite it in terms of the observed squared radii $y = r^2$ and latent $\theta = R^2$ as

$$f(y) = C \int_y^{+\infty} (\theta - y)^{-1/2} g(\theta) d\theta,$$

with $C = 1/(2\int_0^{+\infty}\sqrt{\theta}g(\theta)d\theta)$ and the distribution of θ being G with density g. Absorbing the constant into $g(\theta)$ we can reformulate $f(y)$ as

$$f(y) = \int_y^{+\infty} \varphi(y|\theta)h(\theta)d\theta,$$

with $\varphi(y|\theta) = \frac{1}{2}(\theta - y)^{-1/2}$ and $h(\theta) := g(\theta)/\int_0^{+\infty}\sqrt{\theta}g(\theta)d\theta$. See Groeneboom and Jongbloed (2014), section 4.1 for further details. This leads to a slight modification of our usual NPMLE problem:

$$\min_{h\in\mathcal{H}}\left\{-\sum_{i=1}^{n}\log f(y_i)|f(y_i) = \int \varphi(y_i|\theta)h(\theta)d\theta, i = 1,\ldots,n\right\},$$

where $\mathcal{H}$ denotes the set of functions satisfying

$$\mathcal{H} := \left\{h: \int_0^{+\infty}\sqrt{\theta}h(\theta)d\theta = 1, h(\theta) \geq 0 \quad \text{for all } \theta \in [0,\infty)\right\}.$$

This is again a convex optimization problem, and the final estimator can be obtained by normalizing $f(y)$ to have mass one.

It is clear from the form of φ that the NPMLE is more troublesome here than we have seen previously: Positive mass at any of the observed y_i produces a singularity in the likelihood creating something akin to the familiar Dirac catastrophe of ordinary density estimation. Nevertheless, as with the empirical distribution, the maximum likelihood yields a perfectly sensible estimate of the distribution function, G, as illustrated in the next two examples.

Example 10.1 If the distribution G is $U[0,1]$ the density, $f(y)$, takes the following explicit form, as discussed in Groeneboom and Jongbloed (2014):

$$f(y) = \frac{3}{2}\sqrt{1-y}\mathbb{1}\{0 \leq y \leq 1\}.$$

Example 10.2 If G is standard exponential, again there is an explicit form for $f(y)$:

$$f(y) = \frac{1}{\sqrt{\pi}}\int_y^{+\infty}\frac{1}{\sqrt{\theta - y}}e^{-\theta}d\theta = e^{-y}\mathbb{1}\{y \geq 0\}.$$

For each of these examples we generate $n = 200$ observations, $\{y_1,\ldots,y_n\}$ and illustrate the NPMLE estimates of g and G, respectively in panels (a) and (c) and panels (b) and (d) of Figure 10.6. The smooth (blue) curves in panels (b) and (d) depict the target uniform and exponential distribution functions. Note that the NPMLE estimates of G are necessarily monotone so there is no need for further tweaking, except perhaps for some optional smoothing. See Silverman et al. (1990) and Chan and Qin (2016) for further discussion of EM implementations of related methods.

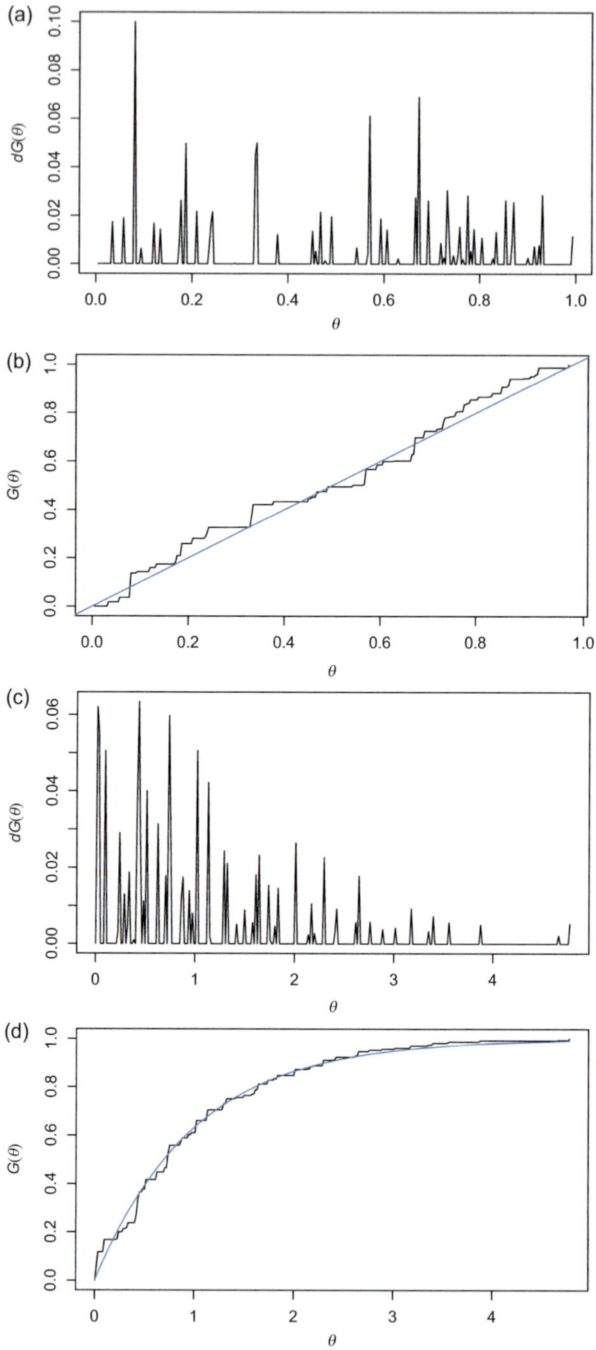

Figure 10.6. NPMLE estimates of g and G for uniform and exponential Wicksell experiments based on 200 sample observations.

10.2.2 Positron Emission Tomography

Positron emission tomography (PET) is a noninvasive imaging technique designed to identify tumors and other medical abnormalities. Following the seminal work of Shepp and Vardi (1982) it has generated intense interest in statistics as an early success of NPMLE methods for imaging. The basic PET principles are illustrated in Figure 10.7. A patient's head represented by the inner ellipse is surrounded by a circular detector ring. A radioactive substance is administered to the patient that induces positrons to be emitted at varying rates within the brain. Each positron is annihilated immediately by an interaction with an electron, and two photons are emitted in opposite directions along the line as shown in the figure. Some of these photon pairs are detected by the circular ring; others go undetected because their angle of emission from the point of occurrence is too great. One can accommodate the three-dimensional nature of the problem, but this will be ignored here. In an effort to keep things simple, all photons will be assumed to be emitted onto a fixed plane. Photons encounter the detector ring at a pair of points depicted by the red dots. The crucial underlying assumption is that the photons are emitted at uniformly distributed angles from their point of origin.

The detection ring is discretized into D arcs. Counts of the observed detection pairs are tabulated, and the objective is then to infer the intensity of the spatial Poisson process of the emission points from these counts. In the 3D geometry of the problem these pairs of detector points are referred to as "tubes." The x–y plane is gridded into rectangular boxes of sufficiently small height and width that Poisson intensity $\lambda(b)$ can be assumed constant within each of them.

The observed rate for the detected counts in tube d from box b is the product of $\lambda(b)$ and a known function $p(b,d) = P(\text{detected in } d \mid \text{emitted in } b)$, which is determined by the discretization of the boxes and the detector ring. Since b and d are both discrete and $p(b,d)$ is known from the geometry, we can formulate a likelihood for the detection problem with our usual NPMLE constraint matrix A having typical element $p(b_i, d_j)$. How to compute the elements of this matrix? Panel (b) of Figure 10.7 is intended to be helpful in this regard. The detector ring has unit radius so it is inscribed by the grid on square $[-1,1]^2$. The ring is segmented into D arcs as illustrated in the figure. If a tube d does not intersect box b then $p(b,d) = 0$. Otherwise, letting r denote the radius of the inscribed disk of each of the boxes, Shepp and Vardi (1982) suggest computing the width, $p(b,d)$, as the distance from the boundary of tube, d, to farthest point on the inscribed circle of the box, b.

Shepp and Vardi (1982) provide a somewhat fanciful physical justification for their suggestion. Boxes that have inscribed circles like the green one that are entirely interior to a tube are also easy; they have width $2r$. The remaining boxes whose inscribed circles, like the blue one in the figure that intersect a tube boundary, are assigned a value equal to the distance from the tube boundary to the furthest point on their inscribed disk inside the tube. These

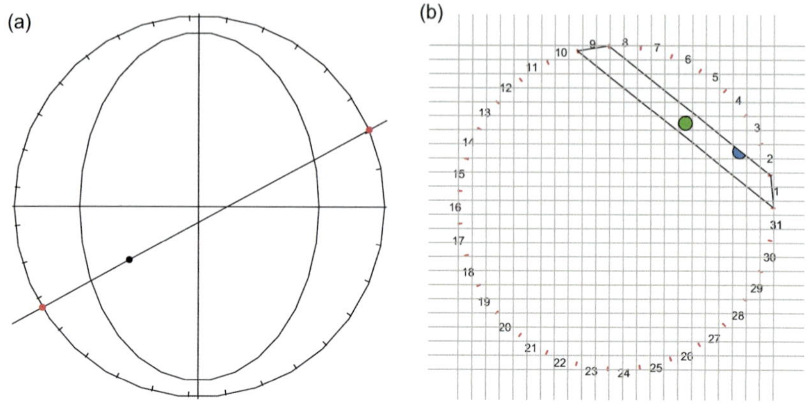

Figure 10.7. Elementary PET geometry: In panel (a), an emission at the (black) point in the patient ellipse generates two photons determining a line at a random angle that in turn determines the two (red) points on the detector ring. In panel (b), a box b that lies entirely within a detector tube d, like the one illustrated in green, has $p(b,d) = 2r$, where r is the radius of the inscribed circle of the box. Boxes that intersect the boundary of a tube have contribution $p(b,d)$ equal to the distance from the tube boundary to the farthest point on the (blue) inscribed semicircle.

values can all be computed before seeing any data, and it seems convenient to do so, although in the original implementation they were computed "on the fly" to conserve computer memory.

Example 10.3 A slight variant of the original Shepp–Vardi test problem is illustrated in Figure 10.8. Poisson intensities are assumed constant within the elliptical regions with relative intensities labeled as in panel (a) of the figure. Given this structure, it is easy to generate a sample of (x, y) points of emission by rejection sampling, after normalizing the relative intensities. In panel (b) of the figure, a `hexbin` two-dimensional histogram illustrates the distribution of observed counts from such a sample. Of course, the whole point is that we cannot observe these counts. Instead, we want to estimate their spatial intensity from the detector pairs. These are easily simulated: For each (x, y) a uniform angle θ is drawn that determines a line through (x, y). Solving for the intersections of this line with the detector ring involves solving a simple quadratic equation. Discretizing these points of intersection yields the "tube counts" that constitute the observed data for the NPMLE tomography problem.

Given a sample of tube counts and the $A = (p(b_i, d_j))$ matrix it is easy to implement one of several variants of the EM algorithm as a fixed point iteration. In Figure 10.9 we illustrate two estimates of the intensity surface based on a large sample of simulated emissions. Panel (a) shows a hexbin plot of the estimated surface after 50 EM iterations, panel (b) after 500 iterations. While neither is quite as precise as the plot based directly on the exact position of

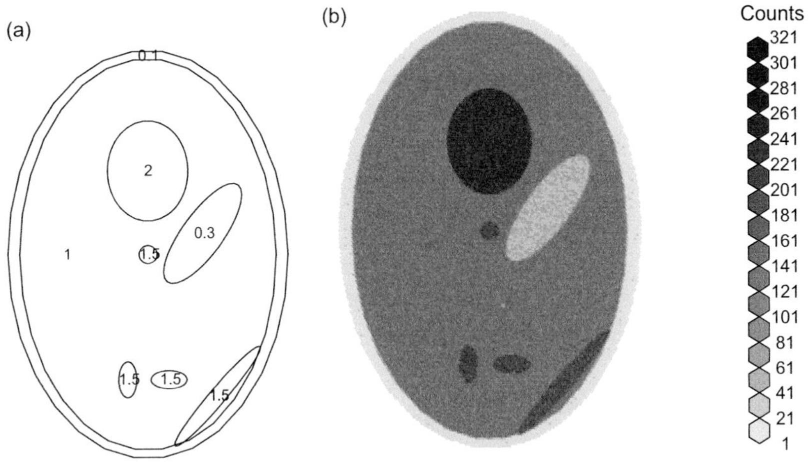

Figure 10.8. Shepp–Vardi PET example: Panel (a) illustrates the structure of the Shepp–Vardi test problem. Emission intensity is assumed to be constant with the ellipses of the figure. These intensities are normalized to produce $\lambda(x, y)$, which integrates to one over the entire patient ellipse and serves as a threshold for rejection sampling. In panel (b), we show a typical realization as a hexbin (histogram) plot of the raw data produced by the rejection sampling based on roughly 2.5 million observations.

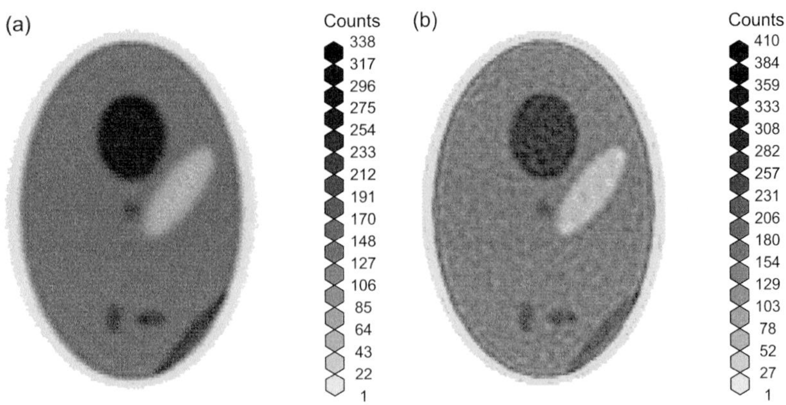

Figure 10.9. EM estimates of the Shepp–Vardi PET example: The two panels illustrate the estimates of the Poisson intensity surface for the Shepp–Vardi test problem. Estimates are based on approximately 2.6 million tube counts. Panel (a) shows a hexbin image of the estimated surface after 50 EM iterations, panel (b) after 500 EM iterations. The latter image offers somewhat better resolution of the boundaries of the phantom regions.

the emissions, the recovered images are quite accurate considering that they were NPMLE estimates based on indirect measurements of the associated tube counts.

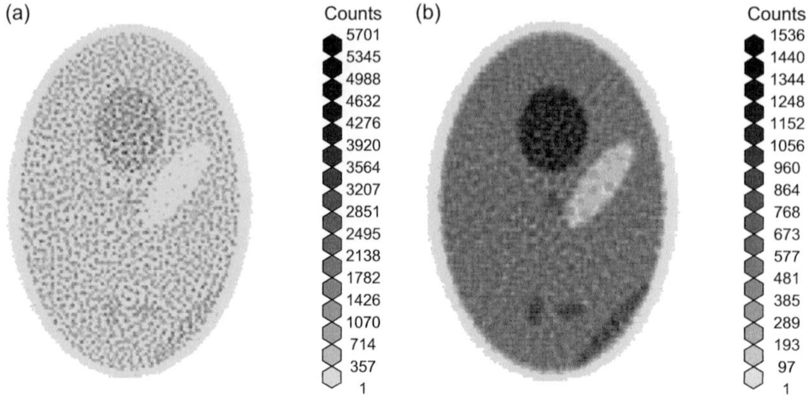

Figure 10.10. Interior point estimates of the Shepp–Vardi PET example: The two panels illustrate the estimates of the Poisson intensity surface for the Shepp–Vardi test problem. Estimates are based on approximately 2.6 million tube counts. Panel (a) shows a hexbin image of the estimated surface based on the interior point fit. Panel (b) shows the same fit after convolution with a bivariate $U[-3r,3r]^2$ kernel.

A natural question at this stage might be: Would further iterations of EM produce something more (or less) convincing? Rather than proceeding with EM, it is more expedient to implement an interior point formulation of the NPMLE. The likelihood requires only minor modifications of the **REBayes** implementation of the Kiefer–Wolfowitz primal problem. There has been considerable speculation about the consequences of a fully iterated version of EM to obtain the NPMLE. Silverman et al. (1990), for example, argue that smoothing an unconverged EM estimate is preferable to iterating to convergence. On the contrary, Vardi in the discussion of their paper argues that, if feasible, it would be better to smooth a fully iterated version of the NPMLE. Fortunately, we don't need to use EM to obtain a fully iterated solution; interior point methods produce an efficient means of computing it. In panel (a) of Figure 10.10 we illustrate a plot of such an interior point estimate. As expected it is much rougher than the partially iterated EM estimates, with lots of small mass points relatively evenly spread over the target domain. In panel (b), we illustrate a simple smoothed version of this estimate using uniform convolution. This experience seems to vindicate Vardi's preference for smoothing the fully iterated estimate. Premature stopping of EM is often advocated as a valid smoothing device, but it seems difficult to judge how much smoothing should be done in this way. Starting from the fully iterated solution allows one to be confident that interesting features of the solution have not been overlooked, and in contrast to prior experience with the slowly converging EM algorithm, the interior point estimate is quite efficient, requiring about one minute, whereas 500 iterations of EM requires 15 minutes.

The Wicksell stereology problem and the PET scan problem both illustrate the usefulness of the NPMLE for indirect estimation of the distribution of latent effects. In the next section we explore some extensions of this approach to random coefficient regression problems.

10.2.3 Random Coefficient Regression

Virtually all of the econometric literature on random coefficient regression involves parametric assumptions about the form of the distribution of the random coefficients. This is most evident in the hierarchical models discussed in Chapter 3 where Gaussian assumptions on the random parameters are almost universal. Why are we entitled to assume latent parameters are Gaussian? Wouldn't it be nice if some evidence could be offered to support such assumptions? The mixture models and the NPMLE methods introduced in this chapter offer some hope that this is feasible, and the stereology and tomography methods reinforce this expectation.

We will consider only the simplest bivariate linear regression setting to simplify the geometric interpretation, so we have the linear model,

$$y_i = a_i + b_i x_i.$$

We observe pairs (y_i, x_i) and would like to say something about the distribution of the pairs, (a_i, b_i), being dissatisfied with the familiar, but boring, $a_i \sim \mathcal{N}(a_0, \sigma^2)$ with $b_i \equiv b_0$. Every point in sample space, (y_i, x_i), gives us a line in parameter space. Pairs of points in sample space give us points in parameter space, since they generate intersections of lines in parameter space. There is a long history of estimators constructed from these pairwise intersections that is sketched in Koenker (2000). Edgeworth (1888) (almost) discovered the simplex algorithm of linear programming by noting that the median regression estimator could be found by moving from vertex to vertex in this so-called dual plot always in the direction of steepest descent. Rousseeuw and Hubert (1999) proposed a highly robust estimator of fixed regression coefficients, (a_0, b_0), by finding the "deepest" point in the scatter of dual plot points in the sense of Tukey's half-space depth. But we are interested in finding the *distribution* of such coefficients, not a single fixed vector. One could easily imagine kernel density estimation methods based on the vertices of the dual plot, but in keeping with our NPMLE orientation we will consider instead methods that are more closely aligned with our tomography discussion.

A line in the dual plot corresponding to a sample observation, (y_i, x_i), is like a line in the tomography setting: We know that (a_i, b_i) is on this line, but we don't know where on the line it is. We will assume from the outset that pairs (a_i, b_i) are independent of pairs (y_i, x_i). This is obviously heroic, but inevitable in the absence of any auxiliary information on the form of dependence. Bounded support for the distribution of (a_i, b_i) is helpful, and in some applications can be easily justified, as for example in ecological regression applications where (a_i, b_i) naturally lives in the unit square.

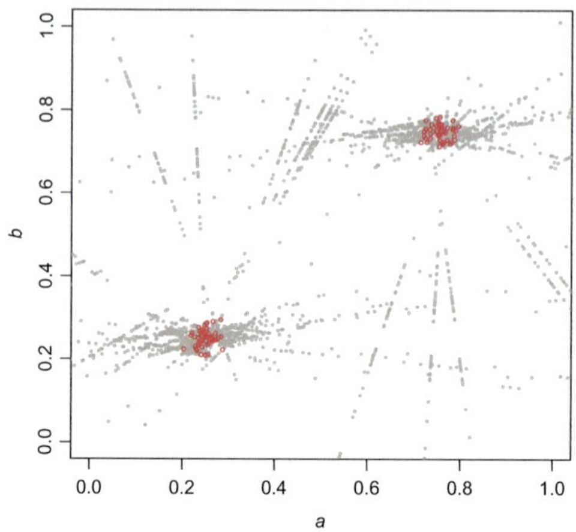

Figure 10.11. Dual plot: Latent coefficients are plotted in red and the dual plot points appear in gray. The gray points are the intersection points of every (i, j) pair of lines $y_i = a_i + b_i x_i$ and $y_j = a_j + b_j x_j$ in the space of (a, b).

Figure 10.11 illustrates a simple bivariate example of the dual plot in a setting in which the coefficient vector is drawn from a bimodal mixture. See Exercise 1.

10.2.4 Ecological Inference

There is an extensive literature on what has come to be known as ecological inference, the seemingly intractable problem of inferring features of individual decision making from aggregated data. A canonical example involves voting turnout. We observe district level data on t_i, the proportion of voting age people who voted in a particular election, and x_i, the proportion of voting age people in the district who identify as white. And we would like to infer something about the propensity to vote by Whites and Hispanics. It is tempting in the face of such a problem to invoke the Tukey maxim: "The combination of some data and an aching desire for an answer does not ensure that a reasonable answer can be extracted from a given body of data." Nevertheless, various proposals have been advanced that offer some prospect of meaningful evidence pertaining to the question posed. Duncan and Davis (1953) suggested that bounds for the parameters could be derived exploiting their bounded support, an approach that has been extensively developed by Manski (2018) and his coauthors in subsequent work. In contrast, Goodman (1953) considered a regression-based approach that Manski (2018) gives a cogent instrumental variables interpretation to and extends by replacing Goodman's linear equalities with linear inequalities yielding new bounds.

In an act of remarkable academic chutzpah, King (1997), published what he called "a solution to the ecological inference problem." His "solution" entailed a random-coefficient interpretation of the problem that brought it into close proximity to the tomography problem we have discussed in the previous subsection. In highly critical reviews, Freedman et al. (1998) and Tam Cho (1998), noted that King's statistical analysis rested on several unverified assumptions and his claims to robustness of the results were misplaced. Ecological inference imposes very stringent assumptions in the effort to extract individual behavioral relationships from aggregate data. In its simplest form considered by Goodman (1953) it posits a linear relationship,

$$t_i = px_i + q(1 - x_i) + \epsilon_i,$$

where, adopting the notation of Freedman et al. (1998), $x_i = n_i^h/n_i$ denotes the proportion of the population in district i who are, for example, Hispanic, and $t_i = v_i/n_i$ denotes the proportion of those in district i who voted for candidate A. We observe, (t_i, x_i, n_i), but we do not observe how $v_i = v_i^h + v_i^a$ is decomposed into Hispanic and non-Hispanic components, which is of primary interest. The constant coefficients of the linear model imply that there is a constant "propensity" of Hispanics to vote for A, and likewise for non-Hispanics. This seems quite far-fetched, even before we consider the possibility that least squares estimates of p and q may produce nonsensical results lying outside the interval $[0,1]$; one could also question the linearity and presumed independence of x_i and ϵ_i. Instead, King focuses on a random-coefficient variant of the original model in which p and q are no longer fixed coefficients but drawn from a bivariate Gaussian distribution suitably truncated to the unit square. Relaxing the parametric assumption on the joint distribution of the coefficients, the random-coefficient regression problem looks very much like the tomography problem, except that the convenient physical assumption that lines in the dual plot are generated at uniformly distributed angles must be jettisoned. Now these angles are determined by the sample observations on the x_i's. Curiously, as noted by Beran et al. (1996), when the x_i's happen to be Cauchy, we are back in the special case of tomography. Otherwise, one has to make some nontrivial modifications of the $p(b,d)$ function to account for the marginal distribution of the x_i's, see Feuerverger and Vardi (2000) for further details. Whether NPMLE tomography methods are suitable for ecological inference remains an intriguing problem for future research. Clearly, they also impose strong linearity and independence assumptions that may be challenged in many applications, and as we have seen, even accepting these conditions, reasonable accuracy requires prodigious sample sizes.

To illustrate the foregoing approach, consider the voting model

$$t_i = p_i x_i + q_i(1 - x_i). \tag{10.2}$$

We have removed the error ϵ_i since when n_i is large, which is typically the case, the equation above gives a reliable approximation. We could, of course, rather than writing down the deterministic relation between t_i and x_i as in (10.2), work with vote counts in each individual location and assume a binomial model for the counts. The following analysis could be adapted to that case.

We maintain the assumption of independence between (p_i, q_i) and x_i. This is obviously a questionable assumption and has been criticized in the literature. One way around it is to bring in additional covariates and assume that independence holds conditional on these covariates. In contrast to King (1997) who makes parametric assumptions on the distribution of the mixing distribution of the random coefficients, G of (p_i, q_i), we propose to estimate G nonparametrically. It is reasonable to assume that G has support on $[0,1]^2$, so

$$P(T = t|X = x) = \int 1\{t = px + q(1-x)\}dG(p,q),$$

which may require some discretization of (T, X). Consider a rectangle grid on the unit square, and denote these rectangular boxes as $\mathcal{B}_1, \ldots, \mathcal{B}_L$. We can let L grow with the sample size N. For a given value of (t,x), all we know from our model is that (p,q) takes some value on the line segment $q = \frac{t}{1-x} - p\frac{x}{1-x}$ restricted to the unit square. Let $Q(t,x) = \{(p,q): t = px + q(1-x)\}$; the likelihood varies with a set of probability weights $\boldsymbol{p} := (p_1, \ldots, p_L) \in [0,1]^L$, such that,

$$L(\boldsymbol{p}) = \sum_i \log g_i, \quad \text{s.t. } g_i = \sum_{\ell=1}^{L} 1\{Q(t_i, x_i) \cap \mathcal{B}_\ell \neq \emptyset\} p_\ell, \quad \sum_{\ell=1}^{L} p_\ell = 1.$$

Maximizing $L(\boldsymbol{p})$ gives rise to a discretized estimator $\hat{G}$ for G. We can also consider smoothed estimators $\tilde{G}$ by distributing estimated mass uniformly inside each rectangle, $\mathcal{B}_\ell$. Let the resulting density be $\tilde{g}$. We can consider in-sample prediction for (p_i, q_i) as the posterior mean of the distribution for (p,q) conditional on $(T,X) = (t,x)$. For example, with a grid $(s_1, \ldots, s_m)$ on $[0,1]$, let the approximated density along the line segment $Q(t,x)$ evaluated at s_j be

$$\tilde{g}(p,q|t,x) := \tilde{g}\left(s_j, \frac{t}{1-x} - s_j\frac{x}{1-x}\right) \Big/ \sum_{k=1}^{m} \tilde{g}\left(s_k, \frac{t}{1-x} - s_k\frac{x}{1-x}\right),$$

and the in-sample prediction for (p_i, q_i) is set as the expected value based on this density. We have applied this method to the voter registration data from 275 counties of four Southern states of the United States. The data is made available in the R package **eco** and was originally analyzed in King (1997). The dataset comes with observed value for (p_i, q_i) in each county. In Table 10.3 we compare the performance on in-sample prediction of our NPMLE method with the parametric method as in King (1997) by assuming that (p_i, q_i) follows a bivariate truncated normal distribution. We also include in the comparison the nonparametric Dirichlet method discussed in Imai et al. (2011). There is a significant improvement using either of the nonparametric methods over the parametric method.

Table 10.3. *In-sample prediction performance: Parametric method assumes a bivariate normal distribution on (p,q). NPMLE estimates the distribution of (p,q) nonparametrically. Dirichlet method uses Dirichlet process prior for the distribution of (p,q).*

	Bias		**RMSE**		**MAE**	
	p	q	p	q	p	q
Parametric	0.274	−0.103	0.315	0.141	0.275	0.103
NPMLE	0.049	−0.019	0.194	0.065	0.134	0.042
Dirichlet	0.047	−0.017	0.166	0.054	0.110	0.034

Exercise

(1) To appreciate the role of the dual plot in random coefficient regression, consider a simple bivariate regression setting of Figure 10.11 in which $Y_i = a_i + b_i x_i$ with $x_i \sim U[-10, 10]$ and (a_i, b_i) drawn iidly from the bimodal mixture $0.5\mathcal{N}_2((0.25, 0.25), \sigma^2 I_2) + 0.5\mathcal{N}_2((0.75, 0.75), \sigma^2 I_2)$, with $\sigma = 0.1$. Draw a sample of 100 observations, construct the dual plot and suggest how it might be used to estimate the density of the random-coefficient distribution.

CHAPTER 11

Inference for Empirical Bayes Procedures

Inference, the willingness to attach a principled measure of precision to one's estimates and forecasts, is both the proudest achievement of Bayesian statistics and its Achilles' heel. Formally, there is no problem: The posterior is baked after stirring together likelihood and prior, and from the posterior credible regions of any desired level can be manufactured. Or should we call them credulity regions? Inevitably, such regions rely upon ingredients that are less than ideal. In the evocative description of an early textbook in econometrics even the likelihood is suspect:

> Econometric theory is like an exquisitely balanced French recipe, spelling out precisely with how many turns to mix the sauce, how many carats of spice to add, and for how many milliseconds to bake the mixture at exactly 474 degrees of temperature. But when the statistical cook turns to raw materials, he finds that hearts of cactus fruit are unavailable, so he substitutes chunks of cantaloupe; where the recipe calls for vermicelli he uses shredded wheat; and he substitutes green garment dye for curry, ping-pong balls for turtle's eggs and, for Chalifougnac vintage 1883, a can of turpentine. [Valavanis (1959)]

And that is just the likelihood; now we must confront the contribution of the prior.

11.1 TESTING FOR UNOBSERVED HETEROGENEITY

We have assumed up until now that parameter heterogeneity is a natural state of affairs. This is a testable hypothesis. A seminal contribution of Chesher (1984) proposed a score test for neglected heterogeneity and showed that it was equivalent to the information matrix test introduced earlier by White (1982). Following Gu (2016), we will reformulate the Chesher testing problem to consider a Neyman (1959) $C(\alpha)$ form of the test.

Suppose we observe independent $Y_1, \ldots, Y_n$ with respective densities $\varphi(y|\theta_i)$. We are interested in testing the homogeneity of the θ_i, which we can represent as

$$\theta_i = \theta_0 + \xi U_i,$$

where U_i are iid with common distribution function, H, and moments $\mathbb{E}U_i = 0$ and $\mathbb{V}U_i = 1$. We would like to test $H_0: \xi = 0$ against the general alternative, $H_a: \xi \neq 0$. Proceeding in the conventional way to compute the score with respect to ξ under the null, we obtain

$$\frac{\partial}{\partial \xi} \log \int \varphi(y_i|\theta_0 + \xi u) dH(u)|_{\xi=0} = \int u dH(u) \frac{\varphi'(y_i|\theta_0)}{\varphi(y_i|\theta_0)} = 0,$$

so the score is identically zero as is the Fisher information for ξ. This poses a problem that can be overcome as in Chesher (1984) by reparameterization, or by considering the second order derivative,

$$S_i(\theta_0) = \frac{\partial^2}{\partial \xi^2} \log \int \varphi(y_i|\theta_0 + \xi u) dH(u)|_{\xi=0} = \int u^2 dH(u) \frac{\varphi''(y_i|\theta_0)}{\varphi(y_i|\theta_0)}$$
$$= \frac{\varphi''(y_i|\theta_0)}{\varphi(y_i|\theta_0)}.$$

Under the null, $n^{-1/2} \sum S_i(\theta_0)$ can be shown to be asymptotically Gaussian with mean 0 and variance $\mathbb{E}S_1^2(\theta_0)$, and therefore provides a foundation for tests of parameter heterogeneity. Adapting LeCam's differentiability in quadratic mean conditions, Gu (2016) proves that for local alternatives with $\xi_n = \mathcal{O}(n^{-1/4})$ the $C(\alpha)$ test is asymptotically optimal with a Gaussian shift limit experiment. This formalization has several advantages over earlier developments including removal of unnecessary symmetry assumptions on the form of the heterogeneity distribution, H. Since the $C(\alpha)$ test is based on curvature of the log-likelihood, it follows that the limit experiment is restricted to a rightward shift under the alternative. Therefore information about the sign of ξ is lost. This means that multivariate versions of the test take a mixture of χ^2 limiting form.

Likelihood ratio tests of parameter homogeneity can be developed along similar lines. Building on work of Gassiat (2002) and Azaïs et al. (2006), Gu et al. (2018) propose a likelihood ratio testing procedure that relies on bootstrapped critical values. Computational advances have made evaluating the likelihood ratio test of parameter homogeneity considerably easier; however obtaining critical values renders this approach still somewhat onerous. Related work that addresses similar issues includes Cho and White (2007), Liu and Shao (2003) and Qu and Zhuo (2021).

Finally, we note that pretesting for parameter homogeneity entails all of the usual difficulties associated with pretesting. When the NPMLE favors the homogeneity hypothesis it may be simpler to adopt the conventional empirical Bayes shrinkage rules that will tend to attract all the estimated parameters toward a common central value in such circumstances.

11.2 CONFIDENCE OR CREDIBILITY?

One may take the view that inference can be subsumed into decision theory: After all, reporting a confidence interval for a parameter, θ, is just a decision to make the report. Cox (1958) argues that there is a useful distinction since inference often abstracts from any prior specification of an "action" space or a loss function. The empirical Bayes perspective brings these aspects back as integral parts of the compound decision framework.

It shouldn't come as a shock at this point to learn that the classical confidence set for the vector, $\theta \in \mathbb{R}^n$, in the Gaussian sequence model, $Y_i|\theta_i \sim \mathcal{N}(\theta_i, 1)$,

$$C_y^0 = \{\theta \in \mathbb{R}_n \mid \|y - \theta\| \leq c_\alpha\},$$

with c_α satisfying $\mathbb{P}(\chi_n^2 \leq c_\alpha^2) = 1 - \alpha$, is inadmissible for $n \geq 3$. This was established formally in a series of papers: Stein (1962), Brown (1966), and Joshi (1967). Somewhat later, Hwang and Casella (1984) showed that the set

$$C_y^+ = \{\theta \in \mathbb{R}_n \mid \|\delta^+(y) - \theta\| \leq c_\alpha\}$$

centered at the James–Stein positive part estimator, $\delta^+(y) = y(1 - a/\|y\|^2)^+$, with $0 < a < 0.8\ (n - 2)$, had strictly better coverage despite having the same volume as the classical confidence set. What may be more surprising is the rather arduous development of these results as recounted in the survey paper of Casella and Hwang (2012). Although strongly motivated by Bayesian considerations these results are firmly frequentist in nature, and therefore definitely call into question the fetish of unbiased centering of confidence sets. Since recentering classical confidence sets at a shrunken point estimate can improve coverage, it is natural to consider ways to adjust the size of the recentered sets to adjust for the improved coverage.

The mechanics of Bayesian inference are seductively simple. One begins with a prior belief about the state of the world, $\theta \in \Theta$; then data arrives so the prior is diligently updated to produce a posterior belief. When asked if you would be willing to bet at 20:1 odds that θ is in some specified set $T \subset \Theta$, one should be prepared to respond by stating which side of the bet you prefer, and after checking your bank balance choose the size of the bet. Computing the posterior probability of T might take a moment or two, but otherwise it is all very mechanical. Similarly, one should be able to report a highest posterior density credible set T_α for any choice of a level α.

The discussion in this section parallels the Bayesian viewpoint on selection bias appearing in Section 4.4. Of course it presumes some confidence in the model underlying the likelihood as well as in the prior. Suspicion, for reasons that are steeped in tradition but otherwise not entirely obvious, seems to focus on the prior. In this section we will briefly focus on the problem of constructing confidence intervals for a scalar parameter before returning to compound decision problems of making multiple intervals.

Focusing on a single coordinate, Bayesian posterior credible intervals can be quite different from the classical confidence intervals of elementary statistics. Suppose, for example, we believe that, $Y|\theta \sim \mathcal{N}(\theta, 1)$ with prior, $\theta \sim G = \mathcal{N}(0, v)$; then the posterior for θ is $\mathcal{N}(wY, w)$ where $w = v/(1 + v)$, and thus a $1-\alpha$ credible interval given that we observe $Y=y$ is $\mathcal{I}_\alpha^B = wy \pm \sqrt{w}\xi_\alpha$, where $\xi_\alpha = \Phi^{-1}(1-\alpha/2)$. In contrast, the conventional frequentist confidence interval for $Y=y$ is $\mathcal{I}_\alpha^F = y \pm \xi_\alpha$, and is substantially wider. Both have a claim to marginal validity in the sense that

$$\mathbb{P}_{\theta|Y=y}\{\theta \in \mathcal{I}_\alpha^B(Y)\} = 1-\alpha$$

and

$$\mathbb{P}_{\theta|Y=y}\{\theta \in \mathcal{I}_\alpha^F(Y)\} = 1-\alpha.$$

However, the frequentist coverage of the Bayesian credible interval $\mathbb{P}_{Y|\theta}\{\theta \in \mathcal{I}_\alpha^B(Y)\}$, and the Bayesian coverage of the frequentist confidence interval $\mathbb{P}_{\theta|Y}\{\theta \in \mathcal{I}_\alpha^F(Y)|Y=y\}$, can be substantially different depending upon the values of θ and y, respectively, as illustrated in Figure 11.1. The effort to reconcile this disparity initially focused on adapting frequentist confidence intervals to reflect prior information on a scalar parameter.

The use of Bayesian ideas to construct frequentist confidence sets can be traced back as least as far as Pratt (1961) and Pratt (1963). Suppose, in the simplest case, G is degenerate and $Y \sim P_\theta$, and we construct a confidence interval, $\mathcal{I}(Y)$, of level $1-\alpha$, that is, such that $P_\theta\{\theta \in \mathcal{I}(Y)\} = 1-\alpha$ for all θ. The length of this interval is

$$\lambda(\mathcal{I}(Y)) = \int \mathbb{1}\{\theta \in \mathcal{I}(Y)\}d\theta,$$

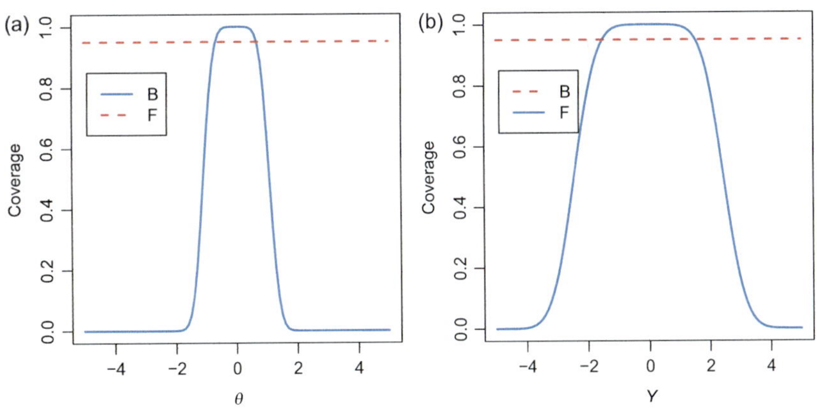

Figure 11.1. Coverage for conventional confidence intervals and Bayesian credible intervals. Panel (a) illustrates frequentist coverage for the conventional confidence interval, $\mathcal{I}_\alpha^F(Y) = Y \pm \xi_\alpha$, and the Bayesian credible interval, $\mathcal{I}_\alpha^B(Y) = wY \pm \sqrt{w}\xi_\alpha$, with $w = v/(1+v)$ based on the prior $\theta \sim \mathcal{N}(0,v)$ and $v = 1/4$. Panel (b) reverses this comparison, showing Bayesian coverage, conditional on Y, for the two intervals. This figure is adapted from lecture notes of Ignatiadis and Sen (2025b).

the Lebesgue measure of $\mathcal{I}(Y)$. Exploiting the familiar duality between confidence sets and hypothesis tests, the expected length of the interval, $\mathcal{I}(Y)$, can be expressed in terms of a test, $\tau_\theta(Y) \in \{0, 1\}$, satisfying $\theta \in \mathcal{I}(Y)$ iff $\tau_\theta = 0$,

$$\begin{aligned}\mathbb{E}\lambda(\mathcal{I}(Y)) &= \int\int \mathbb{1}\{\theta \in \mathcal{I}(y)\} d\theta dP_\theta(y) \\ &= \int P_\theta\{\theta \in \mathcal{I}(Y)\} d\theta \\ &= \int 1 - P_\theta\{\tau_\theta(Y) = 1\} d\theta.\end{aligned}$$

The objective is to construct an interval of minimal length while achieving the required frequentist coverage, that is to solve for all θ,

$$\min_{\mathcal{I}}\{\mathbb{E}\lambda(\mathcal{I}(Y)) \mid P_\theta\{\theta \in \mathcal{I}(Y)\} \geq 1 - \alpha\},$$

or equivalently to maximize the power of the test,

$$\max_{\tau}\{P_\theta\{\tau_\theta(Y) = 1\} \mid P_\theta\{\theta \notin \mathcal{I}(Y)\} \leq \alpha\}.$$

Now let's consider the special case that, $P_\theta = P_0 = \mathcal{N}(0, 1)$, so,

$$\mathbb{E}\lambda(\mathcal{I}(Y)) = \int_{\theta \neq 0} (1 - P_0\{\tau_\theta(Y) = 1\}) d\theta.$$

Note that excluding $\theta = 0$ from the interval doesn't change its expected length, so minimizing $\mathbb{E}[\lambda(I(Y))]$, by the Neyman–Pearson lemma, the most powerful test of null hypothesis θ against the alternative $\theta = 0$ is

$$\tau_\theta(Y) = \mathbb{1}\left\{\frac{p(Y|0)}{p(Y|\theta)} > k(\theta)\right\},$$

with $p(Y|\theta)$ the density of a $\mathcal{N}(\theta, 1)$, and $k(\theta)$ is chosen so that

$$P_\theta(\tau_\theta(Y) = 1) = \alpha.$$

This yields the decision rule for the test,

$$\begin{aligned}\tau_\theta(Y) &= \mathbb{1}\{Y > \theta + \xi_\alpha\} \quad \text{if} \quad \theta < 0, \\ \tau_\theta(Y) &= \mathbb{1}\{Y < \theta - \xi_\alpha\} \quad \text{if} \quad \theta > 0,\end{aligned}$$

with $\xi_\alpha = \Phi^{-1}(1 - \alpha)$. This test has associated confidence interval,

$$\mathcal{I}_0(Y) = [\min\{0, Y - \xi_\alpha\}, \max\{0, Y + \xi_\alpha\}],$$

with expected length $2[(1 - \alpha)\xi_\alpha + \phi(\xi_\alpha)] \approx 3.33$ for $\alpha = 0.05$, whereas the conventional interval has expected length, $2\xi_{\alpha/2} \approx 3.92$, giving a ratio of about 0.85. Thus, if the investigator has a prior "hunch" that θ takes the value 0, so $Y \sim \mathcal{N}(0, 1)$, using the Pratt interval $\mathcal{I}_0$ can result in narrowing the conventional interval by 15% while maintaining frequentist coverage. Of course, if the "hunch" is very wrong the Pratt interval can also be much wider than the conventional one; this is the price one pays for a bad hunch.

If one is not prepared to entertain such dogmatic "hunches," it may be more appealing to consider mixture priors of the form $\theta \sim G$, so Y would have marginal density $\int \varphi(y-\theta)dG(\theta)$. To test the null hypothesis that $Y \sim \mathcal{N}(\theta_0, 1)$ against the alternative that Y comes from this mixture distribution, we consider

$$\tau_{\theta_0}(Y) = \mathbb{1}\left\{\frac{\int \varphi(Y|\theta)dG(\theta)}{\varphi(Y|\theta_0)} > k(\theta_0)\right\},$$

with associated confidence interval, $\mathcal{I}_G(Y)$, of expected length

$$\mathbb{E}\lambda(\mathcal{I}_G(Y)) = \int \int_{\theta \neq \theta_0} (1 - P_\theta(\tau_{\theta_0}(Y) = 1))d\theta_0 dG(\theta).$$

Pratt (1963) considered the Gaussian prior, $G = \mathcal{N}(\mu, \sigma^2)$. To illustrate the performance of these Bayesian intervals, Figure 11.2 compares two versions of the Pratt intervals with the classical, constant width interval. For this figure we assume that $Y|\theta \sim \mathcal{N}(\theta, 1)$ with prior $\theta \sim \mathcal{N}(\mu, \sigma^2)$, with $\mu = 2$ and $\sigma^2 \in \{1/4, 4\}$. When the observed y is near the prior mean, the Pratt intervals are narrower than the classical intervals, but they can be much wider when y is far from μ. In effect we trade somewhat reduced coverage in the likely region for θ for expanded coverage in more remote regions. Yu and Hoff (2018) derive similar Student-t-based intervals for situations in which the variance of Y is unknown, and in multi-group settings they note that information about more

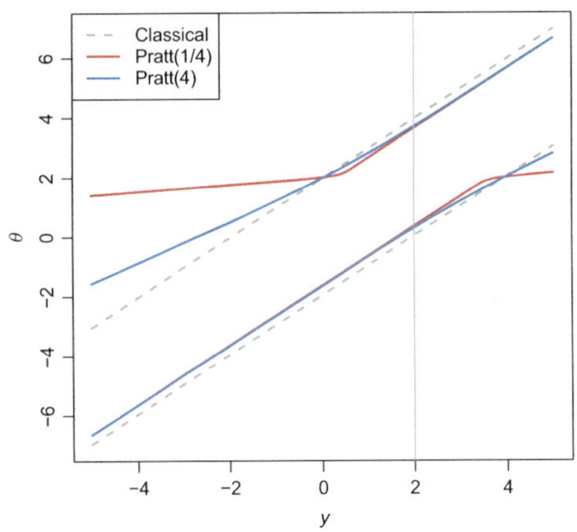

Figure 11.2. Pratt confidence intervals for Gaussian prior: The classical 0.95 confidence interval indicated by the dashed lines is compared with two versions of the Pratt intervals for the prior $\mathcal{N}(\mu, \sigma^2)$ with $\mu = 2$ and $\sigma^2 \in \{1/4, 4\}$. When the observed y is near the prior mean, the Pratt intervals are narrower than the classical interval; however when y is far away from the prior mean, the Pratt intervals can be much wider than the classical interval. This Figure is based on Figure 1b of Yu and Hoff (2018).

general mixing distributions, G, can be acquired, thereby further improving upon the classical intervals.

11.2.1 Confidence and Credibility Bands for Regression

In regression we are often drawn to simple priors like those represented by the ridge or lasso penalties and thus must confront the dreaded problem of selecting tuning parameters: How much do we believe in our prior? Since the answer to this question is usually unclear, we are led into the labyrinthine literature on cross-validation and the dark arts of model selection. Having sinned, by asking the data to help us decide how much we believed in the prior, we must confront a second question: How should we account for this when engaged in inference?

A pragmatic response to both of the foregoing questions is simply to ignore them. Suppose we adopt a data-driven λ-selection rule and treat the induced posterior as if the prior had arrived from the sky. In Gaussian regression and smoothing problems this enables us to immediately write the posterior in closed form. Following Wahba (1983), consider the univariate nonparametric regression model,

$$y_i = g(t_i) + u_i,\ i = 1, \ldots, n,\ t_i \in [0, 1],$$

with u_i iid $\mathcal{N}(0, \sigma^2)$. Solutions to the problem

$$\min_{g \in \mathcal{G}} \sum_{i=1}^{n} (y_i - g(t_i))^2 + \lambda \int_0^1 (g''(t))^2 dt$$

are cubic smoothing splines, $\hat{g}_{n,\lambda} \in C^2$, with knots at the observed points, t_i, and cubic segments in between these points. The squared L_2 penalty on g'' can be interpreted as an improper prior that controls a global measure of curvature of the fitted function. As $\lambda \to \infty$, $\hat{g}$ becomes the linear least squares fit, while as $\lambda \to 0$, $\hat{g}$ interpolates the mean response at each of the unique t_i. If we parameterize $\hat{g}$ by the vector, $\hat{\beta} = (\hat{g}(t_i))$, intermediate values can be interpolated using the continuity conditions imposed on $\hat{g}$. The posterior distribution of β is Gaussian,

$$\beta | y \sim \mathcal{N}(A(\lambda) y, \sigma^2 A(\lambda)),$$

where $A(\lambda) = I + \lambda Q (R + \lambda Q^\top Q)^{-1} Q^\top$, and R and Q are simple tridiagonal matrices depending upon the sample spacings of the ordered design points, t_i. This leads to very efficient computations, but it also means that it is easy to construct pointwise credible bands for g, *conditional on the choice of* λ. This approach can be elaborated to accommodate heteroscedastic noise, and extended to additive models as described by Wood (2006). Silverman (1985) describes a closely related approach that builds upon his asymptotic representation of the Wahba smoothing spline as a nonparametric kernel regression estimator.

How to account for uncertainty about λ selection remains an open question. In practice it seems that conditional bands are often rather insensitive to moderate perturbations of λ. This is hardly unique to the smoothing spline setting; similar issues appear with Dirichlet priors as we have seen in Section 9.3. To some degree they can be alleviated by MCMC methods, but conditioning on data-driven prior parameters often still lurks beneath the surface.

Construction of uniform credible bands poses another challenge for nonparametric regression applications. Again conditioning on λ selection, Krivobokova et al. (2010) propose Hotelling (1939) tube methods for uniform bands for additive spline models. Koenker (2011) suggests similar methods for additive nonparametric quantile regression models employing total variation roughness penalties.

11.2.2 Γ-Minimax Credible Intervals

The parametric and nonparametric empirical Bayes inference methods of the previous section are either implicitly or explicitly grounded in some form of Gaussian prior that produces plausible Bayesian credible regions as long as the prior isn't too unreasonable. When the Gaussian prior assumption, or its scaling by an estimated tuning parameter, is called into question, it is time to consider more conservative methods. Armstrong et al. (2022) (AKPM) have recently proposed an attractive approach to constructing robust confidence intervals for parametric empirical Bayes estimates. Rather than relying on the precise form of the Gaussian prior, they construct an estimate of a least favorable alternative prior and base interval estimates on that. This general approach has its roots in the early work of Robbins (1951) and Good (1952), and is sometimes referred to as Γ-minimax.

To illustrate, consider once again the Gaussian sequence model,

$$Y_i|\theta_i \sim \mathcal{N}(\theta_i, \sigma_0^2),\ i = 1, \dots, n,$$

and suppose provisionally that the θ_i are drawn iidly from $\mathcal{N}(0, \sigma_1^2)$. An oracle, knowing both σ_0 and σ_1, would estimate the θ_i's with

$$\tilde{\theta}_i = (1 - \sigma_0^2/(\sigma_0^2 + \sigma_1^2))y_i \equiv wy_i.$$

Associated credible intervals can be constructed as

$$\mathcal{I}_{\alpha,i} = [\tilde{\theta}_i \pm \xi_\alpha w^{1/2}\sigma_0],$$

where ξ_α denotes a scaling factor chosen to ensure coverage $1 - \alpha$. However, coverage of these intervals can be quite poor when the Gaussian prior assumption is violated. We should stress at this point that "coverage" as it is being used here is unconditional, that is, it refers to average coverage for the composite loss function,

$$L(\theta, \mathcal{I}_\alpha) = n^{-1} \sum_{i=1}^{n} \mathbb{1}\{\theta_i \notin \mathcal{I}_{\alpha,i}\}.$$

This is perfectly consistent with the Robbins notion of compound decision making, but it may offend those who prefer stronger, conditional coverage objectives. For them, there seems little recourse beyond the classical construction of coordinate-by-coordinate intervals.

Proceeding in orthodox frequentist fashion, Armstrong et al. (2022) note that conditional on θ_i, $\tilde{\theta}_i$ has bias $(w-1)\theta_i$ and variance $w^2\sigma_0^2$, so

$$\frac{\tilde{\theta}_i - \theta_i}{w\sigma_0}|\theta_i \sim \mathcal{N}(b_i, 1),$$

where $b_i = (1-1/w)\theta_i/\sigma_0$. Consider $\mathcal{I}_{\alpha,i} = \tilde{\theta}_i \pm c_\alpha w\sigma_0$. The conditional risk of $\mathcal{I}_{\alpha,i}$ is then

$$r(\mathcal{I}_{\alpha,i}) = \mathbb{P}(|Z - b_i| \geq c_\alpha|\theta_i) = \Phi(-c_\alpha - b_i) + \Phi(-c_\alpha + b_i),$$

where Z is standard Gaussian with distribution function Φ. Armstrong et al. (2022) propose to bound the compound risk of the intervals by estimating the least favorable prior that solves

$$\sup_G \mathbb{E}_G\{L(\theta, \mathcal{I}_\alpha) \mid \mathbb{E}_G\theta^2 = \sigma_1^2\},$$

and then to modify the critical value c_α accordingly for this prior. The restriction of $\mathbb{E}_G\theta^2 = \sigma_1^2$ defines a class Γ as all plausible prior distributions. The resulting confidence set minimizes the compound risk for the least favorable prior in the Γ class. One need not buy into the Bayesian view that, $\theta_i \sim G$, for this to be reasonable; instead as we have previously noted one can view the θ_i's as a fixed sequence and interpret the least favorable G simply as an empirical distribution function constrained to satisfy the specified moment condition.

In Figure 11.3 we contrast the AKPM intervals with the Yu and Hoff intervals for two different Gaussian priors. Observed pairs, (Y_i, θ_i), indicated by the black points are generated according to the respective Bayes priors in each panel of the figure. In panel (a) $\theta \sim \mathcal{N}(0, 1/2)$, so shrinkage toward zero is quite strong and the AKPM intervals are narrow compared to both the Yu and Hoff intervals, in blue, and the classical intervals, in green. In panel (b) $\theta \sim \mathcal{N}(0, 2)$, so we are less confident about shrinkage and the three intervals are much more similar. It is important to remember that the coverage guarantees offered by the three intervals in this figure are quite different. The Yu–Hoff intervals, like the classical intervals, promise conditional frequentist coverage of $1-\alpha$, while the AKPM intervals only promise marginal, or average coverage. The AKPM intervals are considerably narrower because they exploit the prior information embodied in the shrinkage and because they offer a weaker coverage guarantee. Rather than insisting on uniform coverage, the coverage criterion only requires coverage "on average." An obvious concern with this marginal coverage criterion is that "difficult" cases can be offset by "easier" cases in a way that may raise fairness concerns. For example, in the setting of panel (a) of Figure 11.3 it appears that most of the AKPM coverage

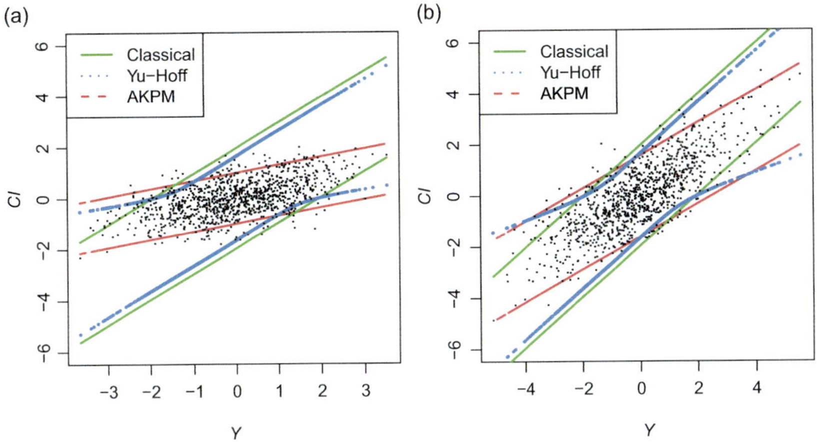

Figure 11.3. Comparison of confidence intervals for two Gaussian priors: The classical 0.95 confidence interval indicated by the (green) solid lines is compared with the (blue) dotted Pratt interval for the Gaussian prior, $\mathcal{N}(\mu, \sigma^2)$, with estimated μ and σ^2, and the (red) dashed Armstron et al. (AKPM) interval. In panel (a) $\sigma^2 = 1/2$, while in panel (b) $\sigma^2 = 2$, and both have $\mu = 0$. The pairs (Y_i, θ_i) indicated by the black points are generated by the respective priors in each panel.

errors occur for the most extreme θ's, while the other intervals' errors are more evenly spread out.

In practice, y_i's typically arise as predictions from some model, so the θ_i's have a nonzero mean, and the y_i's are likely to have associated heteroscedastic variances that need to be estimated; hence Armstrong et al. (2022) show how to modify their procedure to accommodate these features. They also consider imposing an additional moment condition on kurtosis as a way to further constrain the least favorable G. They have also produced an R package **ebci**, (Kolesár, 2021), to facilitate the required computations.

11.3 NONPARAMETRIC EMPIRICAL BAYES CREDIBLE REGIONS

The Γ-minimax approach described in the previous section offers a relatively simple way to assure (asymptotically) correct coverage for confidence intervals centered at classical linear shrinkage estimates. For those who have followed us this far, there should be a lingering suspicion that the Γ-minimax formulation is likely to produce overly conservative intervals in some circumstances. Having argued that nonparametric empirical Bayes methods can often substantially improve upon minimax as well as linear shrinkage rules for estimation, we will now consider how they can be adapted for inference.

11.3.1 Posterior Quantile Credible Intervals Based on the NPMLE $\hat{G}$

Ideally, credible sets should be based on highest posterior density (HPD) regions, although computational cost sometimes dictates simpler procedures. In this section we will confine our attention to intervals based on posterior density, so our $1-\alpha$ sets will ignore potentially multimodal posteriors. Jiang (2019), in his discussion of Efron (2019), notes that the compound decision problem of choosing a simple interval decision rule, $d(Y_i) = [a(Y_i), b(Y_i)]$, solves

$$\min_{a,b} n^{-1} \left\{ \sum_{i=1}^{n} \mathbb{E}\{b(Y_i) - a(Y_i)\}^+ \,\middle|\, n^{-1} \sum_{i=1}^{n} \mathbb{P}\{a(Y_i) \le \theta_i \le b(Y_i)\} = 1 - \alpha \right\}.$$

Equivalently, the oracle Bayes rule, $d^*(Y_i) = [a^*(Y_i), b^*(Y_i)]$, solves

$$\min_{a,b} \left\{ \int \{b(y) - a(y)\}^+ + \lambda \mathbb{1}(a(y) \le \theta_i \le b(y)) dG_n(\theta|y) \right\},$$

where $dG_n(\theta|y) = f(y|\theta)dG_n(\theta)/\int f(y|\theta)dG_n(\theta)$ is the posterior distribution of θ given $Y = y$, and G_n is the empirical distribution of the latent θ_i's. The multiplier, λ is chosen so that

$$\int\int \mathbb{1}(a(y) \le \theta_i \le b(y)) dG_n(\theta|y) f_{G_n}(y) dy = 1 - \alpha,$$

with $f_{G_n}(y) = \int \varphi(y|\theta)dG_n(\theta)$. This is a consequence of the fundamental theorem of empirical Bayes; the loss function balances mean interval length and mean coverage in a natural fashion. For problems with unimodal or monotonic posterior densities, solutions do correspond to HPD intervals and can be characterized as setting interval limits as functions of the Lagrange multiplier, λ. A more stringent coverage requirement for the oracle rule would impose

$$\int \mathbb{1}(a(y) \le \theta_i \le b(y)) dG_n(\theta|y) = 1 - \alpha$$

at each value of y. Such a condition avoids the charge that the weaker mean coverage constraint may unfairly allocate noncoverage probability to some "difficult" cases.

To illustrate the potential advantages of NPMLE credible intervals over Γ-minimax intervals, we consider yet again a simple Gaussian sequence model, $Y_i \sim \mathcal{N}(\theta_i, 1)$ with θ_i's drawn iidly from $G(\theta) = \frac{9}{10}\delta_0 + \frac{1}{10}\delta_{\sqrt{10}}$. Panel (a) of Figure 11.4 depicts estimates of dG based on a sample of $n = 1{,}000$ realizations. The discrete mass points of the NPMLE, denoted as KW, are quite accurate in terms of both location and relative mass, although the main mass at zero is split into two pieces. The Efron g-modeling estimate, discussed in Section 3.3, using his default tuning with five degrees of freedom and $c_0 = 0.1$ is quite similar to the biweight smoothed NPMLE estimate, denoted as KWs. In panel (b) of the figure we compare posterior quantile credible intervals based

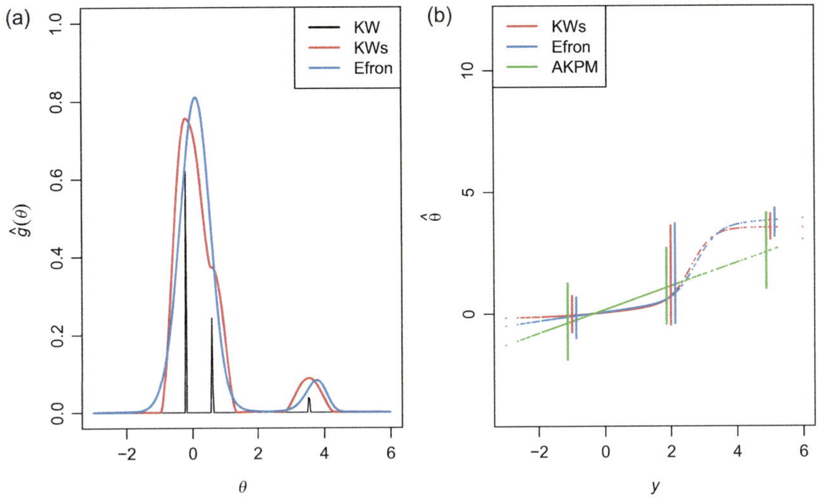

Figure 11.4. Posterior credible interval comparison: Panel (a) depicts three estimates of dG: the NPMLE estimate (denoted KW), a biweight smooth of this discrete estimate (denoted KWs), and the Efron log-spline estimate (denoted Efron). Panel (b) compares posterior quantile credible intervals with the Γ-minimax intervals of Armstrong et al. (2022).

on the Efron and KWs with the intervals proposed by Armstrong et al. (2022) based on the Γ-minimax principle. The latter intervals are of uniform width centered at the (linear) parametric empirical Bayes estimate of the posterior mean. In contrast, the credible intervals for the nonparametric empirical Bayes methods adapt to the changing dispersion of the posterior over the range of Y. Conditional on the observed y near zero, the Efron and KWs intervals are much narrower than the AKPM interval and are centered more accurately near zero. When y is around 2, the nonparametric posteriors are more dispersed since it is difficult to be confident about which of the mass points generated them. Thus the three intervals are roughly the same width. At $y = 4$, the nonparametric intervals reflect confidence that such y's are likely to have been generated from the largest mass point of $\hat{G}(\theta)$. There, and around -1 the KWs and Efron intervals are considerably narrower than the AKPM interval.

What about coverage? Despite the narrower widths of the nonparametric intervals, their coverage for this realization is actually overly conservative, 0.99, rather than the nominal target of 0.95. In spite of this, mean length of the nonparametric intervals is less than two-thirds that of the AKPM intervals. This advantage can partially be attributed to better centering of the Efron and KWs intervals, and partially to the concentration of the posteriors when y is well separated from the region between the two mass points.

Clearly, the flexibility of the NPMLE credible intervals is most advantageous when the posterior mean viewed as a function of y is highly nonlinear and the posterior interquantile range varies considerably with y; otherwise linear shrinkage and credible intervals of constant width seem to be entirely adequate. Thus, discrete location mixtures, like the one illustrated, are particularly favorable, while scale mixtures, or even smooth location mixtures, are less so. To investigate this a bit further we report the results of a small simulation experiment modeled on that appearing in Armstrong et al. (2022). There are three distinct models:

G1 $Y_i = v_j U_i, \quad v_j^2 \in \{0.1, 0.5, 1.0, 2.0\},$
G2 $Y_i = 0.9\delta_0 + 0.1\delta_{v_j} + U_i, \quad v_j^2 \in \{0.1, 0.5, 1.0, 2.0\},$
G3 $Y_i = Z_{i,j} + U_i, \quad v_j^2 \in \{.1, .5, 1.0, 2.0\}.$

The U_i are drawn iidly from $\mathcal{N}(0,1)$, and $Z_{i,j}$ are iid gamma with shape parameter $6v_j$ and rate parameter 3. In the column headings of the table $V = v_j^2$.

We compare the performance of the AKPM intervals with those based on posterior quantiles of the Efron $\hat{G}$ again using its default settings. Table 11.1 reports mean empirical coverage frequencies, in 1,000 replications for each of the model settings for the nominal coverage target 0.95. The AKPM procedure has impressively accurate coverage throughout the experimental design, while there is a slight tendency for the Efron intervals to under-cover. Table 11.2 reports mean widths of the corresponding intervals. As anticipated from Figure 11.4 the Efron intervals are substantially narrower than the AKPM intervals, reflecting both better centering and the adaptive widths of the nonparametric empirical Bayes procedure.

11.4 CONFIDENCE INTERVALS FOR POSTERIOR MEANS

An ambitious new paradigm for empirical Bayes inference has recently been advanced by Ignatiadis and Wager (2022). Given the typical mixture model,

$$Y \sim \varphi(\cdot|\theta), \; \theta \sim G,$$

let $\mu_G(y) = \mathbb{E}_G[h(\theta)|Y = y]$ denote the posterior mean of $h(\theta)$ for some known function h, and let F_G denote the marginal distribution of Y. The objective is to construct intervals,

$$\mathcal{I}_\alpha(y) = [\hat{\mu}_\alpha^-, \hat{\mu}_\alpha^+] \quad \text{s.t.} \quad \liminf_{n\to\infty} \mathbb{P}_G\{\mu_G(y) \in \mathcal{I}_\alpha(y)\} \geq 1-\alpha \quad \text{for all} \quad G \in \mathcal{G}.$$

This objective is quite distinct from the compound decision framework of the previous subsection where intervals were constructed for each observed y_i that were intended to cover θ_i *on average*. Ignatiadis and Wager (2022) motivate their objective with an actuarial example in which auto insurance policy holders have Poisson-distributed accidents with individual specific rate parameters θ_i, and the insurance company would like to construct an interval for the mean number of accidents incurred in a future period by policy holders that had one

Table 11.1. *Empirical coverage for nominal 0.95 credible intervals.*

	G1				G2				G3			
	$V = 0.1$	$V = 0.5$	$V = 1$	$V = 2$	$V = 0.1$	$V = 0.5$	$V = 1$	$V = 2$	$V = 0.1$	$V = 0.5$	$V = 1$	$V = 2$
***n* = 100**												
Efron	0.95	0.91	0.92	0.93	0.94	0.97	0.98	0.99	0.93	0.92	0.92	0.92
AKPM	0.97	0.95	0.94	0.95	0.96	0.94	0.95	0.95	0.96	0.96	0.95	0.94
***n* = 200**												
Efron	0.96	0.92	0.94	0.94	0.93	0.98	0.99	0.99	0.94	0.93	0.93	0.94
AKPM	0.96	0.95	0.95	0.95	0.96	0.94	0.95	0.95	0.96	0.96	0.95	0.95
***n* = 500**												
Efron	0.95	0.91	0.92	0.94	0.92	0.98	0.99	1.00	0.94	0.93	0.92	0.93
AKPM	0.95	0.95	0.95	0.95	0.96	0.95	0.95	0.95	0.97	0.96	0.96	0.95
***n* = 1,000**												
Efron	0.95	0.91	0.89	0.92	0.92	0.98	0.99	1.00	0.94	0.93	0.93	0.93
AKPM	0.97	0.95	0.95	0.95	0.94	0.95	0.95	0.95	0.97	0.96	0.96	0.96

Table 11.2. *Width of nominal 0.95 credible intervals.*

	G1				G2				G3			
	$V = 0.1$	$V = 0.5$	$V = 1$	$V = 2$	$V = 0.1$	$V = 0.5$	$V = 1$	$V = 2$	$V = 0.1$	$V = 0.5$	$V = 1$	$V = 2$
***n* = 100**												
Efron	1.45	2.17	2.67	3.09	1.44	1.93	2.00	1.87	1.67	2.10	2.35	2.58
AKPM	1.84	2.40	2.76	3.19	1.82	2.56	3.03	3.29	2.15	2.44	2.59	2.75
***n* = 200**												
Efron	1.40	2.19	2.72	3.13	1.37	1.89	1.92	1.74	1.64	2.11	2.36	2.64
AKPM	1.76	2.35	2.79	3.20	1.68	2.62	3.08	3.29	2.10	2.40	2.59	2.79
***n* = 500**												
Efron	1.31	2.16	2.67	3.16	1.29	1.84	1.84	1.60	1.59	2.10	2.35	2.62
AKPM	1.68	2.31	2.79	3.21	1.67	2.74	3.09	3.29	2.04	2.39	2.61	2.80
***n* = 1,000**												
Efron	1.27	2.17	2.60	3.09	1.24	1.85	1.79	1.52	1.58	2.12	2.37	2.62
AKPM	1.63	2.30	2.81	3.21	1.63	2.77	3.08	3.29	2.01	2.43	2.62	2.82

accident in the previous sample period. This is a quite natural component in any potential rate-making exercise of an insurance company.

Ignatiadis and Wager (2022) make two proposals to achieve their objective. The first of these they call F-localization; it relies on Massart's form of the Dvoretzky–Kiefer–Wolfowitz inequality. Let

$$\mathcal{F}_n^{DKW}(\alpha) = \left\{ F \in \mathcal{F} \mid \sup_{t \in \mathbb{R}} \mid F(t) - \hat{F}_n(t) \mid \geq \sqrt{\log(2/\alpha)/(2n)} \right\}$$

denote a Kolmogorov–Smirnov ball around the empirical distribution function of the observed Y_i. Then $\mathbb{P}\{F_G \in \mathcal{F}_n^{DKW}(\alpha)\} \geq 1 - \alpha$ for all n and any φ. To make use of this one needs only to observe that the $\mu_G(y)$ functional is a ratio of linear functionals of G, and therefore the interval bounds can be estimated by solving two linear programs using an observation of Charnes and Cooper (1962); see Exercises 2 and 3. A crucial ingredient in these calculations is the restriction of $G \in \mathcal{G}$, where $\mathcal{G}$ denotes a convex set of feasible mixing distribution functions. This may entail bounded support conditions, or classes of location or scale mixtures of some parametric distribution.

The second proposal of Ignatiadis and Wager (2022) seeks to refine their F-localization approach by inverting tests for the posterior mean. This approach is motivated by first considering confidence intervals for linear functionals of G. Then, noting that posterior means are ratios of linear functionals, and adapting a contrivance of Anderson and Rubin (1949), the approach is extended to posterior means. For discrete response models it is natural to use Pearson's goodness of fit criterion in place of the Kolmogorov bounds for F-localization. For binomial mixtures Lord and Cressie (1975) proposed a variant of F-localization further elaborated by Ignatiadis and Wager (2022) that we describe here. Suppose that we observe, for fixed k, a sample of n binomials, as in the Diaconis tack-flicking example of Section 9.3.3,

$$Y_i \sim \text{Bin}(k, \theta_i) \quad \text{with } \theta_i \sim G_0,\ i = 1, \ldots, n.$$

We know that only the first k moments of G_0 are identified; nevertheless we would like to construct confidence intervals for $\mu_{G_0}(y) = \mathbb{E}(\theta \mid Y = y)$ for some fixed value of y, or a simultaneous confidence band for $(\mu_{G_0}(0), \ldots, \mu_{G_0}(k))$. The idea of F-localization is that if we can construct a collection of mixture probabilities $(\phi_G(0), \ldots, \phi_G(k))$ with

$$\phi_G(j) = \int \binom{k}{j} \theta^j (1-\theta)^{k-j} dG(\theta)$$

that covers the true mixture probabilities with probability $1 - \alpha$; then we can characterize a set, $\mathcal{G}_\alpha$, of distributions that will cover the true G_0 with probability $1 - \alpha$. Using this $\mathcal{G}_\alpha$ we can construct intervals that are automatically valid for $\mu_{G_0}(y)$ for all y.

Given the observed frequencies, $\hat{p}_j = n^{-1} \sum_{i=1}^{n} \mathbb{1}\{Y_i = j\},\ j = 0, \ldots, k,$ we can consider the goodness-of-fit statistic,

$$\chi_G^2 = \sum_{j=0}^{k} \frac{(n\hat{p}_j - n\phi_G(j))^2}{n\phi_G(j)}.$$

As $n \to \infty$, we have $\chi_{G_0}^2 \sim \chi_k^2$. Let

$$\mathcal{G}_\alpha = \{G \colon \chi_G^2 \leq \chi_{k,1-\alpha}^2\}$$

with $\chi_{k,1-\alpha}^2$ denoting the $(1-\alpha)$ quantile of the χ^2 distribution with k degrees of freedom. Confidence bounds for $\mu_{G_0}(y)$ can be chosen as

$$\Delta^+(\alpha, y) := \max_{G \in \mathcal{G}_\alpha} \mathbb{E}_G[\theta | Y = y],$$
$$\Delta^-(\alpha, y) := \min_{G \in \mathcal{G}_\alpha} \mathbb{E}_G[\theta | Y = y].$$

So, $\mathbb{P}(\mathbb{E}_{G_0}(\theta | Y = y) \in [\Delta^-(\alpha, y), \Delta^+(\alpha, y)]) = \mathbb{P}(G_0 \in \mathcal{G}_\alpha) = \mathbb{P}(\chi_{G_0}^2 \leq \chi_{k,1-\alpha}^2) = 1 - \alpha$ for all $y \in \{0, 1, \ldots, k\}$.

Figure 11.5 illustrates a simultaneous confidence band for $\mu_{G_0}(y)$ for two binomial settings with $y_i | \theta_i \sim Bin(k, \theta_i)$, and $k = 3$ and $k = 10$. Both panels are based on a sample of size 1,000 and θ taking values in $\{0.3, 0.7\}$ with equal probability. Since the mixing distribution, G_0, is identified only up its first k moments, there is potentially some ambiguity regarding point estimates of the posterior means in these binomial problems, since there are multiple mixing distributions that recover the same observed frequencies $\hat{p}$. This effect is captured by the black line segment in panel (a) where it represents a set-valued estimate. In panel (b) where k is larger, the set of G that recovers $\hat{p}$ is so small that this ambiguity essentially vanishes. Sampling variability of the $\hat{p}$ vector is reflected in the simultaneous band marked by the red $\times$ symbols in the figures.

A deficiency of the NPMLE in categorical data settings like those described here is that it delivers a unique point estimate of G_0 even though we know that G_0 is identified only up to a few moment constraints. For example, in the binomial setting we may have the vector $\hat{p}$ lying outside the model space, and the NPMLE will find a point on the boundary of the model space that is closest to $\hat{p}$ in Kullback–Leibler divergence. When k is relatively small, so the model space is relatively large, this yields a false impression of precision. An advantage of F-localization is that it allows us to check that there is a nonempty intersection of the confidence set for the probability vector p and the model space, the set of feasible probability vectors. If so, we have a way to evaluate the ambiguity of the point estimates. If not, we have evidence that the mixture model representation of the observed data is faulty.

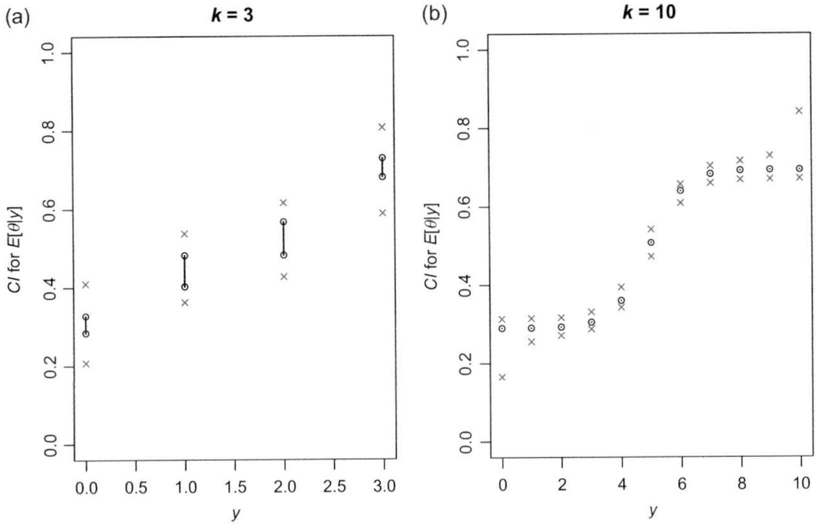

Figure 11.5. F-localization confidence intervals for $\mathbb{E}_{G_0}(\theta|Y = y)$ for two binomial examples. Panel (a) illustrates a setting with $k = 3$ with θ taking values $(0.3, 0.7)$ with equal probability and sample size $n = 1{,}000$. The black line segments represent the range of valid point estimates given the constraints imposed by the set-valued nature of the identification of the mixing distribution, G_0. The outer red $\times$ symbols represent a 95% simultaneous confidence band incorporating the additional sampling variability. Panel (b) illustrates a similar setting except that $k = 10$. The ambiguity of the point estimates collapses to a point in this case, and the uncertainty about the posterior means is due entirely to sampling variability.

11.5 CONFIDENCE INTERVALS FOR RANKING AND SELECTION

A natural criticism of Bayesian methods in general is that inference relies too heavily on the validity of the prior information employed. We have addressed this concern in a variety of earlier sections, notably in Section 4.4, but we revisit it here due to its obvious importance. Any attempt to center confidence intervals at shrunken Bayes estimates risks bias induced by excessive reliance on the prior. This is the critique advanced by Dawid (1994) against the use of naïve priors. Of course naïveté is rather subjective.

In Chapter 7 we have discussed ranking and selection methods intended to choose the best (or worst) elements of a set of candidate individuals, firms or treatments. Loss functions that constrain the number of selected candidates and that control the false discovery rate were considered from a compound decision perspective. Modern multiple testing offers an attractive framework for such decision making. However, it is natural to ask whether ranks themselves or the performance measures used to construct them can be associated with some estimate of their precision. The papers of Mogstad et al. (2024) and Andrews et al. (2024) provide alternative methods for constructing confidence intervals for ranks.

We have argued that selection on the basis of posterior tail probabilities subject to control of false discovery rates offers some advantages over more traditional linear shrinkage methods when underpinned by nonparametric empirical Bayes estimation. In this framework selected candidates have posterior distributions for their latent merit that can be used to construct confidence or credibility intervals. Of course, as we have already noted, care must be taken to ensure that such intervals are reliable. For example, consider the homogeneous Gaussian sequence model, with $Y_i \sim \mathcal{N}(\theta_0, 1)$, $i = 1, \ldots, n$, so ranks are simply a random permutation. In this case, the NPMLE, $\hat{G}$, converges to a point mass at θ_0, and any attempt to construct credible intervals based on posterior quantiles will fail spectacularly. In contrast, smoothing $\hat{G}$, or employing the Efron log-spline estimator, $\tilde{G}$, is likely to produce more plausible intervals.

11.6 CONFORMAL EMPIRICAL BAYES INFERENCE

The rapidly expanding literature on conformal inference, for example, Vovk et al. (2005), Shafer and Vovk (2008) and Romano et al. (2019), raises the obvious question: Can conformal inference be adapted to Bayesian methods in general and empirical Bayes methods in particular? An initial step in this direction is the paper of Fong and Holmes (2021). The prospect is quite attractive even within the restrictive framework of mixture models that we have been considering. We have seen that confidence sets constructed using the smoothed G-modeling approach of Efron (2019) perform remarkably well in our simulation settings, but there is inevitable concern that misspecification of the likelihood, poor choice of tuning parameters for the prior model or some other unanticipated failure may wreak havoc with this approach in some applications.

We will only briefly describe a simple approach to split-sample conformal posterior quantile credible intervals, but there is every reason to believe that there will be rapid continued development of these ideas. Suppose that we would like to compute posterior quantile credible intervals but are concerned that the construction described in Section 11.3.1 may fail to live up to our stringent coverage requirements. We could retreat to the Γ-minimax methods of Armstrong et al. (2022), but conformal inference offers a middle ground designed to reinforce our confidence about our credible intervals.

To illustrate how this might work we return to the familiar empirical Bayes territory of baseball batting averages. Our task will be to predict next year's batting averages based on this year's performance. Point predictions are no longer sufficient though. Confidence intervals for each player are now required.

As in Gu and Koenker (2017a), let H_{it} be the number of hits in N_{it} at bats by player i in period t. This binomial model is transformed to consider

$$Y_{it} = \arcsin\left(\sqrt{\frac{H_{it} + 0.25}{N_{it} + 0.50}}\right),$$

so approximately, $Y_{it} \sim \mathcal{N}(\theta_i, \sigma_{it}^2)$ where $\sigma_{it}^2 = 1/(4N_{it})$. We will adopt the simplest form of conformal inference by splitting our initial year sample into two half-season training and validation subsamples. The first half-season training sample can be used to estimate a posterior for latent batting "ability," θ, for each player,

$$\pi(\theta|Y_{i1} = y_{i1}) = \frac{\theta\phi((y_{i1} - \theta)/\sigma_{i1})/\sigma_{i1} d\hat{G}(\theta)}{\int \phi((y_{i1} - \theta)/\sigma_{i1})/\sigma_{i1} d\hat{G}(\theta)},$$

and thus predictive posteriors,

$$p(y|Y_{i2} = y_{i2}) = \int \phi((y - \theta)/\sigma_{i2})/\sigma_{i2}\pi(\theta|Y_{i2} = y_{i2})d\theta.$$

For each player in the validation sample we can compute quantiles of these predictive posterior distributions and evaluate conformal scores. This could take many forms, but we will adopt the proposal of Romano et al. (2019) and use

$$c_i = \max\{\hat{q}_{i2}(\alpha) - y_{i2}, y_{i2} - \hat{q}_{i2}(1 - \alpha)\},$$

where $\hat{q}_{i2}(\alpha)$ denotes the α posterior quantile of the batter's (predictive) posterior distribution. When player i's observed batting performance in the validation period falls within the predictive interval, $c_i < 0$; when it falls outside, $c_i > 0$. Now denote the $1 - 2\alpha$ quantile of the c_i's, as $\hat{\kappa}$ and modify the original predictive intervals to be

$$\mathcal{I}_i = \{\hat{q}_{i2}(\alpha) - \hat{\kappa}, \hat{q}_{i2}(1 - \alpha) + \hat{\kappa}\}.$$

Note that when $\hat{\kappa}$ is positive we are expanding the original intervals to adjust for under-coverage, while if $\hat{\kappa}$ is negative we are contracting the width of the intervals to correct for over-coverage. There are many variants of this construction, but when carried out properly each guarantees finite sample coverage at the $1-2\alpha$ level provided of course that underlying exchangeability and stationarity conditions are satisfied.

Exercises

(1) Verify the form of the shortened confidence interval for the univariate Gaussian mean constructed by Pratt (1961) and its relative length with respect to the conventional interval.

(2) [Affine Fractional Programming] Given a known matrix $A \in \mathbb{R}^{m \times n}$, vectors $c \in \mathbb{R}^n$, $d \in \mathbb{R}^n$, $b \in \mathbb{R}^m$, and scalars α, β, show that the problem

$$\max_{x \in \mathbb{R}^n} \left\{ \frac{c^\top x + \alpha}{d^\top x + \beta} \mid Ax \leq b,\ d^\top x + \beta \geq 0 \right\}$$

can be written as a linear program by setting $y = tx$ and $t = 1/(d^\top x + \beta)$, and solving

$$\max_{(y,t) \in \mathbb{R}^{n+1}} \left\{ c^\top y + \alpha t \mid Ay \leq bt,\ d^\top y + \beta t = 1,\ t \geq 0 \right\}.$$

(3) Use the preceding exercise to construct a linear program to solve for the Ignatiadis and Wager (2022) F-localization interval bounds, $\mathcal{I}_\alpha(y) = [\hat{\mu}_\alpha^-, \hat{\mu}_\alpha^+]$.

(4) Describe in more detail how to construct the Ignatiadis–Wager confidence bounds for the binomial setting. Hint: Note that convexity is assured by expressing constraints as rotated quadratic cones.

(5) The asymmetry of the confidence intervals depicted in panel (b) of Figure 11.5 seems rather surprising. Using the data from Lord and Cressie (1975) available from **REBayes** with the command `data(psychtest)`, and the code for Figure 11.5 available from the EBR Github site, investigate whether this asymmetry also appears in this "real data" application.

(6) Using the archived baseball data for Gu and Koenker (2017a), construct conformal predictive intervals and evaluate their coverage in a subsequent year.

CHAPTER 12

Computational Considerations

Computational methods for hierarchical Bayesian applications have evolved rapidly with the development of Markov chain Monte Carlo methods introduced in the 1950s. Efficient computational methods for nonparametric empirical Bayes models are relatively recent and therefore less well known. We will focus our exposition in this chapter on the latter developments emphasizing the nonparametric mixture models that have dominated our preceding chapters, with the understanding that there are many excellent resources devoted to the parametric, hierarchical setting. After a brief discussion of computational methods for finite mixture models we will withdraw to the relative safety of nonparametric mixtures where convexity assures us unique solutions and computation is more straightforward.

12.1 FINITE MIXTURES

The first formal estimation of a mixture model in statistics seems to have been an analysis by Karl Pearson (1894) of the ratio of "forehead breadth" to body length of 1,000 crabs sampled from the Bay of Naples by the prominent biologist WFR Weldon. Pearson estimated a two-component normal mixture model by the method of moments, a truly heroic computational effort given the technology of the time. Pearson allowed his two normal components to have distinct means and variances so together with the relative weight of the two components he had five free parameters. Modern EM methods are capable of producing similar results, although they are quite sensitive to the choice of initial values. It is thus tempting to ask: Can we be completely nonparametric in such problems?

The short answer, unfortunately, is "no." The immediate difficulty one encounters is that in contrast to the Gaussian mixture models we have described earlier, there is no fixed scale, or longitudinal dimension to the data. All we have is a single sample, a basket of crabs. If we were to assume that we had a simple location mixture, or a simple scale mixture, it would be easy to estimate the mixing distribution with the NPMLE. But if we try to emulate Pearson and estimate a nonparametric location *and* scale mixture without specifying the number of components we are headed for a Dirac catastrophe. For each observation, we are entitled to assign a distinct mixing value $\theta_i = y_i$, corresponding to these θ_i we are also entitled to assign a $\sigma_i = 0$, and to each of these points $(\theta_i, \sigma_i) = (y_i, 0) \quad i = 1, \dots, n$ we can assign mass $1/n$. As a consequence, the likelihood diverges to infinity. Such catastrophes can be avoided by very cautiously exploring the likelihood surface for interior optima, but there may be several of these and selection of the best one can be difficult.

The moral of this fable is this: Sorting a basket of crabs into groups is more dangerous than it might seem. Kiefer and Wolfowitz were already aware of this; the final paragraph of their 1956 paper points out the fundamental difficulty of the location-scale Gaussian mixture model. Teicher (1967) provides a more formal discussion. Chapter 5 contains some further discussion of the perils of finite mixture models.

These difficulties have led some to abandon mixture models entirely. Wasserman (2012), after a multipart indictment of such models, concludes "that mixtures, like tequila, are inherently evil and should be avoided at all costs." This critique is targeted at finite-parameter mixture models, however, and we have argued that some more flexible nonparametric mixture models are actually quite tractable and potentially useful.

Mixtures are like cocktails: There are the ingredients, their proportions, and perhaps some instructions on how they are to be combined. Thus far we have confined our attention to mixture models whose ingredients are all identical up to some finite dimensional parameter. Our generic model,

$$f(y) = \int \varphi(y|\theta) dG(\theta),$$

presumes a known form for the "base" density, φ, and only G remains unknown. We will adhere to this assumption throughout this chapter, but it would be negligent to pretend that there are not more ambitious formulations of the mixture problem that have attracted the attention of a wide swath of the statistical community. In cluster analysis, for example, it is common to look for a small number of distinct distributions that characterize meaningful groupings of sample observations. Such inquiries typically do not start from some preordained parametric base model; instead, the distributional form of the component groups is left unspecified. This flexibility raises crucial questions of identifiability that have elicited a large literature as discussed briefly in Section 5.2.

For the Gaussian sequence model, Exercise 11 proposes a simple approach to robustify the Gaussian error assumption with the Huber least favorable distribution. This approach admits the possibility of heavier-tailed noise than the traditional Gaussian condition.

12.1.1 Method of Moments for Finite Mixture

In finite mixture models where the mixing distribution, G, is known to have k atoms, a likelihood-based approach can be difficult to use due to nonconvexity.

In such circumstances, the method of moments can offer an attractive strategy for estimation. Returning to the Gaussian sequence model, $Y_i = \theta_i + \sigma U_i$ with σ presumed known, recall from the discussion in Chapter 3 that the moments of G can be expressed in terms of the moments of Hermite polynomials evaluated at the observed Y_i's. These unbiased moment estimators need not correspond to the moments of a valid mixing distribution, G, due to sampling noise; however, they can be projected onto a suitable moment space as described in Chapter 3. Given such a denoised moment vector, $\tilde{\boldsymbol{m}} = (\tilde{m}_1, \ldots, \tilde{m}_{2k-1})$, obtained by the procedure of Wu and Yang (2020), the distribution G can be estimated based on the following result.

Proposition 12.1 Suppose G is a discrete distribution with precisely k atoms. Given $\boldsymbol{m} = (m_1, \ldots, m_{2k-1})$, the first $2k-1$ moments of G, we can uniquely identify G, and the locations of the k atoms are roots of $\boldsymbol{S}_k(t) = 0$ with

$$\boldsymbol{S}_k(t) = det \begin{pmatrix} 1 & m_1 & \ldots & m_k \\ m_1 & m_2 & \ldots & m_{k+1} \\ & & \vdots & \\ m_{k-1} & m_k & \ldots & m_{2k-1} \\ 1 & t & \ldots & t^k \end{pmatrix}.$$

Denote the roots of $\boldsymbol{S}_k(t) = 0$ by $t_1, \ldots, t_k$; these are easily found in R, for example, with the function `polyroot`. The weights of the k atoms can then be found uniquely by solving

$$\begin{pmatrix} 1 & 1 & \ldots & 1 \\ t_1 & t_2 & \ldots & t_k \\ t_1^2 & t_2^2 & \ldots & t_k^2 \\ & & \vdots & \\ t_1^{k-1} & t_2^{k-1} & \ldots & t_k^{k-1} \end{pmatrix} \begin{pmatrix} w_1 \\ w_2 \\ w_3 \\ \vdots \\ w_k \end{pmatrix} = \begin{pmatrix} 1 \\ m_1 \\ m_2 \\ \vdots \\ m_{k-1} \end{pmatrix}.$$

Recall that for any given σ, we have

$$\gamma_k(y, \sigma) = \sigma^k H_k(y/\sigma) = k! \sum_{j=0}^{\lfloor k/2 \rfloor} \frac{(-1/2)^j}{j!\,(k-2j)!} \sigma^{2j} y^{k-2j},$$

such that $\mathbb{E}[\gamma_k(Y, \sigma)] = \mathbb{E}[\theta^k]$. If σ is known, we can construct unbiased estimates as

$$\hat{m}_k = k! \sum_{j=0}^{\lfloor k/2 \rfloor} \frac{(-1/2)^j}{j!\,(k-2j)!} \sigma^{2j} \frac{1}{n} \sum_{i=1}^{n} y_i^{k-2j}.$$

When σ is unknown, Theorem 3.6 then leads to the algorithm suggested by Lindsay (1989) to estimate (σ, G) jointly, which consists of steps described in Algorithm 1.

In contrast to the case where σ is known, the foregoing algorithm involves no denoising step. Wu and Yang (2020) show that with probability one, the

---

Algorithm 1: Lindsay's method-of-moments algorithm for estimation of finite Gaussian mixture models.

---

(1) Estimate $\hat{m}_k(\sigma) = k! \sum_{j=0}^{\lfloor k/2 \rfloor} \frac{(-1/2)^j}{j!(k-2j)!} \sigma^{2j} \frac{1}{n} \sum_{i=1}^{n} y_i^{k-2j}$.

(2) Let $\hat{d}_k(\sigma)$ be the determinant of moment matrix formed from $(\hat{m}_1(\sigma), \ldots, \hat{m}_{2k}(\sigma))$.

(3) Let $\hat{\sigma}$ be the smallest non-negative root of $\hat{d}_k(\sigma) = 0$.

(4) Construct $\check{m}_k = \hat{m}_k(\hat{\sigma})$.

(5) Apply the quadrature method as in Proposition 12.1 with $\check{m}_1, \ldots, \check{m}_{2k-1}$ to obtain an estimator $\hat{G}$.

---

estimated moment vector $(\check{m}_1, \ldots, \check{m}_{2k-1})$ from Lindsay's algorithm lies in the moment space, so no denoising is needed. The same paper also establishes that $\hat{\sigma}$ is a consistent estimator for σ and is minimax rate optimal.

12.2 INFINITE MIXTURES AND THE NONPARAMETRIC MLE

Happily, many of the annoying features of maximum likelihood estimation of finite-dimensional mixture models, including multimodality of the log-likelihood and singularities at the boundary of the parameter space, vanish when we relax the constraints and consider infinite-dimensional mixtures. This was recognized by Kiefer and Wolfowitz (1956) and anticipated by Robbins (1950), but it did not lead to practical optimization methods until Laird (1978) described how to adapt the EM algorithm of Dempster et al. (1977) to this task. Still, efforts to implement EM methods for general mixture models by Heckman and Singer (1984) and others have proven to be challenging. Tuning the EM algorithm involves a number of delicate issues, not the least of which is its convergence criterion. We will describe several alternative approaches to computation of the NPMLE in this chapter. One is a direct implementation of the Kiefer–Wolfowitz estimator based on discretization to a finite-dimensional grid as proposed by Koenker and Mizera (2014); the other is the logspline approach proposed by Efron (2016, 2019).

It is easy to see that the primal NPMLE problem,

$$\min_{G \in \mathcal{G}} \left\{ -\sum_{i=1}^{n} \log f(y_i) \mid f(y_i) = \int \varphi(y_i|\theta) dG(\theta),\ i = 1, \ldots, n \right\}, \tag{12.1}$$

where $\mathcal{G}$ denotes the set of all mixing distributions, is a convex program. It may be noted here that when φ is discrete, n can be interpreted as the number of *distinct* values taken by y_i with the log-likelihood implicitly incorporating appropriate weights to account for repeated observations. The problem (12.1) has a strictly convex objective function, subject to linear equality and inequality constraints. The inequalities arise from the requirement that elements of $\mathcal{G}$ must be nondecreasing, so dG must be non-negative. The infinite-dimensional form of (12.1) may seem to be an impediment to efficient computation, but we will see that this is not really the case. This is most easily seen by considering the dual formulation of the problem, which reduces it to a finite-dimensional objective subject to finite-dimensional linear equality and inequality constraints.

Theorem 12.2. *Koenker and Mizera (2014). The solution, $\hat{G}$, of* (12.1) *exists, and is an atomic probability measure, with no more than n atoms. The locations, $\hat{\theta}_j$, and the masses, $\hat{g}_j$, at these locations can be found via the following dual characterization: The solution, $\hat{\nu}$, of*

$$\max\left\{\sum_{i=1}^{n}\log \nu_i \mid \sum_{i=1}^{n}\nu_i\varphi(Y_i|\theta) \leq n \textit{ for all } \theta\right\} \tag{12.2}$$

satisfies the extremal equations

$$\sum_{j=1}^{m}\varphi(Y_i|\hat{\theta}_j)\hat{g}_j = \frac{1}{\hat{\nu}_i}, \tag{12.3}$$

where $\hat{g}_j$ denotes the mass associated with the m active grid points θ_j – that is, where the constraint function in (12.2) *is equal to n.*

The dual formulation of the NPMLE problem reveals that we have m linear constraints in n variables, and therefore there are at most n active constraints; consequently solutions, $\hat{G}$, must be atomic with no more than n mass points. See Lindsay (1983a, theorem 3.1). The infinite dimensionality of the problem appears only in the requirement that the constraints must hold for all $\theta \in \mathbb{R}$. To help visualize the optimality conditions for the NPMLE we can consider an analogue of the usual (first-order) likelihood equations that characterize the MLE in finite-dimensional problems. Suppose $\hat{G}$ is a solution and consider a one-dimensional perturbation of $\hat{G}$ in the direction H,

$$H_\tau = (1-\tau)\hat{G} + \tau H.$$

Writing our log-likelihood objective as

$$\ell(G) = \sum_{i=1}^{n}\log f_G(y_i),$$

with $f_G(y_i) = \int \varphi(y_i, \theta)dG(\theta)$, we have

$$\frac{\partial}{\partial\tau}\ell(H_\tau) = \sum_{i=1}^{n}\frac{f_H(y_i) - f_{\hat{G}}(y_i)}{f_{H_\tau}(y_i)}$$

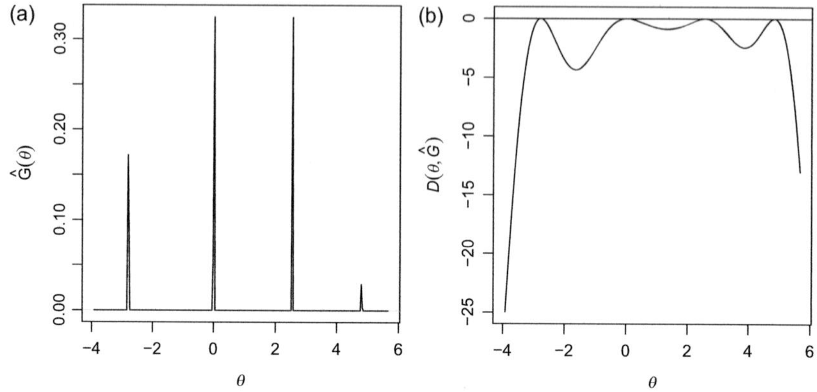

Figure 12.1. Optimality condition for a Gaussian NPMLE solution: Panel (a) depicts the four estimated mass points of $\hat{G}$ and panel (b) shows the Gâteaux derivative of the objective function evaluated at $\hat{G}$. The four tangencies of $D(\delta_\theta, \hat{G})$ with the horizontal line at zero indicate the locations of the mass points.

and

$$\frac{\partial^2}{\partial \tau^2} \ell(H_\tau) = -\sum_{i=1}^{n} \frac{(f_H(y_i) - f_{\hat{G}}(y_i))^2}{f_{H_\tau}^2(y_i)} \leq 0.$$

Thus, $\ell(H_\tau)$ is concave in τ and maximized at $\tau = 0$. Evaluating at $\tau = 0$ we obtain the Gâteaux derivative,

$$D(H, \hat{G}) = \frac{\partial}{\partial \tau} \ell(H_\tau)|_{\tau=0} = \sum_{i=1}^{n} \left(\frac{f_H(y_i)}{f_{\hat{G}}(y_i)} - 1 \right),$$

which at an optimum must be nonpositive for all H. In particular, we can take H to be a point mass at θ, that is, δ_θ, and plot $D(\theta, \hat{G}) \equiv D(\delta_\theta, \hat{G})$ as a function of θ.

This is illustrated in Figure 12.1 for a sample of 100 observations from a discrete Gaussian mixture with equal probability masses at $\{-2.5, 0.5, 3.0\}$. $D(\delta_\theta, \hat{G})$ is evaluated on a moderately fine grid of 300 equally spaced values of θ. This produces a smooth curve that exhibits four tangencies with the $D(\delta_\theta, \hat{G}) = 0$ axis. At all other values of θ, $D(\delta_\theta, \hat{G})$ is strictly negative indicating that the log-likelihood would be reduced were we to introduce a new mass point at such locations. The solution, $\hat{G}$, is depicted in panel (a) where there are three large mass points at approximately the correct locations and a fourth mass point at about $\theta = 5$. The Gâteaux derivative, evaluated at this $\hat{G}$, is shown in panel (b). It is strictly negative at all θ, while the four tangencies correspond to the location of the four mass points. Of the 300 linear constraints imposed by the grid, only four are active and they fully determine the nature of the solution: Location of the masses defining $\hat{G}$ are determined by the zeros of the Gâteaux derivative, and the masses themselves are determined by (12.3).

This derivative characterization of the NPMLE has roots in the literature on optimal experimental design and was further developed by Lindsay (1995). An efficient active set algorithm for computing the NPMLE based on this characterization of the NPMLE has been developed by Wang (2007) and is described in more detail in Section 12.2.3.

12.2.1 Uniqueness and Equivariance of the NPMLE

For mixture models with base density $\varphi(y,\theta)$, Lindsay (1983b) and Lindsay and Roeder (1993) have shown that the NPMLE is unique when φ comes from a continuous exponential family. When φ is discrete, for example, binomial or Poisson, the situation can be somewhat more complicated as we have illustrated in Chapter 4. In discrete settings we observe only a finite number of frequencies and consequently there will be many $\hat{G}$ mixing distributions that can perfectly reproduce these observed frequencies, so there is no unique NPMLE. Such cases are partially identified from a finite set of frequencies, or equivalently moments, of the mixture distribution so we cannot hope to identify a general mixing distribution, G. Thus, from a population viewpoint we will always find ourselves in the quandary that many G serve to generate the same set of population frequencies of a given model. Nevertheless, in any given *sample* it may be impossible to find a $\hat{G}$ that reproduces the observed, marginal frequencies. Indeed, this is quite likely to be the case as Figure 9.4 demonstrates. The NPMLE must in such circumstances find a feasible point, $\hat{G}$, capable of generating marginal frequencies near the observed ones. This projection on to the feasible set produces a unique NPMLE despite the fact that the model is fundamentally underidentified.

We are accustomed to thinking about Bayes estimators as shrinkage methods, a preconception that carries with it the idea that we are "shrinking toward some prior value, usually zero." This is certainly the case for the James–Stein estimator and other soft-thresholding rules, or ridge and lasso penalized regression estimators. An important, but perhaps underappreciated, feature of the NPMLE and the decision rules that flow from it is that there is no privileged value to which shrinkage is attracted. This can be seen especially clearly for location and scale mixtures. Proofs are immediate by noting the invariance of the linear equality constraints of the NPMLE problem.

Proposition 12.3 For base distributions of the location shift form, $\varphi(y-\theta)$, the NPMLE, $\hat{G}$, is location equivariant, that is, if $\hat{G}(\theta)$ is the NPMLE for a sample, $y_1, \ldots, y_n$, then $\hat{G}(\theta + a)$ is the NPMLE for a sample, $y_1 + a, \ldots, y_n + a$ for $a \in \mathbb{R}$.

Proposition 12.4 For base distributions of the scale shift form, $\varphi(y/\theta)$, the NPMLE, $\hat{G}$, is scale equivariant, that is, if $\hat{G}(\theta)$ is the NPMLE for a sample, $y_1, \ldots, y_n$, then $\hat{G}(a\theta)$ is the NPMLE for a sample, $ay_1, \ldots, ay_n$ for $a \in \mathbb{R}_+$.

These results help to explain the good performance of the NPMLE posterior mean in Table 4.1 relative to more formal Bayesian procedures that typically shrink all observations toward zero. In contrast, the NPMLE posterior mean shrinks observations near zero toward zero, but non-null observations are typically shrunk toward an estimated non-null mass point, thereby significantly improving the overall mean squared error. This is a more sophisticated version of the Efron and Morris procedure that shrinks all observations toward the sample mean. It is also related to the self-consistency property of the NPMLE, a fact first noted by Lindsay (1981).

Theorem 12.5. *Let $\hat{G}$ denote a unique solution of the problem (12.1) and*

$$\mathbb{E}_G[h(\theta)|Y = y] = \frac{\int h(\theta)\varphi(y|\theta)dG(\theta)}{\int \varphi(y|\theta)dG(\theta)}.$$

Then, provided that $\partial \log \varphi/\partial\theta$ is well defined on the entire support of φ, we have

$$n^{-1}\sum_{i=1}^{n} \mathbb{E}_{\hat{G}}[h(\theta)\partial \log \varphi(Y|\theta)/\partial\theta \mid Y = y_i] = 0,$$

for any function, $h(\theta)$ that vanishes on the boundary of the support of φ.

As a consequence, if we consider the denoised, posterior means of the sample observations, although each one is biased, the mean bias over the entire sample is zero. In contrast, Lindsay (1981) also shows that the variance of the estimated marginal distribution of Y is less than or equal to the sample variance of the observed y_i's. See Exercises 2 and 3. We note in passing that an analogous result is obtained in the recent literature on log concave density estimators: Sample means are preserved, but sample variances are reduced by the shape-constrained maximum likelihood estimator, see for example, Samworth (2018).

12.2.2 The EM Algorithm

The expectation-maximization EM algorithm of Dempster et al. (1977) has found widespread applicability in both convex and nonconvex problems. Laird (1978) presents a careful characterization of the NPMLE noting that for the Gaussian location mixture, $\hat{G}$ has no more than n mass points, and that these mass points need not occur at the observed sample points. She goes on to propose a variant of the EM algorithm that proceeds by solving for a sequence of finite mixture problems of increasing number of mass points, stopping when improvement in the likelihood become negligible. A related approach was suggested by Simar (1976) for Poisson mixtures. A merger of these strategies was endorsed by Lindsay (1981), and similar methods were adopted by Heckman and Singer (1984). Closely related vertex-exchange algorithms had been developed in the optimal design literature, for example, Böhning (1986).

To the best of our knowledge, Jiang and Zhang (2009) were the first to suggest that the NPMLE could be computed by solving for the fixed-point of the iteration,

$$\hat{g}_j^{(k+1)} = n^{-1} \sum_{i=1}^{n} \frac{\hat{g}_j^{(k)} \varphi(Y_i | \theta_j)}{\sum_{l=1}^{m} \hat{g}_l^{(k)} \varphi(Y_i | \theta_l)},$$

where the location of potential mass points for $\hat{G}$ are given by a prespecified grid, $\{\theta_1, \ldots, \theta_m\}$. This fixed-point iteration formulation of EM is fairly quick to find a rough approximation to the NPMLE solution, but it is very slow to refine the solution to identify the precise location of its discrete mass points.

In Figure 12.2 we illustrate this based on a Gaussian sequence model with $n = 200$ observations and grid dimension $m = 300$. After 100 iterations EM has found a widely dispersed unimodal smooth $\hat{G}$ shown in red. After 10,000 iterations there are 3 distinct modes for the $\hat{G}$ "density," and after 100,000 iterations these modes are somewhat further refined. However, nearly 10 minutes was required to compute the solution with 100,000 iterations. It can be argued that this slow convergence with its smooth approximations to the discrete solution is advantageous. "Early stopping" of the EM iterations can be viewed as a smoothing mechanism for $\hat{G}$, but it may be difficult to tune the convergence tolerance. Lindsay (1995) comments, "One could obviously take the tack that one should iterate on an algorithm until the accuracy of the result approaches the limit of machine accuracy. However, this is not practical if one wants to do simulation studies, or apply bootstrap methods."

The EM algorithm can be seen as a form of gradient descent, see Xu and Jordan (1996), and therefore inherits the convergence properties of the latter.

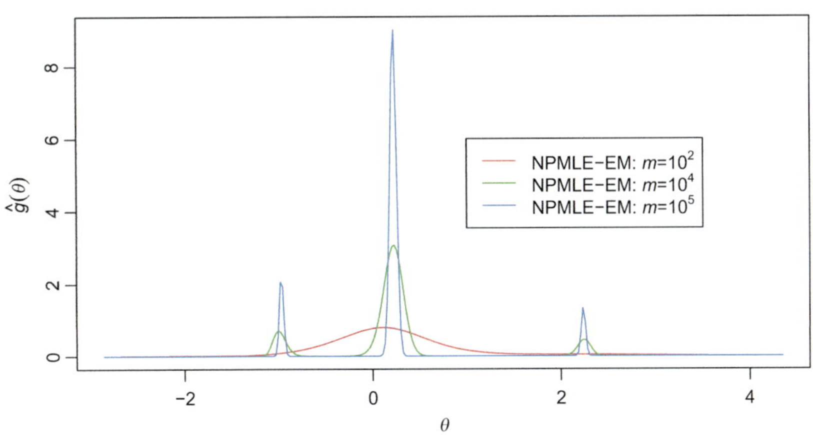

Figure 12.2. Slow convergence of the EM algorithm: The figure shows three NPMLE solutions based on a fixed-point implementation of the EM algorithm for different iteration counts.

In mixture settings with the mixing parameter, θ, of dimension one or two, it is possible to exploit interior point methods for convex optimization that achieve much faster and more accurate solutions.

12.2.3 Active Set Methods

Like many other constrained optimization problems, computing the NPMLE may be viewed as a quest to identify the subset of "active constraints," that is, constraints that are binding at the solution. As we have already noted in Theorem 12.2 and the discussions afterwards, by convexity, this can be reduced to finding a stationary point of the functional derivative of the log-likelihood. Building on work of Lesperance and Kalbfleisch (1992) and earlier work on optimal design, Wang (2007) proposed a constrained Newton method for computing the NPMLE for mixtures. Given an initial guess for $\hat{G}$, Wang computes all the local maxima, say $\theta_1, \ldots, \theta_m$, of the functional derivative, $D(\theta, \hat{G}) = D(\delta_\theta, \hat{G})$. Treating these local maxima as the sole support points of $\hat{G}$, their relative masses can be found by Newton steps subject to a non-negativity constraint. Wang suggests taking only one Newton step at each iteration, then updating $\hat{G}$ by discarding old support points with zero mass and adding new support points found by recomputing the local maxima of $D(\theta, \hat{G})$. Iterations continue until $\max_i D(\theta_i, \hat{G}) = 0$. Like the EM algorithm this approach relies on a finely spaced grid of points on which to evaluate $D(\theta, \hat{G})$; however it is considerably more efficient than EM due to the quadratic convergence of the Newton steps. An R implementation of the algorithm is available in the package `nspmix` (Wang, 2017–2020).

12.2.4 Interior Point Methods

Interior point methods for convex optimization have gradually evolved from their introduction in the 1980s for solving large linear programs. In their simplest form, described in detail in Portnoy and Koenker (1997) for quantile regression problems, they replace linear inequality constraints by log barrier constraints that repel the sequence of iterates away from the boundary of the constraint set, while adjustment of barrier parameters allow them to approach boundary solutions. This can be accomplished quite efficiently because the barrier penalization replaces the boundary constraints with a smooth contribution that admits a smooth Hessian facilitating Newton-like steps. Thus, iterating from an interior point of the constraint set toward the boundary exhibits quadratic convergence in contrast to the sublinear convergence rate of the EM method. The worry, of course, is that problem size may render each iteration of the interior point algorithm too costly. Crucially, because the relevant constraint matrices are typically quite sparse, the linear algebra of these steps can be carried out quite efficiently. Our computational experience is confined to problems with mixing parameter, θ, of dimension one or two, for which gridding of the domain of $\hat{G}$ is entirely manageable. In higher-dimensional mixture settings alternative computational strategies will undoubtedly be needed.

In the Gaussian sequence problem with $n = 200$, using the EM algorithm, 100,000 EM iterations – and nearly 10 minutes – were required to obtain a decent approximate solution. Only 17 iterations of the Mosek interior point solver were required to find a considerably more accurate solution in 0.19 seconds. Lindsay's concerns about the EM algorithm can be circumvented; solutions to machine accuracy are attainable quickly.

Our implementation of interior point methods for computing NPMLEs for various mixture models initially described in Koenker and Mizera (2014) has been developed in the R package **REBayes**, which relies in turn on the convex optimization language Mosek (ApS, 2022a) and its R interface **Rmosek** (ApS, 2022b). A vignette describing the functionality of the **REBayes** package is available in Koenker and Gu (2017). The package contains generic functions `KWDual` for solving the Kiefer–Wolfowitz dual problem,

$$\max_{\nu \in \mathbb{R}^n} \left\{ \sum_{i=1}^{n} \log \nu_i \mid A^\top \nu \leq n \mathbb{1}_m,\ \nu \geq 0 \right\},$$

where A denotes an n by m matrix with ij element $\varphi(y_i|\theta_j)$, and `KWPrimal` for solving the primal problem,

$$\min_{g \in \mathbb{R}^m} \left\{ -\sum_{i=1}^{n} \log f_i \mid Ag = f,\ g \in \mathcal{S}_m \right\},$$

respectively. The two problems are equivalent, but we have observed that the dual problem is typically somewhat more efficiently solved. Various specialized functions designed for particular choices of φ are provided, all of which eventually call on `KWDual` to find a solution.

The choice of the grid $\{\theta_1, \ldots, \theta_m\}$ is obviously a crucial ingredient for specifying the constraint matrix, A. For those familiar with solving ill-posed inference problems like nonparametric instrumental variables problems, it is tempting to suspect that the dimension m of this grid is, in some sense, a regularization parameter, but this is wrong. Refining the grid by making m larger has a negligible impact on solutions; solutions with $m = 300$ are indistinguishable from solutions with the same data and $m = 1{,}000$. This can be seen simply by plotting the solution, $\hat{G}$, or equivalently by plotting the Gâteaux derivative at the solution as described above. In either case a small number of distinct mass points are identified, and increasing m only slightly refines their position but not the number of such points or their relative mass. Dicker and Zhao (2016) show that $\mathcal{O}(n^{1/2})$ grid points are sufficient for Hellinger convergence of the marginal density f_G. See Exercise 1.

Although it is relatively easy to see that the number of distinct mass points of NPMLE solutions $\hat{G}$ is less than or equal to the number of distinct values of the y_i's, it has proven to be considerably more challenging to determine how this number grows with sample size. Recently, Polyanskiy and Wu (2020) have shown that for Poisson and Gaussian mixtures with sub-Gaussian mixing distribution this number grows like $\mathcal{O}(\log n)$. To appreciate the dramatic nature of their results it is worthwhile noting first a circumstance in which the bound n is tight. Suppose in the standard Gaussian sequence model the true mixing distribution, G, consists of widely separated points so the true mixture distribution has n distinct modes; $\hat{G}$ must try to mimic this behavior and consequently may have as many as n mass points.

In the Poisson mixture setting, with $\varphi(y|\theta) = \theta^y e^{-\theta}/y!$, the argument for $\mathcal{O}(\log n)$ mass points for $\hat{G}$ is quite straightforward. Differentiating the Gâteaux derivative, we have

$$\frac{d}{d\theta} D(\theta, \hat{G}) = e^{-\theta} \sum_{i=1}^{n} w_i (y_i \theta^{y_i - 1} - \theta^{y_i})$$

with nonnegative weights, $w_i = (y_i!\, f_{\hat{G}}(y_i))^{-1}$. This is proportional to a polynomial of order $y_{(n)} = \max\{y_1, \ldots, y_n\}$ and consequently can have at most $y_{(n)}$ local maxima. Thus, $D(\theta, \hat{G})$, since it is less than or equal to zero, can have at most $y_{(n)}$ zeros, and for subexponential G, $y_{(n)} = \mathcal{O}(\log n)$, so the number of support points of $\hat{G}$ is of that order. The corresponding argument for the Gaussian mixture model, and exponential family models more generally, is considerably more technical, and we refer the interested reader to Polyanskiy and Wu (2020) for details.

As for some shape-constrained density estimators, the NPMLE for mixture models is self-regularizing; no further penalization is required to achieve a sparse solution that adapts well to the observed mixture distribution. It might be objected that such low-dimensional $\hat{G}$ will not be able to deliver sufficiently accurate estimation of the mixture density; however, this concern is also addressed by Polyanskiy and Wu (2020). They show that in the Gaussian mixture model with any sub-Gaussian mixing distribution G, with mixture density $f(y, G) = \phi * G$, there exists a K-component Gaussian mixture, $f_K(y, G_K) = \sum_{k=1}^{K} g_k \phi(y, \theta_k)$ with $K = C \log n$, such that the total variation distance $\mathrm{TV}(f, f_K) = o(1/n)$. Thus, from any statistical perspective of fitting the mixture density, there is no reason to fit mixing distributions that are more complex than those produced by the NPMLE. In this respect, the NPMLE, $\hat{G}$ can be viewed as analogous to Gaussian quadrature, a discrete approximation that provides a good approximation for linear functionals evaluated against smooth test functions. This is fine for posterior means and other smooth functionals but may need some adjustment for posterior quantiles.

As noted by Lindsay (1995), adding linear equality or inequality constraints to the NPMLE problem introduces no new computational difficulties in principle; the problem remains convex and solvable with modern convex optimization software such as Mosek. Another tractable extension, also mentioned by Lindsay, involves problems where the likelihood appears in a ratio form. This is illustrated by application to size-biased sampling and competing risk survival models in chapter 7 of Lindsay (1995).

12.2.5 Efron's Logspline Method

The Efron (2016) logspline estimator expresses the density of the mixing distribution G in parametric exponential family form,

$$\log g(\theta|\alpha) = \sum_{k=1}^{p} z_k^\top(\theta)\alpha_k - \gamma(\alpha),$$

where $z_k(\theta)$ are elements of a spline basis expansion, and γ denotes the usual constant of integration of the exponential family. This is a variant of earlier proposals of Stone (1990) and Barron and Sheu (1991). Again consider the Gaussian sequence model with $y_i|\theta_i \sim \mathcal{N}(\theta_i, 1)$, letting $(t_1 < \cdots < t_m)$ be some relatively fine grid of $t_i \in \Theta$ and A be an n by m matrix with typical element $\phi(y_i - t_j)$. The penalized Efron log-likelihood is

$$\ell(\alpha) = \sum_{i=1}^{n} \log f_\alpha(y_i) + c_0\|\alpha\|,$$

where the n vector $f_\alpha = (f_\alpha(y_1), \ldots, f_\alpha(y_n))$ can be written as, $f_\alpha = AZ\alpha$ with Z the m by p matrix with typical element $Z_{jk} = z_k(t_j)$. Efron adds a regularization term that shrinks $\hat{g}$ toward the uniform distribution. The choices of the spline basis, its dimension and the regularization parameter, c_0, all require some degree of expert judgment, but the approach has several advantages including relatively easy optimization for moderate p and an elegant inference apparatus.

Efron (2016) refers to his procedure as "empirical Bayes deconvolution" although it is obviously applicable to a far wider range of mixture problems than just Gaussian deconvolution. It is also worth noting that the NPMLE can be quite accurately approximated by letting the parametric dimension of the Efron logspline estimator become large while reducing the penalty parameter, c_0, toward zero. It should be stressed that this is not an especially computationally attractive strategy, but it does reinforce the idea that the two formulations of the maximum likelihood problem are intimately connected.

To compare the performance of the Efron estimator and the Kiefer–Wolfowitz NPMLE we illustrate in Figure 12.3 their behavior in two simple Gaussian mixture models. We include in this comparison a more conventional Fourier method of Stefanski and Carroll (1990), labeled as SC. Their kernel deconvolution estimator assumes that G has a smooth density g. Let $\hat{f}_K(y) = (nh)^{-1}\sum_{i=1}^{n} K((Y_i - y)/h)$ denote a conventional kernel density estimator for the marginal density, and ψ_K denote the characteristic function of K. Then $\hat{g}(\theta) = (nh)^{-1}\sum_{i=1}^{n} L((Y_i - \theta)/h)$ where

$$L(z) = \frac{1}{2\pi}\int e^{itz}\frac{\psi_K(t)}{\psi_\phi(t/h)}dt.$$

The bandwidth for the comparisons, h, is chosen to be $1/3$ in accord with the simulation results in Stefanski and Carroll (1990), together with the choice $K(z) = \frac{1}{\pi z} sin(z)$, the sinc kernel.

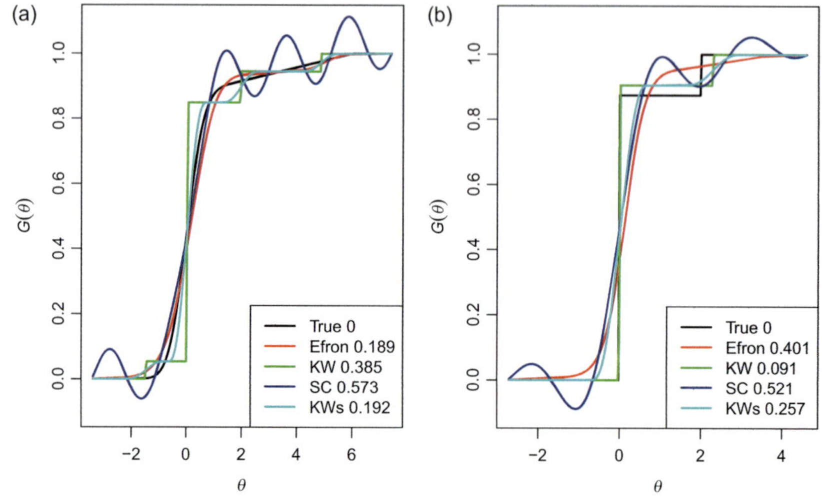

Figure 12.3. Four estimates of the mixing distributions G: In the panel (a) the true mixing distribution is a smooth scale mixture of Gaussians; in panel (b) it is discrete with mass points at 0 and 2. The legend reports Wasserstein (L_1) distances between each of the estimates $\hat{G}_n$ and the true G.

The two variants of the simulation setting are taken from Efron (2016). In the first, G is a smooth scale mixture of Gaussians:

$$G_1(\theta) = \tfrac{1}{8}\Phi(\theta/6) + \tfrac{7}{8}\Phi(2\theta);$$

in the second we have a discrete mixing distribution:

$$G_2(\theta) = \tfrac{1}{8}\delta_0(\theta) + \tfrac{7}{8}\delta_2(\theta).$$

In Figure 12.3 we depict several estimates of G for each of these models based on a sample of size 1,000. Performance, measured by Wasserstein (L_1) distance,

$$W_1(G, \hat{G}_n) = \int |\hat{G}_n(x) - G(x)| dx,$$

is reported in the legend for each estimator. In the smooth setting of panel (a), the Efron estimator is the clear favorite, although a smoothed version of the NPMLE estimator (denoted as KWs) that simply convolves the discrete estimate with a biweight kernel with scale 0.7 does almost as well. In panel (b) where the true G is discrete with only two mass points, the NPMLE estimator is almost oracular. In both settings the kernel-based deconvolution estimator of Stefanski and Carroll (1990) does poorly, particularly in the tails. Probabilistic deconvolution appears to benefit considerably from the additional structure imposed by the likelihood.

As always, there are natural questions to be raised regarding the choice of kernel and bandwidth for such smoothing exercises. As we have suggested earlier we have no particular expertise or ideology about these choices.

Table 12.1. *Mean Wasserstein (L_1) error. For the Efron estimator, we use natural cubic spline with five degree of freedom and $c_0 = 1$. For the SC estimator of Stefanski and Carroll (1990), we use bandwidth $h = 1/3$ and the sinc kernel.*

	Efron	SC	KW	KWs
Smooth	0.185	0.591	0.342	0.180
Discrete	0.409	0.718	0.156	0.280

However, in our experience it seems easier to make such choices *after* seeing the skeletal NPMLE, rather than making them a priori. Adding flesh to the bones of the discrete NPMLE allows one to imagine a suitable shape for the smoothed density that may aid the choice of both the kernel and the bandwidth.

A small simulation experiment to more systematically compare performance of these four estimators in the two settings of Figure 12.3 is reported in Table 12.1. Mean Wasserstein errors are based on 1,000 replications of the experiment. The simulation confirms the observation from Figure 12.3 that smoothing is helpful when G is smooth and not helpful when the target G is discrete. In either case kernel-based Fourier methods perform poorly relative to the likelihood-based methods.

12.2.6 Minimum Distance Methods

Deely and Kruse (1968) proposed a minimum distance method of estimating the mixing distribution G. Let F_n denote the empirical distribution function of a random sample $\{y_1, y_2, \ldots, y_n\}$ from the Gaussian sequence model,

$$Y_i = \theta_i + u_i, \quad u_i \sim \mathcal{N}(0,1),\ u_i \perp\!\!\!\perp \theta_i,\ \theta_i \sim G.$$

Their estimator, $\hat{G}_n$, solves

$$\operatorname{argmin}_{G \in \mathcal{G}} \| F_G - F_n \|_\infty,$$

where $\|F - G\|_\infty = \sup_y |F(y) - G(y)|$, and $F_G(y) := \int \Phi(y \mid \theta) dG(\theta)$.

They show that $\hat{G}_n$ is a consistent estimator for the true mixing distribution G, and that the optimization problem can be formulated as a linear program. To see this fix a grid $u_1, \ldots, u_M$ for the support of G, for example, equally spaced on the interval $[y_{(1)}, y_{(n)}]$, where $y_{(1)} \le y_{(2)} \cdots \le y_{(n)}$ denote the order statistics of the original sample. Define a $2n \times M$ matrix, A, with typical elements

$$a_{ij} = \Phi(y_{(i)} \mid u_j) - \frac{i-1}{n} \qquad \text{for } 1 \le i \le n,$$

$$a_{ij} = \Phi(y_{(i-n)} \mid u_j) - \frac{i-n}{n} \qquad \text{for } n+1 \le i \le 2n.$$

For any M-vector, h, in the unit simplex, $\mathcal{S}_M$, $\sum_j a_{ij} h_j$ measures the difference between $F_G(y_{(i)})$ and $F_n(y_{(i)})$. So our task is to solve

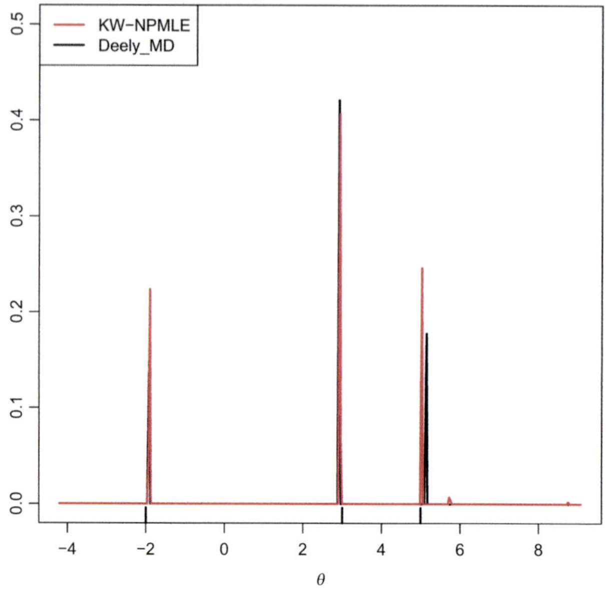

Figure 12.4. Data is generated based on $y_i|\theta_i \sim \mathcal{N}(\theta_i, 1)$ with sample size 500. The true θ_i takes the value $\{-2, 3, 5\}$ with probabilities $\{1/4, 1/2, 1/4\}$. The black line represents the Deely and Kruse minimum distance estimator and the red line represents the Kiefer–Wolfowitz NPMLE for dG. The locations of the true mass points are marked on the x-axis.

$$\min_{h \in \mathcal{S}_M} \max_{1 \le i \le 2n} \left| \sum_{j=1}^{M} a_{ij} h_j \right| .$$

This can be further simplified to the bounded variables linear program,

$$\min_{h \in \mathcal{S}_M, t \in \mathbb{R}} \{t \mid Ah \in [-t, t]^{2n}\}.$$

The original min-max problem can be viewed as a matrix game with mixed strategies, where entries a_{ij} are payoffs of the two players choosing from the action spaces $\{1, 2, \ldots, n\}$ and $\{1, 2, \ldots, M\}$. Figure 12.4 compares the minimum distance estimator of Deely and Kruse (1968) with the Kiefer–Wolfowitz NPMLE estimator based on a sample where the true distribution of G is discrete with three mass points. The solutions are almost indistinguishable in the figure. Only the upper estimated mass points are slightly different, with the NPMLE producing a tiny additional mass point beyond the one located quite precisely at $\theta = 5$.

12.2.7 Leonard's Method

In an underlooked paper Leonard (1984) proposed a variant of the EM algorithm for computing the NPMLE for mixtures. Rather than initially specifying a grid of potential mass point locations as in EM, Leonard suggested restricting the mass associated with support points to be $1/n$, so $\hat{G}$ takes the form

$$\hat{G} = n^{-1} \sum_{j=1}^{n} \delta_{t_j},$$

and we solve for the location of the mass points, $t = (t_j)$. For the standard Gaussian sequence model the log likelihood becomes

$$\ell(t) = \sum_{i=1}^{n} \log \left(n^{-1} \sum_{j=1}^{n} \phi(y_i - t_j) \right),$$

with estimating equations

$$\sum_{i=1}^{n} A_{ij}(y_i - t_j) = 0, \quad j = 1, \ldots, n,$$

where $A_{ij} = \phi(y_i - t_j)/\sum_{j=1}^{n} \phi(y_i - t_j)$, which can be iterated to find a fixed point. As the iterations progress, the t_j tend to coalesce to a few distinct values in the same way that other algorithms do, but crucially this happens more quickly for Leonard's proposal than for the gridded version of the EM algorithm. At convergence the mass at each of the estimated t_j must be an integer multiple of $1/n$, but with n moderately large and only $\mathcal{O}(\log n)$ distinct t_j this is not a stringent constraint. Once estimates of the t_j are obtained, the posterior mean of any of the y_i can be obtained as

$$\hat{E}(\theta | Y = y_i) = \sum_{j=1}^{n} t_j A_{ij}.$$

Leonard's method has a clear missing data interpretation that connects it to the EM algorithm. Consider an expanded model for pairs (Y_i, Z_i), where Z_i takes values in $\{1, \ldots, n\}$, each with probability $1/n$, and $\{Y_i | Z_i = k\} \sim \mathcal{N}(t_k, 1)$. The likelihood for the complete data is then

$$L(Y, Z \mid t) = \prod_{i=1}^{n} \prod_{j=1}^{n} \left(\frac{1}{n} \right)^{\mathbb{1}\{Z_i = j\}} \phi(Y_i - t_j)^{\mathbb{1}\{Z_i = j\}}.$$

The E-step of the EM algorithm would compute

$$\begin{aligned} Q(t, t^0) &= \mathbb{E}_{Z|Y,t^0} \Big[\log L(Y, Z \mid t) \Big] \\ &= \sum_{i=1}^{n} \sum_{j=1}^{n} \mathbb{E}_{Z|Y,t^0} \Big[\mathbb{1}\{Z_i = j\} \Big] (\log(1/n) + \log \phi(y_i - t_j)) \\ &= \sum_{i=1}^{n} \sum_{j=1}^{n} \mathbb{P}(Z_i = j | Y_i, t^0)(\log(1/n) + \log \phi(y_i - t_j)), \end{aligned}$$

where $\mathbb{P}(Z_i = j|Y_i, t^0) = A_{ij}$ for some predetermined values for t^0. The M-step then maximizes $Q(t, t^0)$ over t, which leads back to Leonard's system of estimating equations.

Compared to the EM implementation of Jiang and Zhang (2009), the fixed point iteration of Leonard is considerably more efficient. For a simple illustrative problem with $n = 200$ and $G = \frac{1}{2}\delta_1 + \frac{1}{2}\delta_2$, after 3,000 iterations, Leonard's proposal achieves almost the same precision as the interior point algorithm described in the next subsection, while the gridded EM algorithm is still very imprecise. This can be seen in Figure 12.5, where we plot estimates of $d\hat{G}$ after 3,000 iterations for both the gridded EM method and Leonard's proposed method superimposed on the benchmark **REBayes** estimate. The gridded EM estimate is still quite dispersed, whereas the Leonard estimate essentially coincides with the **REBayes** estimate. Each fixed point iterative method requires about 6 seconds for 3,000 iterations as coded in R. In contrast the interior point **REBayes** method requires only about 0.03 seconds. The attractive feature of the Leonard proposal is that it circumvents the need for any a priori gridding and thus seems potentially more easily adaptable to multidimensional problems.

12.2.8 Mallows's Method

Mallows (2007) proposed an innovative simulation method for solving deconvolution problems that neglect to specify a parametric base distribution. His motivating example involves estimating the distribution of delays in point-

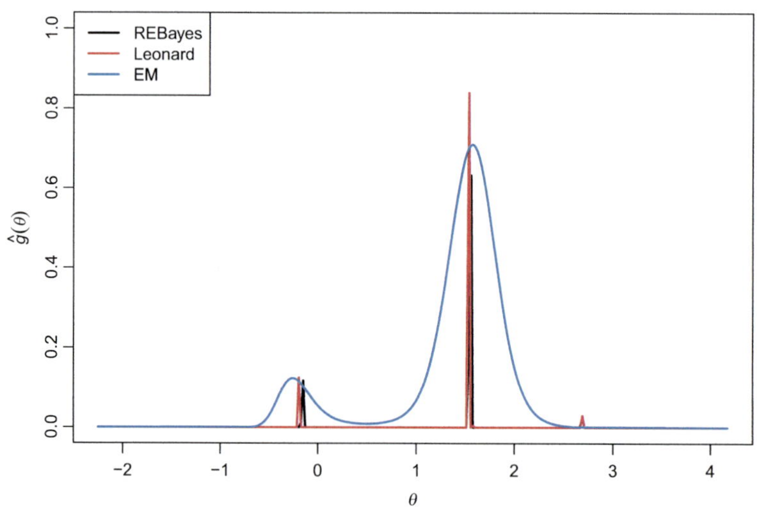

Figure 12.5. Three estimates of $d\hat{G}$ for a simple Gaussian sequence model. After 3,000 iterations the fixed point implementation of Leonard's method essentially coincides with the **REBayes** benchmark solution, while the gridded EM implementation is still quite dispersed.

to-point internet traffic. Suppose we observe random variables, X, measuring the delay in sending a packet from A to B, and Z, the delay in sending a packet from A to C via B. We would like to estimate the marginal distribution of Y, the delay from B to C, assuming the independence of X and Y. Thus, $Z = X + Y$ with $X \perp\!\!\!\perp Y$, and we would like to recover the marginal distribution, G_Y. This appears to be even more challenging than the typical deconvolution problems we have considered so far since we have always assumed that the distribution of X was known.

Given observations, $\boldsymbol{x} = (x_1, \ldots, x_n)$ and $\boldsymbol{z} = (z_1, \ldots, z_m)$, and provisionally assuming $m = n$, Mallows's simulation strategy proceeds by randomly permuting an initial vector $\boldsymbol{y}^0 = (y_1^0, \ldots, y_n^0)$ and computing $\boldsymbol{w} = \boldsymbol{x} + \boldsymbol{y}_\sigma^0$ for some permutation σ. A new $\boldsymbol{y}$ is constructed by arranging the elements of $\boldsymbol{z}$ in the order of the elements of $\boldsymbol{w}$ and then subtracting $\boldsymbol{x}$. Continuing this iteration, for k, yields a vector $\hat{\boldsymbol{y}}^k$ that mimics the original, but unknown vector y, in distribution. In R language this can be concisely represented as shown in Code 12.1.

```
for(i in 1:maxit) y <- sort(z[rank(x + y[rank(runif(n))])] - x).
```
(12.1)

In Figure 12.6 we illustrate the performance of this method for a simple Gaussian sequence model with 500 observations: X and Y are independent standard Gaussian. We plot the sorted observations $\boldsymbol{y}$ against the fitted $\hat{y}_i^k$'s

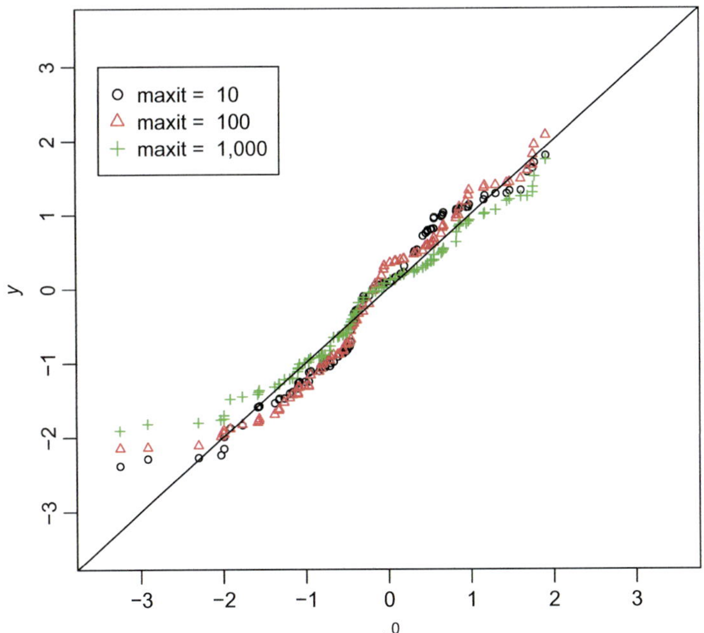

Figure 12.6. QQ Plot of Mallows estimates G_Y against empirical distribution of the true y_i's for three iteration limits.

for several values of the iteration limit k. The 45° line represents a perfect fit between the latent y_i's and the fitted $\hat{y}_i$'s so they would have identical empirical distribution functions. For central order statistics there seems to be some benefit to more iterations, since the green points are closer to the 45° line; however, in the left tail this is reversed and more iterations leads to excessive shrinkage. But how much shrinkage should there be?

To explore this question, we can compare Mallows's method with the NPMLE estimate of the mixing distribution G_Y when we take the base distribution of the NPMLE computation to be a smoothed version of the empirical distribution function of the observed $(x_1, \ldots, x_n)$. For this exercise we use Silverman's penalized density estimator described in Section 3.8 to construct a preliminary estimator of the base density, φ, which in this case is simply the density of X. The distribution G_Y can then be estimated by nonparametric maximum likelihood. In Figure 12.7 the NPMLE estimate of G_Y, the piecewise constant function, is plotted against the empirical distribution function of the Mallows's estimate based on the mean of 1,000 iterations, ignoring the first 50 transient, or burn-in, realizations. In an effort to visualize the variability of

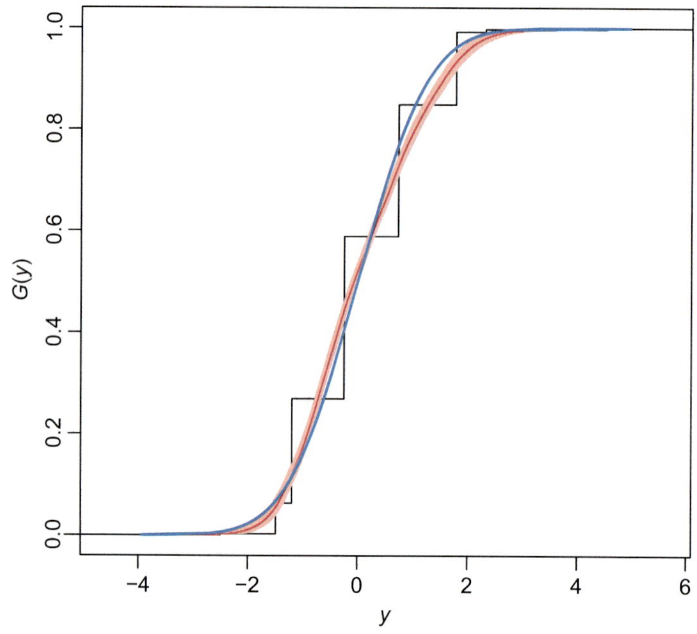

Figure 12.7. Estimates of G_Y for a simple Gaussian–Gaussian mixture model with 500 observations. The step function is the NPMLE using an estimated base distribution from the observed sample, $(x_1, \ldots, x_n)$; the Mallows simulation estimate is the red curve representing the mean of the 1,000 Mallows iterates, excluding the first 50. The pink band is a 0.95 pointwise confidence band based on the same 950 Mallows iterates. The blue curve is the targeted standard Gaussian distribution function.

the Mallows iterations we have also plotted a pointwise 0.95 confidence band based on these iterations. The target standard Gaussian, G_Y, is superimposed in blue. Clearly, the estimated band is overly optimistic about the precision of the mean estimate.

As noted by Arellano and Bonhomme (2021), at each iteration of Mallows's procedure, $\boldsymbol{y}^k = \boldsymbol{z}_\sigma - \boldsymbol{x}$, for some permutation, $\boldsymbol{z}_\sigma$, of the observed $\boldsymbol{z}$ vector, so the procedure can be viewed as an attempt to match elements of the latent $\boldsymbol{y}$ with elements of $\boldsymbol{z}$. This suggests a link to the discrete Monge optimal transport problem, see Galichon (2016, chapter 3) for further exposition. Arellano and Bonhomme (2021) also suggest a multivariate extension of the Mallows procedure to independent-component latent variable models and introduce an optimal transport Wasserstein criterion for estimation that resolves the ambiguity inherent in the stationary distribution of the Mallows simulation method.

12.2.9 Proximal Methods

However satisfied we might be with the performance of interior point methods for computing NPMLEs, there will come a time when the parametric dimension of new problems stretches the effort required for factorization at each iteration to breaking point. When this happens it is time to reconsider first-order, that is, gradient descent, methods. Fortunately, great progress has been made in recent years to produce unified and efficient approaches to convex optimization that are well suited to modern parallelized computation.

Proximal algorithms for convex optimization rely on additive separability of the objective function and efficient computation of optima for separable components of the problem. This structure is well adapted to a wide variety of statistical applications including nonparametric maximum likelihood estimation of mixture models. A brief introduction to these methods will be sketched here; further details are available in Parikh and Boyd (2013) and the extensive references provided there.

Let $f: \mathbb{R}^n \to \mathbb{R} \cup \{\infty\}$ be a closed, proper convex function with effective domain $\operatorname{dom} f = \{x \in \mathbb{R}^n \mid f(x) < \infty\}$. The proximal operator $P_f: \mathbb{R}^n \to \mathbb{R}$ of f is

$$P_f(v) = \operatorname{argmin}_x \{ f(x) + \tfrac{1}{2}\|x - v\|_2^2 \}.$$

$P_f(v)$ can be interpreted as seeking to minimize f without allowing the solution to move too far away from v. By rescaling the function f, so,

$$P_{\lambda f}(v) = \operatorname{argmin}_x \{ f(x) + \tfrac{1}{2\lambda}\|x - v\|_2^2 \},$$

we can control the relative strength of this trade-off. $P_f(v)$ can be viewed as a generalized projection: If f is simply the indicator of a convex set $\mathcal{C}$, so $f(x) = 0$ if $x \in \mathcal{C}$ and $f(x) = \infty$ otherwise, we have

$$P_f(v) = \operatorname{argmin}_{x \in \mathcal{C}} \|x - v\|_2^2,$$

the Euclidean projection of v onto $\mathcal{C}$.

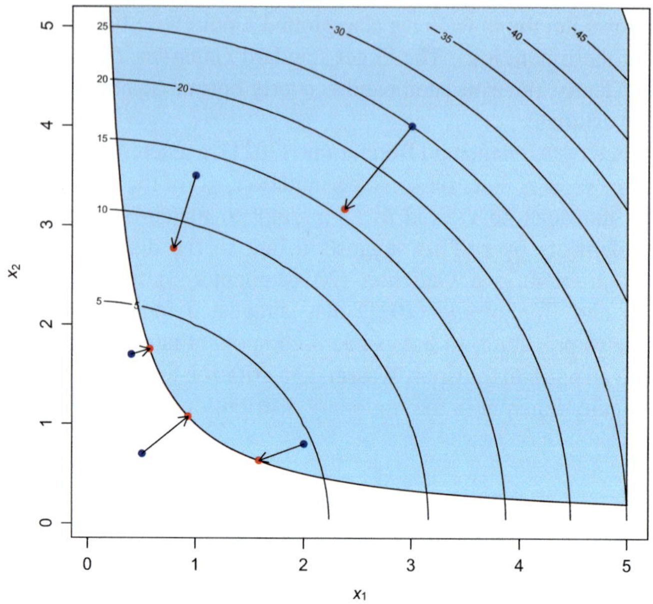

Figure 12.8. The proximal operator $P_f(v)$ projects points; points v outside the shaded constraint set are mapped to the constraint boundary, while points inside the constraint set are mapped toward the boundary by an amount controlled by the choice of λ.

To illustrate the behavior of the proximal operator, P_f, Figure 12.8 depicts the action of P_f for the function

$$f(x) = \begin{cases} \|x\|_2 & \text{if } x_1 x_2 \geq 1, \\ \infty & \text{otherwise.} \end{cases}$$

Points v are mapped by the proximal operator toward the constrained optimum at $(1, 1)$: When v lies outside the constraint set it is sent to the nearest boundary point; when v lies inside the constraint set it is directed toward the optimum by an amount controlled by λ.

To pursue the connection to projection a bit further, recall that the infimal convolution, Rockafellar (1970), of two closed proper convex functions f and g on $\mathbb{R}^n$ is

$$(f \Box g)(v) = \inf_x \{f(x) + g(v - x)\}.$$

If we take $g(x) = \frac{1}{2}\|\cdot\|_2^2$, then

$$M_{\lambda f}(v) = \inf_x \left\{f(x) + \tfrac{1}{2\lambda}\|x - v\|_2^2\right\}$$

is called the Moreau envelope of the function λf. We may view $M_{\lambda f}(v)$ as a smoothed, or regularized, version of f. As such it has several advantages:

It has domain $\mathbb{R}^n$ even when f does not, it is continuously differentiable even though f may not be, and perhaps most importantly, f and $M_{\lambda f}$ have the same minimizers. Parikh and Boyd (2013) interpret M_f in the following way: Letting f^* denote the convex conjugate of f, that is $f^*(y) = \sup_x\{y^\top x - f(x)\}$, we may write

$$M_f = \left(f^* + \tfrac{1}{2}\|\cdot\|_2^2\right)^*,$$

so M_f results from adding a smooth regularization to f^* and then transforming back to obtain a smooth approximation of f. The connections between P_f and M_f are very intimate. $P_f(x)$ is the unique point that achieves the infimum of M_f, that is,

$$M_f(x) = f(P_f(x)) + \tfrac{1}{2}\|x - P_f(x)\|_2^2,$$

and

$$\nabla M_{\lambda f}(x) = \tfrac{1}{\lambda}(x - P_{\lambda f}(x)).$$

The latter expression, when rewritten as

$$P_{\lambda f}(x) = x - \lambda \nabla M_{\lambda f}(x),$$

reveals that $P_{\lambda f}(x)$ can be viewed as a gradient step of length λ for the regularized function $M_{\lambda f}$. This interpretation also suggests the fixed-point iteration,

$$x^{k+1} = P_{\lambda f}(x^k),$$

which can be shown to converge under quite general conditions. As noted by Parikh and Boyd (2013), such methods are closely related to gradient flow methods for solving differential equations, and in special cases to the EM algorithm.

It is common in statistical applications to encounter optimization problems with additively separable convex components. Suppose we consider only two components,

$$\min_x\{f(x) + g(x)\}.$$

One, or even both, components may represent constraints since they may take on infinite values. A familiar example would be f as a (negative) log-likelihood and g a lasso-type parametric penalty. When P_f and P_g are easily computed, but P_{f+g} is not, the following iteration can be attractive:

$$\begin{aligned} x^{k+1} &= P_{\lambda f}(z^k - u^k), \\ z^{k+1} &= P_{\lambda g}(x^k + u^k), \\ u^{k+1} &= u^k + x^{k+1} - z^{k+1}. \end{aligned}$$

This alternating direction method of multipliers (ADMM) algorithm has broad applicability and has been shown to converge under very mild conditions.

Fougner and Boyd (2015) discuss implementation details for an extension of the ADMM approach introduced in Parikh and Boyd (2014) to problems of the following "graph form":

$$\min_{(x,y)}\{f(y) + g(x) \mid y = Ax\}.$$

Now, (x, y) is constrained to the graph $\mathcal{G} = \{(x, y) \in \mathbb{R}^{n+m} \mid y = Ax\}$. In this implementation of the Kiefer–Wolfowitz NPMLE, f is taken as the negative log-likelihood values and g as the indicator function of the box constraints that require the masses of $\hat{G}$ to lie in the unit interval. The modified ADMM algorithm becomes

$$\begin{aligned}(x^{k+1/2}, y^{k+1/2}) &= (P_{\lambda g}(x^k - \tilde{x}^k), P_{\lambda f}(y^k - \tilde{y}^k))\\ (x^{k+1}, y^{k+1}) &= \Pi_A(x^{k+1/2} - \tilde{x}^k, y^{k+1/2} - \tilde{y}^k)\\ (\tilde{x}^{k+1}, \tilde{y}^{k+1}) &= (\tilde{x}^k + x^{k+1/2} - x^{k+1}, \tilde{y}^{k+1/2} + y^{k+1/2} - y^{k+1}),\end{aligned}$$

where Π_A denotes the (Euclidean) projection operator into the set $\mathcal{G}$. This projection has a relatively simple structure and has the advantage that the linear system representing the solution need only be solved once, contrasting sharply with interior point methods that repeatedly need to solve distinct linear systems.

ADMM algorithms, like other first-order gradient descent methods, have the advantage that they are efficiently parallelizable. All that is needed is to compute the proximal operators for f and g, and we have a gradient descent strategy based the regularized problem, a strategy that avoids the burden of matrix factorization at each iteration of the interior point methods.

Fougner and Boyd (2015) discuss many implementation issues, and Fougner (2014) describes a C++ library with both Matlab and R interfaces. The R interface for this proximal operator graphical solver available in the **pogs** package makes it relatively easy to implement ADMM versions of various NPMLE methods structured in a similar fashion to that available in the `KWDual` of the **REBayes** package. The idiosyncratic aspects of the various base distributions, φ, appear only in the constraint matrix, A, allowing each case to be solved with a common implementation of the **pogs** solver. Like other first-order methods ADMM can achieve modest accuracy quite quickly but struggles to achieve the accuracy of the interior point approach.

In Figure 12.9 we compare solutions to a standard Gaussian sequence mixture model with $n = 20{,}000$ observations. The true mixing distribution is $G(\theta) = 0.375\delta_2(\theta) + 0.625\delta_0(\theta)$, which is quite accurately estimated by the NPMLE. However, the ADMM solution of the **pogs** solution after 10,000 iterations is still noticeably more spread out than the interior point solution produced by the **REBayes** implementation using Mosek's interior point implementation. At this scale with $m = 300$ grid points, the interior point solution is also considerably faster: 0.2 seconds versus 3.1 seconds for the ADMM solution. Sufficiently larger problems would presumably reverse

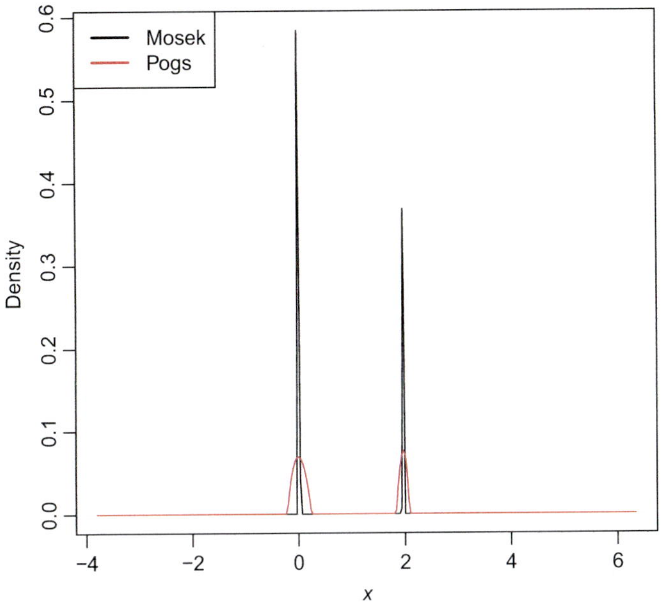

Figure 12.9. Comparison of the Mosek interior point and Pogs/ADMM solutions to a simple Gaussian sequence mixture model.

this comparison. Recent work by Zhang et al. (2024) on Gaussian mixtures in $\mathbb{R}^d$ with $d > 2$ supports this assertion.

12.3 OPTIMAL TRANSPORT METHODS

Optimal transport has proven to be an important tool in many fields within and beyond the confines of economics and econometrics. Galichon (2016) presents a valuable appraisal of applications of optimal transport throughout economics. In this section we will describe some relatively new developments linking optimal transport to Gaussian deconvolution and thus to empirical Bayes methods.

Consider two discrete measures, μ and ν: Measure μ puts mass a_i on points x_i $i = 1, \ldots, m$, and measure ν puts mass b_j on points y_j $j = 1, \ldots, n$. Let M denote the m by n matrix of squared distances, $M_{ij} = (x_i - y_j)^2$, between the points of support of the underlying random variables $X \sim \mu$ and $Y \sim \nu$. The classical (Kantorovich) optimal transport problem involves finding a "transport plan" or coupling, P, that minimizes the cost of transport,

$$W(a,b) = \min_{P \in U(a,b)} \langle M, P \rangle = \sum_i \sum_j M_{ij} P_{ij}$$

where M_{ij} denotes the cost of moving mass from x_i to y_j, and $U(a,b) = \{P \colon P\mathbb{1}_m = a, \quad P^\top \mathbb{1}_n = b\}$ is the set of joint distribution of X and Y that has marginal μ and ν, respectively. This is a linear programming problem. For modest m and n it can be solved efficiently by conventional methods. For large problems, Cuturi (2013) has shown that penalization of this (Kantorovich) objective can lead to significantly more efficient computation of P. Cuturi's entropic Wasserstein problem is

$$W_\gamma(\mu,\nu) = \min_{P\in U(a,b)} \langle M, P\rangle + \gamma E(P),$$

where $E(P) = \sum_{ij} P_{ij}(\log P_{ij})$, and $\gamma > 0$. The entropy penalty blurs the solution of the unregularized LP problem, while letting $\gamma \to \infty$ produces a coupling P that turns out to be the product measure of μ and ν.

To see the advantage of the entropy penalty, consider the Lagrangian,

$$L(P,\alpha,\beta) = \sum_{ij} P_{ij}M_{ij} + \gamma P_{ij}(\log P_{ij}) + \alpha^\top(P\mathbb{1}_m - a) + \beta^\top(P^\top \mathbb{1}_n - b).$$

Differentiating, we have

$$\partial L/\partial P_{ij} = M_{ij} + \gamma(\log P_{ij} + 1) + \alpha_i + \beta_j;$$

solving, we can write

$$P_{ij} = e^{-1}e^{-\alpha/\gamma}e^{-M_{ij}/\gamma}e^{-\beta/\gamma} \equiv u_i K_{ij} v_j.$$

The constraint $P \in U(a,b)$ implies

$$\begin{aligned}\mathrm{diag}(u)K\mathrm{diag}(v)\mathbb{1}_n &= a,\\ \mathrm{diag}(v)K^\top\mathrm{diag}(u)\mathbb{1}_m &= b,\end{aligned}$$

or

$$\begin{aligned}\mathrm{diag}(u)Kv &= a,\\ \mathrm{diag}(v)K^\top u &= b,\end{aligned}$$

or, employing elementwise division,

$$\begin{aligned}u &= a/Kv,\\ v &= b/K^\top u.\end{aligned}$$

Thus, the problem of finding the coupling, P, is reduced to solving these two equations for the vectors u and v. Everything else, K, a and b are known data, as is γ. Efficient solutions are achieved by simply iterating back and forth between these two equations starting from an arbitrary v. In the optimal transport literature this is usually referred to as the Sinkhorn algorithm, (Sinkhorn, 1964), but may be more familiar to a statistical audience as iterative proportional fitting, as in Bishop et al. (1975).

Cuturi and Doucet (2014) show that the dual of the W_γ problem is

$$W_\gamma(a,b) = \max_{(x,y)\in\mathbb{R}^{m+n}} x^\top a + y^\top b - \gamma\sum_{ij}\exp((x_i+y_j-M_{ij})/\gamma - 1),$$

yielding first order conditions,

$$a_i \Bigg/ \left(\sum_j \exp(y_j/\gamma)\exp(-M_{ij}/\gamma) \right) = \exp(x_i/\gamma),$$

$$b_i \Bigg/ \left(\sum_j \exp(x_i/\gamma)\exp(-M_{ij}/\gamma) \right) = \exp(y_j/\gamma).$$

Replacing $\exp(y_j/\gamma)$ by v_j and $\exp(x_i/\gamma)$ by u_i takes us back to the same updating formulae derived for the primal.

Finding the coupling P_γ is all well and good, but what have we really accomplished? In the world of Robbins (1950) and Kiefer and Wolfowitz (1956), ν is the empirical distribution of the y's, and μ is the mixing distribution usually represented as a distribution function by G. The formulation so far presumes that μ is given, but of course it isn't, it is what we are looking for, so in effect solving the problem of computing the entropic Wasserstein distance yields just one *evaluation* of the objective function. A connection between optimal transport and empirical Bayes methods has been developed in Rigollet and Weed (2018) who show that if we optimize W_γ over μ, we obtain the NPMLE for G in the Gaussian sequence model.

To make this more explicit we will describe a general approach of Cuturi and Peyré (2016) to variational Wasserstein problems. Fixing $b_j = 1/n$, for $j = 1, \dots, n$ to represent the empirical distribution of the y_i's, let

$$\begin{aligned} H_b(a) &= W_\gamma(a,b) \\ &= \max_{(x,y)\in\mathbb{R}^{m+n}} \left\{ x^\top a + y^\top b - \gamma \sum_{ij} \exp((x_i + y_j - M_{ij})/\gamma - 1) \right\}, \end{aligned}$$

and consider the convex conjugate, that is, the Fenchel–Legendre transform,

$$\begin{aligned} H_b^*(g) &= \max_a g^\top a - H_b(a) \quad \text{for all } g \in \mathbb{R}^m, \\ &= \max_a \left\{ - \max_{(x,y)\in\mathbb{R}^{m+n}} \left\{ -g^\top a + x^\top a + y^\top b - \gamma \sum_{ij} \exp((x_i + y_j - M_{ij})/\gamma - 1) \right\} \right\} \\ &= \max_a \left\{ - \max_{(\tilde{x},y)\in\mathbb{R}^{m+n}} \left\{ \tilde{x}^\top a + y^\top b - \gamma \sum_{ij} \exp((\tilde{x}_i + g_i + y_j - M_{ij})/\gamma - 1) \right\} \right\}, \end{aligned}$$

where $\tilde{x}_i = x_i - g_i$. The inner maximum is the dual of the problem,

$$\min_{P\in U(a,b)} \langle M - g\mathbb{1}_n^\top, P\rangle + \gamma E(P),$$

and thus,

$$H_b^*(g) = \max_a \left\{ - \min_{P \in U(a,b)} \langle M - g\mathbb{1}_n^\top, P\rangle + \gamma E(P) \right\}$$
$$= - \min_a \left\{ \min_{P \in U(a,b)} \langle M - g\mathbb{1}n^\top, P\rangle + \gamma E(P) \right\}.$$

At this point we have an entropy-penalized optimal transport problem with only one fixed marginal; imposing the constraint $P^\top \mathbb{1}_m = b$ yields the Lagrangian,

$$\min_g \left\{ \sum_{ij} (M_{ij} - g_i) P_{ij} + \gamma \sum_{ij} P_{ij} \log(P_{ij}) + \sum_j \lambda_j \left(\sum_i P_{ij} - b_j \right) \right\},$$

with first order conditions with respect to P_{ij},

$$M_{ij} - g_i + \gamma(\log P_{ij} + 1) + \lambda_j = 0,$$

so

$$\log P_{ij}^* = \gamma^{-1}(g_i - M_{ij} - \lambda_j) - 1.$$

Since $\sum_i P_{ij}^* = b_j$, we have $\exp(-\lambda_j/\gamma - 1) = b_j / \sum_i \alpha_i K_{ij}$, where $\alpha_i = \exp(g_i/\gamma)$ and $K_{ij} = \exp(-M_{ij}/\gamma)$. So we can write

$$P_{ij}^* = \alpha_i K_{ij} b_j / \sum_i \alpha_i K_{ij}.$$

This explicit form for the optimal coupling yields

$$H_b^*(g) = -\gamma \sum_{ij} \alpha_i K_{ij} \frac{b_j}{\sum_i \alpha_i K_{ij}} \log \left(\frac{b_j}{\sum_i \alpha_i K_{ij}} \right)$$
$$= -\gamma \sum_j \left(\left(\sum_i \alpha_i K_{ij} \right) \frac{b_j}{\sum_i \alpha_i K_{ij}} \left(\log b_j - \log \left(\sum_i \alpha_i K_{ij} \right) \right) \right)$$
$$= -\gamma \sum_j \left(b_j \log b_j - b_j \log \left(\sum_i \alpha_i K_{ij} \right) \right).$$

Since $b_j \equiv 1/n$, maximizing $H_b^*(g)$ over g is equivalent to solving the reparameterized problem,

$$\max_{a \in \mathcal{S}_m} \sum_j \log \left(\sum_i K_{ij} a_i \right).$$

The restriction of a to the unit simplex has been suppressed in the prior computations, but is clearly necessary if μ is to be a proper probability measure. Our original optimal transport problem is thus recognizable as the familiar NPMLE problem for the homoscedastic Gaussian mixture problem with $\gamma = 2\sigma^2$.

If we now replace the quadratic cost matrix, M, of the optimal transport problem, which led us to the Gaussian kernel, following the same argument delivers a new NPMLE for a new mixture problem. Thus, the Rigollet and

Weed (2018) assertion is far more general than the application to Gaussian deconvolution might suggest. Indeed they note in their proposition 2 that the same arguments apply to a much larger class of deconvolution problems, for instance we might consider location mixtures of Laplace (double exponential) distributions on $\mathbb{R}$. This would correspond to optimizing an entropy-penalized Wasserstein problem with cost specified not as squared distance but as Euclidean distance itself, that is,

$$W_1(\mu, \nu) = \min_P \int \|x - y\| dP(x, y).$$

This Laplace base model lies outside the comfort zone of our usual exponential family setting, but the NPMLE machinery is still applicable.

It remains to be seen whether the optimal transport view of such problems can produce real computational improvements, but the close connection between optimizing entropic Wasserstein distances and nonparametric maximum likelihood comes as a pleasant surprise. See Kent et al. (2021) and Yan et al. (2023) for further steps in this direction.

12.4 PROFILING AND THE METHOD OF LOG SPACINGS

As we have seen in Section 6.3 on models for income dynamics and in Chapter 8 on survival models, it is sometimes relatively easy to introduce fixed structural parameters into mixture models and estimate them by maximizing profile likelihoods in conjunction with their associated mixing distribution. Indeed, Wilk's phenomenon, (Fan et al., 2001), was seen to provide a valid form of inference for these parameters in some cases. However, statistical life is not always so convenient, and there are other circumstances in which profiling can be much more challenging. A prominent example of the latter situation involves estimation of the scale parameter of the base distribution in the Gaussian sequence model. In some applications there is compelling auxiliary information available for this task; if not, identification fails.

Lemma 12.6. *Consider $Y_i = \theta_i + \sigma U_i$ with $\theta_i \perp\!\!\!\perp U_i$, $\theta_i \sim_{iid} G$ and $U_i \sim_{iid} \mathcal{N}(0, 1)$; then (σ, G) is not identifiable.*

Proof: We have

$$V(Y) = E[V(Y|\theta)] + V[E(Y|\theta)] = \sigma^2 + V(\theta),$$

so $\sigma^2 = V(Y) - V(\theta)$. Without any further restriction on G, sharp bounds for σ^2 are $[0, V(Y)]$. Suppose the true data generating process is (σ_0^2, G_0). It is easy to see that for any $\tau \geq 0$, $(\sigma_0^2 - \tau^2, G^*)$ with G^* the convolution of G_0 with $\mathcal{N}(0, \tau^2)$ yields the same marginal distribution for Y, and thus is observationally equivalent. The lower bound for σ is rationalized by setting τ equal to σ_0, and the upper bound is rationalized by G_0 being a degenerate distribution. ■

It is instructive to consider the profile likelihood estimator for σ in this case. For each fixed $\sigma > 0$, the nonparametric maximum likelihood estimator $\hat{G}_\sigma$ exists and is unique. As we decrease σ, the NPMLE $\hat{G}_\sigma$ converges weakly to the empirical CDF of the data, and the profile likelihood tends to infinity. As we increase σ, the number of distinct mass points of the NPMLE, $\hat{G}$, decreases, and eventually $\hat{G}$ becomes degenerate taking the value $\bar{Y}_n$ with probability one.

When likelihood misbehaves, becoming unbounded and yielding inconsistent estimates, the situation can sometimes be ameliorated by replacing the evaluation of the likelihood by a sum of log probability spacings. This has been proposed by Roeder (1990) and Roeder (1992) for the normal mixture model with unknown base variance and was considered earlier by Cheng and Amin (1983) and Ranneby (1984). We will briefly review the link between these methods and conventional maximum likelihood for parametric models and then elaborate on their use in normal mixture models for estimating bounds for the parameter σ.

Let $X_1, \ldots, X_n = Y_{(1)}, \ldots, Y_{(n)}$ be the order statistics of the sample $Y_1, \ldots, Y_n$, and suppose the true distribution of Y_i is F_{θ_0} with density f_{θ_0} supported on the real line, where θ_0 is the true unknown parameter and F is the known parametric distribution. Let $X_0 = -\infty$ and $X_{n+1} = +\infty$ and define the interval $I_i = [X_{i-1}, X_i]$; then the probability spacings are defined as $D_i(\theta) = F_\theta(I_i) = F_\theta(X_i) - F_\theta(X_{i-1})$ for a distribution F_θ with $i = 1, 2, \ldots, n+1$. The log probability spacing method estimates θ by maximizing

$$LPS(\theta) := (n+1)^{-1} \sum_{i=1}^{n+1} \log D_i(\theta).$$

The connection to maximum likelihood can be seen by considering the Kullback–Leibler divergence,

$$\begin{aligned} KL(f_{\theta_0}, f_\theta) &= \int f_{\theta_0}(y) \log \frac{f_{\theta_0}(y)}{f_\theta(y)} dy \\ &= \int f_{\theta_0}(y) \log f_{\theta_0}(y) dy - \int f_{\theta_0}(y) \log f_\theta(y) dy. \end{aligned}$$

Minimizing $KL(f_0, f_\theta)$ is equivalent to maximizing $\int f_{\theta_0}(y) \log f_\theta(y) dy$ whose sample counterpart is the likelihood on the realized sample. By the mean value theorem, we have

$$\begin{aligned} F_{\theta_0}(x_i) - F_{\theta_0}(x_{i-1}) &= (x_i - x_{i-1}) f_{\theta_0}(\bar{x}_i), \\ F_\theta(x_i) - F_\theta(x_{i-1}) &= (x_i - x_{i-1}) f_\theta(\check{x}_i), \end{aligned}$$

so

$$(n+1)^{-1} \sum_{i=1}^{n+1} \log \frac{F_{\theta_0}(x_i) - F_{\theta_0}(x_{i-1})}{F_\theta(x_i) - F_\theta(x_{i-1})} = (n+1)^{-1} \sum_{i=1}^{n} \log \frac{f_{\theta_0}(\bar{x}_i)}{f_\theta(\check{x}_i)} \tag{12.4}$$

converges to $KL(f_{\theta_0}, f_\theta)$. Minimizing (12.4) is equivalent to maximizing $LPS(\theta)$. When terms in the likelihood become unbounded for some values of θ, this typically induces inconsistency of the MLE. See for example, Cheng and Amin (1983). We can see that $LPS(\theta)$, is approximating the same quantity but is guaranteed to have each of the terms in the sum bounded from above.

With a normalization that does not change the maximizer of $LPS(\theta)$, let

$$S_n(\theta) = (n+1)^{-1} \sum_{i=1}^{n+1} \log[(F_\theta(x_i) - F_\theta(x_{i-1}))(n+1)].$$

Since $F_{\theta_0}(X_i)$ is uniformly distributed, $F_{\theta_0}(x_i) - F_{\theta_0}(x_{i-1})$ is the spacing of ordered uniform random variables supported on $[0,1]$. Using a result in Darling (1953), we have as $n \to \infty$,

$$S_n(\theta_0) \xrightarrow{p} -\gamma,$$
$$\sqrt{n}(S_n(\theta_0) + \gamma) \xrightarrow{d} \mathcal{N}\left(0, \frac{\pi^2}{6} - 1\right),$$

where γ is the Euler constant. Note that when evaluated at the true value θ_0, the limiting distribution of the centered and normalized $LPS(\theta)$ becomes a pivotal distribution. This provides immediate opportunities for inference and confidence set construction.

Roeder (1990, 1992) discuss the use of log probability spacings for Gaussian mixture models and provide an attractive strategy for estimation of σ, when the profile likelihood method clearly fails as discussed above.

In the Gaussian sequence model, $Y_i = \theta_i + \sigma_0 U_i$ with $U_i \sim \mathcal{N}(0,1)$ and $\theta_i \sim G_0$, denote the true marginal density for Y_i as

$$f_0(y) := f(y; G_0, \sigma_0) = \int \phi((y-\theta)/\sigma_0)/\sigma_0 dG_0(\theta).$$

And now define

$$LPS(G,\sigma) = (n+1)^{-1} \sum_{i=1}^{n+1} \log D_i(G,\sigma)$$

with $D_i(G,\sigma) = F(X_i, G, \sigma) - F(X_{i-1}, G, \sigma)$, where F is a marginal distribution of Y_i with density

$$f(y) = f(y; G, \sigma) = \int \phi((y-\theta)/\sigma)/\sigma dG(\theta).$$

Observing that $F(X_i, G_0, \sigma_0)$ follows a uniform distribution,

$$S_n(G,\sigma) = (n+1)^{-1} \sum_{i=1}^{n+1} \log[D_i(G,\sigma)(n+1)],$$

then as $n \to \infty$,

$$\sqrt{n}(S_n(G_0,\sigma_0) + \gamma) \xrightarrow{d} \mathcal{N}\left(0, \frac{\pi^2}{6} - 1\right).$$

This suggests that as $n \to \infty$,

$$\mathbb{P}(|\sqrt{n}(S_n(G_0,\sigma_0)+\gamma)| < c_{\alpha/2}) \to 1-\alpha,$$

where c_α is the $1-\alpha$ quantile of the limiting distribution above. We can form a confidence set with level α for the marginal density of Y_i as

$$\{f(y,G,\sigma) : |\sqrt{n}(S_n(G,\sigma)+\gamma)| < c_{\alpha/2}\}.$$

A simple profiling strategy can be based on $\hat{G}_h := \text{argmax}_{G\in\mathcal{G}} LPS(G,h)$; then the confidence set of the marginal density can be expressed as

$$\{f(y,\hat{G}_\sigma,\sigma) : |\sqrt{n}(S_n(\hat{G}_\sigma,\sigma)+\gamma)| < c_{\alpha/2}\}$$

and equivalently, the confidence set for σ as

$$\{\sigma : |\sqrt{n}(S_n(\hat{G}_\sigma,\sigma)+\gamma)| < c_{\alpha/2}\}.$$

Figure 12.10 plots the profiling function for three different data-generating processes. DGP2 with G Gaussian seems to be the most difficult with the widest confidence interval for σ with $\alpha = 0.2$.

DGP1: $\sigma_0 = 0.5$, $G_0 = \frac{1}{3}\delta_0 + \frac{1}{3}\delta_2 + \frac{1}{3}\delta_4$.
DGP2: $\sigma_0 = 0.5$, $G_0 = \mathcal{N}(0,1)$.
DGP3: $\sigma_0 = 0.5$, $G_0 = U[0,2]$.

Table 12.2 reports the coverage frequency and width of the confidence interval for σ with $\alpha = 0.2$ over 250 repetitions for four different sample sizes $n \in \{500, 1{,}000, 2{,}000, 4{,}000\}$ for the three DGPs with critical value $c_{0.1}$. As sample size increases, the coverage probability mostly exceeds the nominal 80% and the width of the confidence interval for σ declines, albeit slowly, as sample size increases. While profiling using log-likelihood does not provide any information on σ, profiling using log-spacings does provide some useful information. The last column of Table 12.2 reports the naïve bound of $[0, \sqrt{Var(Y)}]$ for σ. For DGP1 the method of log-spacings does provide a much narrower confidence interval for σ. Roeder (1992) discusses the potential power improvement using higher-order spacings, and it would be an interesting area for further study of such approaches. In principle, the pivotal property of the centered and re-scaled log-probability spacing statistics under the true distribution continues to hold for general mixture models; hence the profiling method using spacings for structural parameters can be attractive especially when profiling using likelihood fails. Another example of this type is the estimation of the shape parameter of the Weibull mixture model as discussed in Chapter 4.

12.5 THE REBAYES PACKAGE

To convey some sense of the feasible scope of applications of nonparametric maximum likelihood methods for mixture models we will briefly describe the

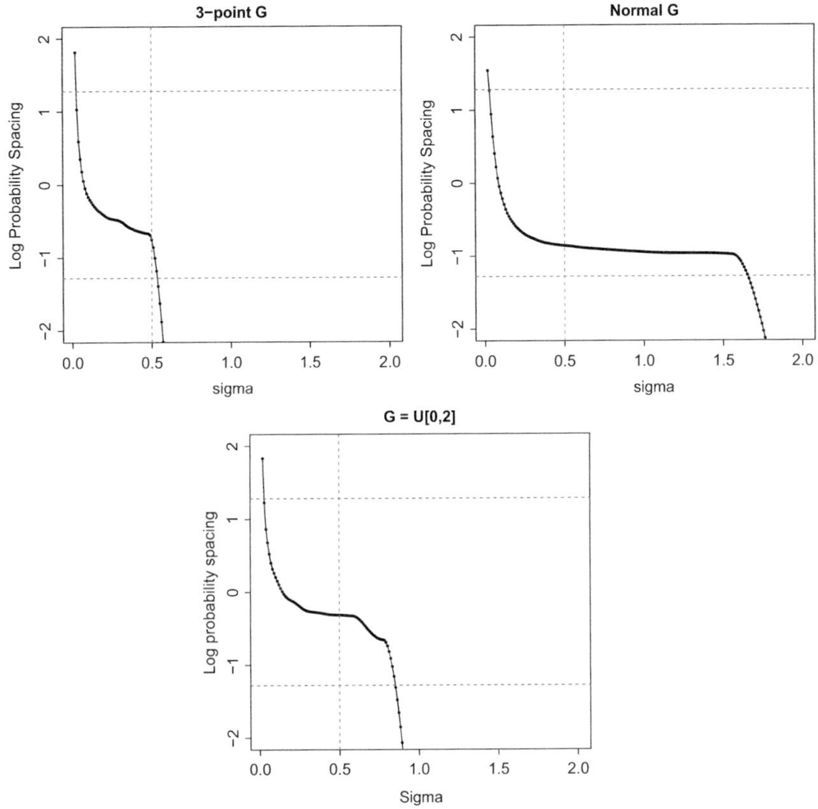

Figure 12.10. The profile function for σ with σ taking on values between $[0, 2]$ for the three DGPs described in the text. The vertical blue dotted line in each plot marks out the true σ_0, and the horizontal red dotted lines indicate the critical values $c_{0.1}$. Sample size for all three DGPs are $n = 4,000$.

current functionality of the R package **REBayes** with the understanding that future development may significantly expand upon what is described here.

REBayes Primary Model Fitting Functions

`GLmix`: Gaussian location mixtures with possibly heterogeneous scale parameters
`TLmix`: Student *t* location mixtures
`GVmix`: Gaussian scale mixtures
`GLVmix`: Gaussian location-scale mixtures for longitudinal data
`Gammamix`: Gamma scale mixtures
`Weibullmix`: Weibull scale mixtures
`Gompertzmix`: Gompertz scale mixtures
`Umix`: Uniform mixtures
`Bmix`: Binomial mixtures

Table 12.2. *Coverage and width for log-spacing confidence intervals for σ in the Gaussian sequence model. The last column reports the coverage and width of a naïve bound for σ, $[0, (\hat{V}(Y_i))^{1/2}]$, with $n = 500$. As n increases, coverage remains at 1, and the width of the naïve intervals remains fairly constant.*

	$n = 500$	$n = 1{,}000$	$n = 2{,}000$	$n = 5{,}000$	Naïve
Coverage					
DGP1	0.880	0.904	0.876	0.912	1.000
DGP2	0.788	0.812	0.868	0.844	1.000
DGP3	0.856	0.860	0.860	0.904	1.000
Width					
DGP1	0.574	0.531	0.506	0.504	1.709
DGP2	1.148	1.113	1.120	1.094	1.118
DGP3	0.814	0.774	0.751	0.740	0.764

`Pmix`: Poisson mixtures
`BPmix`: Binomial Poisson mixtures

In accordance with standard model fitting functionality in R, the **REBayes** functions listed above have associated `plot` and `predict` methods. The former is intended to enable users to plot the estimate, $\hat{G}$, of the mixing distribution, while the latter allows users to compute in-sample and out-of-sample predictions of the latent parameters for the posterior mean, posterior mode or posterior quantiles based on the estimated $\hat{G}$. Functions are also provided to smooth the atomic, $\hat{G}$, estimates by convolution with a biweight or triweight kernel, and the plotting and prediction methods can be applied to the smoothed estimates. Several illustrative examples of **REBayes** usage are included in the package and can be accessed, for example, with the command `demo(GLmix1)`. A complete list of these demos can be seen with the command `demo(package = "REBayes")`. Similarly, several data sets are included in the package and can be accessed with the command, for example, `data(bball)` for the baseball example in Section 1.4, and a complete list of the available data sets in the package can be obtained with the command `data(package = "REBayes")`. Full documentation of the **REBayes** functions and data sets is accessible with the command `?fname`.

The common structure of all of the **REBayes** NPMLE fitting functions involves a call to `KWDual` that provides three arguments: an A matrix specifying the linear equality constraints; a vector, d, specifying the upper bound on these constraints; and a vector, w, that represents the weights appearing in the objective function of the problem. Other control parameters specifying convergence tolerances, verbosity of the solution, and so on, can be passed to `KWDual` via the R ellipsis mechanism. The function `KWDual` formulates the problem in a manner suitable for Mosek and returns the solution to the control of R. Prior to version 9 of Mosek, the logarithmic form of the NPMLE objective function could be specified directly. Version 9 and presumably future Mosek versions specify problems with a linear objective subject to convex cone constraints. The function `KWDual` of **REBayes** accommodates both formulations adapting to the installed version of Mosek.

To help visualize the geometry of this transition, consider the finite-dimensional dual problem as implemented in Version 8 of Mosek,

$$\min_{\nu} \left\{ \sum_i w_i \log(\nu_i) \mid 0 \leq A^\top \nu \leq n\mathbb{1}_m,\ \nu \geq 0 \right\},$$

where, to preserve the minimization sense, the $w_i = -1$. We have a strictly convex objective constrained by linear inequalities. In Version 9 a new formulation was required that moved the nonlinearity of the log objective into the constraints. To accomplish this we need to replace the explicit log terms with the auxiliary variables, $t \in \mathbb{R}^n$, and then link the ν_i's with the t_i's via the exponential cone constraints, $t_i \leq \log \nu_i,\ i = 1, \ldots, n$. These can be written as $(\nu_i, 1, t_i) \in \mathcal{K}$, with canonical exponential cone $\mathcal{K} = \{x \in \mathbb{R}^3 | x_1 \geq x_2 \exp(x_3/x_2), x_1, x_2 > 0\}$, illustrated in Figure 12.11. Thus, our constraint $t_i \leq \log \nu_i,\ i = 1, \ldots, n$ becomes $\nu_i \geq \exp(t_i)$.

This gives us the $i = 1, \ldots, n$ convex cone constraints:

$$\begin{pmatrix} e_i^\top & 0 \\ 0 & 0 \\ 0 & e_i^\top \end{pmatrix} \begin{pmatrix} \nu \\ t \end{pmatrix} + \begin{pmatrix} 0 \\ 1 \\ 0 \end{pmatrix} \in \mathcal{K},$$

where e_i denotes the ith standard unit basis vector of $\mathbb{R}^n$. The x_2 coordinate of the exponential cones is identically set to one, and we have $2n$ variables

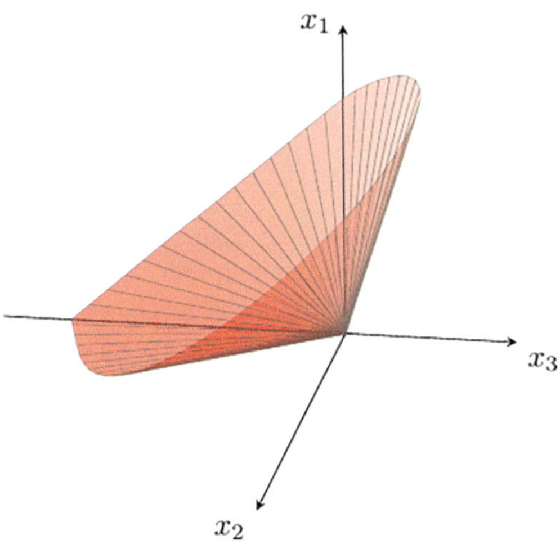

Figure 12.11. Boundary of the canonical exponential cone $\mathcal{K}$. Source: ApS (2022a).

$\{\nu_1, \ldots, \nu_n\}$ and $\{t_1, \ldots, t_n\}$. The objective function is now linear in the t, as $w^\top t$, and we must augment the A matrix to annihilate the t contribution. For example, $0 \leq \begin{pmatrix} A^\top & 0 \end{pmatrix} \begin{pmatrix} \nu \\ v \end{pmatrix} \leq n\mathbb{1}_m$. As before $\nu \in \mathbb{R}^n_+$, but t lives in all of $\mathbb{R}^n$. Expanding the dimension of the problem unknowns in this way may seem to increase its difficulty; however the expanded formulation is actually more efficient, and the memory requirements are no greater due to the magic of sparse linear algebra. See Dahl and Andersen (2022) for a detailed description of the interior point methods underlying the Mosek implementation.

When the dimension of the grid of potential support points for G becomes large, as in problems with multivariate latent structure, the current implementation in `KWDual` may become unwieldy. Recent work by Zhang et al. (2024) using Moreau–Yosida regularization suggests that somewhat bigger problems can be more efficiently tackled with modified second-order methods.

An additional feature of the **REBayes** package is the function `medde` (Maximum entropy deregularized density estimation) that implements a variety of penalized density estimation methods. Examples include: the Silverman (1982) estimator described in Section 3.8, a monotonized version of the Bayes rule density estimator of Brown and Greenshtein described in Koenker and Mizera (2014) and a variety of shape-constrained density estimators minimizing Renyi entropy described in Koenker and Mizera (2010). Illustrative demos of these procedures in the **REBayes** package can be accessed with the commands: `Silverman`, `Brown` and `Renyi`, respectively.

12.6 THE RCBR PACKAGE

Another R package, also available from the CRAN repository, is the **RCBR** package designed to estimate the random coefficient binary response models described in Chapter 10. This package incorporates the hyperplane arrangement algorithms required in Gu and Koenker (2022a) and a variety of related functionality.

12.7 REPRODUCIBILITY

In accordance with the modern imperative that published computational methods and results be fully documented and reproducible, we have created a GitHub site containing code and data to enable readers to reproduce any of the figures and tables appearing in the text. This site can be accessed via the link https://github.com/rkoenker/EBR. Tables of contents provided there should assist in locating the files required to reproduce each figure and table. Questions and suggestions for improvements can be addressed to either author.

Exercises

(1) Show that for a fixed sample $\{y_1, \ldots, y_n\}$ from the Gaussian sequence mixture model, the NPMLE $\hat{G}_m$ based on an equally spaced grid of dimension m converges to a fixed function $\hat{G}_\infty$ as $m \to \infty$.

(2) Suppose $Y_i \sim \mathcal{N}(\theta_i, 1)$; show that the mean of the posterior means under the NPMLE $\hat{G}$ is equal to the sample mean, that is,

$$n^{-1}\sum_{i=1}^{n} \mathbb{E}_{\hat{G}}(\theta|Y = y_i) = n^{-1}\sum_{i=1}^{n} y_i = \bar{y}.$$

(3) Under the conditions of the previous exercise, verify the inequality

$$n^{-1}\sum_i y_i^2 - \bar{y}^2 \leq 1 + n^{-1}\sum_i \mathbb{E}_{\hat{G}}(\theta^2|Y = y_i) - \left(n^{-1}\sum_i \mathbb{E}_{\hat{G}}(\theta|Y = y_i)\right)^2.$$

(4) Verify the equivalence of the min-max formulation of the Deely–Kruse minimum distance estimator with the bounded variables linear program in Section 12.2.6. See Karlin (1959) for further interpretation from the theory of games.

(5) An early example of the use of nonparametric maximum likelihood is the Grenander (1956) estimator of a monotone density. Like the NPMLE for mixtures, the Grenander estimator is also self-regularizing. It has a simple mechanical interpretation: Imagine stretching a string over an observed empirical distribution function and then pulling the string taut. The string will touch F_n at a few points and will linearly interpolate between these "tangencies." Differentiating this linear interpolant yields a piecewise constant estimator of the density. Show that this description of the Grenander estimator as the least concave majorant of F_n is equivalent to solving for the NPMLE for a mixture of uniform random variables, $U[0,\theta]$. Hint: See the demo Grenander in the **REBayes** package.

(6) Prove Proposition 12.1. Hint: Use theorem 2A(a) of Lindsay (1989).

(7) Estimation of the distribution, F, of a positive random variable, X, when realizations x of X are observed with probability proportional to x can also be formulated as a NPMLE: Suppose the true distribution of X is F with density f, but rather than random sampling based on f, we sample from the density proportional to $xf(x)$. Given observations $y_1, \ldots, y_n$ of such a length-biased sampling scheme, show that the NPMLE of F is

$$\hat{F}(x) = \left[\sum_{i=1}^{n}(1/y_i)\right]^{-1} \sum_{i=1}^{n}(1/y_i)\mathbb{1}(y_i \leq x).$$

(8) Generalize the preceding exercise to the case that we sample from the density proportional to $w(x)f(x)$.

(9) Lindsay (1995) generalizes-length biased sampling NPMLE further to consider a class of mixture problems with a "ratio structure." Suppose that we seek to solve

$$\sup_G \prod_{i=1}^{n}\left[\frac{\int \psi_i(\theta)dG(\theta)}{\int \Psi(\theta)dG(\theta)}\right],$$

for some positive valued function, Ψ. Show that this is equivalent to the NPMLE mixture problem

$$\sup_H \prod_{i=1}^n \int \frac{\psi_i(\theta))}{\Psi(\theta)} dH(\theta),$$

where

$$dH(\theta) = \frac{\Psi(\theta) dG(\theta)}{\int \Psi(\theta) dG(\theta)}.$$

And that given an NPMLE estimate $\hat{H}$ of H, an estimate of G can be recovered as

$$d\hat{G}(\theta) = \frac{(1/\Psi(\theta)) d\hat{H}(\theta)}{\int (1/\Psi(\theta)) d\hat{H}(\theta)}.$$

(10) To illustrate the bivariate binomial model of employment discrimination of Kline and Walters (2021) described briefly in Section 9.3.4, consider the **REBayes** example in `demo(B2mix1)` and marvel at the accuracy of the NPMLE. Since the number of Bernoulli trials varies from 8 to 12 in this artificial example, partial identification is only of moderate concern: Explain why. For coders: Suggest a way to reformulate the code in the **REBayes** function `B2mix` using tensor algebra.

(11) Consideration of the classical empirical Bayes Gaussian sequence model may lead to anxiety over the validity of the Gaussian noise assumption. What happens if Gaussian noise is replaced by something that acknowledges the possibility of a few outliers? Huber's least favorable model for the Gaussian contamination model naturally suggests itself. Suppose, instead of the standard Gaussian base model, we consider

$$\varphi_\epsilon(u) = \begin{cases} (1-\epsilon)\phi(k)\exp(-k(u-k)) & u > k, \\ (1-\epsilon)\phi(u) & |u| \le k, \\ (1-\epsilon)\phi(k)\exp(k(u+k)) & u < -k, \end{cases}$$

where Huber's k, the value at which the influence function of the Huber M-estimator flips from being linear in the center to being constant in the tails, is related to the contamination proportion, ϵ, by the expression $2\phi(k)/k - 2\Phi(-k) = \epsilon/(1-\epsilon)$. An R function, `HLmix`, to solve problems of the form

$$\min_{G \in \mathcal{G}} \left\{ \sum_{i=1}^n \log f_G(y) \mid f_G(y) = \int \varphi_\epsilon(y-\theta) dG(\theta) \right\}$$

is available in **REBayes**.

Compare root mean square error performance for denoising with the posterior means of the Huber base distribution versus the Gaussian base for two test scenarios:

(a) $Y_i = \theta_i + U_i$, with $\theta_i \sim 0.8\delta_0 + 0.2\delta_3$ and $U \sim 0.9\Phi(u) + 0.1\Phi(u/3)$.
(b) $Y_i = \theta_i + U_i$, with $\theta_i \sim 0.8\delta_0 + 0.2\delta_3$ and $U \sim \Phi(u)$.

Hint: See Koenker (2024).

CHAPTER 13

Conclusion

Variety, it's said, is the spice of life; it is also the raison d'être of the discipline of data analysis. There will always be a temptation to compress the meaning of scientific observation into a table of mean effects, but there is usually something more to be gained by exploring the heterogeneity underlying the central tendency.

In prior work on quantile regression we sought to escape the confines of the conventional conditional mean signal plus homogeneous noise model of classical regression analysis. Heterogeneous treatment effects are now acknowledged to be a critical aspect of program evaluation and we have seen that covariates only rarely exhibit a pure location-shift effect.

Heterogeneity in latent variable effects has long been recognized as something that needs to be accounted for. In panel data models it has often been treated simply as a nuisance phenomenon, something that can be "projected away"; however, increasingly it is seen as something deserving a more diligent investigation. Kiefer and Wolfowitz (1956) first noted that the incidental parameters critique of Neyman and Scott (1948) could be ameliorated by estimating the distribution of these effects rather than treating them as isolated fixed parameters. That insight, together with the fundamental efforts of Herbert Robbins and Charles Stein, opened a new path for statistical data analysis. Compound decision theory by combining problems and borrowing strength for each problem from the entire collection leads to improved overall performance. The empirical Bayes perspective can be viewed as a middle way – drawing inspiration from both the Wald tradition of frequentist decision theory and the subjectivist decision theory of Savage.

We have tried to illustrate the empirical Bayes approach in a wide variety of empirical settings, but the scope for further exploration is vast. New developments of computational methods will undoubtedly bring new opportunities in large scale data analysis. A unified way to incorporate covariate effects into the latent variable framework of empirical Bayes methods remains a major challenge, see for example, Mukherjee et al. (2023). Inference has lagged behind estimation in the development of empirical Bayes methods and deserves more attention. New data structures pose new challenges: Time series, models of spatial dependence, networks and myriad other settings need further development.

Of special consequence is the linkage of empirical Bayes methods to Robbins's other great love – sequential analysis:

> We are indebted to Wald for the first significant contribution to the theory of sequential design. His book [Wald (1947)] states the problem in full generality and gives the outline of a general inductive method of solution. The probability problems involved are formidable, since dependent probabilities occur in all their complexity, and explicit recipes are not yet available for handling problems of practical interest. Nevertheless, enough is visible to justify a prediction that future results in the theory of sequential design will be of the greatest importance to mathematical statistics and to science as a whole. [Robbins (1952)]

There is growing interest in such problems motivated by refinements of clinical trial procedures and experimental practices more generally, as well as the rapid progress of machine learning. In addition to the legacy of Robbins's own contributions there is the early contribution of Martinsek (1987) and the recent contributions of Hirano and Porter (2025) and Lattimore and Szepesvári (2020). Further progress is just around the corner.

References

Aalen OO (1988) Heterogeneity in survival analysis. *Statistics in Medicine* 7: 1121–1137

Aalen OO (1992) Modelling heterogeneity in survival analysis by the compound Poisson distribution. *Annals of Applied Probability* 2:951–972

Aalen OO, Borgan O, Gjessing H (2008) *Survival and Event History Analysis*. Springer-Verlag

Abadie A, Kasy M (2019) Choosing among regularized estimators in empirical economics: The risk of machine learning. *The Review of Economics and Statistics* 101:743–762

Abbring JH, van der Berg GJ (2007) The unobserved heterogeneity distribution in duration analysis. *Biometrika* 94:87–99

Allman ES, Matias C, Rhodes JA (2009) Identifiability of parameters in latent structure models with many observed variables. *Annals of Statistics* 37:3099–3132

Alvarez J, Arellano M (2003) The time series and cross-section asymptotics of dynamic panel data estimators. *Econometrica* 71:1121–1159

Andersen EB (1970) Asymptotic properties of conditional maximum-likelihood estimators. *Journal of the Royal Statistical Society B* 32:283–301

Anderson TW, Rubin H (1949) Estimation of the parameters of a single equation in a complete system of stochastic equations. *The Annals of Mathematical Statistics* 20:46–63

Andrews D, Bickel P, Hampel F, Huber P, Rogers W, Tukey JW (1972) *Robust Estimates of Location: Survey and Advances*. Princeton University Press

Andrews DF, Mallows CL (1974) Scale mixtures of normal distributions. *Journal of the Royal Statistical Society B* 36:99–102

Andrews I, Kitagawa T, McCloskey A (2024) Inference on winners. *Quarterly Journal of Economics* 139:305–358

Angrist J, Hull P, Walters CR (2023) Methods for measuring school effectiveness. In: Machin SJ, Woessmann L, Hanushek EA (eds) *Handbook of the Economics of Education*, vol 7. Elsevier

Anscombe F, Robbins H, Morris C, Sobel M (1990) A discussion with Herbert Robbins, www.youtube.com/watch?v=IIO2urt8jHI

Antoniak C (1974) Mixtures of Dirichlet process with applications to Bayesian nonparametric problems. *Annals of Statistics* 2(6):1152–1174

ApS M (2022a) Mosek modeling cookbook, release 3.3.0, https://docs.mosek.com/MOSEKModelingCookbook-a4paper.pdf

ApS M (2022b) Rmosek package, release 10.0.16, https://docs.mosek.com/10.0/rmosek.pdf

Arellano M (2003) *Panel Data Econometrics*. Oxford University Press

Arellano M, Bonhomme S (2021) Recovering latent variables by matching. *Journal of the American Statistical Association* 118:693–706

Armstrong TB, Kolesár M, Plagborg-Møller M (2022) Robust empirical Bayes confidence intervals. *Econometrica* 90:2567–2602

Ashenfelter O (1978) Estimating the effect of training programs on earnings. *The Review of Economics and Statistics* 60:47–57

Ashenfelter O, Card D (1985) Using the longitudinal structure of earnings to estimate the effect of training programs. *Review of Economics & Statistics* 67:648–660

Avriel M (1972) r-convex functions. Math Programming 2:309–323

Azaïs JM, Gassiat É, Mercadier C (2006) Asymptotic distribution and local power of the log-likelihood ratio test for mixtures: Bounded and unbounded cases. *Bernoulli* 12(5):775–799

Azevedo EM, Deng A, Montiel Olea JL, Rao J, Weyl EG (2020) A/B testing with fat tails. *Journal of Political Economy* 128:4614–4672

Balestra P, Nerlove M (1966) Pooling cross section and time series data in the estimation of a dynamic model: The demand for natural gas. *Econometrica* 34:585–612

Barndorff-Nielsen O (1965) Identifiability of mixtures of exponential families. *Journal of Mathematical Analysis and Applications* 12:115–121

Barron AR, Sheu CH (1991) Approximation of density functions by sequences of exponential families. *Annals of Statistics* 19:1347–1369

Basu P, Cai T, Das K, Sun W (2018) Weighted false discovery rate control in large-scale multiple testing. *Journal of the American Statistical Association* 113:1172–1183

Beckett L, Diaconis P (1994) Spectral analysis for discrete longitudinal data. *Advances in Mathematics* 103:107–128

Benjamini Y, Hochberg Y (1995) Controlling the false discovery rate: A practical and powerful approach to multiple testing. *Journal of Royal Statistical Society B* 57: 289–300

Beran R, Feuerverger A, Hall P (1996) On nonparametric estimation of intercept and slope distributions in random coefficient regression. *Annals of Statistics* 24: 2569–2592

Berger JO (1985) *Statistical Decision Theory and Bayesian Analysis*, 2nd ed. Springer-Verlag

Berman R, van den Bulte C (2022) False discovery in A/B testing. *Management Science* 68:6762–6782

Bertrand M, Mullainathan S (2004) Are Emily and Greg more employable than Lakisha and Jamal? a field experiment on labor market discrimination. *American Economic Review* 94:991–1013

Bickel PJ (1982) On adaptive estimation. *Annals of Statistics* 10:647–671

Bishop YM, Fienberg SE, Holland PW (1975) *Discrete Multivariate Analysis: Theory and Practice*. MIT Press

Blackwell D, MacQueen J (1973) Ferguson distribution via Pólya urn schemes. *Annals of Statistics* 1(2):353–355

Böhning D (1986) A vertex-exchange-method in d-optimal design theory. *Metrika* 33:337–347

Bonhomme S, Robin J (2010) Generalized nonparametric deconvolution with an application to earnings dynamics. *Review of Economic Studies* 77:491–533

Bonhomme S, Jochmans K, Robin JM (2016) Estimating multivariate latent-structure models. *The Annals of Statistics* 44:540–563

Bradley R, Terry M (1952) Rank analysis of incomplete block designs: I. The method of paired comparisons. *Biometrika* 39:324–345

Brown LD (1966) On the admissibility of invariant estimators of one or more location parameters. *Annals of Mathematical Statistics* 37:1087–1136

Brown LD (1968) Inadmissibility of the usual estimators of scale parameters in problems with unknown location and scale parameters. *Annals of Mathematical Statistics* 39:29–48

Brown LD (1971) Admissible estimators, recurrent diffusions and insoluble boundary value problems. *Annals of Mathematical Statistics* 42:855–903

Brown LD (2008) In-season prediction of batting averages: A field test of empirical Bayes and Bayes methodologies. *Annals of Applied Statistics* 2:113–152

Brown LD, Greenshtein E (2009) Nonparametric empirical Bayes and compound decision approaches to estimation of a high dimensional vector of normal means. *Annals of Statistics* 37(4):1685–1704

Brown LD, Greenshtein E, Ritov Y (2013) The Poisson compound decision problem revisited. *Journal of the American Statistical Association* 108:741–749

Browning M, Ejrnæs M, Alvarez J (2010) Modelling income processes with lots of heterogeneity. *Review of Economic Studies* 77:1353–1381

Bühlmann H, Gisler A (2005) *A Course in Credibility Theory and Its Applications*. Springer-Verlag

Butucea C, Comte F (2009) Adaptive estimation of linear functionals in the convolution model and applications. *Bernoulli* 15:69–98

Calonico S, Cattaneo MD, Farrell MH, Titiunik R (2023) rdrobust: Robust data-driven statistical inference in regression-discontinuity designs. https://CRAN.R-project.org/package=rdrobust, R package version 2.2

Cameron AC, Trivedi PK (2005) *Microeconometrics: Methods and Applications*. Cambridge University Press

Carey J, Curtsinger J, Vaupel J (1993) Fruit fly aging and mortality. Response to letters to the editor. *Science* 260:1567–1569

Carey J, Liedo P, Orozco D, Vaupel J (1992) Slowing of mortality rates at older ages in large medfly cohorts. *Science* 258:457–461

Carlin BP, Louis TA (2000) *Bayes and Empirical Bayes Methods for Data Analysis*, 2nd ed. Chapman-Hall

Carpenter B, Gelman A, Hoffman MD, Lee D, Goodrich B, Betancourt M, Brubaker M, Guo J, Li P, Riddell A (2017) Stan: A probabilistic programming language. *Journal of Statistical Software* 76:1–32

Carvalho C, Polson N, Scott J (2009) Handling sparsity via the horseshoe. *Journal of Machine Learning Research* 5:73–80

Casella G, Hwang JT (2012) Shrinkage confidence procedures. *Statistical Science* 27:51–60

Castillo I, van der Vaart A (2012) Needles and straw in a haystack: Posterior concentration for possibly sparse sequences. *Annals of Statistics* 40:2069–2101

Chamberlain G (1980) Analysis of covariance with qualitative data. *Review of Economic Studies* 47:225–238

Chamberlain G, Hirano K (1999) Predictive distribution based on longitudinal earnings data. *Annales d' Économie et de Statistique* 55/56:211–242

Chamberlain G, Leamer EE (1976) Matrix weighted averages and posterior bounds. *Journal of the Royal Statistical Society B* 38:73–84

Chan KCG, Qin J (2016) Nonparametric maximum likelihood estimation for the multisample Wicksell corpuscle problem. *Biometrika* 103:273–286

Charnes A, Cooper WW (1962) Programming with linear fractional functionals. *Naval Research Logistics Quarterly* 9:181–186

Chen J (2025) Empirical Bayes when estimation precision predicts parameters, *Econometrica*, forthcoming.

Chen X, Liao Z (2014) Sieve m inference on irregular parameters. *Journal of Econometrics* 182(1):70–86

Chen X, Tamer ET, Torgovitsky A (2011) Sensitivity analysis in semiparametric likelihood models, Cowles Foundation discussion paper

Cheng R, Amin N (1983) Estimating parameters in continuous univariate distributions with a shifted origin. *Journal of the Royal Statistical Society B* 45:394–403

Chesher A (1984) Testing for neglected heterogeneity. *Econometrica* 52(4):865–872

Cho J, White H (2007) Testing for regime switching. *Econometrica* 75:1671–1720

Clevenson M, Zidek J (1975) Simultaneous estimation of the means of independent Poisson laws. *Journal of the American Statistical Association* 70:112–120

Coey D, Hung K (2022) Empirical Bayes selection for value maximization. Proceedings of the 31st ACM SIGKDD Conference on Knowledge Discovery and Data Mining, 2, 357–368.

Compiani G, Kitamura Y (2016) Using mixtures in econometric models: A brief review and some new results. *The Econometrics Journal* 19:C95–C127

Copas JB (1969) Compound decisions and empirical Bayes. *Journal of the Royal Statistical Society B* 31:397–425

Cosslett SR (1983) Distribution-free maximum likelihood estimator of the binary choice model. *Econometrica* 51:765–782

Cox DR (1958) Some problems connected with statistical inference. *Annals of Mathematical Statistics* 29:357–372

Cox DR (1962) Comment on L.J. Savage's lecture: Subjective probability and statistical practice. In: Barnard G, Cox D (eds) *The Foundations of Statistical Inference*, Methuen

Cox DR (1972) Regression models with life tables. *Journal of the Royal Statistical Society B* 34:187–220

Cox DR (1975) A note on partially Bayes inference and the linear model. *Biometrika* 62:651–654

Cuturi M (2013) Sinkhorn distances: Lightspeed computation of optimal transport. In: *Proceedings of the 26th International Conference on Neural Information Processing Systems*, vol 2, pp 2292–2300

Cuturi M, Doucet A (2014) Fast computation of Wasserstein barycenters. In: Xing EP, Jebara T (eds) *Proceedings of the 31st International Conference on Machine Learning*, vol 32, pp 685–693

Cuturi M, Peyré G (2016) A smoothed dual approach for variational Wasserstein problems. *SIAM Journal on Imaging Sciences* 9:320–343

Dahl J, Andersen ED (2022) A primal-dual interior-point algorithm for nonsymmetric exponential-cone optimization. *Mathematical Programming* 194:341–370

Darling DA (1953) On a class of problems related to the random division of an interval. *Annals of Mathematical Statistics* pp 239–253

Davies PL, Kovac A (2004) Densities, spectral densities and modality. *Annals of Statistics* 32:1093–1136

Dawid AP (1994) Selection paradoxes of Bayesian inference. In: *Multivariate Analysis and Its Applications*, vol 24. Institute of Mathematical Statistics

Deely J, Kruse R (1968) Construction of sequences estimating the mixing distribution. *Annals of Mathematical Statistics* 39:286–288

Del Negro M, Schorfheide F (2011) Bayesian macroeconometrics. In: Geweke J, Koop G, van Dijk H (eds) *Oxford Handbook of Bayesian Econometrics*, Oxford University Press, pp 293–389

Dempster A, Laird N, Rubin D (1977) Maximum likelihood from incomplete data via the EM algorithm. *Journal of the Royal Statistical Society B* 39:1–38

Diaconis P (1987) Application of the method of moments in probability and statistics. In: Landau HJ (ed) *Moments in Mathematics*, American Mathematical Society, pp 125–142

Diaconis P (2009) Review of *Probabilistic Symmetries and Invariance Principles*, by Olav Kallenberg. *AMS Bulletin* 46:691–696

Diaconis P, Skyrms B (2018) *Ten Great Ideas about Chance*. Princeton University Press

Dicker LH, Zhao SD (2016) High-dimensional classification via nonparametric empirical Bayes and maximum likelihood inference. *Biometrika* 103:21–34

Doan T, Litterman R, Sims C (1984) Forecasting and conditional projection using realistic prior distributions. *Econometric Reviews* 3:1–100

Donoho D, Chen S, Saunders M (1998) Atomic decomposition by basis pursuit. *SIAM Journal of Scientific Computing* 20:33–61

Duncan OD, Davis BJ (1953) An alternative to ecological correlation. *American Sociological Review* 18:665–666

Dyson F (1926) A method for correcting series of parallax observations. *Monthly Notices of the Royal Astronomical Society* 86:686–706

Eckles D, Ignatiadis N, Wager S, Wu H (2025) Noise-induced randomization in regression discontinuity designs, *Biometrika*, 112.

Edgeworth F (1888) On a new method of reducing observations relating to several quantities. *Philosophical Magazine* 25:184–191

Efron B (2010) *Large-Scale Inference: Empirical Bayes Methods for Estimation, Testing, and Prediction*. Cambridge University Press

Efron B (2011) Tweedie's formula and selection bias. *Journal of the American Statistical Association* 106:1602–1614

Efron B (2014) Two modeling strategies for empirical Bayes estimation. *Statistical Science* 29:285–301

Efron B (2016) Empirical Bayes deconvolution estimates. *Biometrika* 103:1–20

Efron B (2019) Bayes, oracle Bayes and empirical Bayes. *Statistical Science* 34: 177–201

Efron B, Morris C (1973a) Combining possibly related estimation problems. *Journal of the Royal Statistical Society B* 35:379–421

Efron B, Morris C (1973b) Stein's estimation rule and its competitors – An empirical Bayes approach. *Journal of the American Statistical Association* 68:117–130

Efron B, Morris C (1977) Stein's paradox in statistics. *Scientific American* 235:119–127

Efron B, Olshen RA (1978) How broad is the class of normal scale mixtures? *Annals of Statistics* 5:1159–1164

Efron B, Thisted R (1976) Estimating the number of unseen species: How many words did Shakespeare know? *Biometrika* 63:435–447

Efron B, Tibshirani R, Storey J, Tusher V (2001) Empirical Bayes analysis of microarray experiments. *Journal American Statistical Association* 96:1151–1160

Elbers C, Ridder G (1982) True and spurious duration dependence: The identifiability of the proportional hazard model. *Review of Economic Studies* 49:403–409

Escobar M (1994) Estimating normal means with a Dirichlet process prior. *Journal of the American Statistical Association* pp 268–277

Escobar M, West M (1994) Bayesian density estimation and inference using mixtures. *Journal of the American Statistical Association* 90:577–588

Fan J, Zhang C, Zhang J (2001) Generalized likelihood ratio statistics and Wilks phenomenon. *Annals of Statistics* 29:153–193

Feller W (1943) On a general class of "contagious" distributions. *Annals of Mathematical Statistics* 14:389–400

Feller W (1971) *Introduction to Probability Theory and Its Applications*, vol II, 2nd ed. Wiley

Ferguson T (1967) *Mathematical Statistics: A Decision-Theoretic Approach*. Academic Press: New York

Ferguson T (1973) A Bayesian analysis of some nonparametric problems. *Annals of Statistics* 1:209–230

Ferguson T (1983) Bayesian density estimation by mixtures of normal distributions. In: Rizvi H, Rustagi J (eds) *Recent Advances in Statistics*, Academic Press: New York, pp 287–302

Feuerverger A, Vardi Y (2000) Positron emission tomography and random coefficients regression. *Annals of the Institute of Statistical Mathematics* 52:123–138

de Finetti B (1964) Foresight: Its logical laws and subjective sources. In: Kyburg HE, Smokler H (eds) *Studies in Subjective Probability*, Wiley, pp 93–158

Fisher RA, Corbet AS, Williams CB (1943) The relation between the number of species and the number of individuals in a random sample of an animal population. *Journal of Animal Ecology* 12:42–58

Fong E, Holmes C (2021) Conformal Bayesian computation. In: *Advances in Neural Information Processing Systems* https://api.semanticscholar.org/CorpusID:235417223

Fougner C (2014) POGS: Proximal operator graph solver. https://github.com/foges/pogs

Fougner C, Boyd S (2015) Parameter selection and pre-conditioning for a graph form solver, http://stanford.edu/~boyd/papers/pogs.html

Freedman DA, Klein SP, Ostland M, Roberts MR (1998) Review of: A solution to the ecological inference problem by G King. *Journal of the American Statistical Association* 93:1518–1522

Galichon A (2016) *Optimal Transport Methods in Economics*. Princeton University Press

Galton F (1892) *Hereditary Genius: An Inquiry into Its Laws and Consequences*, 2nd ed. Macmillan

Gassiat E (2002) Likelihood ratio inequalities with applications to various mixtures. In: *Annales de l'Institut Henri Poincare (B) Probability and Statistics*, vol 38. Elsevier, pp 897–906

Gautier E, Kitamura Y (2013) Nonparametric estimation in random coefficients binary choice models. *Econometrica* 81:581–607

Gelfand A, Smith A (1990) Sampling-based approaches to calculating marginal densities. *Journal of the American Statistical Association* 85:398–409

Gelman A (2021) Actually, I'd just do full Bayes. https://statmodeling.stat.columbia.edu/2016/03/19/actually-id-just-do-full-bayes/

Genovese C, Wasserman L (2002) Operating characteristics and extensions of the false discovery rate procedure. *Journal of the Royal Statistical Society B* 64:499–517

Gentleman R, Geyer C (1994) Maximum likelihood for interval censored data: Consistency and computation. *Biometrika* 81:618–623

Geweke J, Keane M (2000) An empirical analysis of earnings dynamics among men in the PSID: 1968–1989. *Journal of Econometrics* 96:293–356

Goldberger AS (1962) Best linear unbiased prediction in the generalized linear regression model. *Journal of the American Statistical Association* 57:369–375

Good IJ (1952) Rational decisions. *Journal of the Royal Statistical Society: B* 14: 107–114

Good IJ (1953) On the population frequencies of species and the estimation of population parameters. *Biometrika* 40:237–264

Good IJ (1971) 46656 varieties of Bayesians. *American Statistician* 25:62–63

Good IJ (1976) The Bayesian influence, or how to sweep subjectivism under the carpet. In: Hooker C, Harper W (eds) *Foundations of Probability Theory, and Statistical Inference*, Reidel

Goodman LA (1953) Ecological regressions and behavior of individuals. *American Sociological Review* 18:663–669

Green EJ, Strawderman WE (1991) A James–Stein type estimator for combining unbiased and possibly biased estimators. *Journal of the American Statistical Association* 86:1001–1006

Greenshtein E, Ritov Y (2019) Comment: Empirical Bayes, compound decisions and exchangeability. *Statistical Science* 34:224–228

Grenander U (1956) On the theory of mortality measurement, part II. *Skandinavisk Aktuarietidskrift* 39:125–153

Groeneboom P, Hendrickx K (2018) Current status linear regression. *Annals of Statistics* 46:1415–1444

Groeneboom P, Jongbloed G (2014) *Nonparametric Estimation under Shape Constraints: Estimators, Algorithms and Asymptotics*. Cambridge University Press

Groeneboom P, Wellner J (1992) Information bounds and nonparametric maximum likelihood estimation, *DMV Seminar*, vol 19. Birkhäuser Verlag

Gu J (2016) Neyman's $C(\alpha)$ test for unobserved heterogeneity. *Econometric Theory* 32(6):1483–1522

Gu J, Koenker R (2017a) Empirical Bayesball remixed: Empirical Bayes methods for longitudinal data. *Journal of Applied Econometrics* 32:575–599

Gu J, Koenker R (2017b) Unobserved heterogeneity in income dynamics: An empirical Bayes perspective. *Journal of Business and Economic Statistics* 35:1–16

Gu J, Koenker R (2019) RCBR: An R package for binary response with random coefficients. www.econ.uiuc.edu/~roger/research/ebayes/ebayes.html

Gu J, Koenker R (2022a) Nonparametric maximum likelihood methods for binary response models with random coefficients. *Journal of the American Statistical Association* 117:732–751

Gu J, Koenker R (2022b) Ranking and selection from pairwise comparisons: Empirical Bayes methods for citation analysis. *AEA Papers and Proceedings* 112:624–629

Gu J, Koenker R (2023) Invidious comparisons: Ranking and selection as compound decisions. *Econometrica* 91:1–41

Gu J, Russell TM (2023) Partial identification in nonseparable binary response models with endogenous regressors. *Journal of Econometrics* 235:528–562

Gu J, Shen S (2018) Oracle and adaptive false discovery rate controlling methods for one-sided testing: Theory and application in treatment effect evaluation. *The Econometrics Journal* 21:11–35

Gu J, Koenker R, Volgushev S (2018) Testing for homogeneity in mixture models. *Econometric Theory* 34:850–895

Gu J, Russell TM, Stringham T (2025) Counterfactual identification and latent space enumeration in discrete outcome models, forthcoming, *Review of Economic Studies*

Guvenen F, Karahan F, Ozkan S, Son J (2022) What do data on millions of U.S. workers reveal about lifecycle earnings dynamics? *Econometrica* 89:2303–2339

Haastrup S (2000) Comparison of some Bayesian analyses of heterogeneity in group life insurance. *Scandinavian Actuarial Journal* 1:2–16

Hahn J (1994) The efficiency bound of the mixed proportional hazard model. *The Review of Economic Studies* 61:607–629

Hall P, Zhou XH (2003) Nonparametric estimation of component distributions in a multivariate mixture. *The Annals of Statistics* 31(1):201–224

Hausdorff F (1921) Summationsmethoden und momentfolgen. *Mathematische Zeitschrift* 9:74–109

Hayfield T, Racine J (2008) Nonparametric econometrics: The np package. *Journal of Statistical Software* 27:1–32

Heckman J, Singer B (1983) The identification problem in econometric models for duration data. In: Hildenbrand W (ed) *Advances in Econometrics*, Cambridge University Press, p 3978

Heckman J, Singer B (1984) A method for minimizing the impact of distributional assumptions in econometric models for duration data. *Econometrica* 52:63–132

Heckman JJ, Smith JA (1999) The pre-programme earnings dip and the determinants of participation in a social programme. implications for simple programme evaluation strategies. *The Economic Journal* 109:313–348

Henderson N, Newton M (2016) Making the cut: Improved ranking and selection for large-scale inference. *Journal of the Royal Statistical Society B* 78:781–804

Henry M, Kitamura Y, Salanié B (2014) Partial identification of finite mixtures in econometric models. *Quantitative Economics* 5:123–144

Hewitt E, Savage L (1955) Symmetric measures on Cartesian products. *Transactions of the American Mathematical Society* 80:470–501

Hill BM (1975) A simple general approach to inference about the tail of a distribution. *Annals of Statistics* 3:1163–1174

Hirano K (2002) Semiparametric Bayesian inference in autoregressive panel data models. *Econometrica* 70:781–799

Hirano K, Porter J (2020) Asymptotic analysis of statistical decision rules. In: Durlauf SN, Hansen LP, Heckman J, Matzkin RL (eds) *Handbook of Econometrics*, vol 7a. Elsevier, pp 283–354

Hirano K, Porter JR (2025) Asymptotic representations for sequential decisions, adaptive experiments, and batched bandits. Review of Economic Studies, forthcoming.

Hocking D, Joulin A, Bach F, Vert JP (2011) Clusterpath: An algorithm for clustering using convex fusion penalties. *Proceedings of the 28th International Conference on International Conference on Machine Learning*, pp 745–752

Holland P (1990) Letter to Herbert Robbins dated April 25. Robbins Archive, Low Library, Columbia University

Holm S (1979) A simple sequentially rejective multiple test procedure. *Scandinavian Journal of Statistics* 6:65–70

Honoré BE (1990) Simple estimation of a duration model with unobserved heterogeneity. *Econometrica* 58:453–473

Honoré BE (1997) A note on the rate of convergence of estimators of mixtures of Weibulls, preprint, Princeton

Horowitz J (1993) Semiparametric estimation of a work-trip mode of choice model. *Journal of Econometrics* 58:49–70

Horowitz JL (1999) Semiparametric estimation of a proportional hazard model with unobserved heterogeneity. *Econometrica* 67:1001–1028

Horowitz J, Markatou M (1996) Semiparametric estimation of regression models for panel data. *Review of Economic Studies* 63:145–168

Hospido L (2012) Modelling heterogeneity and dynamics in the volatility of individual wages. *Journal of Applied Econometrics* 27:386–411

Hotelling H (1939) Tubes and spheres in n-space and a class of statistical problems. *American Journal of Mathematics* 61:440–460

Hougaard P (1986) Survival models for heterogeneous populations derived from stable distributions. *Biometrika* 73:387–396

van Houwelingen J, Stijnen T (1983) Monotone Empirical Bayes estimators for the continuous one-parameter exponential family. *Statistica Neerlandica* 37:29–43

Hu Y (2017) The econometrics of unobservables: Applications of measurement error models in empirical industrial organization and labor economics. *Journal of Econometrics* 200:154–168

Hu Y, Schennach SM (2008) Instrumental variable treatment of nonclassical measurement error models. *Econometrica* 76:195–216

Huber PJ (1964) Robust estimation of a location parameter. *Annals of Mathematical Statistics* 35:73–101

Hwang JT, Casella G (1984) Minimax confidence sets for the mean of a multivariate normal distribution. *Statistical Decisions* 1:3–16

Ichimura H, Thompson T (1998) Maximum likelihood estimation of a binary choice model with random coefficients of unknown distribution. *Journal of Econometrics* 86:269–295

Ignatiadis N, Sen B (2025a) Empirical partially Bayes multiple testing and compound χ^2 decisions. *Annals of Statistics*, 53, 1–36

Ignatiadis N, Sen B (2025b) Topics in theoretical statistics: Empirical Bayes. *Notes for Statistics* GR8201

Ignatiadis N, Wager S (2022) Confidence intervals for nonparametric empirical Bayes analysis. *Journal of the American Statistical Association* 117:1149–1166

Ignatiadis N, Saha S, Sun DL, Muralidharan O (2021) Empirical Bayes mean estimation with nonparametric errors via order statistic regression on replicated data. *Journal of the American Statistical Association* 118:1–13

Imai K, Lu Y, Strauss A (2011) Eco: R package for ecological inference in 2x2 tables. *Journal of Statistical Software* 42:1–23

Ishwaran H (1996) Uniform rates of estimation in the semiparametric Weibull mixture models. *Annals of Statistics* 24:1560–1571

Ishwaran H (1999) Information in semiparametric mixtures of exponential families. *Annals of Statistics* 27:159–177

Jackson DA, O'Donovan TM, Zimmer WJ, Deely JJ (1970) $\mathcal{G}_2$-minimax estimators in the exponential family. *Biometrika* 57:439–443

James W, Stein C (1961) Estimation with quadratic loss. In: *Proceedings of the Fourth Berkeley Symposium on Mathematical Statistics and Probability*, University of California Press, p 361

Jana S, Polyanskiy Y, Wu Y (2022) Optimal empirical Bayes estimation for the Poisson model via minimum-distance methods, https://arxiv.org/abs/2209.01328

Jeffreys H (1961) *Theory of Probability*, 3rd ed. Oxford University Press

Jiang W (2019) Comment: Empirical Bayes interval estimation. *Statistical Science* 34:219–223

Jiang W, Zhang CH (2009) General maximum likelihood empirical Bayes estimation of normal means. *Annals of Statistics* 37:1647–1684

Jin J (2008) Proportion of non-zero normal means: Universal oracle equivalences and uniformly consistent estimators. *Journal of the Royal Statistical Society B* 70: 461–493

Johns MV (1986) Fully nonparametric empirical Bayes estimation via projection pursuit. In: Ryzin JV (ed) *Adaptive Statistical Procedures and Related Topics*, Institute of Mathematical Statistics, pp 164–178

Johns M (1957) Non-parametric empirical Bayes procedures. *Annals of Mathematical Statistics* 28:649–669

Johns M, Van Ryzin J (1971) Convergence rates for empirical Bayes two-action problems i. discrete case. *Annals of Mathematical Statistics* 42:1521–1539

Johns M, Van Ryzin J (1972) Convergence rates for empirical Bayes two-action problems ii. continuous case. *Annals of Mathematical Statistics* 43:934–947

Johnstone IM (2017) Gaussian estimation: Sequence and wavelet models, https://imjohnstone.su.domains//GE_08_09_17.pdf

Johnstone I, Silverman B (2004) Needles and straw in haystacks: Empirical Bayes estimates of possibly sparse sequences. *Annals of Statistics* 32:1594–1649

Johnstone IM, Silverman BW (2005) Ebayesthresh: R and S-plus programs for empirical Bayes thresholding. *Journal of Statistical Software* 12:1–38

Joshi V (1967) Inadmissibility of the usual confidence sets for the mean of a multivariate normal population. *Annals of Mathematical Statistics* 38:1868–1875

Judge G, Bock ME (1978) *The Statistical Implications of Pre-Test and Stein-Rule Estimators in Econometrics*. North Holland

Kadane JB (1980) Predictive and structural methods for eliciting prior distributions. In: Zellner A (ed) *Bayesian Analysis in Econometrics and Statistics*, North-Holland

Kadane JB, Wolfson LJ (1998) Experiences in elicitation. *Journal of the Royal Statistical Society D* 47:3–19

Kadane JB, Dickey JM, Winkler RL, Smith WS, Peters SC (1980) Interactive elicitation of opinion for a normal linear model. *Journal American Statistical Association* 75:845–854

Karlin S (1959) *Mathematical Methods and Theory in Games, Programming, and Economics*. Addison-Wesley

Kasahara H, Shimotsu K (2009) Nonparametric identification of finite mixture models of dynamic discrete choices. *Econometrica* 77:135–175

Kent C, Li J, Blanchet J, Glynn PW (2021) Modified Frank Wolfe in probability space. In: Ranzato M, Beygelzimer A, Dauphin Y, Liang P, Vaughan JW (eds) *Advances in Neural Information Processing Systems*, vol 34. Curran Associates, Inc., pp 14448–14462

Keynes JM (1921) *A Treatise on Probability*. Macmillan

Kiefer J, Wolfowitz J (1956) Consistency of the maximum likelihood estimator in the presence of infinitely many incidental parameters. *Annals of Mathematical Statistics* 27:887–906

Kimeldorf GS, Wahba G (1970) A correspondence between Bayesian estimation on stochastic processes and smoothing by splines. *Annals of Mathematical Statistics* 41:495–502

King G (1997) *A Solution to the Ecological Inference Problem: Reconstructing Individual Behavior from Aggregate Data*. Princeton University Press

Klein R, Spady R (1993) An efficient semiparametric estimator for binary response models. *Econometrica* 61:387–421

Kline P, Rose EK, Walters CR (2022) Systemic discrimination among large us employers. *The Quarterly Journal of Economics* 137:1963–2036

Kline PM, Walters CR (2021) Reasonable doubt: Experimental detection of job-level employment discrimination. *Econometrica* 89:765–792

Koenker R (2000) Galton, Edgeworth, Frisch, and prospects for quantile regression in econometrics. *Journal of Econometrics* 95:347–374

Koenker R (2011) Additive models for quantile regression: Model selection and confidence bandaids. *Brazilian Journal of Probability and Statistics* 25:239–262

Koenker R (2013) Adaptive estimation of regression parameters for the Gaussian scale mixture model. In: Beran J, Feng Y, Hebbel H (eds) *Empirical Economic and Financial Research: A Festschrift for Siegfried Heiler*, Springer-Verlag, pp 373–378

Koenker R (2024) Robust estimation of the Gaussian sequence model: An r vinaigrette, www.econ.uiuc.edu/~roger/research/vinaigrettes/HEB.pdf

Koenker R, Geling O (2001) Reappraising medfly longevity: A quantile regression survival analysis. *Journal of the American Statistical Association* 96:458–468

Koenker R, Gu J (2013) Frailty, profile likelihood and medfly mortality. In: Lahiri S, Schick A, Sengupta A, Sriram T (eds) *Contemporary Developments in Statistical Theory: A Festschrift for Hira Lal Koul*, Springer

Koenker R, Gu J (2015–2024) REBayes: An R package for empirical Bayes methods, https://cran.r-project.org/package=REBayes

Koenker R, Gu J (2017) REBayes: An R package for empirical Bayes mixture methods. *Journal of Statistical Software* 82:1–26

Koenker R, Gu J (2019) Comment: Minimalist g-modeling. *Statistical Science* 34: 209–213

Koenker R, Gu J (2024) Empirical Bayes for the reluctant frequentist. *Journal of Political Economy Microeconomics*, forthcoming

Koenker R, Mizera I (2010) Quasi-concave density estimation. *Annals of Statistics* 38:2998–3027

Koenker R, Mizera I (2014) Convex optimization, shape constraints, compound decisions, and empirical Bayes rules. *Journal of the American Statistical Association* 109:674–685

Koenker R, Ng P, Portnoy S (1994) Quantile smoothing splines. *Biometrika* 81:673–680

Kolesár M (2021) EBCI: Robust empirical Bayes confidence intervals. R package version 1.0.0, https://CRAN.R-project.org/package=ebci

Krivobokova T, Kneib T, Claeskens G (2010) Simultaneous confidence bands for penalized spline estimators. *Journal of the American Statistical Association* 105: 852–863

Kruskal JB (1976) More factors than subjects, tests and treatments: An indeterminacy theorem for canonical decomposition and individual differences scaling. *Psychometrika* 41:281–293

Kruskal JB (1977) Three-way arrays: Rank and uniqueness of trilinear decompositions, with application to arithmetic complexity and statistics. *Linear Algebra Applications* 18:95–138

Laird N (1978) Nonparametric maximum likelihood estimation of a mixing distribution. *Journal of the American Statistical Association* 73:805–811

Laird N, Louis T (1989) Empirical Bayes ranking methods. *Journal of Educational Statistics* 14:29–46

Lambert D, Tierney L (1984) Asymptotic properties of maximum likelihood estimates in the mixed Poisson model. *Annals of Statistics* 12:1388–1399

Lancaster T (2000) The incidental parameter problem since 1948. *Journal of Econometrics* 95:391–413

Lancaster T (2002) Orthogonal parameters and panel data. *The Review of Economic Studies* 69:647–666

Lattimore T, Szepesvári C (2020) *Bandit Algorithms*. Cambridge University Press

Lazar NA (2003) Bayesian empirical likelihood. *Biometrika* 90:319–326

Le Cam L (1990) Maximum likelihood: An introduction. *International Statistical Review* 58:153–171

Leamer EE (1978) *Specification Searches: Ad Hoc Inference with Nonexperimental Data*. Wiley

Leamer EE, Chamberlain G (1976) A Bayesian interpretation of pretesting. *Journal of the Royal Statistical Society B* 38:85–94

Leonard T (1984) Some data-analytic modifications to Bayes–Stein estimation. *Annals of the Institute of Statistical Mathematics* 36(1):11–21

Lesperance ML, Kalbfleisch JD (1992) An algorithm for computing the nonparametric MLE of a mixing distribution. *Journal of the American Statistical Association* 87:120–126

Li KC (1985) From Steins unbiased risk estimates to the method of GCV. *Annals of Statistics* 13:1352–1377

Li T, Vuong Q (1998) Nonparametric estimation of the measurement error model using multiple indicators. *Journal of Multivariate Analysis* 65:139–165

Lindley DV, Smith AF (1972) Bayes estimates for the linear model. *Journal of the Royal Statistical Society B* pp 1–41

Lindley DV, Tversky A, Brown RV (1979) On the reconciliation of probability assessments. *Journal of the Royal Statistical Society A* 142:146–180

Lindsay BG (1980) Nuisance parameters, mixture models, and the efficiency of partial likelihood estimators. *Philosophical Transactions of the Royal Society of London Series A, Mathematical and Physical Sciences* 296(1427):639–662

Lindsay B (1981) Properties of the maximum likelihood estimator of a mixing distribution. In: Taillie C, Patil GP, Baldessari BA (eds) *Statistical Distributions in Scientific Work*, D. Reidel, pp 95–109

Lindsay B (1983a) The geometry of mixture likelihoods: A general theory. *Annals of Statistics* 11:86–94

Lindsay B (1983b) The geometry of mixture likelihoods, part II: The exponential family. *Annals of Statistics* 11:783–792
Lindsay BG (1989) Moment matrices: Applications in mixtures. *Annals of Statistics* 17:722–740
Lindsay B (1995) Mixture models: Theory, geometry and applications. In: NSF-*CBMS Regional Conference Series in Probability and Statistics*
Lindsay BG, Basak P (2000) Moments determine the tail of a distribution (but not much else). *The American Statistician* 54:248–251
Lindsay BG, Roeder K (1993) Uniqueness of estimation and identifiability in mixture models. *Canadian Journal of Statistics* 21:139–147
Lindsay B, Clogg C, Grego J (1991) Semiparametric estimation in the Rasch model and related exponential response models, including a simple latent class model for item analysis. *Journal of American Statistical Association* 86:96–107
Liu J (1996) Nonparametric hierarchical Bayes via sequential imputations. *Annals of Statistics* 24(3):911–930
Liu L, Moon HR, Schorfheide F (2020) Forecasting with dynamic panel data models. *Econometrica* 88:171–201
Liu X, Shao Y (2003) Asymptotics for likelihood ratio tests under loss of identifiability. *Annals of Statistics* 31:807–832
Lo A (1984) On a class of Bayesian nonparametric estimates: 1. density estimates. *Annals of Statistics* 12:351–357
Lönnstedt I, Speed T (2002) Replicated microarray data. *Statistica Sinica* 12:31–46
Lord FM, Cressie N (1975) An empirical Bayes procedure for finding an interval estimate. *Sankhyā: The Indian Journal of Statistics B* 37:1–9
Lu M, Stephens M (2016) Variance adaptive shrinkage: Flexible empirical Bayes estimation of variances. *Bioinformatics* 32:3428–3434
Lunn D, Jackson C, Best N, Thomas A, Spiegelhalter D (2012) *The BUGS Book: A Practical Introduction to Bayesian Analysis*. Chapman and Hall/CRC
Mallows CL (1973) Some comments on C_p. *Technometrics* 15:661–675
Mallows C (2007) Deconvolution by simulation. In: Liu R, Strawderman W, Zhang CH (eds) *Complex Datasets and Inverse Problems: Tomography, Networks and Beyond: Essays in Memory of Yehuda Vardi*, IMS Lecture Notes Monograph Series, vol 54. Institute of Mathematical Statistics
Manski CF (1975) Maximum score estimation of the stochastic utility model. *Journal of Econometrics* 3:205–228
Manski CF (2004) Statistical treatment rules for heterogeneous populations. *Econometrica* 72:1221–1246
Manski CF (2007) Minimax-regret treatment choice with missing outcome data. *Journal of Econometrics* 139:105–115
Manski CF (2018) Credible ecological inference for medical decisions with personalized risk assessment. *Quantitative Economics* 9:541–569
Manski CF, Tetenov A (2016) Sufficient trial size to inform clinical practice. *Proceedings of the National Academy of Sciences* 113:10518–10523
Mao CX, Lindsay BG (2004) Estimating the number of classes in multiple populations: A geometric analysis. *Canadian Journal of Statistics* 32(3):303–314
Mao CX, Lindsay BG (2007) Estimating the number of classes. *Annals of Statistics* 35(2):917–930
Marin JM, Pudlo P, Robert CP, Ryder RJ (2012) Approximate Bayesian computational methods. *Statistics and Computing* 22:1167–1180

Maritz J, Lwin T (1989) *Empirical Bayes Methods*, 2nd ed. Chapman-Hall

Martinsek A (1987) Empirical Bayes methods in sequential estimation. *Sequential Analysis* 6:119–137

Massart P (1990) The tight constant in the Dvoretzky–Kiefer–Wolfowitz inequality. *Annals of Probability* 18:1269–1283

Matias C, Taupin ML (2004) Minimax estimation of linear functionals in the convolution model. *Mathematical Methods of Statistics* 13:282–328

McCall BP (1996) Unemployment insurance rules, joblessness, and part-time work. *Econometrica* 64:647–682

McCullagh P (1994) Does the moment-generating function characterize a distribution. *American Statistician* 48:208

McCullagh P, Polson NG (2018) Statistical sparsity. *Biometrika* 105:797–814

Meghir C, Pistaferri L (2004) Income variance dynamics and heterogeneity. *Econometrica* 72:1–32

Michigan Kidney Epidemiology and Cost Center (2018) Technical notes on the dialysis facility compare quality of patient care star rating methodology for the October 2018 release. https://data.cms.gov/dialysis-facility-reports

Milnor J (1954) Games against nature. In: Thrall R, Coombs C, Davis R (eds) *Decision Processes*, Wiley

Misak S (2020) *Frank Ramsey: A Sheer Excess of Powers*. Oxford University Press

Mogstad M, Romano J, Shaikh A, Wilhelm D (2024) Inferences for ranks with applications to mobility across neighborhoods and academic achievement across countries. *Review of Economic Studies* 91:476–518

Montiel Olea JL, O'Flaherty B, Sethi R (2021) Empirical Bayes counterfactuals in Poisson regression with an application to police use of deadly force, https://ssrn.com/abstract=3857213

Moreira MJ (2009) A maximum likelihood method for the incidental parameter problem. *Annals of Statistics* 37:3660–3696

Morris C (1983) Natural exponential families with quadratic variance functions: Statistical theory. *Annals of Statistics* 11:515–529

Mukherjee S, Sen B, Sen S (2023) A mean field approach to empirical Bayes estimation in high-dimensional linear regression, https:arxiv.org/abs/2309.16843

Mundlak Y (1961) Empirical production function free of management bias. *Journal of Farm Economics* 43:44–56

Mundlak Y (1978) On the pooling of time series and cross section data. *Econometrica* 46:69–85

Murphy SA (1995) Asymptotic theory for the frailty model. *Annals of Statistics* 23: 182–198

Murphy SA, van der Vaart AW (2000) On profile likelihood. *Journal of the American Statistical Association* 95:449–465

Narasimhan B, Efron B (2018–2024) A G-modeling program for deconvolution and empirical Bayes estimation, http://statweb.stanford.edu/~ckirby/brad/papers/2016G-ModelingProgram.pdf

Nerlove M (1971) Further evidence on the estimation of dynamic economic relations from a time series of cross sections. *Econometrica* 39:359–382

Nerlove M (2002) *Essays in Panel Data Econometrics*. Cambridge University Press

Neyman J (1959) Optimal asymptotic tests of composite statistical hypotheses. In: Grenander U (ed) *Probability and Statistics, the Harald Cramer Volume*. Wiley

Neyman J, Scott EL (1948) Consistent estimates based on partially consistent observations. *Econometrica* 16:1–32

Norberg R (1989) Experience rating in group life insurance. *Scandinavian Actuarial Journal* 194–224

Owen A (1990) Empirical likelihood ratio confidence regions. *Annals of Statistics* 18:90–120

Owen A (2001) *Empirical Likelihood*. Chapman & Hall

Parikh N, Boyd S (2013) Proximal algorithms. *Foundations and Trends in Optimization* 1:123–221

Parikh N, Boyd S (2014) Block splitting for distributed optimization. *Mathematical Programming Computation* 6:77–102

Patra RK, Sen B (2016) Estimation of a two-component mixture model with applications to multiple testing. *Journal of the Royal Statistical Society B* 78:869–893

Pearson K (1894) Contributions to the mathematical theory of evolution. *Philosophical Transactions of the Royal Society of London, Series A* 185:71–110

Pensky M (2017) Minimax theory of estimation of linear functionals of the deconvolution density with or without sparsity. *Annals of Statistics* 45:1516–1541

Petrone S, Rizzelli S, Rousseau J, Scricciolo C (2014a) Empirical Bayes methods in classical and Bayesian inference. *Metron* 72:201–215

Petrone S, Rousseau J, Scricciolo C (2014b) Bayes and empirical Bayes: Do they merge? *Biometrika* 101:285–302

Plummer M (2017) JAGS User Manual. Version 4.3.0 https://people.stat.sc.edu/hansont/stat740/jags_user_manual.pdf

Polyanskiy Y, Wu Y (2020) Self-regularizing property of nonparametric maximum likelihood estimator in mixture models, https://arxiv.org/abs/2008.08244

Polyanskiy Y, Wu Y (2021) Sharp regret bounds for empirical Bayes and compound decision problems, https://arxiv.org/abs/2109.03943

Pop-Eleches C, Urquiola M (2013) Going to a better school: Effects and behavioral responses. *American Economic Review* 103:1289–1324

Portnoy S (2015) Maximizing probability bounds under moment-matching restrictions. *The American Statistician* 69:41–44

Portnoy S, Koenker R (1989) Adaptive L-estimation for linear models. *Annals of Statistics* 17(1):362–381

Portnoy S, Koenker R (1997) The Gaussian hare and the Laplacian tortoise: Computability of squared-error versus absolute-error estimators, with discussion. *Statistical Science* 12:279–300

Pratt JW (1961) Length of confidence intervals. *Journal of the American Statistical Association* 56:549–567

Pratt JW (1963) Shorter confidence intervals for the mean of a normal distribution with known variance. *Annals of Mathematical Statistics* 34:574–586

Qu Z, Zhuo F (2021) Likelihood ratio based tests for Markov regime switching. *Review of Economic Studies* 88:937–968

R Core Team (2021) *R: A Language and Environment for Statistical Computing*. R Foundation for Statistical Computing, https://www.R-project.org/

Ramsay J, Heckman N, Silverman B (1996) Spline smoothing with model-based penalties. *Behavior Research Methods, Instruments, & Computers* 29:99–106

Ramsey FP (1931) Truth and probability. In: Braithwaite RB (ed) *The Foundations of Mathematics and Other Logical Essays*, Routledge, Kegan Paul, pp 156–198

Ranneby B (1984) The maximum spacing method. an estimation method related to the maximum likelihood method. *Scandinavian Journal of Statistics* 11:93–112

Rao CR (1973) *Linear Statistical Inference and Its Applications*. Wiley

Rasch G (1960) *Probabilistic Models for Some Intelligence and Attainment Tests*. University of Chicago Press

Rigollet P, Weed J (2018) Entropic optimal transport is maximum-likelihood deconvolution. *Comptes Rendus Mathematique* 356:1228–1235

Robbins H (1950) A generalization of the method of maximum likelihood: Estimating a mixing distribution (abstract). *Annals of Mathematical Statistics* 21:314–315

Robbins H (1951) Asymptotically subminimax solutions of compound statistical decision problems. In: *Proceedings of the Berkeley Symposium on Mathematical Statistics and Probability*, vol I. University of California Press

Robbins H (1952) Some aspects of the sequential design of experiments. *Bulletin of the American Mathematical Society* 59:527–535

Robbins H (1956) An empirical Bayes approach to statistics. In: *Proceedings of the Third Berkeley Symposium on Mathematical Statistics and Probability*, vol I. University of California Press

Robbins H (1977) Prediction and estimation for the compound Poisson distribution. *Proceedings of the National Academy of Science* pp 2670–2671

Robbins H (1982) Estimating many variances. In: Gupta SS, Berger JO (eds) *Statistical Decision Theory and Related Topics III*, Elsevier, pp 251–261

Robbins H (1988) The u, v, method of estimation. In: Gupta SS, Berger JO (eds) *Statistical Decision Theory and Related Topics IV*, Elsevier, pp 265–270

Robbins H (1990) Letter to Paul Holland dated May 1. Robbins Archive, Low Library, Columbia University

Robbins H, Zhang CH (1988) Estimating a treatment effect under biased sampling. *Proceedings of the National Academy of Sciences* 85:3670–3672

Robbins H, Zhang CH (1989) Estimating the superiority of a drug to a placebo when all and only those patients at risk are treated with the drug. *Proceedings of the National Academy of Sciences* 86:3003–3005

Robbins H, Zhang CH (1991) Estimating a multiplicative treatment effect under biased allocation. *Biometrika* 78:349–354

Robinson GK (1991) That BLUP is a good thing: The estimation of random effects. *Statistical Science* 6:15–51

Rockafellar RT (1970) *Convex Analysis*. Princeton University Press

Rodriguez G (2005) Unobserved heterogeneity, https://data.princeton.edu/pop509/UnobservedHeterogeneity.pdf

Roeder K (1990) Density estimation with confidence sets exemplified by superclusters and voids in the galaxies. *Journal of the American Statistical Association* 85:617–624

Roeder K (1992) Semiparametric estimation of normal mixture densities. *Annals of Statistics* pp 929–943

Romano JP, Wolf M (2005) Stepwise multiple testing as formalized data snooping. *Econometrica* 73:1237–1282

Romano Y, Patterson E, Candès E (2019) Conformalized quantile regression. In: Wallach H, Larochelle H, Beygelzimer A, d'Alché Buc F, Fox E, Garnett R (eds) *Advances in Neural Information Processing Systems*, vol 32. Curran Associates, Inc.

Rousseeuw PJ, Hubert M (1999) Regression depth. *Journal of the American Statistical Association* 94:388–402

Saha S, Guntuboyina A (2020) On the nonparametric maximum likelihood estimator for Gaussian location mixture densities with application to Gaussian denoising. *Annals of Statistics* 48(2):738–762

Samworth RJ (2018) Recent progress in log-concave density estimation. *Statistical Science* 33:493–509

Savage LJ (1954) *Foundations of Statistics*. Wiley

Schwarz G (1978) Estimating the dimension of a model. *Annals of Statistics* 6:461–464

Senn S (2008) A note concerning a selection "paradox" of Dawid's. *The American Statistician* 62:206–210

Serfling RJ (1980) *Approximation Theorems of Mathematical Statistics*. Wiley

Shafer G, Vovk V (2008) A tutorial on conformal prediction. *Journal of Machine Learning Research* 9:371–421

Shah N, Wainwright M (2018) Simple, robust and optimal ranking from pairwise comparisons. *Journal of Machine Learning Research* 18:1–38

Shen Y, Wu Y (2022) Empirical Bayes estimation: When does g-modeling beat f-modeling in theory (and in practice)?, Annals of Statistics, forthcoming.

Shepard D, Zeckhauser R (1980) Long-term effects of interventions to improve survival in mixed populations. *Journal of Chronic Disease* 33:413–433

Shepp LA, Vardi Y (1982) Maximum likelihood reconstruction for emission tomography. *IEEE Transactions on Medical Imaging* 1:113–122

Silverman BW (1982) On the estimation of a probability density function by the maximum penalized likelihood method. *Annals of Statistics* 10:795–810

Silverman BW (1985) Some aspects of the spline smoothing approach to non-parametric regression curve fitting. *Journal of the Royal Statistical Society B* 47:1–52

Silverman BW, Jones MC, Wilson JD, Nychka DW (1990) A smoothed EM approach to indirect estimation problems, with particular, reference to stereology and emission tomography. *Journal of the Royal Statistical Society B* 52:271–324

Simar L (1976) Maximum likelihood estimation of a compound Poisson process. *Annals of Statistics* 4:1200–1209

Sinkhorn R (1964) A relationship between arbitrary positive matrices and doubly stochastic matrices. *Annals of Mathematical Statistics* 35(2):876–879

Smyth GK (2004) Linear models and empirical Bayes methods for assessing differential expression in microarray experiments. *Statistical Applications in Genetics and Molecular Biology* 3:1–25

Soloff JA, Guntuboyina A, Sen B (2025) Multivariate, heteroscedastic empirical Bayes via nonparametric maximum likelihood, *Journal of the Royal Statistical Society: Series B, 87, 1–32*

Solomentsev E (2020) Riesz theorem (2). In: *Encyclopedia of Mathematics*, Springer, http://encyclopediaofmath.org/index.php?title=Riesz_theorem(2)&oldid=48570

Stefanski LA, Carroll RJ (1990) Deconvolving kernel density estimators. *Statistics* 21:169–184

Stein C (1956) Inadmissibility of the usual estimator of the mean of a multivariate normal distribution. In: *Proceedings of the Third Berkeley Symposium on Mathematical Statistics and Probability*, vol I. University of California Press, pp 197–206

Stein C (1962) Confidence sets for the mean of a multivariate normal distribution. *Journal of the Royal Statistical Society B* 24:265–296

Stein C (1981) Estimation of the mean of a multivariate normal distribution. *Annals of Statistics* pp 1135–1151

Stein C (1986) Lectures on the theory of estimation of many parameters. *Journal of Soviet Mathematics* 34:1373–1403

Stephens M (2017) False discovery rates: A new deal. *Biostatistics* 18:275–294

Stigler GJ, Stigler SM, Friedland C (1995) The journals of economics. *Journal of Political Economy* 103:331–359

Stigler SM (1990) A Galtonian perspective on shrinkage estimators. *Statistical Science* 5:147–155

Stigler SM (1994) Citation patterns in the journals of statistics and probability. *Statistical Science* 9(1):94–108

Stone C (1990) Large-sample inference for log-spline models. *Annals of Statistics* 18:717–741

Stone M (1977) An asymptotic equivalence of choice of model by cross-validation and Akaike's criterion. *Journal of the Royal Statistical Society* 39:44–47

Storey JD (2002) A direct approach to false discovery rates. *Journal of the Royal Statistical Society: B* 64:479–498

Storey JD (2003) The positive false discovery rate: A Bayesian interpretation and the q-value. *The Annals of Statistics* 31:2013–2035

Stoye J (2009) Minimax regret treatment choice with finite samples. *Journal of Econometrics* 151:70–81

Stoye J (2012) Minimax regret treatment choice with covariates or with limited validity of experiments. *Journal of Econometrics* 166:138–156

Strasser H (2012) The covariance structure of CML-estimates in the Rasch model. *Statistics & Risk Modeling* 29:315–342

Sun W, Cai TT (2007) Oracle and adaptive compound decision rules for false discovery rate control. *Journal of the American Statistical Association* 102:901–912

Sun W, McLain AC (2012) Multiple testing of composite null hypotheses in heteroscedastic models. *Journal of the American Statistical Association* 107:673–687

Tam Cho WK (1998) Iff the assumption fits: A comment on the King ecological inference solution. *Political Analysis* 7:143–163

Teicher H (1961) Identifiability of mixtures. *Annals of Mathematical Statistics* 32:244–248

Teicher H (1967) Identifiability of mixtures of product measures. *Annals of Mathematical Statistics* 38:1300–1302

Thisted R, Efron B (1987) Did Shakespeare write a newly-discovered poem? *Biometrika* 74:445–455

Tibshirani R (1996) Regression shrinkage and selection via the lasso. *Journal of the Royal Statistical Society B* 58:267–288

Tukey JW (1960) A survey of sampling from contaminated distributions. In: Olkin I (ed) *Contributions to Probability and Statistics*, Stanford University Press

Uspensky JV (1937) *Introduction to Mathematical Probability*. McGraw-Hill

van der Vaart A (1996) Efficient maximum likelihood estimation in semiparametric mixture models. *Annals of Statistics* 24:862–878

Valavanis S (1959) *Econometrics, An Introduction to Maximum Likelihood Methods*. McGraw-Hill

Vandenberghe L, Boyd S (1996) Semidefinite programming. *SIAM Review* 38:49–95

Varin C, Cattelan M, Firth D (2016) Statistical modelling of citation exchange between statistics journals. *Journal of the Royal Statistical Society A* 179:163

Vaupel J (2005) Lifesaving, lifetimes and lifetables. *Demography* 13:597–614

Vaupel J, Carey J (1998) Compositional interpretations of medfly mortality. *Science* 260:1666–1667

Vaupel J, Manton K, Stollard E (1979) The impact of heterogeneity in individual frailty on the dynamics of mortality. *Demography* 16:439–454

Vovk V, Gammerman A, Shafer G (2005) *Algorithmic Learning in a Random World*. Springer

Wahba G (1983) Bayesian "confidence intervals" for the cross-validated smoothing spline. *Journal of the Royal Statistical Society B* 45:133–150

Wald A (1947) *Sequential Analysis*. Wiley

Wald A (1950) *Statistical Decision Functions*. Wiley

Walters CR (2024) Empirical Bayes methods for labor economics. In: Christian Dustmann TL (ed) *Handbook of Labor Economics*, vol 5. Elsevier

Wang Y (2007) On fast computation of the non-parametric maximum likelihood estimate of a mixing distribution. *Journal of the Royal Statistical Society B* 69:185–198

Wang Y (2017–2020) nspmix: Nonparametric and semiparametric mixture estimation, https://cran.r-project.org/web/packages/nspmix/index.html

Wasserman L (2012) Mixture models: The twilight zone of statistics, https://normaldeviate.wordpress.com/2012/08/04/mixture-models-the-twilight-zone-of-statistics/

Weinstein A, Ma Z, Brown LD, Zhang CH (2018) Group-linear empirical Bayes estimates for a heteroscedastic normal mean, *Journal of the American Statistical Association*, 113, 698–710

White H (1982) Maximum likelihood estimation of misspecified models. *Econometrica* 50:1–25

Wicksell SD (1925) The corpuscle problem: A mathematical study of a biometric problem. *Biometrika* 17:84–99

Wijsman RA (1990) *Invariant Measures on Groups and Their Use in Statistics*, vol 14. Institute of Mathematical Statistics

Wood GR (1992) Binomial mixtures and finite exchangeability. *Annals of Probability* 20:1167–1173

Wood SN (2006) *Generalized Additive Models*. Chapman and Hall

Wu Y, Yang P (2020) Optimal estimation of Gaussian mixtures via denoised method of moments. *Annals of Statistics* 48:1981–2007

Xie X, Kou SC, Brown LD (2012) SURE estimates for a heteroscedastic hierarchical model. Journal of the *American Statistical Association* 107:1465–1479

Xu L, Jordan M (1996) On convergence properties of the EM algorithm for Gaussian mixtures. *Neural Computation* 2:129–151

Xue X, Wang Y (2023) A nonparametric mixture approach to density and null proportion estimation in large-scale multiple comparison problems. *Australian & New Zealand Journal of Statistics* 65:49–75

Yan Y, Wang K, Rigollet P (2023) Learning Gaussian mixtures using the Wasserstein–Fisher–Rao gradient flow. *Annals of Statistics*, 52, 1774–1795. and year by 2024.

Yu C, Hoff PD (2018) Adaptive multigroup confidence intervals with constant coverage. *Biometrika* 105:319–335

Zabell SL (1992) Predicting the unpredictable. *Synthese* 90:205–232

Zermelo E (1929) Die Berechnung der Turnier–Ergebnisse als ein Maximum-Problem der Wahrscheinlichkeitsrechnung. *Mathematische Zeitschrift* 29:436–460

Zhang CH (2009) Generalized maximum likelihood estimation of normal mixture densities. *Statistica Sinica* 19:1297–1318

Zhang Y, Cui Y, Sen B, Toh KC (2024) On efficient and scalable computation of the nonparametric maximum likelihood estimator in mixture models, *Journal of Machine Learning Research*, 25, 1–46.

Subject Index

Names Index

"These are the men who pretend to understand a book by scouting through the index, as if a traveller should go about to describe a palace, when he had seen nothing but the privy." [Jonathan Swift (1704)]

Other titles in the series (*continued from page ii*)

E. Ghysels, N. Swanson, & M. Watson (eds.), *Essays in Econometrics: Collected Papers of Clive W. J. Granger, Vols. I &II*, 2001
S. Strøm (ed.), *Econometrics and Economic Theory in the 20th Century: The Ragnar Frisch Centennial Symposium*, 1999
A. C. Cameron & P. K. Trivedi, *Regression Analysis of Count-Data*, 1998
D. Jacobs, E. Kalai, & M. Kamien (eds.), *Frontiers of Research in Economic Theory: The Nancy L. Schwartz Memorial Lectures*, 1998
D. M. Kreps & K. F. Wallis (eds.), *Advances in Economics and Econometrics: Theory and Applications, Seventh World Congress, Vols. I, II, & III*, 1997
R. Guesnerie, *A Contribution to the Pure Theory of Taxation*, 1995
C. Sims (ed.), *Advances in Econometrics, Sixth World Congress, Vols. I &II*, 1994
H. White, *Inference, Estimation and Specification Analysis*, 1994
J-J. Laffont (ed.), *Advances in Economic Theory, Sixth World Congress, Vols. I & II*, 1992
W. Härdle, *Applied Nonparametric Regression Analysis*, 1990
A. Roth & M. Sotomayor, *Two-Sided Matching*, 1990
T. Lancaster, *The Econometric Analysis of Transition Data*, 1990
L. G. Godfrey, *Misspecification Tests in Econometrics*, 1989
H. Moulin, *Axioms of Cooperative Decision-Making*, 1988
T. Bewley (ed.), *Advances in Economic Theory, Fifth World Congress, Vols. I, II, & III*, 1987
C. Hsiao, *Analysis of Panel Data*, 1986
J. Heckman & B. Singer, *Longitudinal Analysis of Labor Market Data*, 1985
A. Mas-Colell, *The Theory of General Economic Equilibrium: A Differentiable Approach*, 1985
R. J. Bowden & D. A. Turkington, *Instrumental Variables*, 1985
B. Peleg, *Game Theoretic Analysis of Voting in Committees*, 1984
F. M. Fisher, *Disequilibrium Foundations of Equilibrium Economics*, 1983
J.-M. Grandmont, *Money and Value*, 1983
G. Debreu, *Mathematical Economics*, 1983
G. S. Maddala, *Limited Dependent and Qualitative Variables in Econometrics*, 1983
W. Hildenbrand (ed.), *Advances in Economic Theory*, 1983
W. Hildenbrand (ed.), *Advances in Econometrics*, 1983

Printed in the United Kingdom by TJ Clays Ltd.